Wake UP America !!!

Restore OUR Republic

Fight for Freedom

OR

Succumb to Slavery

The Coming Cleansing
& Restoration

Copyright

<u>Wake UP America!!!</u>

3rd Edition (updated information, new graphics, new diagrams.)

Cover Design: Paul Van Der Horst

Printed in the United States of America

ISBN #ISBN-13: 978-0615556796

ISBN-10: 0615556795

Table of Contents

What This Book Is About

**The primary purpose of this book is to contribute to the mission
to restore the Republic of the United States of America.**

<u>Wake UP America!!!</u> uniquely connects the normally disconnected dots of both spiritual and secular determinants of America's past, present and future. We are spiritual beings having physical experiences, not physical beings having spiritual experiences. The world typically separates these two. This book combines them to provide a holistic overview of world issues and presents a way to solve our dilemma.

Connecting spiritual and secular determinants reveal things as they were, as they are and as they are to come. When man's spirit leaves his physical body, the body dies. The spirit gives life to the body. All organisms - and organizations - are similarly affected. Spiritual principles form the foundation of organizations, including governments. When secular relativism erodes foundations of spiritual truths on which organizations are built, they fall. Truth is light that enables vision. Without vision the people perish. This book adds light to the mind and enables people to see clearly to discern truth from error. It a vision to a preferred future.

People tend to protect what they fall in love with. I hope this book will help people fall in love with Liberty, Freedom, America, the U.S. Constitution and with our Republic - and protect them.

America has a divine mission to be a 'shining city on a hill' that shines the light of liberty to all the World; 'for out of Zion shall go forth The Law.' This book invites men of good will everywhere to unite in a common mission to restore OUR Republic; to rise up and act to correct our course and enable America to fulfill her divine mission.

The U.S. Government has moved to the far left from its original far right position as framed by our Founding Fathers in the Declaration of Independence and the U.S. Constitution. The last 100 year shift to the left has been carefully orchestrated and executed by progressives, socialists, Marxists, and communists who intend to destroy America & the liberty of all mankind. Government is supposed to be servant of the We The People, but it has become a master. It's gargantuan size, out-of-control spending, ignoring the Constitution, and invasive control is like a bloated bloodsucking tick draining its host.

The same metal can cast a Liberty Bell that rings for freedom or chains of slavery that cries out for freedom. For the first 270 years Americans preserved their liberties. For the past 100 years Marxists/socialists/communists disguised as liberal left progressives have slowly and methodically forged chains of government enslavement.

This book is about truth and principles; not politics. I do not favor one political party over another. I do not care if you vote Republican, Democrat, Libertarian, and Independent, white, black, male or female.

Like Thomas Jefferson, *"I have sworn upon the altar of God eternal hostility against every form of tyranny over the mind of man."* To be neutral now when freedom hangs by a thread is treason to America and disloyalty to God who inspired our Founding Fathers to write The Declaration of Independence and the U.S. Constitution.

Questions

- Are you concerned about the direction America is heading?
- Are you concerned that our government has become UN-Constitutional?
- Are you concerned about our high unemployment rate and the current depression?
- Do you lack trust in our government and politicians?
- Are you angry that you have to work until May 15th each year just to pay income taxes?
- Do you wonder where all that government stimulus money really went?
- Are you angry that government wastes trillions of YOUR tax dollars?
- Are you angry that your representatives in Washington ignore you?
- Are you concerned about propaganda from our bought and paid for 'mainstream' media?
- Are you concerned about illegal invasion across our borders?
- Are you unsure of where Muslims really stand on the subject of freedom and liberty?
- Are you concerned that the America today is not the one you grew up in?
- Are you worried about the future for your children and grandchildren?
- Have you had enough of excessive government regulations in your life and business?
- Do you wonder if high gas prices are really justified?
- Do you wonder who controls Washington politicians?
- Are you concerned about our un-sustainable national debt?
- Do you wonder how insurrections in the Middle East, Europe & America will affect you?
- Are you concerned that the U.S. in involved in too many foreign wars?
- Are you concerned about the declining value of the U.S. dollar and your 401K?
- Are angry about invasive TSA, NSA, IRS,FDA, HEW & EPA control?
- Do you wonder how we can get out of this mess?

If you have these concerns and questions, this book is for you.

If you do not have these concerns and questions, you really need this book!

Learn where America Roots are, why the War continues,
America's ascent, decline, & awful situation,
And an action plan of what We The People MUST Do & CAN Do Now.

Introduction

America is in crisis at a fork in the road of history. One leads to freedom, the other to slavery. Restoring our Constitutional Republic leads to freedom. Succumbing to current trends enslaves.

The genesis of this book occurred in 2010AD when I awoke in the middle of the night with thoughts pouring into me. I arose and filled up an architect size D (24"x36") sheet of paper with notes and went back to bed. The next morning I wondered why I had been given what I had. As I pondered the point I realized that my grown children like I was at their age; so involved in making a living and taking care of family. In addition the tsunami of distracting entertainment options divert them from becoming aware of America's decline. World conditions are more concerning that I have ever seen. From the vantage point of six decades of hindsight, a significantly changed America now exists from the one I knew as a boy. I realize that my children, and their generation, lack historical perspective that I see. More importantly, they have not been taught the true roots of America. Therefore, I started writing this book for them. In the process of research and writing to arm my children with truth, reviewers suggested that all Americans would benefit from this book.

America is way off course to fulfill its divine role as a 'light on a hill'. My desire is that this book will wake up America and unite people in a collective effort to restore our Republic. I am aware of no other book that paints a picture of both sufficient breadth and depth to expand understanding and empower people to act on the foundation of truth in order to correct America's current course. I seek to contribute in the battle to protect our liberties, to make truth more available, to honor God by bringing to fruition the seeds of inspiration He gave me, to bless my family, my children, my grandchildren, and posterity yet unborn. This book is my humble effort to bless America during these historic and turbulent times.

I have never written a book before. If I did, I may not have tackled this one for it has consumed way more time than I ever expected! I am not a Washington elitist. I am a son of good parents whose love of their children has blessed me. I am a husband of 44+ years to a good woman who is a faithful companion in my continuous process of striving to become better, and father of 5 children and 15 grandchildren – all of whom have taught and are teaching me much about life.

I write to you as one of you; a common man that Abraham Lincoln said 'God must love because He made so many of us.' This common man has normal aspirations to be a good son, husband, father and citizen of this great country. I desire to contribute something worthy for having lived here on Earth; something of value for my fellow man.

I am a man who loves God, family and America. My Father loved America for the opportunities she offered that his native Netherlands could not. He loved America so much that at 32 years of age, he enlisted as a soldier in WWII and served in the Pacific theater. The younger soldiers, 18-22 years old, called him 'Grandpa'. I suppose part of my love for America derives from my good patriot father. I am grateful to that 'greatest generation' that I do not have to speak German or Japanese. My love for America was evident at a young age and has grown over the years. Old Glory waving, singing The Star Spangled Banner, and The Pledge of Allegiance all bring a lump to this Patriot's throat...and proudly so.

This book seeks to clear away the clouds of confusion from our current condition so that we can see clearly what has happened, what is happening, what will happen if we do not change our course. It provides a way to chart our course to a preferred future. It provides a 'big picture' overview of the issues affecting our life from an unusually broad perspective – from the pre-mortal life to Earth's telestial end. Many other books exist that delve deeply into separate issues presented here as 'tip of the iceberg' overviews. However, I present ample evidence on each issue for the reader to grasp its importance. I provide a unique compilation of the individual puzzle pieces of truth selected from a wide range of sources over many millennia and 'connect the dots' to enhance understanding.

Like the morning sunlight pushes back the nights' darkness to bring a brighter day, seeing the whole picture of truth pushes back the darkness of ignorance. Truth provides sure footing on which to plant one's feet in order to advance on the path of life toward a better future. I hope this book will empower patriots with the sword of truth, clear vision, enable better choices, and increase effectiveness to affect positive change.

The following counsels from presidents, prophets, educators, scholars and statesmen that have guided me and motivated me through the months of research and writing:

- *"No greater immediate responsibility rests upon...all citizens of this Republic, than to protect the freedom vouch safed by the Constitution of the United States."* (America in History and Prophecy p. 45)

- *"...if we had done our homework and were faithful, we could step forward at this time and help save this country. The fact that most of us are unprepared to do it is an indictment we will have to bear. The longer we wait, the heavier the chains, the deeper the blood, the more the persecution, and the less we can carry out our God-given mandate and world-wide mission."* (America in History and Prophecy p.48)

- *"... men should be anxiously engaged in a good cause, and do many things of their own free will, and bring to pass much righteousness;... the power is in them, wherein they are agents unto themselves...."* (America in History and Prophecy p.48)

- Those who save the U.S. Constitution will be *"... choice spirits who, not waiting to be commanded in all things, [who] use their own free will, the counsel of the prophets, and the Spirit of the Lord as guidelines and who entered the battle...in freedom's cause."* (America in History and Prophecy p.47)

- *"I am not bound to win, but I am bound to be true. I am not bound to succeed, but I am bound to live by the light that I have. I must stand with anybody that stands right, and stand with him while he is right, and part with him when he goes wrong."* (Abraham Lincoln)

- *"For there are many yet on the earth...who are blinded by the subtle craftiness of men, whereby they lie in wait to deceive, and who are only kept from the truth because they know not where to find it."* (J. Smith 1839)

- *"Ye hear of wars in far countries, and you say that there will soon be great wars in far countries, but ye know not the hearts of men in your own land."* (J. Smith 1831)

- *"A foreign power had inroaded the nation which, from every human indication, it appeared would seize the government and supplant it with monarchy. I stood trembling at the prospect, when, lo, a power arose in the west which declared itself in favor of the Constitution in its original form; to this suddenly rising power every lover of constitutional rights and liberties throughout the nation, gave hearty support."* (America In History & Prophecy p. 45-46)

- Edward Everett Hale's poem:

> *I am only one, but I am one.*
> *I can't do everything, but I can do something.*
> *What I can do, that I ought to do,*
> *And what I ought to do,*
> *By the grace of God, I shall do!*

For the past 100 years, abundant evidence reveals that organized forces slowly, secretly and strategically eroded our Republic and our freedoms. Recently, our government pushed America off a financial debt cliff. We must restore Our Republic before we lose all our freedoms.

I write to all people who treasure truth and freedom. I will gladly stand with them in this cause. While I am a Christian, I will defend everyman's right to worship God according to the dictates of his own conscience so long as the practice of that religion does not interfere with the life, liberty, property or pursuit of happiness of others.

Pilgrims, Puritans and other Christian immigrants established America. It is way past time for the 86% Christian majority of America to unite with one voice to expose and remove the secret societies that have gained power over the world and us. I invite people of all faiths and all men of good character with high moral standards who love freedom to join the cause to restore our Republic; the government our Founding Fathers established. The silent majority must be silent no more!

I believe America is at a fork in the road of life; Fight for Freedom OR Succumb to Slavery. Our U.S. Constitution is in jeopardy and is 'hanging by a thread'.

The path of Freedom requires an uphill climb from our current degraded state by cleansing our collective hearts of impure and improper thoughts, desires, appetites, passions, words and deeds. We must plant in our minds the seeds of purity and disciplined living according to high moral principles to provide the required foundation upon which the U.S. Constitution will function. This path will restore our country to be the light on a hill we were created to be.

The path of slavery lies down the current slippery slope of succumbing to the ever-increasing control of our gargantuan, out-of-control, progressive/socialist government. The end of this path - as proven by all socialist/communist/fascist governments of the past, including Stalin, Lenin, Marx, Hitler, Mussolini, Mao – inevitably leads to the tyranny of enslavement by a dictator.

Which road we choose as a society is the great question of our day. No other choice is so important for our future. The choice we make will affect generations of our posterity. We will be accountable to God for our choices. I hope that this book will inspire good men everywhere to stand together with one voice to preserve the power that facilitates human progress.

I plead with my fellow citizens to Wake UP America! ...and choose Freedom!

About the Author

This part is included simply because that is what most readers want to know, not because I am of much significance compared to the great ones among us.

The most important part about the author is to know that, above all else, God has blessed him with truth and a good family; both ancestry and posterity. His children were the first reason to write this book.

The author earned five college degrees in environmental science, planning, design and landscape architecture at Summa Cum Laude or Magna Cum Laude levels, was on the Dean's List for all ten semesters, the first 4.0 graduate in the 50 year history of a college where he was the Valedictorian at the State University of New York. Phi Kappa Phi Honor Society inducted him and the Fairchild-Hiller Corporation presented him the America Awareness Award as the result of his valedictory address. He completed his formal education at Syracuse University/SUNY. His passions include alpine skiing, canoeing, hiking, mountain biking, guitar, song writing and playing the violin.

He served most of his professional career licensed in the State of Georgia at The Georgia Institute of Technology. A highlight was serving as the Campus Master Planner during the preparation and hosting of the 1996 Summer Olympic Games in Atlanta at the Georgia Tech Olympic Village and project manager for the International Village Center. He has authored several large planning and implementation documents and many designs to transform concepts to reality in order to support human enterprise, progress, achievement, and fulfillment. Concurrent to his service as a member of the General Faculty, he maintained a professional consulting practice. He also invented and designed several products that he is working to manufacture and market. Recent initiatives include design of sustainable, near net-zero energy, passive solar, healthy, green homes.

He has a 'pursuit of excellence' mentality and a drive for continuous education and understanding of new fields of study. He has spent a lifetime learning theology, history, psychology, sociology, philosophy, healing modalities, health sciences, environmental sciences and political science. Six decades of learning and living brings a better holistic view of life that connects the disparate dots of normally segregated areas of fields of study into a big picture of understanding of where we came from, how we got where we are, and what we must do to create a preferred future for ourselves, our children, grandchildren and posterity.

Acknowledgements

First and foremost I am grateful for the Spirit of the Lord that woke me up in the middle of the night and inspired me to write this book,...and continued to wake me up in the middle of the night with additions, insights, editing and organization refinements during the months of writing. I hope to get a good nights' sleep after publication!

I thank patriots who have fought and continue to fight for freedom from tyranny.

I am grateful for good parents. My Dad, William, taught me to love America, how to work and to be good and honest. I am grateful he emigrated from Holland at age 16 with his twin brother, seeking a better life in America. The twins worked 12 hrs./day 6 days/week when they arrived and then went to the movies at night to learn English to become true, non-hyphenated, Americans. Dad proudly served in WWII to defend our freedoms. His courage, dedication and hard work was a good example for me. His coming to America blessed me to be born here. I hope from heaven that he is proud that I stood up for America by writing this book.

I am grateful for my 97 year-old 'sharp-as-a-tack' Mother, Gertrude, who spent days learning how to use a computer for the first time just to read the first draft. She provided useful comments and encouragement from her perspective of a 'near centurion'.

I am grateful for my brother Lynn who taught our family that you do the right things and endure to the end as he demonstrated by serving his wife who suffered with Alzheimer's for 9 years.

I am grateful for an understanding wife Chris who supported me in this mission to research and write this book. She also gave guidance, encouragement and spent many hours as editor.

I am grateful for good children and grandchildren with whom familial love is enduring. Their love and time shared is a treasure way beyond what merchants offer.

I am grateful for all the influences of love that shimmer as golden threads in the fabric of life. Love creates memories of June roses in December, and a hope of Spring Daffodils.

I am grateful to be an American and to live in this land that is choice above all other lands.

Without all these good influences this book would be less than it is. Because of them I have hope in the future.

Dedication

I dedicate this book to Our Founding Fathers
and to all Patriots who love the United States of America.

We who enjoy the sweet fruits of America's Tree of Liberty
Owe a debt of gratitude
to those who fought to provide, and are fighting to preserve,
our God-given inalienable Rights.
It is upon their shoulders we stand today.
Too often, we take for granted their sacrifices.

To them all – **THANK YOU!**

1

Discerning Truth

*If "... the truth...shall make you free", Jhn 8:32,
then falsehoods make you slaves.*

To discern America's crisis one must have the tools to discern truth. Sadly, propaganda and historical revisionists have dulled the sharp edge to discern between truth and falsehood.

What is truth? Truth is things as they were, as they are and as they will be. Many 'expert' TV 'talking heads' and pundits throughout the World claim to know the 'facts' and what is true. Yet they profess viewpoints ranging from A to Z; many times in direct opposition with one another. Furthermore, there are people who intentionally lie and 'spin' the truth in order to get gain and power. Therefore, it is hard to know what and who to believe. However, there is a way to know truth from falsehood.

This chapter seeks to lay a foundation of truth upon which you can firmly stand. It briefly reminds us of where we came from, why were are here, and where we are going. It reveals WHO we really are. To know who we really are is a cornerstone of the foundation of truth. In this chapter you will learn HOW to know truth independent of me or any man. The reader will also learn about relative intelligence and where to find truth. Finally, you will discover the roots and fruits of the following opposites; truth and falsehoods, clarity and deception, and good and evil power.

When YOU know the truth from the right source you will less likely be deceived. This chapter creates an essential paradigm that will enhance understanding of America's past, present and future. It provides principles which if applied enhance understanding not only of the rest of the book but also for all of life.

Only truth endures. Falsehoods finally fall and are burned up along with those who embrace them.

Included in this book is truth from both secular and sacred sources. It matters not what religion, culture, race or any other categorized source truth comes from. Truth is the only secure foundation upon which to stand.

Application of this knowledge is essential in choosing how to act in the face of so many conflicting voices in our confusing world. This chapter presents principles that are essential to understand and apply in order to come to knowledge of the truth of all things and find freedom from those who spin webs of deceit to enslave your soul.

Intelligence

Albert Einstein is generally recognized as the most intelligent person in history. He used 7% of his brain. The rest of us use 3-5%, on average.

Sometimes you hear,' I have a PhD' or 'I am an MD' or 'I am lawyer' or 'I have "X" college degrees' ...you get the picture. So what! All those proclamations provide is a metric of endeavor; what people studied, what they are educated in, but not necessarily how intelligent they are. Granted, difficult courses of study do require more intelligence and usually greater effort, but we're still talking in the range of 5% brain use – not really very impressive.

What about IQ's? They are just another metric of what you know and your ability to reason, but – and this will be hard for those with high degrees, multiple degrees, much experience in practice and high IQ's – we're still only talking about 5% brain use.

It IS important to learn, to apply ourselves to the extent of our ability and to gain all the education we can. But realize we can never know it all. An old legend about Uncle Zek reveals some truth about us all. He said after he made a wrong choice based on all that he 'knew' to be true... *"it ain't what I knowed that done me in. It's what I knowed that wasn't so!"* The point is, it is important not to discount new information on the basis of our limited intellect and pre-conceptions. If we do, we dam our progress, like a dam that stops the flow of a stream.

It is essential that we empower ourselves to see things as they really were, as they really are and as they really will be. But when we reach the extent of our own understanding, which at 3-5% brain-use is very limited indeed, who should we turn to?

Regarding intelligences it was recorded by the prophet Abraham that God said, *"I am the Lord thy God, I am more intelligent than they all."*

America's Founding Fathers often turned to God, Our Father in Heaven. His greater intelligence will guide beyond the dead ends of our own reasoning and limited intellect. But how do we do that? The answer is found in this chapter as it relates to America.

Choices

Choices are often more simple than they appear. However, we often confuse the issues by allowing our emotions or guilt to distort the lens of our sight. Often those presenting the options, make truth hard to see intentionally by cloaking the devouring consequences in sheep's clothing. Ultimately, each choice boils down to the simple alternatives of good or evil.

Good choices lead to freedom. Evil choices lead to slavery. Yes, there are shades of grey; more freedom or less freedom, more slavery or less slavery, but the accumulated effect leads toward one or the other.

America's current choices are similar to our choices in the pre-mortal life where two opposing plans were presented.

Lucifer offered a plan that provided safety and security but denied us our freedom to choose. Thus he became Satan, the father of lies, because he uses lies to deceive men to lead them into captivity. He insured that no one would sin or be lost, but we would be like marionettes dancing on the strings he pulled. Under Lucifer's plan he would become our God and replace our Heavenly Father. He then created a state of fear to persuade us to accept his plan by warning that some of you will be lost if you don't follow my plan. Lucifer's plan and fear tactics deceived 1/3 of God's children who chose to follow him. Their choice of security over freedom turned out to be enslavement to Lucifer who became Satan.

Jehovah (Jesus Christ's name in the pre-mortal life and in the Old Testament), the first born spirit son of God, presented Heavenly Father's Plan of Salvation and Happiness. His plan included continuation of moral agency (freedom to choose) on Earth like we had in heaven. Heavenly

Father's Plan has some serious risks. We would sin, become unclean and not able to return to God's presence because no unclean thing can enter the presence of God. Our eldest brother, Jehovah, offered to atone for our sins (become our Savior and Redeemer) and make a way for us to repent and be cleansed from sin thus enabling our return to live with Heavenly Father after proving ourselves worthy in mortality.

Our Father in Heaven choose the first Plan and for Jehovah to become our Savior. Lucifer's rebellion to overthrow God and to remove our moral agency persuaded 1/3 of our pre-mortal life brothers and sisters to follow him. Their choice was allowed by God – due to the eternal principle of moral agency - and Lucifer with his followers was cast down to this Earth.

Those were the choices in the pre-mortal life – freedom or slavery. Your presence on Earth with mortal bodies indicates you choose Jehovah's plan in the pre-mortal life. Congratulations!

Today, in all mankind's machinations, these two plans or forces – freedom or slavery - are behind every action. Today as in the past, the roots of slavery are carefully cloaked beneath the tantalizing fruits of security.

Our task is to discern truth – which path leads to freedom and which path leads to enslavement – and choose.

Emotions of our hearts often drive choices against our heads' advice. The head, not the heart, is designed to be the leader of the soul. So consider your emotional state when choosing. To choose wisely, first find a place of emotional balance. Then choose freedom.

Know Thyself

Consider the following story: A young man traveled to a new town. Near the edge of town he met an old sage. After greetings, the young man asked the old sage, "How are the people in your town?" The old sage responded, "How are the people in the town where you came from?" Well he answered, "They're wonderful; friendly, giving, caring for each other, working together to build a good community". The old sage said. "That's the kind of folks you will find here too." So the young man went on his way and discovered the old sage to be right.

Later that day a second young man traveled the same road and met the old sage. After their greetings, this young man asked the old sage, "How are the people in your town?" The old sage responded, "How are the people in the town where you came from?" Well he answered, "They're bad; not to be trusted, unfriendly, unkind, selfish and rude." The old sage said. "That's the kind of people you will find here too." So this second young man went on his way and discovered the old sage to be right.

Both travelers found not people as they really are, but they saw the people as they saw life. Their expectations became their reality. The point is - We See Life We Are, Not How It Is.

What we Seek we Find

Pain is a very powerful teacher. Although it is human to avoid life's tests, trials teach many life lessons that we were sent here to learn.

One trial for me was quite revealing; it involved seven eye surgeries, three Lasik's to the cornea, two scalpels to remove cataracts and two YAG lasers. Each one increased clarity of my vision.

Although I did not know it, my eyes' lenses became cloudy slowly over time. The optometrist could see it with his special equipment. So I went under the knife, two knives per eye actually. During the surgery only my eye was numbed after a couple of uncomfortable needles (I *hate* needles) were inserted below and above my eyeball. As the knives were inserted from the top and sides of each eyeball my mind stopped seeing the room's contents. All I could see was a swirling light show of many colors. I was blind except for those swirling lights which must have been a combination of the surgery lamp refracting through my pupil and bouncing off the shiny blade and the little vacuum inserted to suck out the clouded lens. A new clear lens was inserted and 'hooked' into place. After a good night's sleep and a few days of wearing an eye patch, I could see out of my new lens.

I wasn't aware of the effect of the surgery until sitting on the couch one day I happened to put a hand over one eye and then the other. Our living room wall is painted white. Yet with one eye, the one with the new lens, the white appeared bright white. With the other it appeared ochre. I retested my sight and was amazed how the new lens brightened my world. I could see differently; better!

Spiritual lenses are made clearer or cloudier by experience. The lens through which we look at life influences what we see in life – sometimes dramatically! For example, a child who grows up in a loving nurturing home tends to trust life and have an optimistic outlook. A gang-raped teenage girl tends to fear life and lack trust in men – and for good reason!

If there is no space between stimulus and response – we react, often with regret later. If we create a space between stimulus and our response, by counting to 10...or 100 when necessary, we can choose our response; which usually produces a better outcome - difficult for A-type personalities – easier for B-type. The sum total of our choices determines what we become, and after all, this life is a test to see what we choose to become.

The point is: life's experiences 'color' our lenses and sometime distort them. Since we see life through our own lenses we see life 'how we are', not 'how life is'. Because of this no one sees life completely clearly - no one except God. More on that subject later.

Consider the following story of two men in a hospital room that reveals what we see is influenced by our choices.

> Two men, both seriously ill, occupied the same hospital room. One man was allowed to sit up in his bed for an hour each afternoon to help drain the fluid from his lungs. His bed was next to the room's only window.

> The other man had to spend all his time flat on his back. The men talked for hours on end. They spoke of their wives and families, their homes, their jobs, their involvement in the military service, where they had been on vacation.

> Every afternoon when the man in the bed by the window could sit up, he would pass the tim7e by describing to his roommate all the things he could see outside the window. The man in the other bed began to live for those one hour periods where his world would be broadened and enlivened by all the activity and color of the world outside.

> The window overlooked a park with a lovely lake. Ducks and swans played on the water while children sailed their model boats. Young lovers walked arm in arm amidst flowers of every color and a fine view of the city skyline could be seen in the distance. As the man by the window described all this in exquisite detail, the man on the other side of the room would close his eyes and imagine the picturesque scene.

One warm afternoon the man by the window described a parade passing by. Although the other man couldn't hear the band - he could see it in his mind's eye as the gentleman by the window portrayed it with descriptive words.

Days and weeks passed.

One morning, the day nurse arrived to bring water for their baths, only to find the lifeless body of the man by the window, who had died peacefully in his sleep. She was saddened and called the hospital attendants to take the body away. As soon as it seemed appropriate, the other man asked if he could be moved next to the window. The nurse was happy to make the switch, and after making sure he was comfortable, she left him alone.

Slowly, painfully, he propped himself up on one elbow to take his first look at the real world outside. He strained to slowly turn to look out the window beside the bed. It faced a blank wall. The man asked the nurse what could have compelled his deceased roommate who had described such wonderful things outside this window. The nurse responded that the man was blind and could not even see the wall.

The point is one man chose to see that which was beautiful which lifted his spirits as well as his roommates.

The question for us is – what are we choosing to see?

A Clear Lens

"A nation of well-informed men who have been taught to know and prize the rights which God has given them cannot be enslaved. It is in the religion of ignorance that tyranny begins." Benjamin Franklin

Ignorance is enslavement. Truth is freedom. Truth sets us free from the slavery of ignorance and empowers us to act with confidence.

To see clearly it is essential to know the answers to three questions:

1. Where did I come from before this life?

2. Why am I here?

3. Where am I going after I die?

Correct answers to these questions create the proper paradigm of life through which truth reveals itself.

Consider a man walking on a remote beach or desert. He comes upon a shiny object partially buried in the sand. Picking it up he discovers that it is a watch. He could draw one of two conclusions using deductive reasoning:

- Option #1 is that this watch evolved from the elements of sand and organized itself with all those diverse working parts precisely coordinated to tell time. An evolutionary miracle to be sure!

- Option #2 is that this watch was made by a higher intelligence – a watchmaker -and subsequently lost by someone on this stretch of sand.

To believe that people evolved from sea slime is like believing a watch evolved from sand. Common sense reveals the insanity of this line of reasoning. Common sense tells us that the watch was created by a higher intelligence. Common sense tells us that people were created by a higher intelligence; they are the offspring of God.

Simple common sense reveals much truth. Man, the highest form of life, need only apply his reasoning powers to see the fallacy of the theory of evolution. Observed through the lens of clarity all Nature testifies that there is a higher intelligence who created all things. Earth is just the right distance from the Sun so that we do not either freeze or fry. It rotates on its axis on a regular schedule and orbits around the sun on a regular schedule, as do the other planets in our solar system. Our earth is the only planet in our solar system that sustains such a wonderful diversity of life. All of nature's majesty, beauty and symbiotic relationships reveal that there is a God of Nature. Our solar system, our Earth with its regular seasons is all evidence of order created by a higher intelligence. That higher intelligence is God who is our Father in Heaven. To see nature with the correct understanding is to see God's creations and organization, and to appreciate them like never before.

There is a scientific truth called entropy; the propensity for matter to go from order to disorder. Your home or garden left unattended in time becomes less organized and run down, eventually deteriorating back to its elemental parts. Life is like that. Life does not evolve on its own from lower forms to higher forms. Yes, there is adaptation of species, but an ameba never becomes a monkey and a monkey never becomes a man. Life does not organize into higher forms any more than beach sand organizes into a watch - no matter how much time we give it.

In truth, all creation is evidence of a higher intelligence that creates and governs the universe. He is God.

The current fad is 'the big bang' theory. The key word here is THEORY. It is nothing more than a theory. It cannot be proved, because it is false. Use common sense that God gave you. For a 'big bang' to have created our universe organized into galaxies and solar systems, and that plants, animals and humans evolved from the explosion is as absurd as thinking that an explosion in a print shop could produce an encyclopedia. The possibility is extremely remote! Even if it did happen, it could not heal its torn pages or reproduce new editions. But plants, animals and humans can!

Now consider for a moment another alternative to creation; the _theory_ of evolution. In fact, exhaustive scientific research disproves this theory. Darwin himself stated that he was not promoting evolution, but rather the theory of species adaptation. However, people with evil intent have spun Darwin's theory of species adaptation into the theory of evolution. Why would they do that? They do it in order to discredit the truth of creation to gain power and control.

If you are one of Darwin's evolutionists, I submit that the rest of this book will have little value for you unless you consider for the moment your 3-5% level of intelligence. There just might be something 'you know that isn't so'.

Embracing false theories like evolution creates a distorted lens through which all you see must be somehow explained by evolution. Evolutionists 'find answers' because that is what they seek. But is it truth? Distorted lenses destroy seeing things as they really are. It leads even the most 'learned' minds to be ever learning but never coming to the knowledge of the truth. Of course the opposite argument can be made; that creationists find the answers they are looking for because that is what they seek.

The most important question is not whether you can defend your position with eloquence and scientific data. The most important question is, is it true? The 'truth's' that science discovers over man's recorded history have changed. Many truths (like the earth being flat) become ridiculous based on new information. Evolutionists become creationists the same way. Truth never changes, but once found, truth does change people.

For those who still choose to believe evolution over creation - science over faith - consider the following story of an exchange between a professor and a student: (while the author is unknown and the story has morphed over time, the overall logic is worth pondering)

'Let me explain the problem science has with religion. The atheist professor of philosophy pauses before his class and then asks one of his new students to stand.

'You're a Christian, aren't you, son?' 'Yes sir, 'the student says.

'So you believe in God?' 'Absolutely.'

Is God good?' 'Sure! God's good.'

'Is God all-powerful? Can God do anything?' 'Yes'

'Are you good or evil?' 'The Bible says I'm evil.'

The professor grins knowingly. 'Aha! The Bible!' He considers for a moment. 'Here's one for you. Let's say there's a sick person over here and you can cure him. You can do it. Would you help him? Would you try?' 'Yes sir, I would.'

'So you're good...!' 'I wouldn't say that.'

'But why not say that? You'd help a sick and maimed person if you could. Most of us would if we could. But God doesn't.'

The student does not answer, so the professor continues. 'He doesn't, does he? My brother was a Christian who died of cancer, even though he prayed to Jesus to heal him. How is this Jesus good? Can you answer that one?'

The student remains silent. 'No, you can't, can you?' the professor says. He takes a sip of water from a glass on his desk to give the student time to relax. 'Let's start again, young fella. Is God good?' 'Er...yes,' the student says.

'Is Satan good?' The student doesn't hesitate on this one. 'No.'

'Then where does Satan come from?' The student falters. 'From God'

'That's right. God made Satan, didn't he? Tell me, son. Is there evil in this world?' 'Yes sir.'

'Evil's everywhere, isn't it? And God did make everything, correct?' 'Yes'

'So who created evil?' The professor continued, 'If God created everything, then God created evil, since evil exists, and according to the principle that our works define who we are, then God is evil.'

Again, the student has no answer. 'Is there sickness? Immorality? Hatred? Ugliness? All these terrible things, do they exist in this world?' The student squirms on his feet. 'Yes.'

'So who created them?' The student does not answer again, so the professor repeats his question.

'Who created them?' There is still no answer. Suddenly the lecturer breaks away to pace in front of the classroom. The class is mesmerized.

'Tell me,' he continues onto another student. 'Do you believe in Jesus Christ, son?' The student's voice betrays him and cracks. 'Yes, professor, I do.'

The old man stops pacing. 'Science says you have five senses you use to identify and observe the world around you. Have you ever seen Jesus?' 'No sir. I've never seen Him.'

'Then tell us if you've ever heard your Jesus?' 'No, sir, I have not.'

'Have you ever felt your Jesus, tasted your Jesus or smelt your Jesus? Have you ever had any sensory perception of Jesus Christ, or God for that matter?' 'No, sir, I'm afraid I haven't.'

'Yet you still believe in him?' 'Yes'

'According to the rules of empirical, testable, demonstrable protocol, science says your God doesn't exist... What do you say to that, son?' 'Nothing,' the student replies.. 'I only have my faith.'

'Yes, faith,' the professor repeats. 'And that is the problem science has with God. There is no evidence, only faith.'

The student stands quietly for a moment, before asking a question of His own. 'Professor, is there such thing as heat?' 'Yes. '

'And is there such a thing as cold?' 'Yes, son, there's cold too.'

'No sir, there isn't.' The professor turns to face the student, obviously interested. The room suddenly becomes very quiet. The student begins to explain. 'You can have lots of heat, even more heat, super-heat, mega-heat, unlimited heat, white heat, a little heat or no heat, but we don't have anything called 'cold'. We can hit down to 458 degrees below zero, which is no heat, but we can't go any further after that. There is no such thing as cold; otherwise we would be able to go colder than the lowest -458 degrees. Everybody or object is susceptible to study when it has or transmits energy, and heat is what makes a body or matter have or transmit energy. Absolute zero (-458 F) is the total absence of heat. You see, sir, cold is only a word we use to describe the absence of heat. We cannot measure cold. Heat we can measure in thermal units because heat is energy. Cold is not the opposite of heat, sir, just the absence of it.'

Silence across the room. A pen drops somewhere in the classroom, sounding like a hammer.

'What about darkness, professor. Is there such a thing as darkness?' 'Yes,' the professor replies without hesitation. 'What is night if it isn't darkness?'

'You're wrong again, sir. Darkness is not something; it is the absence of something. You can have low light, normal light, bright light, flashing light, but if you have no light constantly you have nothing and it's called darkness, isn't it? That's the meaning we use to define the word. In reality, darkness isn't. If it were, you would be able to make darkness darker, wouldn't you?'

The professor begins to smile at the student in front of him. This will be a good semester. 'So what point are you making, young man? My point is, your philosophical premise is flawed to start with, and so your conclusion must also be flawed.'

The professor's face cannot hide his surprise this time. 'Flawed? Can you explain how?'

'You are working on the premise of duality,' the student explains... 'You argue that there is life and then there's death; a good God and a bad God. You are viewing the concept of God as something finite, something we can measure. Sir, science can't even explain a thought.' 'It uses electricity and magnetism, but has never seen, much less fully understood, either one. To view death as the opposite of life is to be ignorant of the fact that death cannot exist as a substantive thing. Death is not the opposite of life, just the absence of it.' 'Now tell me, professor. Do you teach your students that they evolved from a monkey?'

'If you are referring to the natural evolutionary process, young man, yes, of course I do.'

'Have you ever observed evolution with your own eyes, sir?' The professor begins to shake his head, still smiling, as he realizes where the argument is going. A very good semester, indeed.

'Since no one has ever observed the process of evolution at work and cannot even prove that this process is an on-going endeavor, are you not teaching your opinion, sir? Are you now not a scientist, but a preacher?'

The class is in uproar. The student remains silent until the commotion has subsided. 'To continue the point you were making earlier to the other student, let me give you an example of what I mean.'

The student looks around the room. 'Is there anyone in the class who has ever seen the professor's brain?' The class breaks out into laughter.

'Is there anyone here who has ever heard the professor's brain, felt the professor's brain, touched or smelt the professor's brain? No one appears to have done so.

So, according to the established rules of empirical, stable, demonstrable protocol, science says that you have no brain, with all due respect, sir.' 'So if science says you have no brain, how can we trust your lectures, sir?'

Now the room is silent. The professor just stares at the student, his face unreadable. Finally, after what seems an eternity, the old man answers. 'I guess you'll have to take them on faith.'

'Now, you accept that there is faith, and, in fact, faith exists with life,' the student continues. Now, sir, is there such a thing as evil?' Now uncertain, the professor responds, 'Of course, there is. We see it every day. It is in the daily example of man's inhumanity to man. It is in the multitude of crime and violence everywhere in the world. These manifestations are nothing else but evil.'

To this the student replied, 'Evil does not exist sir, or at least it does not exist unto itself. Evil is simply the absence of God. It is just like darkness and cold, a word that man has created to describe the absence of God. God did not create evil. Evil is the result of what happens when man does not have God's love present in his heart. It's like the cold that comes when there is no heat or the darkness that comes when there is no light.'

The professor sat down.

Does God Exist?

A man went to a barbershop to have his hair cut and his beard trimmed. As the barber began to work, they began to have a good conversation. They talked about so many things and various subjects. When they eventually touched on the subject of God, The barber said: 'I don't believe that God exists.

'Why do you say that?' asked the customer.

'Well, you just have to go out in the street to realize that God doesn't exist.
Tell me, if God exists, would there be so many sick people? Would there be abandoned children?

If God existed, there would be neither suffering nor pain.
I can't imagine a loving God who would allow all of these things.'

The customer thought for a moment, but didn't respond because he didn't want to start an argument. The barber finished his job and the customer left the shop.

Just after he left the barbershop, he saw a man in the street with long, stringy, dirty hair and an untrimmed beard.

He looked dirty and unkempt. The customer turned back and entered the barbershop again and he said to the barber: 'You know what? Barbers do not exist.'

'How can you say that?' asked the surprised Barber.
'I am here, and I am a barber. And I just worked on you!' 'No!' the customer exclaimed.
'Barbers don't exist because if they did, there would be no people with dirty long hair and untrimmed beards, like that man outside.'

'Ah, but barbers DO exist! That's what happens when people do not come to me.'
'Exactly!' affirmed the customer. 'That's the Point!

God, too, DOES exist! That's what happens when people do not go to Him and don't look to Him for help. That's why there's so much pain and suffering in the world.' (author unknown)

The Tree Of God's Power & The Tree Of Satan's Power

At the root of all actions and events there are only two taproots; God and Satan. Both have power. Both are real. However, the source of their power is different and produces opposite fruits.

It is critical to understand the source of God's power and Satan's power. Understanding these sources will enable you to discern what power source politicians, government and business is using to influence and control us.

The Tree of God's Power: The taproot is honor obtained through love. Everything God does flows from the fountain of His eternal and infinite love of His children; US!. God keeps His own commandments; perfectly. So when He asks us to keep His commandments it is comforting to know that He has 'been there, done that' and is doing that! Commandment keeping leads to Godly power and true joy.

Note that the tree trunk and branches of these roots produce that which is good; self-less service to improve mankind, honesty, freedom to choose, integrity, truth, trustworthiness, abundance and eternal progression. God's powers are the fruits of these roots and shoots. If we come to know God as our Father in Heaven and the laws that He

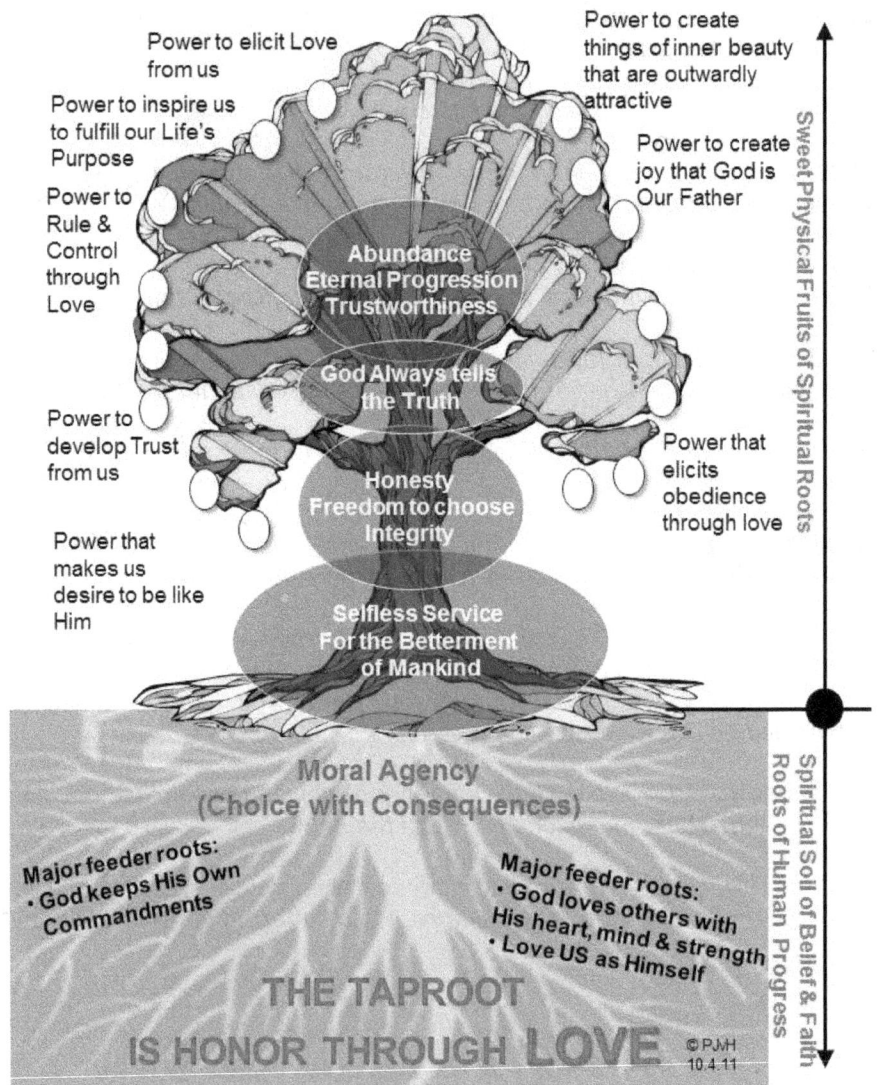

The Tree of God's Power

Power to elicit Love from us

Power to create things of inner beauty that are outwardly attractive

Power to inspire us to fulfill our Life's Purpose

Power to create joy that God is Our Father

Power to Rule & Control through Love

Abundance
Eternal Progression
Trustworthiness

God Always tells the Truth

Power to develop Trust from us

Power that elicits obedience through love

Honesty
Freedom to choose
Integrity

Power that makes us desire to be like Him

Selfless Service
For the Betterment
of Mankind

Sweet Physical Fruits of Spiritual Roots

Moral Agency
(Choice with Consequences)

Major feeder roots:
• God keeps His Own Commandments

Major feeder roots:
• God loves others with His heart, mind & strength
• Love US as Himself

Spiritual Soil of Belief & Faith
Roots of Human Progress

THE TAPROOT
IS HONOR THROUGH LOVE

©PJH
10.4.11

lives by we come to understand what many people do not understand. For example why is there evil in the world? Why does God allow suffering? When we exercise faith in Christ we come to understand Our Father in Heaven and we love Him, we are inspired by Him and we trust Him. Keeping God's commandments results in knowing Him, knowing the truth, knowing who we are and we develop inner goodness that reflects in the beauty and handsomeness of our countenances. We willingly submit to His leadership because we know that He wants the best for us and doing so optimizes our progression and joy.

Through faith and living God's commandments we come to know that we are indeed the offspring of God created in His image. Application is the key! Learning without doing results in not knowing. We must do to know! John 15:10 records God's law in this way, "If ye keep my commandments, ye shall abide in my love; even as I have kept my Father's commandments, and abide in his love." And in 1 Jhn 2:3 we read, *"And hereby we do know that we know him, if we keep his commandments."* [emphasis added]

The Tree of Satan's Power: The taproot is control obtained through fear. This was Lucifer's (Satan) tactic used in the War in Heaven. He tried to instill fear into us by saying in effect 'Don't follow Jehovah because some of you will be lost through sin and becoming unclean, and you know that no unclean thing can dwell in God's presence. So, you better follow me. I will take care of you so not one soul will be lost.'

The Tree of Satan's Power

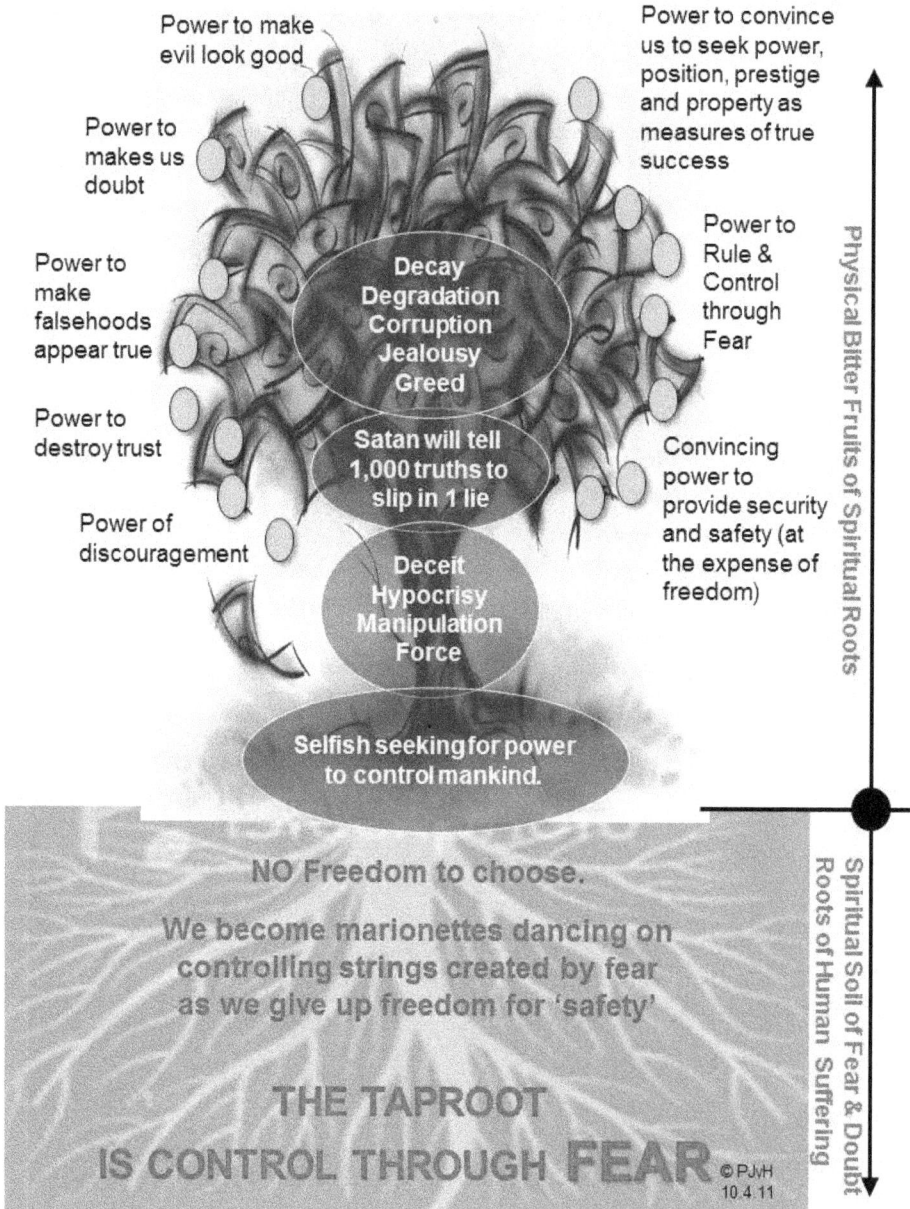

Power to make evil look good

Power to convince us to seek power, position, prestige and property as measures of true success

Power to makes us doubt

Power to make falsehoods appear true

Power to Rule & Control through Fear

Power to destroy trust

Decay Degradation Corruption Jealousy Greed

Satan will tell 1,000 truths to slip in 1 lie

Convincing power to provide security and safety (at the expense of freedom)

Power of discouragement

Deceit Hypocrisy Manipulation Force

Selfish seeking for power to control mankind.

Physical Bitter Fruits of Spiritual Roots

NO Freedom to choose.

We become marionettes dancing on controlling strings created by fear as we give up freedom for 'safety'

Spiritual Soil of Fear & Doubt
Roots of Human Suffering

THE TAPROOT IS CONTROL THROUGH FEAR

© PJvH
10.4.11

The trunk and branches of this approach to gaining power include selfish power mongering, deceitful speech and actions, hypocrisy, manipulation and force. Satan will entice with a thousand truths to slip in one lie and divert you down the wrong path of life. The leaves of Satan's tree of power are money $$$$, the love of which brings greed, jealousy, corruption, degraded behavior and the decay of civilizations.

The effect of being under Satan's power is to feel doubt, fear and mistrust of others.

The important thing to remember about these two Trees is that both God and Satan have power, but they use opposite forces to obtain power. God uses honor developed through His actions of love for us. Satan uses control gained through creating a climate of fear. Watch for these roots and fruits of power throughout this book and throughout life. This paradigm will enable you to discern between good and evil intent in all mankind.

Joseph Goebbels, Hitler's Nazi Propaganda Minister, said, *"If you tell a lie big enough and keep repeating it, people will eventually come to believe it. The lie can be maintained only for such time as the State can shield the people from the political, economic, and/or military consequences of the lie. It thus becomes vitally important for the State to use all of its powers to repress dissent, for the truth is the mortal enemy of the lie, and thus by extension, the truth is the greatest enemy of the State."*

The Tree Of Clarity & The Tree Of Distortion

Clear lenses improve vision. Sometimes we see what we choose to see. But seeing reality requires more. Who we are, our experiences, who taught us, how we were brought up, how we think, form mental filters through which our brains interpret, or 'see', life.

Like the trees of Truth and Falsehoods, the following diagrams of The Trees of Clarity and The Tree of Distortion have opposite tap and major feeder roots. And from the roots trees grow and bear the fruits. In these 'pictures worth a thousand words' are illustrations of the relationships between roots and fruits concerning clarity and distortion.

Despite similar genetics people's spiritual roots ingest ideologies that dramatically affect the clarity or distortion with which they see life. Different ideologies produce different behavior. On one hand we see a Mother Teresa whose ideology of service produced the good fruits of loving kindness to multitudes. On the other hand we see both the Nazis of WWII and the Muslim terrorist today whose evil ideologies of world domination produced bitter fruits of suffering and death to millions.

The taproot of the **Tree of Clarity** is **GOD** that produced what Benjamin Franklin called 'The American Religion. Yale University asked Ben Franklin, *'what is The America Religion?'* He responded: *'God lives, we will face him when we die, He will judge us, and therefore we should serve Him. The best way to serve Him is to serve our fellow man.'* Christians and Jews embrace this common set of beliefs. Living according to these truths influenced our Founding Fathers to create the Declaration of Independence and the U.S. Constitution. They are the life giving branches on which the sweet fruits of our Republic are produced. Note that the Tree of Clarity produced our <u>inalienable</u> rights of Life, Liberty and the Pursuit of Happiness (the original right was Property) that are granted by our Creator. Since they are <u>inalienable</u> rights the State cannot take them away.

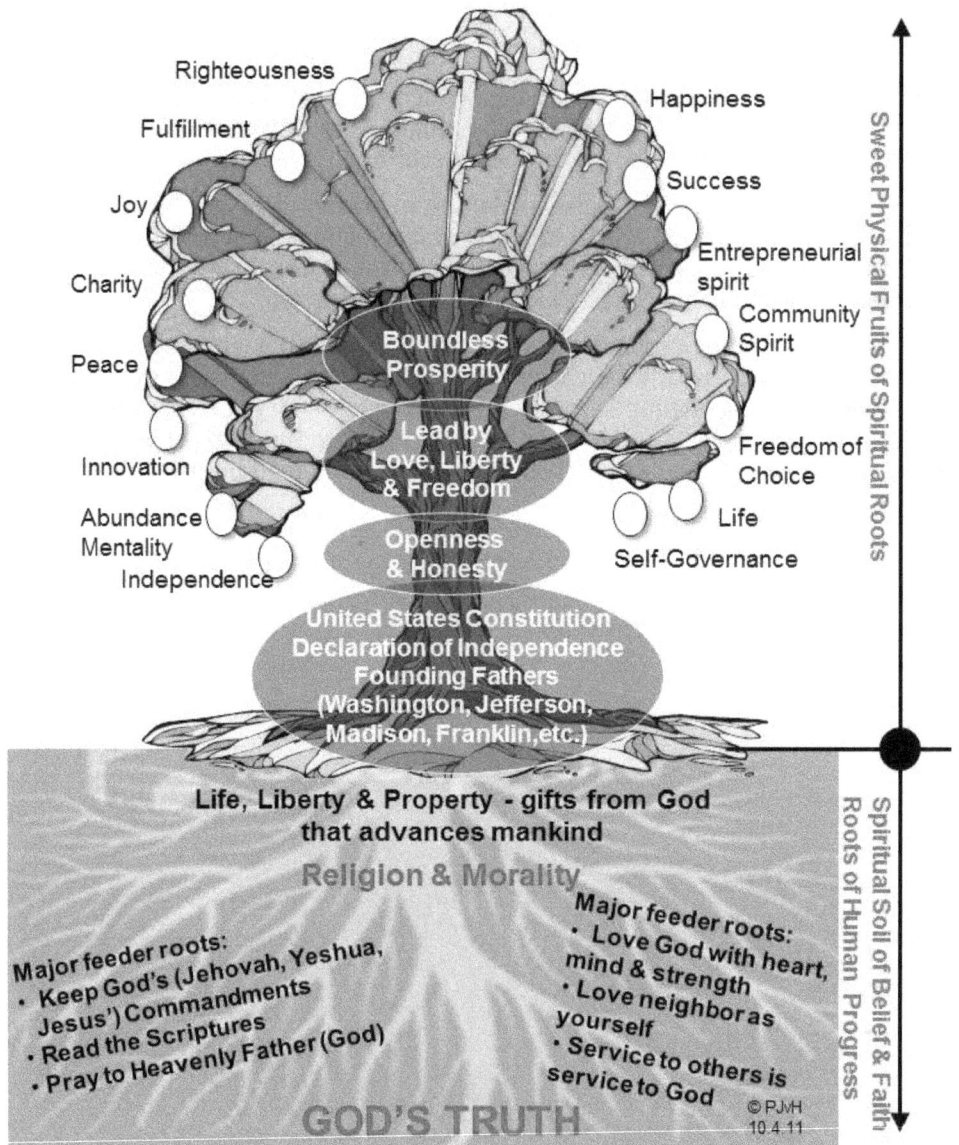

The Tree of Clarity

Righteousness
Fulfillment
Joy
Charity
Peace
Innovation
Abundance Mentality
Independence

Happiness
Success
Entrepreneurial spirit
Community Spirit
Freedom of Choice
Life
Self-Governance

Boundless Prosperity

Lead by Love, Liberty & Freedom

Openness & Honesty

United States Constitution
Declaration of Independence
Founding Fathers
(Washington, Jefferson, Madison, Franklin, etc.)

Life, Liberty & Property - gifts from God that advances mankind

Religion & Morality

Major feeder roots:
• Keep God's (Jehovah, Yeshua, Jesus') Commandments
• Read the Scriptures
• Pray to Heavenly Father (God)

Major feeder roots:
• Love God with heart, mind & strength
• Love neighbor as yourself
• Service to others is service to God

GOD'S TRUTH

© PJvH 10.4.11

Sweet Physical Fruits of Spiritual Roots

Spiritual Soil of Belief & Faith
Roots of Human Progress

15

The taproot of the **Tree of Distortion** is **SATAN** which produces a mentality that mankind achieves according to the law of the jungle, survival of the fittest, and that man accumulates more of the world's goods according to his superior intelligence, connections and sometimes, deceit. Under this paradigm even deceit is justified because there is no God, therefore there is no accountability to Him after this life, and therefore whatever is done in this life is OK because we answer to no one.

From these roots power mongers develop ideologies and governments of enslavement (communism, socialism, fascism, Marxism, Nazism etc.) with their predictable, and historically documented bitter fruits of human suffering. For example, Mao killed 70 million of his own people, Stalin - 20 million Russians, Hitler - 12 million Jews & Christians.

Note that The Tree of Distortion produced <u>alienable</u> rights of Life, Liberty and the Pursuit of Happiness (the original right was Property) granted by the State. If they are <u>alienable</u> rights granted by the State, they can be taken away by the State.

The Tree of Distortion

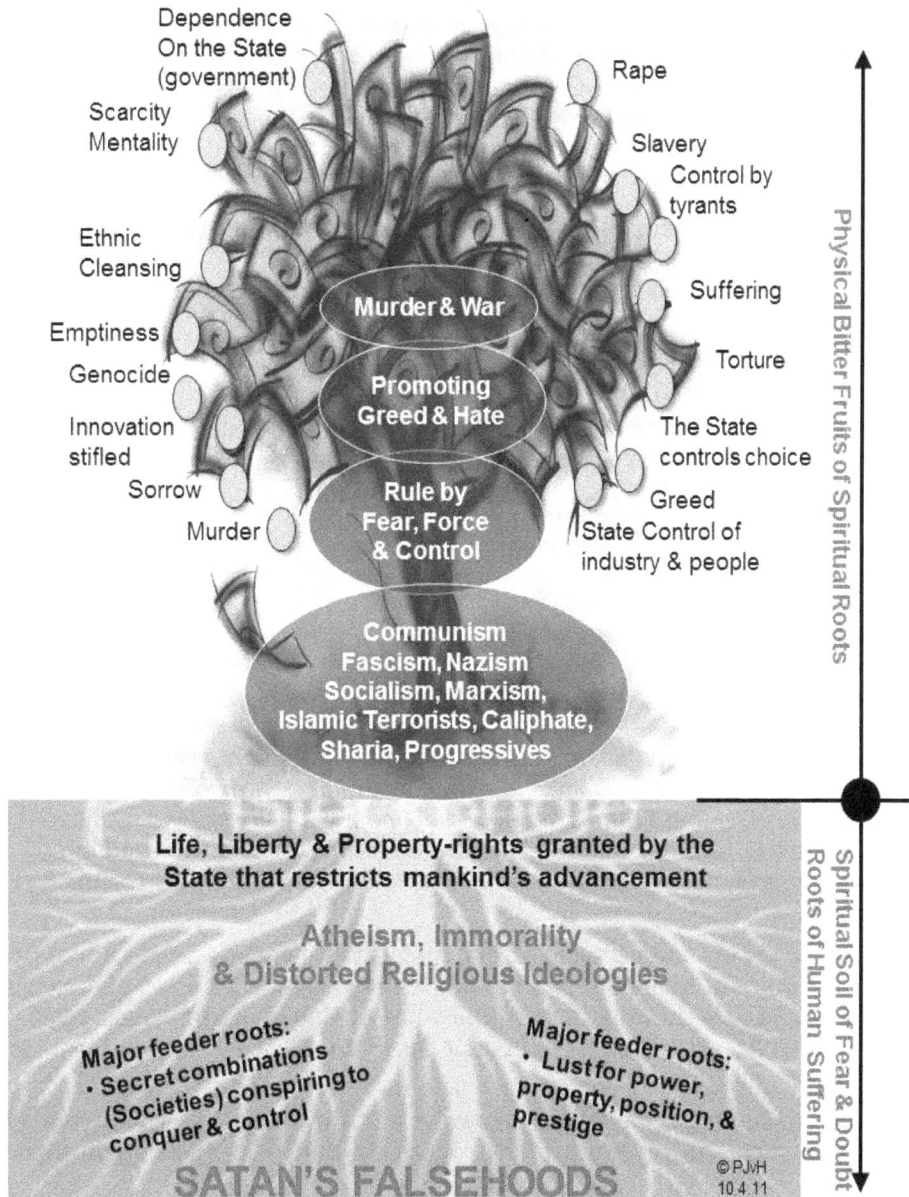

Dependence On the State (government)

Scarcity Mentality

Rape

Slavery Control by tyrants

Ethnic Cleansing

Suffering

Emptiness

Torture

Genocide

Murder & War

Innovation stifled

Promoting Greed & Hate

The State controls choice

Sorrow

Rule by Fear, Force & Control

Greed State Control of industry & people

Murder

Communism Fascism, Nazism Socialism, Marxism, Islamic Terrorists, Caliphate, Sharia, Progressives

Physical Bitter Fruits of Spiritual Roots

Life, Liberty & Property-rights granted by the State that restricts mankind's advancement

Spiritual Soil of Fear & Doubt Roots of Human Suffering

Atheism, Immorality & Distorted Religious Ideologies

Major feeder roots:
• Secret combinations (Societies) conspiring to conquer & control

Major feeder roots:
• Lust for power, property, position, & prestige

SATAN'S FALSEHOODS

© PJvH 10.4.11

We Must be Rooted in Truth

I have presented logical, common sense, explanations that God exists and other truths relating to our relationship to Him including the forces affecting our lives. I can testify personally of these truths, independent of any man.

However, what is critical is for each person to know these truths for themselves. How can each person come to knowledge of the truth? The answer is by exercising the full extent of our intellect, by studying, by searching, by pondering – and lastly, and most importantly, by seeking confirmation of what we think is right from Our Father in Heaven. That requires faith in Him.

Faith is a choice! We can choose to believe in God, exercise faith in Him by living His commandments and thus increasingly enlighten our minds which leads to greater knowledge of His never-changing truths. Or, we can choose not to believe in God, exercise faith in our own limited intellect, which darkens our minds toward the evolutionary falsehoods of Satan to the eventual hopeless dead-end of ever-changing scientific 'evidence.'

If Einstein used 7% of his brain and typical man uses about 3-5%, what is the rest of that gray matter doing and what is it there for? The rest of that stuff is our sub-conscious mind and it helps perform various autonomic functions in the body like digesting, breathing etc. The greater part of it is connected to the ether, the holy spirit of God, His power and intelligence that fills the immensity of space; in short, all truth.

Before the power of your 3-5% 'great' intellect leads you to the dead-end of your own reasoning and you reject this information, please understand the most powerful principle of truth-finding. There is another 'thinking part of us. Scientists have concluded that there are more neurons in the heart than in the brain. Your heart thinks! Praying to God taps not only into the other 95% of your sub-conscious brain, but your heart and to your entire spirit. Dr. Deepak Chopra, the former head of the New England School of Medicine who taught at Tufts and Yale, stated that at the molecular level we humans are rivers of information and intelligence. Combining all these levels of our intelligence enables us to connect with God, the source of all truth.

We are all blessed with the light of Christ; knowing right from wrong. However, discernment is enhanced when we invite God's spirit to aid understanding. There is a way for you to KNOW the truth – independent of me or any other man. The way is to study, ponder and then pray to God to know what is true. The Apostle James teaches it this way – *"If any of you lack wisdom let him ask of God, who giveth liberally, but have him ask in faith nothing wavering."* (James 1:5-6) The ancient prophet Moroni stated: *"... I would exhort you that ye would ask God, the Eternal Father, in the name of Christ, if these things are not true; and if ye shall ask with a sincere heart, with real intent, having faith in Christ, he will manifest the truth of it unto you, by the power of the Holy Ghost. And by the power of the Holy Ghost ye may know the truth **of all things**."* (**THE TRUTH OF ALL THINGS!**

Answers to prayer and personal revelation most often come in the form of peace, and warmth and light. The voice of God's Spirit is more often felt than heard as an audible sound. It is comforting to the soul. The scriptures refer to the voice of God as a still, small voice. Please, if you do not know, try God on His word. I testify that Our Father loves us and wants us to know the truth. God will answer your prayers!

I ask you to sincerely pray about this work, and all works. Discern for yourselves what is true. Let God – not man – testify truth to your spirit. In that way, and only in that way, you will not be deceived and you will know for yourself what is true. And truth is the most precious thing, for it sets us free from the bondage of ignorance.

You <u>must</u> know who you are. The truth is that you are a spiritual son or daughter of God our Heavenly Father. You have the spiritual inheritance of divinity in your soul! Know this. Know who God is. Know why you are here, what your purpose is here. Learn where you are going when you leave here. These are essential to know in order to see the truth of life and understand this book.

God knows all things. He loves us more than anyone else. God is a god of truth and cannot lie. He wants us to know the truth and has provided a way for us to know.

Please reader if you do not know who you are, ask God, your Father in Heaven. He will answer. You will feel the warmth of peace in your soul as He confirms truth in your soul. God communicates with us spirit to spirit – from Father to child, whom we are!

Summary Points:

- God is the original author of truth and liberty.
- There are many confusing and conflicting voices in the world.
- Discerning truth is essential to know how to act.
- There are only two root forces at work in the world; good and evil.
- Truth and goodness come from God. Lies and evil comes from Satan.
- Discerning between truth and lies is essential. The way to know truth is to ask God who is Our Father in Heaven – the source of all truth. IF we ask Him with real intent to do something about it when He answers (meaning we will apply what we learn from Him), with faith in His son Jesus Christ, and in the sincerity of our hearts, He will answer us by the power of the Holy Ghost. One of the most common ways He will answer is that you will feel peace in your soul concerning the thing you asked about.
- Study plans for our welfare and our Country. Evaluate where that plan will lead; and it will reveal their roots. Plans lead either to more freedom or more dependency. Outcomes reveal the roots of God or Lucifer. Knowing the roots of politicians' positions and promises empowers us to make better voting choices.
- Like the ancient mariners who looked to the North Star to successfully navigate Earth's oceans, we must look to the North Star of our lives who is God (Jesus Christ, Jehovah, Yahweh, The God of Nature) to successfully navigate today's oceans of uncertainty.
- Not understanding truth opens the door to secularism and empowers evil men to gain control over us.

Action Steps:

1. If you do not already know, please take time to KNOW who you are through the power of study and prayer to Your Father in Heaven. You are his child. He wants you to know.
2. Test it. Check it out for yourself. Gain your own testimony of truth. Doing so will empower you to act like nothing else will.
3. Please use this essential tool of receiving answers to prayer and personal revelation to know truth of all things, including what is presented in each chapter of this book. Pray before reading and after reading to know the truth of all things from the source of all truth.

End of Chapter

2

America's Real Roots

*"Even so every good tree bringeth forth good fruit;
but a corrupt tree bringeth forth evil fruit."* Matt 7:17

Roots, shoots, and fruits reveal much about trees. Good roots feeding from good soil produce good shoots that create good fruits. Likewise, people, civilizations, and countries have spiritual roots, shoots, and fruits. It is essential to understand America's real roots for they explain where we came from and how we became a light to the world.

Understanding America's crisis requires understanding her roots. America's roots are truth and liberty; its origins extend farther back in history than most people realize. God's truths were woven into the fabric of America from the beginning. We must know truth, promote truth and live truth.

The Tree of Truth - The Tree of Falsehoods

America has her roots in the Tree of Truth.

The fruits of our lives originate in the roots of our choices. The old adage –you are what you eat applies to our thoughts as well. What we ingest in our minds affects decisions. Decisions determine destiny. What we see, hear, smell, touch, think and do create our reality. Thoughts, desires, appetites, passions, words are roots of life's fruits. Spiritual roots bear physical fruits.

The Trees of Truth and Falsehoods have opposite roots. From roots trees grow and bear fruit.

Despite similar genetics of the original seeds, uptake from the root systems can either facilitate growth to help fulfill the measure of creation (to become what they were created to be) or distort dendroform (the shape and character of the tree) and bear bitter fruit. Roots, and what they absorb, affect outcome and can produce very different fruits.

People have spiritual roots; things they believe, understand and know. Like physical tree roots, spiritual roots affect outcome. What we ingest into our minds affects how we think and behave. Ralph Waldo Emerson had it right when he said, *"Sow a thought and you reap an action; sow an act and you reap a habit; sow a habit and you reap a character; sow a character and you reap a destiny."* In computer language - garbage in, garbage out, and the corollary is true too, wisdom in enables wise choices.

In Daniel Chapter 2 we learn about how in our day God will establish His Kingdom 'as a stone cut out of a mountain without hands'. His Kingdom is the sledge hammer of truth that will break in pieces the image that Nebuchadnezzar's saw which represented latter-day kingdoms built by men. Truth is both the sword that cuts asunder and the hammer that brakes in pieces Satan's falsehoods.

The diagrams of **The Tree of Truth** and **The Tree of Falsehoods** on the following pages convey a thousand words to better understand the root and fruit relationships operating in our lives.

From the taproot of **GOD** in **The Tree of Truth** our desires, appetites and passions become good. God is a God of Truth and cannot lie. He is the author of clarity and all that is good. Knowing God and seeking His will influences the mind to seek that which is good. Advancing up this narrow path of life develops honor which creates trust. Trust is the foundation upon which human relationships thrive. Trust empowers progress in righteous endeavors. Continuing on this path and applying the principles derived from God refines and advances the human spirit. The end result are sweet fruits of the Tree of Truth. Trees are known by their fruits; apple, pear, cherry, etc. Likewise, we know the Tree of Truth by its fruits.

"...Hereby know ye the Spirit of God: [which is truth] Every spirit that confesseth that Jesus Christ is come in the flesh is of God: And every spirit that confesseth not that Jesus Christ is come in the flesh is not of God: and this is that spirit of anti-Christ, [who is] in the world. They are of the world: therefore speak they of the world, and the world heareth them. We are of God: he that knoweth God heareth us; he that is not of God heareth not us.

***Hereby know we the spirit of truth, and the spirit of error**. (Jhn 4:1-3,5-6*

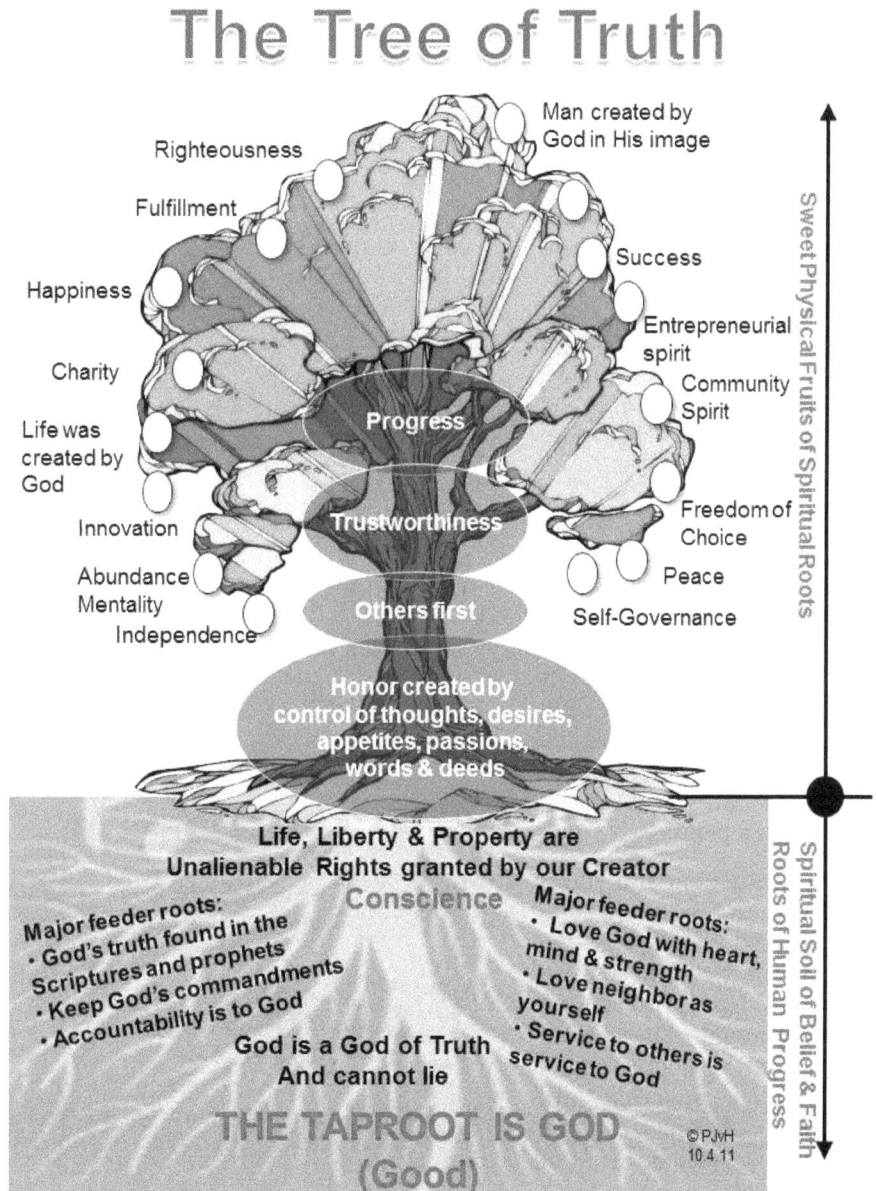

The Tree of Truth

Man created by God in His image
Righteousness
Fulfillment
Success
Happiness
Entrepreneurial spirit
Charity
Community Spirit
Life was created by God
Progress
Innovation
Trustworthiness
Freedom of Choice
Abundance Mentality
Others first
Peace
Independence
Self-Governance
Honor created by control of thoughts, desires, appetites, passions, words & deeds

Sweet Physical Fruits of Spiritual Roots

Life, Liberty & Property are Unalienable Rights granted by our Creator
Conscience
Major feeder roots:
• God's truth found in the Scriptures and prophets
• Keep God's commandments
• Accountability is to God
Major feeder roots:
• Love God with heart, mind & strength
• Love neighbor as yourself
• Service to others is service to God
God is a God of Truth And cannot lie
THE TAPROOT IS GOD (Good)
© PJvH 10.4.11

Spiritual Soil of Belief & Faith Roots of Human Progress

From the taproot of **LUCIFER** in **The Tree of Falsehoods** our desires, appetites and passions become evil. Satan is a liar from the beginning, the author of confusion and all that is evil. Satan orients the mind to seek evil. Descending down this wide road of death develops dishonor which creates distrust. Distrust is the sandy foundation upon which human relationships fail. Note that the often hidden and underlying desires of the Tree of Falsehoods are the leaves of money $$$$ and the lust for power, position, power and prestige that destroy and degrade the human spirit. The end result is the bitter fruits that the Tree of Falsehoods produce.

Satan presents drugs, tobacco, alcohol, food, alternative lifestyles, and gambling as 'feel-good alternatives' to reality; and they do! They do provide an escape from dealing with life, temporarily that is. Then after the bait is taken and the hook is set the evil 'fisher of men' reels in his catch and enslaves the soul with addiction to substance and feelings. In the end, the 'take this or do that and you will be free' bait ends up with the opposite; loss of freedom to choose.

God's commandments are guard-rails along the path of life designed to keep us within the bounds of safe travel. Thus God counsels us to avoid the very things Satan promotes. God wants to be empower us to be free. Satan wants us to destroy us to be enslaved.

Good presents itself as what it is. It does not deceive. It teaches correct principles and invites people to follow. Evil poses as good. Evil calls good evil and evil good. Evil teaches a close resemblance to correct principles but always deviates from it on one or more points.

Tyrants coerce, nudge and if needed, force 'sheeple' (people who act like sheep – they follow the leader even when the leader is leading them to slaughter) to do what they want. Their control increases in degrees until insidious flaxen chords become chains of enslavement.

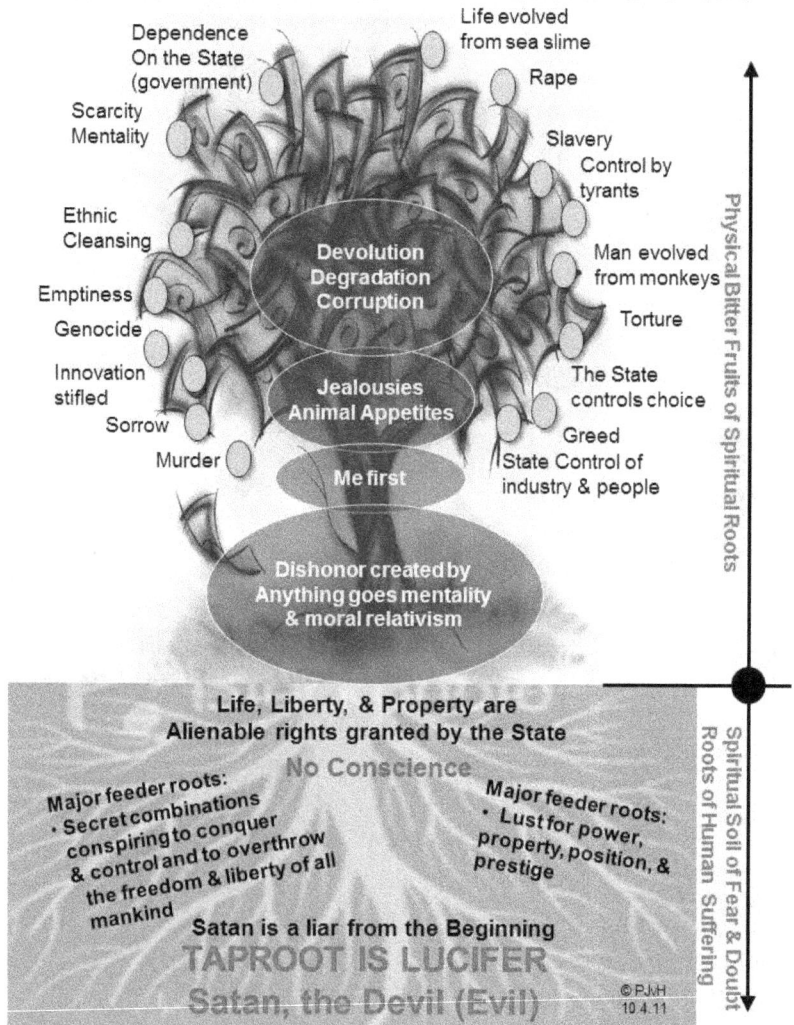

The Tree of Falsehoods

Dependence On the State (government)
Scarcity Mentality
Ethnic Cleansing
Emptiness
Genocide
Innovation stifled
Sorrow
Murder

Life evolved from sea slime
Rape
Slavery Control by tyrants
Man evolved from monkeys
Torture
The State controls choice
Greed
State Control of industry & people

Devolution Degradation Corruption

Jealousies Animal Appetites

Me first

Dishonor created by Anything goes mentality & moral relativism

Physical Bitter Fruits of Spiritual Roots

Spiritual Soil of Fear & Doubt Roots of Human Suffering

Life, Liberty, & Property are Alienable rights granted by the State
No Conscience

Major feeder roots:
· Secret combinations conspiring to conquer & control and to overthrow the freedom & liberty of all mankind

Major feeder roots:
· Lust for power, property, position, & prestige

Satan is a liar from the Beginning
TAPROOT IS LUCIFER
Satan, the Devil (Evil)

© PJH 10.4.11

Spiritual Roots of America's Fruits

The forces affecting America and indeed all human life on Earth today started in the pre-mortal existence. The pre-mortal War In Heaven was a war between two ideologies; freedom and slavery. America's spiritual roots extend far back into the pre-mortal existence where we choose God's freedom over Satan's slavery. America's existence is a continuation of ancient root choices.

America has always faced tough choices, and for good reason. John the Revelator records the event as follows: *"And the great dragon was cast out, that old serpent, called the Devil, and Satan, which deceiveth the whole world: he was cast out into the earth, and his angels were cast out with him."* (Rev 12:8) Lucifer in his wrath declared that he would reign with blood and horror on this earth. And he has. His influence is the root source of all the evil acts from Adam to today.

An estimated 120 billion people lived on earth from Adam to 2011. So if we do the math it results in approximately 180 billion sons and daughters of God living in the pre-mortal life. 1/3 of God's children followed Lucifer in the preexistence and were cast out of heaven down to earth. Therefore approximately 60 billion evil spirits live disembodied on earth with us. Their mission is to make us miserable like they are. They are miserable because they made the wrong choice in the preexistence, they are denied physical bodies like we have and their god is Satan. There are approximately 6.6 billion people living on earth today. That means that for each person there are approximately 10 evil spirits for each one of us! We are greatly outnumbered! Those Satanic spirits hate that we enjoy the God-given freedoms guaranteed under America's U.S. Constitution. So they fight to destroy America's freedoms using all the weapons available – everything that is anti-American including communism, socialism, progressivism, Nazism, Marxism etc. No wonder this life is so hard sometimes! No wonder there is so much temptation and evil! These evil spirits do not sleep and are relentless in their pursuit of our sorrow and slavery just as they are enslaved to Satan. (Before you criticize the math – yes I realize that not all of God's children have come to earth for their mortal experience by 2012 – but this is the best approximation available with present knowledge. The overall meaning is still valid for our purposes.)

Having physical bodies is a great advantage; it enables us to progress to become more like our Father in Heaven if we make the right choices to follow God's teachings. Remember that spirits with physical bodies have power over spirits without physical bodies, no matter how many there are. Therefore, 'the devil made me do it is false. We have a choice and we have the power over him, especially if we enlist the help of Jesus Christ in our effort.

Thus, the correct lens through which we must view life is that the War in Heaven is still raging on this earth – the war between good and evil – the war between God and Satan – the war between freedom and slavery – the war between America's freedoms and the World's tyranny.

Lucifer (Satan) is still trying to influence men to do evil and God is still inviting men to do good. Satan is still trying to control us along with his millions of followers. God is still encouraging us to choose good over evil that enables us to retain our freedom.

Satan's distorted view of life is where man judges what is right and wrong depending on circumstances. It is a view that man's opinions are superior to God's commandments. And Satan is making headway. In 1993 80% of adults believed that there are clear guidelines about right and wrong, good and evil. By 2002 75% believe that the difference between right and wrong is relative.

Those who believe in Satan's lie that man evolved from some ancient sea slime feel no accountability toward God. No accountability means you never have to face the music for bad choices, bad behavior, or lying, cheating, murder etc.; a convenient, but false, ideology that produced the bitter fruit called 'relative morality.'

The truth is there ARE moral absolutes. There IS right and wrong. God defines truth and falsehoods, right and wrong, good and evil. The Ten Commandments is a good place to start. Satan tries to sell us his substitutes called 'moral relativism.' Many teachers in schools and professors in colleges and universities are teaching and practicing relative morality. Knowingly or not, they are Satan's agents.

God's law preserves life and liberty (freedom to choose). This was the issue over which the War in Heaven was fought. America's law is the Declaration of Independence and the U.S. Constitution – the supreme law of the land – that insures God's inalienable rights of life and liberty.

Joseph Smith said, "The Constitution of the United States is a glorious standard, and it is founded in the wisdom of God. It is a heavenly banner." President Lorenzo Snow said, "We trace the hand of the Almighty in framing the Constitution of our land and believe that the Lord raised up men purposely for the accomplishment of this object"

It is clear that the spiritual roots of America are in God's law from the pre-mortal life. America IS God's doing. America IS God's land that is choice above all other lands on the face of the Earth. God created the land we call America so His laws could bless His children!

America's power, or loss of it, is derived from the sources of power illustrated in the following two Trees:

America's Cleansings

God has cleansed the Earth of evil before. In the days of Noah God cleansed evil from the Earth with a universal flood. He did this when the now-divided continents were together in one land mass. It was a time when disobedience to God's commandments degraded mankind so severely that God chose to protect His future children from being infected with this evil by removing the evil hosts that carried it and start civilization over again. After the flood of Noah the Earth was divided 'in the days of Peleg' into separate continents we see today.

Peter warned of false teachers when he wrote *"...there were false prophets also among the people, even as there shall be false teachers among you, who privily shall bring in damnable heresies, even denying the Lord that bought them, and bring upon themselves swift destruction."* (2 Pet 2:1) Some things never change. Today we also have false teachers whose goal is to separate us from our Father. Branches separate from the vine dies. Man separated from the source of life also dies spiritually and is therefore easier to control.

God also cleansed the Americas – twice. After Noah's flood two great civilizations were destroyed; first the Jaredites and then the Nephites. In sequence, they rose to be great nations, turned to evil and were destroyed from off this land when they became ripe with iniquity. ('destroyed' in this context means their civilization – their social order - no longer existed, not that every person was killed.) God reserves this land of America, which is choice above all other lands, for those who will worship him and remain righteous. The descendants of these former civilizations are the Aztec, Mayan, Incas, and Native American tribes.

For American's today, we need to ask ourselves a key question- how righteous or evil are we? Subsequent chapters of this book will seek to reveal evidence that will enable the reader to answer that question accurately.

Americans - Owners or Stewards?

Many people think our life is ours and that we own the earth. Whatever gain we enjoy it is solely because of one's greater intelligence, or pure luck. This mindset typically derives from belief in evolution. Since their ancestors were the slime of the sea, they answer to no one and death is the end of existence – dust to dust so to speak. They OWN themselves and the Earth.

The truth is that we were endowed by God our Creator with the opportunity to come to earth. We are here to be tested and to prove ourselves worthy of returning home to live with our Father in Heaven by demonstrating that we will choose to keep His commandments. The truth is that we are not our own, we were bought with the price of the best blood that ever coursed through the veins of man; the blood of Jesus Christ. Consider Paul's writings in 1 Cor: 6:19-20 *"..know ye not that* your *body is the temple of the Holy Ghost which is in you, which ye have of God, and ye are not your own? For ye are bought* with a price*: therefore glorify God in* your body*, and in* your spirit*, which are God's.* This understanding derives from knowing the truth of creation; who you really are. We are STEWARDS of our bodies and of the Earth.

To expand understanding on this subject the following story is revealing:

> A sophisticated, 'elite', powerful and very learned man came to God and said, 'we don't need you anymore. We grow our own food, build our own houses, trade our own stocks, heal ourselves with our medicines, clone our own animals and we can even clone humans.'
>
> God said. 'O.K., have at it!'
>
> So the man picked up a handful of dirt to start his own world.
>
> And God said, 'Oh no, no, no!...get your own dirt!'

When we get too full of ourselves, it is well to remember that in the beginning God created the Earth where upon we dwell for a short season of mortality. Our lives here are a gift from God who created us and the Earth for His purposes which are to enable us, His children, to progress, gain immortality and eternal life.

Therefore, we are stewards over 'our' bodies and 'our' Earth and will be accountable for both to God whose children we are and whose Earth this is.

America's Roots in which God?

Are we rooted in God, our Father in Heaven, or in the God of this world who is Satan?

When trees are severed from their roots, they die. Likewise when a country is severed from its roots, it dies. When people are severed from their root connection with God, they forget who they are - sons and daughters of God - and then they become subject to every wind of doctrine and every philosophy of man, especially those charismatic types with strong persuasion powers.

This is how Progressives work; they separate people and America from their roots. Progressives disconnect us from who we really are by advancing 'theories' as fact. Like the theory of evolution as how man came to be. Contrast that with creation fact; that we are sons and daughters of Heavenly Father. When we remember that, we are empowered by that root knowledge.

If Progressives can separate our connection with God, they can easily persuade us to their way of thinking and control us. It's all about control and power!

God established America through the hands of righteous men whom He raised up. Lose our connection to this truth and America becomes led first by socialists and Marxists, then by communists - eventually by a tyrannical dictator.

There are two basic ways to motivate people; love and fear. Christ uses the persuasive power of teaching correct principles and having patience with us while we learn to apply them. Satan's way is to create a climate of fear and to pose as a savior to 'protect us' with intent to enslave.

These two basic motivational techniques enable better judgment of the landscape of life. Applying these principles enables us to see intent clearly. Consider Rahm Emanuel - Obama's first term czar - when he says *"you never want a serious crisis to go to waste"*. Rahm knows that crises create fear, and fear can be used to gain more control over the people so that the 'elite' can further gorge themselves on the labors of the common man.

Summary Points:

- America's real roots are with God; the original author of truth and liberty.

- There are many confusing and conflicting ideologies in the world; the U.S. Constitution and America's Republic comes from God.

- When politicians, or anyone, present their plan for our welfare and our Country, study where that plan will lead; and the roots of their plan will reveal the future fruits. Plans lead either to more freedom or more dependency. Roots are either in God or Lucifer. Knowing the roots of politicians' positions and promises to make better voting choices.

- Knowing America's real roots - its true history - empowers and clarifies voters choice so that we vote on principle - NOT on party, color, gender, race etc...

Action Steps:

Apply knowledge of Americas real roots when you vote to restore and advance our Republic.

End of Chapter

3

The War Continues on Earth

"And Cain talked with Abel his brother:
and it came to pass, when they were in the field,
that Cain rose up against Abel his brother, and slew him". Genesis 4:8

All the pain, suffering, injury, murders, and wars since the beginning of time have their roots in the War in Heaven. That war continues today. It is the war between good and evil. It is the war between God's way and Satan's way. God's plan on Earth is His Plan of Salvation that provides for moral agency and is embodied in the Scriptures. Satan's plan on Earth is the enslavement of man that deprives man of agency and is embodied in communism, socialism, fascism, Marxism, Nazism, modern day Progressivism and Islamic Sharia law.

For the purposes of this book I will not distinguish between the evil cousins of communism, socialism, fascism, Marxism, Nazism, modern day Progressivism and Islamic Sharia law; they are simply cuts from the same cloth of evil. For those who wish to 'split evil hairs,' definitions of these ideologies are included in Appendix B – Definitions.

"...communism is just another form of socialism, as is fascism.... liberals want you to know how much they are doing for you – with your tax money, of course. But they don't want you to realize that the path they are pursing is socialistic and that socialism is the same as communism in its ultimate effect on our liberties. When you point this out they want to shut you up; they accuse you of maligning them, of casting aspersions, of being political. No matter whether they label their bottle as liberalism, progressivism, or social reform, I know the contents of the bottle is poison to this Republic and I'm going to call it poison." (An Enemy Hath Done This, P. 43)

Examples of those influenced by Satan include mass-murderers like Khan, Mao, Stalin, Hitler, Hirohito, Hussein, Ahmadinejad and Mohammed in his later life. Men seeking power and control over others start all conflicts, including in our day, WWI, WWII, Korean, Vietnam and the War on Terror.

Since WWII communists have brought under bondage, enslaved, on average approximately 6,000 persons/hour; that's 52 million/year!

Americans were compelled to fight in WWII by Hirohito's attack on Pearl Harbor. Etched in the base of the WWII Memorial in Washington DC are these words: *"Americans came to liberate, not to conquer. To restore freedom and end tyranny."*

Tyranny raises its evil head as long as good men do nothing. Consider the obvious evil ideologies in world history; Marxists, fascist, Nazis, communists, socialists. While there are minor differences in these ideologies, they are 'birds of feather;' evil with Satanic roots whose end-game is to enslave mankind.

Components of these ideologies are present also in modern Progressives; a movement started during Woodrow Wilson's presidency continuing in most presidency's including Obama's, the 'one world order' advocates, George Soros, Islamic Muslim jihadists, the Nazi rooted Muslim Brotherhood, Rockefeller Foundation, Ford Foundation, Bilderberg group, Tri-Lateral

Commission, Council on Foreign Relations, United Nations etc. They are all modern day wolves in sheep's clothing.

The Soros controlled media and his scores of communist/socialist organizations are nothing less than a propaganda machine that feeds the sheeple what he wants them to hear in order to advance the 'one world order' agenda.

Actors and rhetoric on the world stage change but the underlying objectives of those actors' remains the same: they either promote Jehovah's (AKA Jesus, Yeshua, Yahweh) freedom and liberty, agency and light, OR they promote Lucifer's (AKA Satan, the devil, the deceiver) serfdom and slavery, bondage and darkness. Therefore, look for the outcome of their propositions, for 'by their fruits ye shall know them.' They lead either to freedom or slavery; to heaven or hell.

It is by the light of Christ that is given to all men by which we can know good from evil and discern truth from error. That is why the liberal progressive left has and continues to work so hard to discredit religion, to take prayer and the Bible out of schools, to re-write history and discredit and sometimes demonize our Founding Fathers and people who stand on the moral foundation of religious doctrine. In fact, progressive's intent is to destroy man's religion, history and the U.S. Constitution; what Glenn Beck refers to the faith, hope and charity foundations of our Republic.

Investigation into history reveals that after 100 years of effort the Progressives have achieved many of their goals.

The U.S. Supreme Court issued two bans on prayer in public schools both of which were designed to destroy the influence of religion in the public realm. The first ban came in 1962 and the second was issued in 1963. The bans were the result of a court case sponsored in part by Madelyn Murray O'Hair. The ban not only outlawed prayer in public schools but it also banned Bible reading in public schools.

When you compare modern day histories of our Founding Fathers with original sources it reveals that progressive revisionists have for decades succeeded in re-writing history and demonizing the good men through whom God worked to establish the U.S. Constitution.

Progressives continue to destroy the U.S. Constitution. Just consider the growing un-constitutional acts by our elected representatives and un-constitutional laws passed by Congress. Case in point: When Minnesota Representative Michelle Bachmann asked speaker of the house, Nancy Pelosi, where in the Constitution is the authority for Obamacare, she responded sarcastically, "Are you kidding, are you kidding!?" To Pelosi, Obama and many of our politicians, the U.S. Constitution is an antiquated document to be ignored and an obstacle in their way of controlling us. The U.S. Constitution stands in their way of the destruction of capitalism and the imposition of socialism – and ultimate control.

"SOCIALISM" the new SLAVERY

History Repeats

History repeats when people are ignorant of history.

Prior to WWII a member of the German aristocracy owned large homes and several major industries. He reported that very few people were true Nazis and that German pride was high and their lives were busy with family, work and recreation. (like America today) Many thought the Nazis were few in number and regarded as fools. The majority basically ignore them. Then, before we realized what was happening the majority lost control to these fools. My family lost our homes and business. The Nazis put many of the former aristocracy in concentration camps. These active fanatic minority were responsible for the murder of 12 million undesirables.

Russia was composed of primarily of peace-loving citizens before Stalin rose to power. Under his tyranny the violent few communists murdered 20 million of their own people.

China's citizens was primarily peace-loving before Mao Tse Tung rose to power. Yet the Chinese Communist leadership under Mao murdered 70 million of peace-loving Chinese citizens.

Japan's citizens were primarily peace loving prior to WWII. Yet in the name of religion and to gain power and control a few fanatical Shinto leaders murdered peace-loving people across southeast Asia including 12 million Chinese.

Now in America today leading 'experts' and progressive, liberal left talking heads teach is that Islam is a religion of peace and that most Muslims are peace-loving. While that may be true, the message misses the point.

Today the Muslim Brotherhood Islamic fanatic jihadists rule Islam, like the Nazis did in Germany. The fanatics are responsible for murder of innocents, rape of women, enslavement of women under sharia law, 'honor' killings of their own daughters and wives, murder of homosexuals, and teach violent jihad in mosques throughout the world including in America. The Muslim Brotherhood worked with the Nazis in WWII. They are the mother of Hamas, Hezbollah, Al-Qaida and a host of other terrorist organizations today.

The point is...... Peace loving Germans, Russians, Chinese, Japanese, Bosnians, Afghanis, Iraqis, Palestinians, Somalis, Nigerians, Algerians in history – and many other peace-loving majority – have died because they did not speak up and speak out against the few radicals.

Today our lame-stream media's propaganda promotes our destruction by discounting Muslim acts and infiltration into our government.

The pre WWII Nazis and the Communists were cooperating to overthrow the existing German regime. When it came down to who finally controls what they turned against each other.

Similar collaboration is happening in many countries of the Middle East with the 2011 uprisings. Most were orchestrated by U.S. progressive liberal left groups (SEIU, Code Pink etc. along with Barack Obama and Hillary Clinton to work with the Muslim brotherhood, unions and other liberal left/socialist/radical groups in the Middle East to cause chaos and overthrow the regimes in Egypt, Tunisia, Libya, Syria. The plan then is to use their concocted 'responsibility to protect' doctrine devised by Samantha Powers to entrap Israel into defending herself, and then paint Israel as evil. They then will levy accusations against Israel that will 'justify' destroying them. Israel is the last outpost of freedom in the Middle East. As Israel goes so does America.

As of this writing there is uncertainty which militant group will ultimately control most the Middle Eastern countries, but the Muslim Brotherhood is heavily involved in gaining power.

Barack Obama's choices reveal his preference for Muslims to control and institute a Caliphate with sharia law. Why did Obama choose to help protect Egyptians where 400 persons were killed prior to U.S. covert involvement, and also in Libya where 1,000 persons were killed prior to U.S. overt involvement via the United Nations, and do absolutely NOTHING about the 35,000 persons killed by Mexican drug cartels and dumped in mass graves on the U.S./Mexico border? Where is the common sense here? Where is the justice NOT to defend America's borders and citizens?

Summary Points:

• All the wars on Earth are a continuation of the War in Heaven.

• All our wars on Earth boil down to freedom to choose or force into dependence (slavery).

Action Steps:

1. Pray to God to know the truth of these things.

2. The truth will create the correct paradigm to correctly judge behavior; especially in politicians, international banksters and others in the power struggle to control and dominate.

End of Chapter

4

The American Experiment
Why & How We Became Great

The United States of America is a Miracle that changed the World,
A 5,000 year leap in the history of mankind

The basis of American ascent to greatness is compiled in this chapter. This summary of our true American history include the original guiding principles that formed our Government. They reveal why America exists and why she became great.

America Exists Because God Has Willed It

God Accomplished His Will Through Men as the following quotes reveal:

An ancient American prophet had a vision of future America - *"And I looked and beheld a man* [Christopher Columbus] *among the Gentiles, ...and I beheld the Spirit of God, that it came down and wrought upon the man; and he went forth upon the many waters, even unto ... the promised land. [America]"*

The Mayflower Compact signed by each of the Pilgrims was based on Biblical principles drawn from their redemption through the blood of Christ. *"Having undertaken the glory of God and advancement of the Christian faith..."*

The New England Confederation - 1643 the colonies of Massachusetts, Connecticut, New Plymouth and New Haven joined together to form America's first united government – The New England Confederation, which stated clearly their reasons for coming to Massachusetts Bay: *"Whereas we all came into these parts of America with one and the same end and aim, namely, to advance the kingdom of our Lord Jesus Christ."*

William Bradford, Governor of Plymouth Colony stated the reason the Pilgrims came to America, *"...for the propagating and advancing the Gospel of the kingdom of Christ in those remote parts of the world."* (William Bradford, History of Plymouth Plantation, p. 24).

John Winthrop leader of the Puritans, warned them of the consequence of forgetting their goal of being a testimony to the world of God's grace, *"[W]e are a company professing ourselves fellow-members of Christ...we must consider that we shall be as a city upon a hill, the eyes of all people are upon us; so that if we shall deal falsely with out God in this work we have undertaken and so cause Him to withdraw His present help from us, we shall be made a story and a byword through the world."* (John Winthrop, The Winthrop Papers, Stewart Mitchell, ed., Mass. Historical Society, 1931, Vol. II, pp. 292-295).

The First Charter of Virginia – April 10, 1606 *"We, greatly commending, and graciously accepting of, their Desires for the Furtherance of so noble a Work, which may, by the Providence of Almighty God, hereafter tend to the Glory of His Divine Majesty, in propagating of Christian Religion to such People, as yet live in Darkness and miserable Ignorance of the true Knowledge and Worship of*

God, and may in time bring the Infidels and Savages, living in those Parts, to human Civility, and to a settled and quiet Government."

Charter of Massachusetts – 1629 *"Our said people...be so religiously, peaceably, and civilly governed [that] their good life and orderly conversation may win and incite the natives of ...[that] country to the knowledge and obedience of the only true God and Savior of mankind, and the Christian faith, which...is the principal end of this plantation [colony].*

Charter of North Carolina – 1662 *"{E}xcited with a laudable and pious zeal for the propagation of the Christian faith...only inhabited by...people who have no knowledge of Almighty God.*

Charter of Rhode Island – 1663 *"...their sober, serious and religious intentions of Godly edifying themselves and one another in the holy Christian faith..."*

Charter of Pennsylvania – 1680-81 *"...out of a commendable desire to ...[convert] the savage natives by gentile and just manners to the love of civil society and Christian religion..."*

On July 4, 1776, fifty-six men gathered in Philadelphia, Pennsylvania and drafted the Declaration of Independence. In declaring their independence from an earthly foreign power the Founding Fathers declared their dependence upon Almighty God. From The Declaration of Independence we read:

"When in the course of human events, it becomes necessary for one people to dissolve the political bands which have connected them with another, and to assume among the powers of the earth the separate and equal station to which the laws of nature and nature's God entitles them..." We hold these truths to be self-evident that all men are created equal, that they are endowed by their Creator with certain unalienable rights..." "We, therefore, the Representatives of the United States of America, in general Congress assembled, appealing to the Supreme Judge of the world..." "And for the support of this Declaration, with a firm reliance on the protection of Divine Providence, we mutually pledge to each other our lives, our fortunes, and our sacred honor.

George Washington – *"I am sure there was never was a people, who had more reason to acknowledge a diving interposition in their affairs, than those of the United States....so often manifested during our revolution...[the people must] consider the omnipotence of God who is alone able to protect them."*

A prophet of God saw that *"... the Gentiles who had gone forth out of captivity [the Puritans, Pilgrims etc.] did humble themselves before the Lord; and the power of the Lord was with them. And I beheld that their mother Gentiles [England] were gathered together upon the waters, and upon the land also, to battle against them. And I beheld that the power of God was with them, and also that the wrath of God was upon all those that were gathered together against them to battle. And I, ...beheld that the Gentiles that had gone out of captivity were delivered by the power of God out of the hands of all other nations."*

The American Religion

Benjamin Franklin summarized the following five points of 'America's religion'; the fundamental religious belief expressed by nearly all of the Founders:

1. That there exists a Creator who made all things and mankind should recognize and worship Him.
2. That the Creator has revealed a moral code of behavior for happy living which distinguishes right from wrong.
3. That the Creator holds mankind responsible for the way they treat each other.
4. That all mankind live beyond this life.
5. That in the next life mankind are judged for their conduct in this one.

"All five of these tenets run through practically all of the Founders' writings. These are the beliefs which the Founders sometimes referred to as the 'religion of America,' and they felt these fundamentals were so important in providing 'good government and the happiness of mankind' that they wanted them taught in the public schools along with morality and knowledge." ([See Northwest Ordinance of 1787, Article 3]; Skousen, The 5,000 Year Leap, page 78)

"The religion of America is the religion of all mankind." Samuel Adams

"Our cause is the cause of all mankind." Benjamin Franklin

"Out of love for me, become a good American....the welfare of America is closely bound up with the welfare of all mankind." Marquis de Lafayette

"In vain would that man claim the tribute of patriotism, who should labor to subvert these great pillars of human happiness – religion and morality." (George Washington: Basic American Documents, pp. 108-9)

President George Washington, in his Farewell Address, advised his fellow citizens that **"Religion and morality" were the "great Pillars of human happiness, these firmest props of the duties of Men and citizens." "National morality,"** he added, could not exist **"in exclusion of religious principle." "Virtue or morality,"** he concluded, as the products of religion, were **"a necessary spring of popular government."**

George Washington: ***"It is impossible to rightly govern the world without God and the Bible."***

James Madison: *"We have staked the whole future of American civilization not on the power of Government, far from it. **We have staked the future of all of our political institutions upon the capacity of each and all of us to govern ourselves according to the Ten Commandments of God.**"*

Daniel Webster: *"If we abide by the principles taught in the Bible, our country will prosper. But if we and our posterity neglect the instructions and authority in this book, no man can tell how sudden a catastrophe may overtake us and bury our glory in profound obscurity."*

95% of the Founding Fathers were Christian.

Patrick Henry, Delegate, Virginia House of Burgesses said, *"The rising greatness of our country...is greatly tarnished by the general prevalence of deism which, with me, is but another name for vice* *and depravity....I hear it is said by the deists that I am one of their number; and indeed that some good people think I am no Christian. This thought gives me much more pain than the appellation of Tory [being called a traitor], because <u>I think religion of infinitely higher importance than politics.... Being a Christian...is a character which I prize far above all this world has or can boast</u>."*

Benjamin Rush, Signer of the Declaration said, *"I anticipate nothing but suffering to the human race if the present systems of paganism, deism, and atheism prevail in the world."* *"<u>My only hope of salvation is in the infinite transcendent love of God manifested to the world by the death of his Son upon the cross. Nothing but his blood will wash away my sins. I rely exclusively upon it. Come, Lord Jesus!</u> Come quickly!"*

John Witherspoon, Signer of the Declaration declared, *"I shall now conclude my discourse by preaching God's Savior to all who hear me, and entreating you in the most earnest manner to <u>believe in Jesus Christ, for 'there is no salvation in any other'</u> [Acts 4:12....<u>If you are not reconciled to God through Jesus Christ, if you are not clothed with the spotless robe of His righteousness, you must forever perish.</u>" "<u>The Ten Commandments...are the sum of the moral law.</u>"*

Roger Sherman, Signer of the Declaration and Constitution *"<u>I believe that there is one only living and true God, existing in three persons, the Father, the Son, and the Holy Ghost.</u>"*

Richard Stockton, Signer of the Declaration *"I think it proper here not only to subscribe to the entire belief of the great and leading doctrines of the Christian religion, such as the being of God, the universal defection and depravity of human nature, the divinity of the person and the completeness of the redemption purchased by the blessed Savior, the necessity of the operations of the Divine Spirit; of Divine faith accompanied with an habitual virtuous life, and the universality of the Divine Providence: ...<u>the fear of God is the beginning of wisdom</u>, that <u>the way of life held up in the Christian system is calculated for the most complete happiness that can be enjoyed in this mortal state.</u>"*

Samuel Adams, Signer of the Declaration *"Principally and first of all, I recommend my soul to that Almighty Being who gave it and my body I commit to the dust, <u>relying upon the merits of Jesus Christ</u> for a pardon of all my sins."*

George Mason, Father of the Bill of Rights *"<u>My soul I resign into the hands of my Almighty Creator</u>, whose tender mercies are all over His works, ...humbly hoping from His unbounded mercy and benevolence, <u>through the merits of my blessed Savior</u>, a remission of my sins."*

Robert Treat Paine, Signer of the Declaration *"I am constrained to express my adoration of <u>the Supreme Being, the Author of my existence, in full belief of His Providential goodness and His forgiving mercy revealed to the world through Jesus Christ</u>, through whom I hope for never ending happiness in a future state."*

John Quincy Adams, *"<u>My hopes of a future life are all founded upon the Gospel of Christ</u> and I cannot cavil or quibble away [evade or object to]...the whole tenor of His conduct by which He sometimes positively asserted and at others countenances [permits] His disciples in asserting that He was God."*

James Kent, Father of American Jurisprudence *"My object in telling you this is that if anything happens to me you might know, and perhaps it would console you to remember, that on this point my mind is clear; <u>I rest my hopes of salvation on the Lord Jesus Christ.</u>"*

Francis Scott Key, Author, "The Star Spangled Banner" *"May I always hear that you are following the guidance of <u>that blessed Spirit that will lead you into all truth, leaning on the Almighty arm</u>*

that has been extended to deliver you, trusting only in the only Savior and going on in your way to Him rejoicing."

"I have sworn upon the altar of God eternal hostility against every form of tyranny over the mind of man." Thomas Jefferson

"We hold these truths to be self-evident, that all men are created equal, that they are endowed by their Creator with certain unalienable Rights that among these are Life, Liberty and Property." Thomas Jefferson

"Life, liberty and property do not exist because men have made laws. Life, liberty and property existed before man-made laws. This triad of life requirements caused men to make laws in the first place. That to secure these rights governments are instituted among men, deriving their just powers from the consent of the governed." (Bastiat – The Law)

Note that the U.S. Constitution was based on the law of heaven. God stated 'my honor is my power.' God has all power because of His honor and all the intelligences of the universe honor God. Thus He derives His power from the consent of the governed.

God created man with certain inalienable rights, and man, in turn, created government to help secure and safeguard those rights. Therefore, it follows that man is superior to his creation. Man is superior to government and should remain master over it, not the other way around. A government is nothing more or less than a relatively small group of citizens who have been hired by the rest of us to perform certain functions and discharge responsibilities which have been authorized. Government itself has no innate power or privilege to do anything. Its only source of authority and power is from the people who have created it. Remember....*'WE THE PEOPLE....do ordain and establish this Constitution for the United States of America."* The people who create government and give to that government only such powers as they themselves have. Each of us has the natural right from God to defend his life, liberty and property; the basic requirements for life itself.

The proper role of government is limited to that which the individual citizen has the right to act. Thus, the limited role of government is to defend its citizens from bodily harm, theft and involuntary servitude. It cannot claim the power to redistribute wealth or force reluctant citizens to preform acts of charity against their will. Either of these actions is legalized plunder! George Washington warned that *"Government is not reason, it is not eloquence - it is force! Like fire it is a dangerous servant and a fearful master!"*

Since government only has the right that its creator has, and men create government, a simple test question reveals whether government is acting according to Nature's Law. Do I as an individual have a right to use force upon my neighbor to accomplish this goal? If I do not, then neither does government.

Once government moves from its proper defensive role and oversteps its Constitutional bounds into the legalized plunder of taking from those who worked to earn and give to those who will not work, it mushrooms into welfare states that drive nations toward totalitarianism.

The American philosophy is a simple: No government ever created wealth. People who work create wealth. Economic security is impossible without abundance. Abundance is impossible without industrious production. Production is impossible with a willing and eager labor force which requires incentive to work. The freedom to obtain and enjoy the fruits of one's labor is the greatest incentive to work. This profit motive of work decreases as governmental control through taxation and regulation increases.

America became great because it followed Thomas Jefferson's advice for charity to originate from caring individuals at the community level. But when government do-gooders legalize plunder to force workers to give to those who will not work, then it has crossed the line of Constitutional authority.

Government fulfilled its proper role of providing a sound money supply based on the silver and gold of the Constitution. When it violated its Constitution authority and issued irredeemable paper money it became part of the problem of inflation/deflation cycles that rob mankind of their wealth.

America became great because in the early years government lived within Constitutional bounds.

Abraham Lincoln: *"I believe the Bible is the best gift God has ever given to man. All the good from the Savior of the world is communicated to us through this Book. I have been driven many times to my knees by the overwhelming conviction that I had nowhere else to go. I can see how it might be possible for a man to look down upon the earth and be an atheist, but I cannot conceive how he could look up into Heaven and say there is no God."*

Abraham Lincoln *"My concern is not whether God is on our side; my greatest concern is to be on God's side, for God is always right."*

America has deep Christian roots; roots that extend from the pre-mortal life to Adam and down to our day. The Christian religion uses the Old and New Testament of the Bible. The Old Testament was compiled by the house of Judah. The first five books of the Old Testament were written by Moses, a Levite. The Ten Commandments found in Exodus is the foundation of both Jew and Christian. Thus, America has a Judeo-Christian foundation.

Jehovah offered to become our savior and redeemer in the pre-mortal life and we accepted Him there to fulfill that mission. Adam, the first man, sacrificed the firstlings of his flocks in similitude of the only begotten son of God that would come. All prophets and sacrifices from Adam to Jesus Christ (4,000 years) looked forward to the coming of the Lamb of God who would offer Himself as the last great sacrifice for sin in the meridian of time. Jesus replaced the law of sacrifice with the law of sacrament at the Last Supper. For the past 1979 years (2012AD-33AD=1979) all prophets and sacrament services looked back in remembrance of Jesus Christ's Atonement. Therefore, the God of the Old Testament (Jehovah/Yaweh) and the God of the New Testament (Jesus Christ) is the same God. In the Old Testament Moses records, *"In the beginning God created the heaven and the Earth."* (Gen 1:1) In the New Testament John records, *"In the beginning was the Word, and the Word was with God, and the Word was God. The same was in the beginning with God. All things were made by him; and without him was not anything made that was made."* (John 1:1-3) Moses recorded that in the beginning God created the heaven and the earth (4,000 BC). John recorded that the 'Word' (Jesus) created all things. Therefore the New Testament Jesus created all things. Jesus in the Old Testament is known by Jehovah and Yahweh. Thus we see that Christianity started in the pre-mortal life, was practiced by Adam & Eve in 4,000 BC and is therefore a 6,000 year old religion. Jews are descendants of Judah, the fourth son of Jacob and Leah, who was born around 1,600BC.

Clearly, Christianity is the World's oldest religion which started 'in the beginning'. It was established by God in the pre-mortal life and God taught the Gospel to the first man Adam.

Democracy Or Republic?

Another reason America became great is that we are a Republic. We are NOT a democracy. Democracy is mob rule. Democracies always end up in anarchy and eventual destruction.

A woman asked, "what have you given us Dr. Benjamin Franklin?" He replied, *"A republic if you can keep it."* A republic is governed by rule of law.

God's Role In The Establishment Of The U.S. Government

God stated through his prophet *"...for this purpose have **I [The Lord God] established the [US] Constitution of this land, by the hands of wise men [Founding Fathers] whom I raised up unto this very purpose**, and redeemed the land by the shedding of blood." "And that law of the land which is constitutional, [the US Constitution] supporting that principle of freedom in maintaining rights and privileges, belongs to all mankind, and ...as pertaining to law of man, whatsoever is more or less than this, cometh of evil."* [emphasis added] (America In History & Prophecy p 26, 40)

1856 Maryland History Text - *"20 years before the Revolutionary War, when **George Washington** was 23 years old he commanded 100 Virginia buckskins who had joined 1200 British troops to march on Fort Duquesne during the French and Indian War. The French and Indians ambushed killing (86 British officers) and 714 men. George Washington was the only officer not shot. The next day Washington wrote his mother that he had bullet holes in his jacket and fragments in his hair but he was not hit. Fifteen years later in 1770 Washington returned to the Pennsylvania woods. An Indian chief told Washington he was in charge of the Indian braves. He told the braves to fire at Washington. They fired repeatedly at Washington (the chief fired personally 17 times). The Indian traveled all the way just to meet **the man God would not let die in battle**."* [emphasis added]

General George Washington wrote to Congress during those war years to report the progress of their fight for liberty. [during the Revolutionary War] He reported that **67 different times, in their destitute and trapped situations, if it hadn't been for the hand of God, the troops would have been slaughtered and the battles lost.** (See Carrington, *Battles of the American Revolution, 1876*) [emphasis added]

*"I've lived, Sir, a long time, and the longer I live, the more convincing Proofs I see of this Truth — That **God governs in the Affairs of Men**. And if a sparrow cannot fall to the ground without his Notice, is it probable that an Empire can rise without his Aid? We have been assured, Sir, in the Sacred Writings, that except the Lord build the House they labor in vain who build it. I firmly believe this, — and I also believe that without his concurring Aid, we shall succeed in this political Building no better than the Builders of Babel: We shall be divided by our little partial local interests; our Projects will be confounded, and we ourselves shall become a Reproach and Bye word down to future Ages."* (Benjamin Franklin - Speech to the Constitutional Convention --28 June 1787)

28 Basic Principles - The Basis For The U.S. Constitution

Source: The 5,000 Year Leap, Cleon Skousen, National Center for Constitutional Studies, 1981

1: The only reliable basis for sound government and just human relations is Natural Law.

2: A free people cannot survive under a republican constitution unless they remain virtuous and morally strong.

3: The most promising method of securing a virtuous and morally stable people is to elect virtuous leaders.

4: Without religion the government of a free people cannot be maintained.

5: All things were created by God, therefore upon Him all mankind are equally dependent, and to Him they are equally responsible.

6: All men are created equal.

7: The proper role of government is to protect equal rights, not provide equal things.

8: Men are endowed by their Creator with certain unalienable rights.

9: To protect man's rights, God has revealed certain principles of divine law.

10: The God-given right to govern is vested in the sovereign authority of the whole people.

11: The majority of the people may alter or abolish a government which has become tyrannical.

12: The United States of America shall be a republic.

13: A constitution should be structured to permanently protect the people from the human frailties of their rulers.

14: Life and liberty are secure only so long as the right to property is secure.

15: The highest level of prosperity occurs when there is a free-market economy and a minimum of government regulations. (This encompasses the freedom to try, to buy, to sell, to fail.)

16: The government should be separated into three branches: legislative, executive, and judicial.

17: A system of checks and balances should be adopted to prevent the abuse of power.

18: The unalienable rights of the people are most likely to be preserved if the principles of government are set forth in a written constitution.

19: Only limited and carefully defined powers should be delegated to government, all others being retained in the people.

20: Efficiency and dispatch require government to operate according to the will of the majority, but constitutional provisions must be made to protect the rights of the minority.

21: Strong local self-government is the keystone to preserving human freedom.

22: A free people should be governed by law and not by the whims of men.

23: A free society cannot survive as a republic without a broad program of general education.

24: A free people will not survive unless they stay strong.

25: "Peace, commerce, and honest friendship with all nations - entangling alliances with none."

26: The core unit which determines the strength of any society is the family; therefore, the government should foster and protect its integrity.

27: The burden of debt is as destructive to freedom as subjugation by conquest.

28: The United States has a manifest destiny to be an example and a blessing to the entire human race.

French writer Alexis de Tocqueville, after visiting America in 1831, said, *"I sought for the greatness of the United States in her commodious harbors, her ample rivers, her fertile fields, and boundless forests - and it was not there. I sought for it in rich mines, her vast world commerce, her public school systems, and in her institutions of higher learning - and it was not there. I looked for it in her democratic Congress and her matchless Constitution - and it was not there. Not until I went into the churches of America and heard her pulpits flame with righteousness did I understand the secret of her genius and power.* ___America is great because America is good,___ ___and if America ever ceases to be good, America will cease to be great!"___

The fabric of America is woven by the horizontal strands of the Declaration of Independence and the US Constitution, and the vertical strands of religion and morality. These strands in both directions are required for the fabric of American to hold up under the onslaught of evil forces of communism, socialism, fascism, Nazism, progressivism, Islamic Sharia law etc....

Another way to look at America is in the metaphor of a 3-legged stool. Our Republic's 3 legs are the US Constitution, religion and morality.

Government Control & Self-Government

"We base all our experiments on the capacity of mankind for self-government." James Madison

"We base the American Experiment on the ability of man to live according to the Ten Commandments of God." James Madison

"The Constitution is not an instrument for the government to restrain the people; it is an instrument for the people to restrain the government - lest it come to dominate our lives and interests". Patrick Henry

Liberty <u>without</u> self-discipline according to Judeo-Christian-defined morals leads to immorality and corruption. Immorality leads to corruption which justifies greater government control.

Liberty <u>with</u> self-discipline derived from the Judeo-Christian-defined morals creates honor and trustworthiness. These noble character traits serve to retain our freedoms of life, liberty and property and to limit government control.

The war raging now in politics regarding government control over us is simply an extension of and current expression of the original issues fought over in the War in Heaven. The fight is between good and evil; freedom and slavery. While to some that may seem simplistic, if one takes the time to 'follow the money' or in this case 'follow the power' it will lead to freedom or slavery, to moral agency or control, and finally to Christ or Lucifer.

There is an inverse relationship between the ability of people to self-govern based on religious and moral principles and the ability for satanic ideologies to take root in our lives. The more people are religious, the more moral they are, and the more they are guided by moral principles to make choices and the less government control they need. The less religious - more godless - people are the more moral relativism and the 'flavor of the day' behavior is promoted, accepted and lived, even when it is destructive and the more government control is needed.

Morals are defined by God, not man. Amorality is the fertile soil of tyranny.

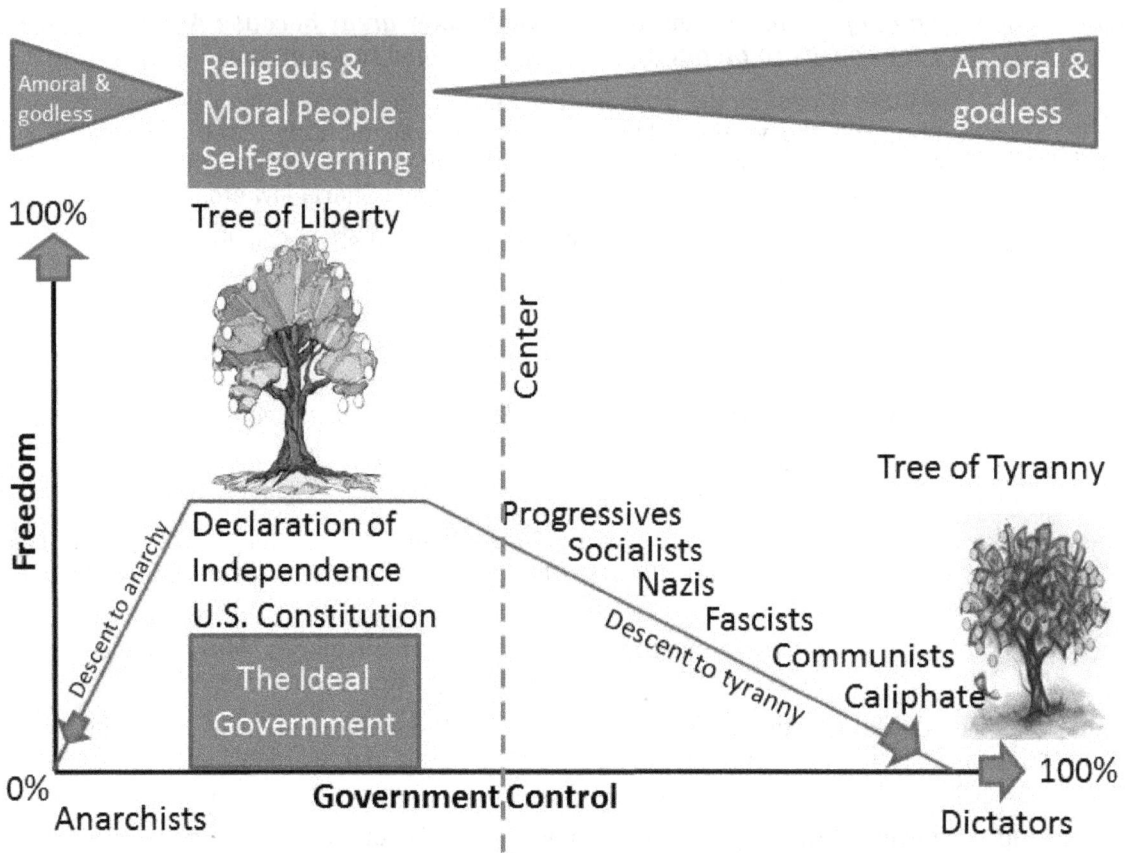

Note that the U.S. Constitution is to the left of center. It is the ideal balance between freedom and control. It uses minimal government control and allows maximum self-government guided by the morality of religious people.

Moving to the right of the U.S. Constitution where people are separated from moral principles established by God. There they are subject to evil influences in increasing degrees starting with Progressives and ending with Communist/Caliphate – tyranny, slavery and destruction.

Moving to the left of the U.S. Constitution people are again separated from moral principles established by God and are subject to the evil of anarchy – lawlessness, chaos and destruction.

Abraham Lincoln's Gettysburg Address:

America became great by carrying forth the torch of liberty our Founding Fathers lit and by upholding the U.S. Constitution through living the American religion. We also owe a debt to the American soldiers who gave their last full measure of devotion to preserve our liberty. We must carry the torch of freedom and pass it on to the next generation. Abraham Lincoln's infamous Gettysburg address best illustrates this point.

"Four score and seven years ago <u>Our Fathers brought forth on this continent, a new nation, conceived in Liberty, and dedicated to the proposition that all men are created equal</u>.

"Now we are engaged in a great civil war, testing whether that nation, or any nation so conceived and so dedicated, can long endure. We are met on a great battle-field of that war. We have come to dedicate a portion of that field, as a final resting place for those who here gave their lives that that nation might live. It is altogether fitting and proper that we should do this.

"But, in a larger sense, we cannot dedicate -- we cannot consecrate -- we cannot hallow -- this ground. The brave men, living and dead, who struggled here, have consecrated it, far above our poor power to add or detract. The world will little note, nor long remember what we say here, but it can <u>never forget what they did here. It is for us the living, rather, to be dedicated here to the unfinished work which they who fought here have thus far so nobly advanced. It is rather for us to be here dedicated to the great task remaining before us</u> -- <u>that from these honored dead we take increased devotion to that cause for which they gave the last full measure of devotion</u> -- that <u>we here highly resolve that these dead shall not have died in vain</u> -- <u>that this nation, under God, shall have a new birth of freedom</u> -- and <u>that government of the people, by the people, and for the people, shall not perish from the earth</u>."

Story Of The Star Spangled Banner—Insight Into The America Spirit

The spirit of America is represented in many ways. Perhaps one of the most noteworthy is the story behind our National Anthem.

America declared war on Great Britain in June 1812 in response to trade disagreements. British troops invaded Washington, D.C. in August 1814 and burned the White House, Capitol Building, and Library of Congress. Then they targeted Baltimore.

When the British arrived in Baltimore, they saw a large American Flag commissioned in 1913 by Major George Armistead, commander of Fort McHenry. Each star measured 24" wide. The Flag was 42 feet long and 30 feet tall.

The British took prisoner Dr. William Beanes, a friend of Francis Scott Key. Francis Key joined Colonel John Skinner, a American government agent charged to arrange prisoner trades, on a journey to Chesapeake Bay. They saw the British fleet sailing toward Baltimore. Key and Skinner boarded the Tonnant, flagship of the British fleet where they were told that they could not return to Baltimore until the British conquered the city. The British transferred them to the British ship Suprize from which they witnessed the attack on Fort McHenry.

The British bombardment began at 7AM September 13, 1814 and lasted for 25 hours. The British fired 1500 bombshells that has fuses to cause them to explode when they reached the target. However, many of them blew up in mid-air lighting up the sky with bombs bursting in air fireworks. Rockets from the British ships left fiery contrails across the sky.

Key and Skinner watched the bombardment throughout the day and night. Next morning they searched the Fort for a sign that would tell if America surrendered or fought on. They they saw a joyous sight of the American flag, shell torn, but still blowing in the morning breeze!

Key was a true patriot who watched and prayed under emotional stress of fear, anxiety for the safely of his Country, State and loved ones. He later gave the following speech at Frederick, MD: *"I saw the flag of my country waving over a city—the strength and pride of my native State—a city devoted to plunder and desolution by its assailants. I witnessed the preparation for its assaults, and I saw the array of its enemies as they advanced to the attack. I heard the sound of battle; the noise of the conflict fell upon my listening ear, and told me that 'the brave and the free' had met the invaders. Through the clouds of the war the stars of that banner still shone in my view, and I saw the discomfited host of its assailants driven back in ignominy to their ships. Then, in that hour of deliverance and joyful triumph, my heart spoke; and "Does not such a country and such defenders of their country deserve a song?" was its question. With it came an inspiration not to be resisted; and even though it had been a hanging matter to make a song, I must have written it. Let the praise, then, if any be due, be given, not to me, who only did what I could not help doing, not to the writer, but to the inspirers of the song!"*

"Oh say can you see by the dawn's early light

What so proudly we hailed At the twilight's last gleaming

Whose broad strips and bright stars through the perilous fight

O'er the ramparts we watched were so gallantly streaming

And the rockets' red glare, the bombs bursting in air,

Gave proof through the night that our flag was still there.

Oh say does that stars spangled banner yet wave

O'er the land of the free and the home of the brave."

Francis Scott key said, "he remembered what **George Washington** had said --- he said, *"**The thing that sets the American Christian apart from all other people in the world is he will die on his feet before he'll live on his knees."***

The Tree of Liberty And The Tree of Tyranny

America choose the Tree of Liberty.

Like the trees of Truth and Falsehoods, and the trees of Clarity and Distortion, the Tree of Liberty and the Tree of Tyranny have opposite roots. Please study the following diagrams of the Tree of Liberty and the Tree of Tyranny. Despite similar genetics of original seeds (they are both trees), uptake from the root systems can either product the sweet fruits of liberty or the bitter fruits of tyranny.

Governments have spiritual roots; values and principles that the people and politicians believe, understand, know and live by. Like physical tree roots, spiritual roots produce fruits due to what they ingest.

When trees become severed from their physical roots they die. Likewise, when people, communities, governments, societies and civilizations become separated from their spiritual roots they also die; first spiritually, then physically.

In a garden if weeds are not uprooted, they can overrun the good plants that bring forth good fruit. Likewise, in the garden of life, when weeds of control planted by evil leaders are not uprooted they can overcome the good fruits of liberty.

WHAT IS LIBERTY and its synonym FREEDOM? Is there a difference between freedom and liberty of the soul?

Abraham Lincoln was of the opinion that *"the world has never had a good definition of* [liberty]. *We all declare for liberty," he said; "but in using the same word we do not mean the same thing. With some, the word liberty may mean for each man to do as he pleases with himself and the product of his labor; while with others* [liberty] *may mean for some men to do as they please with other men and the product of other men's labor."*

Freedom of choice is a gift of God, but man can, through the use of this God-given agency, deprive other men of this freedom. Tyranny robs men of freedom. Freedom is not free, it often requires blood sacrifice to preserve or restore. It must be vigilantly preserved by those who love it. Sometimes it must be regained through war to defeat tyrants who deprive mankind of God's great gift of freedom.

There are three kinds of freedom; personal, political, economic. These are all subsets of true freedom – the freedom of the soul.

Personal freedom is the freedom to act. Some people speak about a nice sounding misnomer 'free agency.' There is no such thing as free agency; the right to choose without receiving the attendant consequences. All choices have consequences; that is moral agency. Moral agency is our right to choose. Each choice has attendant consequences. We can, and must, choose what to think, what to say and what to do. But we cannot choose the consequences of these choices; they come in the package called 'choice.'

One only need to consider the tragic lives of drug addicts doing whatever is necessary for his next 'fix', or the alcoholic craving his next drink, or those enslaved by pornography, or the gambler looking for his next big win. None of these people have true freedom to act; they all are slaves to their appetites – addicted to physical enticements. They arrived at those tragic places by the exercise of their moral agency. They choose to do drugs, to drink alcohol, to continue down the road of lust and to believe in the big win next time rather than the law of the harvest. So moral agency is wonderful, but it does not always lead to the

personal freedom to act. Exercise of moral agency increases or decreases a person's freedom to act by the choices he makes. Every wrong decision restricts the amount of freedom to act and vice versa.

The Tree of Liberty is alive with the right to choose our government representatives. It is freedom to think, to worship, to devote your energies to what you desire.

Economic freedom is to have the liberty to buy and sell what and when you choose. It is to have the freedom to pursue a career or to be an entrepreneur. One can also choose laziness, enslave himself to the government through accepting welfare and loose his dignity in the process. People should work to the extent of their ability in order to maintain their dignity as a human being. People can lose economic freedom through unwise exercise of moral agency. For example, anciently, the Egyptians, instead of exercising their moral agency to provide for themselves against a day of need, depended upon the government. First they used their money. When that was gone, they gave their livestock, then their lands, and finally they were compelled to sell themselves into slavery, that they might eat. (Gen 41:54-56; 47:13-26)

Freedom of the soul is more encompassing than the other three. While moral agency, political freedom and economic freedom contribute to freedom of the soul, they do not guarantee it. Obedience to the law of Christ is the ultimate freedom of the soul – the highest form of liberty. The bondage of sin is the ultimate enslavement. One can have freedom of the soul through obedience to Christ's law even though he may be deprived of personal, political and economic freedom.

On The Tree of Liberty the taproot is GOD.

Because of its taproot and associated major feeder roots the Tree of Liberty produces religion and morality; the foundation for self-government on which the U.S. Constitution rests. The U.S. Constitution has been the foundation of mankind and America's ascent to greatness.

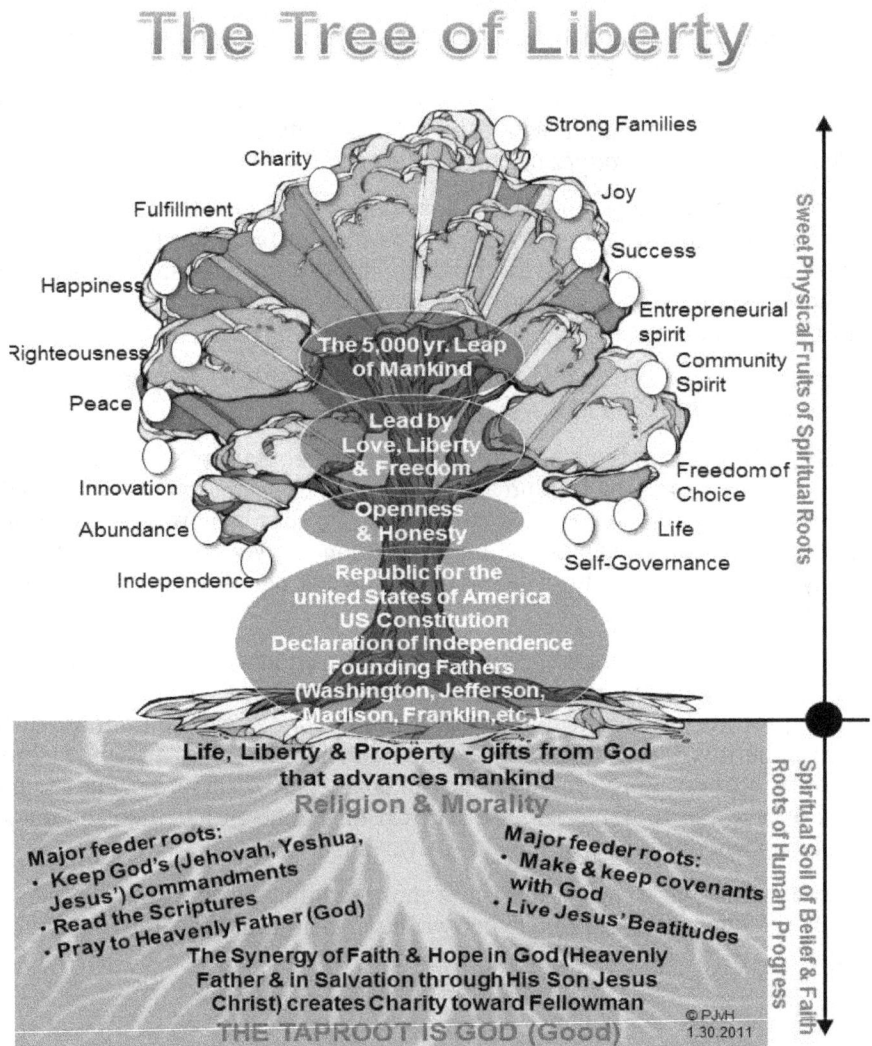

The Tree of Liberty

On the Tree of Tyranny the taproot is LUCIFER (Satan). Because of its taproots and associated major feeder roots, the Tree of Tyranny produces atheism and immorality; the foundation of communism, fascism, socialism, Nazism, and Muslim radical terrorists. These ideologies believe that the ends justify the means. Even deceit is justified because there is no God in their hearts to define morality.

Note that the leaves of the tree of Tyranny is money $$$$$$ - their god; the holder of which gains power, prestige, position and property. The evil roots identified produce all the bitter fruits illustrated. Examples of bitter fruits of the Tree of Tyranny include Mao who killed 70 million of his people, Stalin, 20 million, Hitler, 12 million; Gaddafi, Hussein, Mussolini, Kim Jong-Il, Tito – the list is long, but the roots of these tyrants is always Lucifer and their governments are always tyrannical.

The Tree of Tyranny

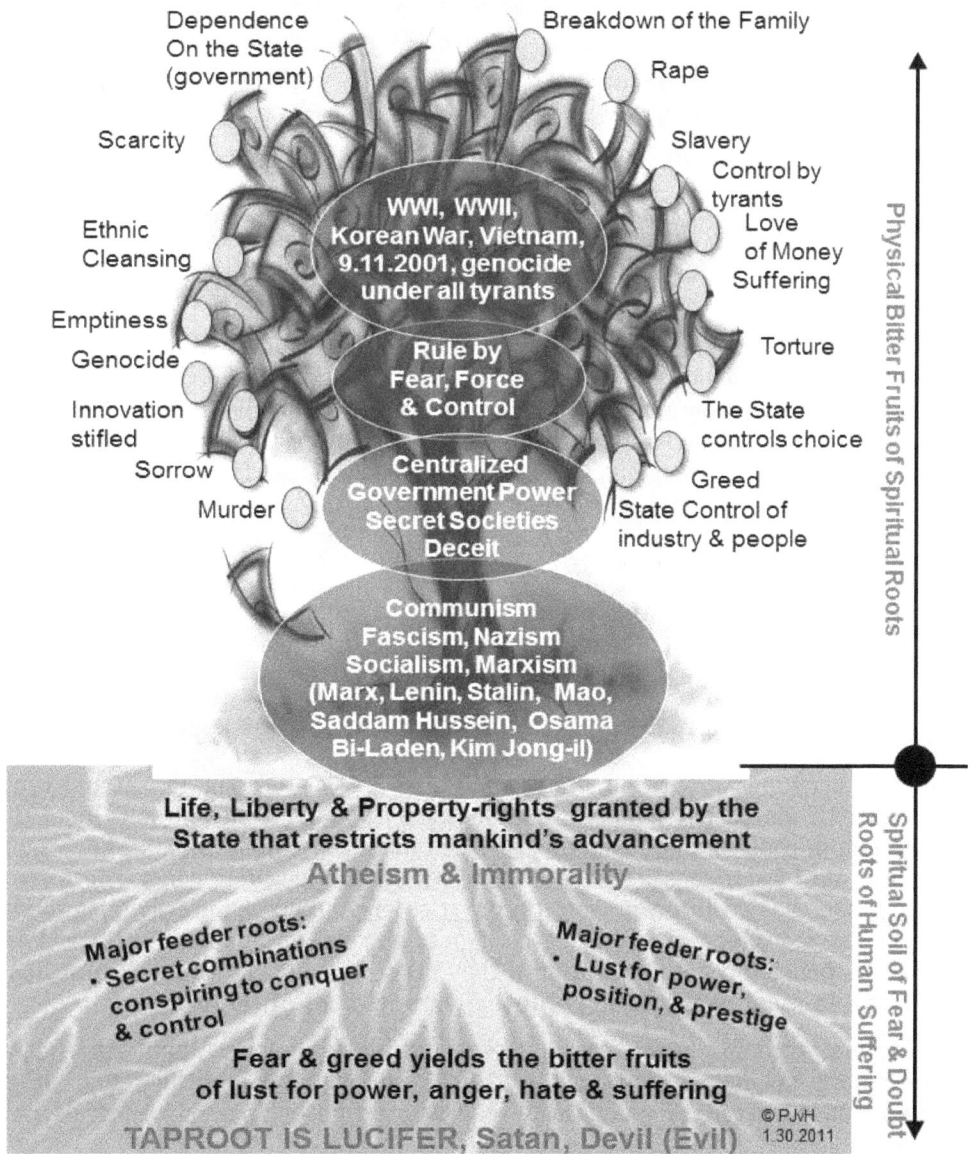

Dependence On the State (government)

Breakdown of the Family

Rape

Scarcity

Slavery

Control by tyrants

Ethnic Cleansing

Love of Money

WWI, WWII, Korean War, Vietnam, 9.11.2001, genocide under all tyrants

Suffering

Emptiness

Genocide

Torture

Innovation stifled

Rule by Fear, Force & Control

The State controls choice

Sorrow

Greed

Murder

Centralized Government Power Secret Societies Deceit

State Control of industry & people

Communism Fascism, Nazism Socialism, Marxism (Marx, Lenin, Stalin, Mao, Saddam Hussein, Osama Bi-Laden, Kim Jong-il)

Physical Bitter Fruits of Spiritual Roots

Life, Liberty & Property-rights granted by the State that restricts mankind's advancement

Atheism & Immorality

Major feeder roots:
• Secret combinations conspiring to conquer & control

Major feeder roots:
• Lust for power, position, & prestige

Spiritual Soil of Fear & Doubt Roots of Human Suffering

Fear & greed yields the bitter fruits of lust for power, anger, hate & suffering

© PJvH 1.30.2011

TAPROOT IS LUCIFER, Satan, Devil (Evil)

It is critical to note the following differences in God's way and Lucifer's way. There are two levels of intelligences in the universe; those who act and those who are acted upon.

> **God's way is to invite people to come unto Christ and be perfected in him. His way is based on principles of moral agency (freedom of choice and accountability), faith, repentance, baptism and the gift of the holy ghost that enables progression. God's end-game is our independence to act and not to be acted upon.**

> **Lucifer's way is to create a state of fear to manipulate people in order for them to give up freedom in exchange for security. His way is based on principles of dependency, force and control. Satan's end-game is dependency on him to be acted upon, like slave puppets dancing on the strings he pulls.**

God's way will always offer choices that promote the progression of His children. His choices always aligns with His law. His commandments are designed to bless us because He loves us. We choose whether or not to obey.

Lucifer's way will usually offer choices that look similar to God's, but are different in the details. If you consider the eventual outcome, they always lead to enslavement to his evil control.

Most often the choices we face are not between good or evil and black or white. More often they are between evil, bad, good, better and best. We must use our intellect, ponder the outcomes, make a decision, pray for God's confirmation of our choice, and if we receive it, move forward in order to do His will.

Promoters of both Liberty and Tyranny governmental systems use the same language to sell their ideas. Hitler's National Socialist Party (Nazis) was sold to the people as prosperity and equality for all. And in the beginning, it was. However, after the sheeple took the bait and were hooked on the government provided welfare and prosperity programs through socialism, the sheep's clothing came off the wolf of Nazism and the people suffered greatly. This same sly and treacherous bait is being offered by Obama today. Obama is a smooth talker facilitated by conniving script writers and his delivery is mesmerizing to some sheeple. But he does the opposite of what he says!; classic signs of a narcissist and hypocrite.

Recognizing these essential differences enables correct evaluation of politicians' plans for your future and empowers people to make better choices for their elected representatives.

A Chinese Insight: Religion, Republics & Capitalism

A <u>Marxist economist from China</u> <u>had come to study western capitalism and republics.</u> Near the conclusion of his research he commented that '<u>I had no idea how critical religion is to the functioning of republics and capitalism.</u>' It is one of the unique things I have seen in America. <u>In your past, most Americans attended a church or synagogue every week. These are institutions that people respected....</u>*where* <u>you were taught that you should voluntarily obey the law; ...to respect other people's property, not steal,</u> to be honest, to voluntarily pay their taxes. People believe that even if the police did not catch them if they broke a law, God would. **<u>Republics work because most people most of the time voluntarily obey most of the laws.</u>'**

The same is true for capitalism. It works because religions taught Americans to keep their promises and not lie. An advanced economy cannot function without this integrity. Capitalism works because most people voluntarily keep their promises. In many countries, banks will not lend money to small businesses because there is no trust, and taking people who do not repay money to court is ineffective.

Trust, honesty, integrity are the foundations of republics and capitalism. These moral standards are best taught by religion.

America has tried to institute republics in other countries, and it failed if there was not a strong religious foundation in those countries that support the sanctity of life, the equality of people, the importance of respecting others' property, and the importance of personal honesty. Attempts to establish republics in countries where non-Judeo-Christian religions fail to teach those moral codes has failed miserably.

For example, in religions in Russia exist but they influence few people, thus communism controls because religion fails to establish moral codes. Consequently, murder, bribery and stealing are common.

A republic only works where there is a strong foundation of religion.

Today in America we are living on the momentum of moral codes taught in the past that have become embedded in our culture even though more and more people are irreligious. However, culture is not a stalwart protector of republics enabling values. When people stop going to their churches, or if our churches lose their power over our culture, our system will not sustain itself.

Churches are the most effective institution in teaching moral code that is the foundation of republics and capitalism.

What other institutions will teach these values to Americans with the power required to guide their daily behavior?

Religion is being methodically separated from the public square based on civil liberties. Religious dilution includes removing prayer from schools, the Bible from schools, The Ten Commandments from state courthouses, nativity scenes in public squares, religious songs in schools. The enemies of religion have framed the debate to advance their agenda. The ironic truth is that religious institutions whose role on the public stage they hope to minimize are in fact among the fundamental enablers of the civil liberties.

Republics and capitalism work only when most people most of the time voluntarily obey the laws. Religion is the best teacher and maintainer of moral laws. So we should be strengthening those institutions that enable our civil liberties; churches and synagogues.

It is surprising that a Marxist Chinese observed what is blind to most Americans.

We must repent and remove the evil that has crept into our thinking. The Ten Commandments and the Gospel of Jesus Christ is the best source of morality that inculcates the values and principles to do right – to keep the Golden Rule. Living this moral code will re-form the foundation upon which the U.S. Constitution must have to function. If we succeed, we can look forward with a brightness of hope in a preferred future for America. If we fail, we will sink further into slavery to evil government and banksters. We are at a critical fork in the journey of American life; freedom or slavery.

Why & How America Became Great

America became great due in large part to living Dean Alfange's creed: *"I do not choose to be a common man, It is my right to be uncommon ... if I can, I seek opportunity ... not security. I do not wish to be a kept citizen. Humbled and dulled by having the State look after me. I want to take the calculated risk; To dream and to build. To fail and to succeed. I refuse to barter incentive for a dole; I prefer the challenges of life To the guaranteed existence; The thrill of fulfillment To the stale calm of Utopia. I will not trade freedom for beneficence Nor my dignity for a handout I will never cower before any master Nor bend to any threat. It is my heritage to stand erect. Proud and unafraid; To think and act for myself, To enjoy the benefit of my creations And to face the world boldly and say: This, with God's help, I have done All this is what it means To be an American entrepreneur."*

Hans Rosling's presents an informative 200 Countries, 200 Years, History in 4 Minutes on YouTube. It is worth watching. He summarizes how America led the world to greater wealth and health.

<u>Why</u> America became great is due to the innate desire of the human soul to become, to advance, to create.

<u>How</u> America became great and ascend to be the 'light on the hill' is due to the freedoms established by The Declaration of Independence and the U.S. Constitution the free markets of Capitalism's economic the growth engine.

America became great because men and women lived moral laws derived from the Bible and the values and principles defined in our founding documents. Christian Pilgrims and Puritans seeking religious freedom from tyrants braved the Atlantic to seek the 'new world' and established colonies dedicated to God. Subsequent immigrants, primarily from Europe, followed. They came here legally, formed governments and established the melting pot called 'America' by learning English, dropping the hyphenations of former countries, and uniting to build a land of freedom.

Summary Points:

- God's hand is in the founding of America.

- God worked through His servants to create the Declaration of Independence and the Constitution of the United States of America.

- America's re-discovery and settlements from the Pilgrims to the Founding Fathers was inspired by God.

- The foundation of government was based upon the principles of God derived from the Bible.

- America's foundation is Judeo-Christian. Moses wrote the first five books of the Bible. We can thank the Jews for the preservation of them. Christians re-founded America (remember the Native Americans were already here) and based their government and judicial system of law on the Bible.

- The Declaration of Independence (July 4, 1776) and the Constitution of the United States, (September 17, 1787) including the Bill of Rights, are the foundational law of America.

These governing guides enabled a free people to be entrepreneurs in a free economy called capitalism to develop the greatest nation on Earth.

- The God of the Old Testament and the God of the New Testament is the same God, just known by different names. In the Old Testament - Lord, Jehovah, Yahweh. In the New Testament - God, Lord, Jesus, Christ.

- Biblical principles forged into the Declaration of Independence and the Constitution of the United States of America and followed by early Patriots made America good.

- America became great because, generally, men lived God's laws.

- America is great because America is good. If America ceases to be good she will cease to be great!

- America represents a 5,000 year leap in human achievement based upon our Constitutional granted freedoms.

- IN GOD WE TRUST sums up the foundation of America.

- Liberty without self-discipline derived from the Judeo-Christian-defined morals leads to immorality and corruption. These traits of debauchery empower and justify greater government control over our lives.

- Liberty with self-discipline derived from the Judeo-Christian-defined morals creates honor and trustworthiness. These noble character traits serve to retain our freedoms of life, liberty and property and to limit government control. God's way is freedom of choice.

- Lucifer's way is force and control.

- America is a Republic – NOT a democracy .

- We must water, nurture and grow the Trees of Truth, Clarity & Liberty.

- God's way is to invite people to come unto christ and be perfected in him. His way is based on principles of moral agency (freedom of choice and accountability), faith, repentance, baptism and the gift of the holy ghost that enables progression. God's end-game is our independence to act and not to be acted upon.

- Lucifer's way is to create a state of fear to manipulate people in order for them to give up freedom in exchange for security. His way is based on principles of dependency, force and control. Satan's end-game is dependency on him to be acted upon, like slave puppets dancing on the strings he pulls.

Action Steps:

Apply the principles in this chapter to evaluate political candidates and vote for those – regardless of party affiliation – which align their values and principles with our core American values.

End of Chapter

Truth vs. Falsehood

All things have opposites. Otherwise, there could be no choices to make.

There is opposition (counterfeits) in all things. This is a key to understand and 'see' clearly. Opposites include good & evil, truth & falsehood, etc.... This chapter will present God's truth on which America was founded vs. Satan's falsehoods.

In this chapter I will set the record straight about who is good and who is evil; not that all Americans are good nor are all non-Americans evil. That is absurd. All people sin and have need of repentance. There is no one truly good but God. The point is that the foundation of America is God's truth which is good. Satan is alive and well. He uses evil men who serve him knowingly or unknowingly by putting their lust for power, property, position and prestige above honor and integrity. They craftily conspire to change the argument and call good evil and evil good.

President of Iran, Mahmoud Ahmadinejad, had the audacity recently to call Israel 'little Satan' and America 'big Satan.' Well did Isaiah warn *"Woe unto them that call evil good, and good evil; that put darkness for light, and light for darkness; that put bitter for sweet, and sweet for bitter!"* (Isa 5:20) The roots of this perversion of truth is with Satan.

Following is a comparative chart of some of the key issues of our time.

ISSUE	GOD'S TRUTH	SATAN'S FALSEHOODS
Faith	Faith in Jesus Christ is essential to salvation. "...a man is not justified by the works of the law, but by the faith of Jesus Christ, ... that we might be justified by the faith of Christ,..." Galatians 3:26	Faith in government to take care of you. Have faith in science to provide answers to your bad habits
Hope	Our hope should be in Christ. *"If in this life only we have hope in Christ, we are of all men most miserable."* 1 Cor 15:19. Lord Jesus Christ, which is our hope 1 Tim1:1. *"Blessed be the God and Father of our Lord Jesus Christ, ...hath begotten us again unto a lively hope by the resurrection of Jesus Christ from the dead."* 1 Peter 1:3	Hope in the government to take care of you – communism, socialism, fascism, example: Obamacare
Charity	Under Christianity and the U.S. Constitution is Free-will tithing and fast offerings to help those in need.	Under Socialism is forced redistribution of wealth by stealing from those who work (using guilt, intimidation and taxes), by stealing their power from

ISSUE	GOD'S TRUTH	SATAN'S FALSEHOODS
	Charity suffereth long, and is kind; charity envieth not; charity vaunteth not itself, is not puffed up,..." 1 Cor 13:4	our liberty to give to those who will not work for 'the public good'.
Honesty	Judaism & Christianity "Thou shalt not bear false witness against thy neighbour." Ex 20:16	Communism, socialism, progressivism, godless, & Islam's philosophy of Al-Taqiyya – that states when it is possible to achieve an aim by lying ..., it is permissible to lie if attaining the goal is permissible...and obligatory to lie if the goal is obligatory – are ALL Stan's opposition in varying degrees, to God's Truth..
Salvation	Our Heavenly Father is God. Individual salvation – we come before the judgment bar of Christ to be judged individually. For God hath not appointed us to wrath, but to obtain salvation by our Lord Jesus Christ, 1 Thes 5:9 Christianity – salvation comes by accepting Jesus Christ as our Savior, doing His will, and bringing souls unto Christ so that together we may enjoy eternal life. It's an honor to love like Jesus loved and help others live.	Government is god. Collective salvation. (Obama & Rev. Jeremiah Wright) Government promises to save us – from global warming, (now conveniently called climate change), from fiscal irresponsibility, from debt, from bad habits, from ..... with the hidden price of economic, political and social slavery attached to it. Islam – salvation comes by killing infidels (non-Muslims) so you can enjoy 72 virgins in heaven. It's an obligation and honor to kill for Allah.
Freedom & Slavery	Moral agency under law. All men are born free. Freedom is endowed by God (our Creator). Independent living.	Coercion with anarchy. Freedom is granted by the government. Government welfare state

ISSUE	GOD'S TRUTH	SATAN'S FALSEHOODS
	"Today two mighty forces are battling for the supremacy of the world. The destiny of mankind is in the balance. <u>It is a question of God and liberty or atheism and slavery</u>.... "Those forces are known and have been designated by Satan on the one hand and Christ on the other. <u>In these days, they are called 'domination by the state' on one hand, 'personal liberty,' on the other; communism on one, free agency on the other.</u>" (America In History & Prophecy p. 45) *"Reduced to its lowest terms, the great struggle which now rocks the whole earth [is] a struggle of the individual versus the state.... Upon its final issue, liberty lives or dies....<u>The plain and simple issue now facing us in American is freedom or slavery</u>....We have largely lost the conflict so far waged. But there is time to win the final victory, if we sense our danger and fight."* (America In History & Prophecy p. 45-46)	Dependency (slavery) to the government. Satan argued that men given their freedom would not choose correctly, therefore he would compel them to do right and save us all. Today Satan argues that men given their freedom do not choose wisely; therefore a so-called brilliant, benevolent few must establish the welfare government and force us into a greater socialistic society...the people must be controlled. We are assured of being led into the promised land as long as we let them put a golden ring in our nose. In the end we lose our freedom and the promised land also. No matter what you call it—communism, socialism, or the welfare state— our freedom is sacrificed.
Governments	<u>The United States Constitution /United Order</u> Based upon principles of freedom, moral agency, self-rule, enterprise, initiative & love. Power comes FROM the PEOPLE TO the government. (We The People...do ordain and establish this Constitution....)	<u>Communism/socialism /fascism/Nazism, Marxism /progressivism/godless/Sharia Law/One World Government....</u> Are all ideologies that are 'wolves in sheep's clothing.' Based upon principles of satanic force & control. They manipulate people to serve the government master according to ability and redistribute wealth to each according to his needs.

ISSUE	GOD'S TRUTH	SATAN'S FALSEHOODS
	Perpetuates over time, increases creativity, enterprise, industry, dignity and self-worth.	Power comes FROM the GOVERNMENT TO the people.
		Self-destructing ideologies (if we do not support them with trade and foreign aid!) Turn worker against receiver, destroying initiative, enterprise, industry, dignity and self-worth.
	The Haves give to the Have-Nots from the fountain of love in their hearts.	Cannot long survive under the weight of satanic economic falsehoods. Bred seeds of rebellion amongst their subjects who eventually rise up and overthrow the evil.
	The supreme law of the land with 3 branches – Executive, Legislative & Judicial that are the checks and balances to government **Of the People, By the People and For the People**	The Haves who work for a living are forced to redistribute their earnings to the Have-Nots who won't work.
	Limited government. Problems are solved best at the local level, then state, then federal.	Government OF big business, BY special interest groups and FOR foreign communists/socialist/one world order/sharia law advocates etc...
	God instituted governments to benefit man. God will hold men accountable for their actions as representatives of the people in making laws and administering them, for the good and safety of society.	Monarchs and tyrants are the supreme law of the land.
	There can be no peaceful government unless good laws are adopted and obeyed in order to insure freedom of choice, the right to own and control property and the protection of life.	Islam-Caliphate-Sharia (religion-government-law) Three INSEPARABLE branches that constitute Muslim theocracy where the government is Of the Imams, BY the Imams and For the Imams at the expense of the people.
	Governments require civil officers and magistrates to enforce laws fairly and justly. Honorable men and women should be sought out to represent the people in these positions of responsibility.	

ISSUE	GOD'S TRUTH	SATAN'S FALSEHOODS
	Man is required to sustain and uphold good government as long as those governments protect their inalienable rights. Governments should make and uphold laws the protect religious freedom. They do not have the right to institute a state religion and no one religion should be given special government favors. All should be treated equally and fairly. Man is justified in defending himself, his family, friends and property and the government, from the unlawful assaults and encroachments in times of emergency, where immediate and timely help by law enforcement officers is unavailable.	Big centralized Federal government seeks to control everything (the States, communities, and people) because the Washington 'elite' are smarter and can do it better.
Constitution of The United States of America	God established the U.S. Constitution through our Founding Fathers. "... I [God] ...established the Constitution of [America] by the hands of wise men whom I raised up unto this very purpose..." (America In History & Prophecy p. 40) "I am grateful that the God of heaven...put his stamp of approval upon the Constitution and to indicate that it had come into being through wise men whom he raised up unto this very purpose." (America In History & Prophecy p. 41)	The Constitution is an outdated document, a set of negative liberties that must be disregarded, overlooked and destroyed to promote progressivism, socialism, and godless communism.
Religion in government	"...no government armed with power capable of contending with human passions unbridled by morality and religion. Avarice, ambition, revenge, or gallantry, • would break the strongest cords of our Constitution as a whale goes through a net. Our Constitution was made only for a moral and religious people. It is wholly inadequate to the government of any other." — John Adams is a signer of the Declaration of Independence, the Bill of Rights and our second President. October 11, 1798. Gouverneur Morris, Signer of the Constitution. "...religion is the only solid base of morals and those morals are the only possible	Separation of church and state. [a statement not to be found in either the Declaration of Independence or the US Constitution] Separation of God and Country. Who needs religion, we have government. Islam/Caliphate/Sharia is government, religion, control and law combined.

ISSUE	GOD'S TRUTH	SATAN'S FALSEHOODS
	support of free governments, therefore <u>*education should teach the precepts of religion and the duties of man towards God.*</u>" God IS in government. God's law is the basis for judicial law and the U.S. Constitution. However, there is no State sponsored religion. Each person has the freedom of religious practice as long as it does not infringe on the God-given inalienable rights granted in the U.S. Constitution. James Wilson, *Signer of the Constitution; U. S. Supreme Court Justice, "Human law must rest its authority ultimately upon the authority of that law which is Divine. . .* <u>*religion and law are twin sisters, friends, and mutual assistants.*</u>" George Washington, General of the Revolutionary Army, president of the Constitutional Convention, First President of the United States of America, Father of our nation, "<u>*Religion and morality are the essential pillars of civil society.*</u>" "<u>*True religion offers to government its surest support*</u> . . . <u>*It is impossible to rightly govern the world without God and the Bible.*</u>" Benjamin Franklin, Signer of the Declaration of Independence "<u>*[O]nly a virtuous people are capable of freedom. As nations become corrupt and vicious, they have more need of masters*</u>." "*Whereas* <u>*true religion and good morals are the only solid foundations of public liberty and happiness . .*</u>." Continental Congress, 1778 James Madison, author of the US Constitution – 4th US President - "<u>*We have staked the future of all our political institutions upon the capacity of mankind to self-government, upon the capacity of each and all of us to govern ourselves, to control ourselves, to sustain ourselves according to the Ten Commandments of God.*</u>"	There is no separation possible in Muslim ideology. Islam IS government.

ISSUE	GOD'S TRUTH	SATAN'S FALSEHOODS
Founding Fathers	Our Founding Fathers were good men whom God inspired to write the Declaration of Independence, the U.S. Constitution and America. Kings and rulers and the peoples of all nations are invited to adopt similar governmental systems to the U.S. Constitution. Doing so will fulfill the ancient prophecy of Isaiah that _"out of Zion shall go forth the law and the word of the Lord from Jerusalem."_ (Isaiah 2:3) The U.S. Constitution is <u>the supreme law</u> of our land. _"...the Constitution of the United States of America is just as much from my Heavenly Father as the Ten Commandments."_ _(America In History & Prophecy p 40_ 95% of the Founding Fathers were Christian. 70% of the Founding Fathers were republican abolitionists; they were against slavery. Thomas Jefferson tried to abolish it seven times through the courts of law in Virginia and Congress.	Progressives re-write history to promote their political agenda of force and control. A.D. 1958 - Organized Attacks - The results of the investigation ordered by the 83rd Congress became public, revealing a massive organized attack against the Founding Fathers, their reputations, and the relevancy of the Constitution. A summary of this information can be obtained in "The Reese Committee Report." Teach lies about the Founding fathers; that they did not believe in God, and were white slave-holding supremists.
Communism, socialism, Marxism, fascism, Nazism, Islam	All cousins of evil – Satan's counterfeit to the U.S. Constitution. Communism is not a political party - it is a system of government that is the opposite of our Constitutional government. Communism would destroy our American Constitutional government. To support Communism is an act of treason. No patriotic American citizen may become either a Communist or supporter of Communism.	Obama's acts reveal socialist and communist preference. Many of Obama's czar appointees are avowed communists and socialists (Van Jones & Anita Dunn etc.) Barack Obama has stated that he will stand with the Muslims should the political winds shift in an ugly direction.
Secret Combinations (Societies)	Secret combinations are most abominable and wicked above all, in the sight of God. Whatever nation upholds secret	Council on Foreign Relations, Trilateral Commission Skull &

ISSUE	GOD'S TRUTH	SATAN'S FALSEHOODS
	combinations, shall be destroyed. These murderous secret combinations are built up to get power and gain. *"Wickedness is rapidly expanding in every segment of our society. It is more highly organized, more cleverly disguised, and more powerfully promoted than ever before. Secret combinations lusting for power, gain, and glory are flourishing. A secret combination that seeks to overthrow the freedom of all lands, nations, and countries is increasing its evil influence and control over America and the entire world."* (America In History & Prophecy p. 56)	Crossbones, Bilderberg Group, Bohemian Grove, Thule Society and Illuminati – all created with the sole purpose to destroy people's freedom, the US Constitution, religion and morality; and to supplant it with political, economic and social slavery in the form of One World Order blend of communism, Marxism, socialism and fascism.
Marriage	Marriage between a man and a woman is ordained of God and that the family is central to the Creator's plan for the eternal destiny of His children. (Proclamation on the Family)	U.S. Supreme Court - June 26, 2015, declared Gay marriage is legal in all 50 states. The end-game of the gay rights movement is to replace religious freedom with massive coercive government control overs the lives, minds an beliefs of people once protected by the First Amendment. The gay marriage ruling is a foot-in-the-door to force communism on the American people.
Morality	Defined by God's commandments & teachings Morality is defined by God. The definition does not change with the changing definition of morality by immoral men.	The 'New morality.' Is defined by man's desires after they remove God from public life so they can manipulate people. There is no standard of morality; morality is defined by everyman's carnal desire. For man left unto himself is carnal devilish, sensual.
Abortion & Human Life	Life is God's to give and take away. Thou shalt not kill	Pro-choice Abortion is OK and promoted by government

ISSUE	GOD'S TRUTH	SATAN'S FALSEHOODS
	Pro-Life & Pro-Choice! God favors adoption over abortion except in the cases of incest and rape. Even then the decision must be made after consultation with medical experts, religious leaders and after much prayer. Only evil men present abortion as a either/or choice with the intent to divide people. Abortion is more complex moral issue. Understanding God's truth unites people. Abortion is murder except in certain cases. Adoption not abortion except in cases of rape, incest & where the life of the mother is at risk.	using our tax dollars to pay for abortions under Obamacare.
Sex & Homosexuality	God has commanded that the sacred powers of procreation are to be employed only between man and woman, lawfully wedded as husband and wife. *"Know ye not that the unrighteous shall not inherit the kingdom of God? Be not deceived: neither fornicators, nor idolaters, nor adulterers, nor effeminate, nor abusers of themselves with mankind."* 1 Corinthians 6:9	Homosexuality is an acceptable alternative lifestyle 'sleeping' together – sexual relationships OK with consenting adults
Pornography	God calls it perversion, a black hole of addiction that destroys participants and families.	Satan calls it $12 Bil./yr. adult entertainment.
Immigration	We believe in being subject to kings, presidents, rulers, and magistrates, in obeying, honoring, and sustaining the law. A of F 1: 12 Illegal immigration is illegal!	The federal government says it's OK to break the law. We will provide entitlements to you so you can receive for free what Citizens have to work for. Politicians buy votes from illegal aliens that way. Acorn will even help you vote – 70 times!
Alcoholism drunkenness	Keep the Lord's Law of Health	A social disease that gov't programs *treat* (not *cure!*)
Cheating	Thou shalt not bear false witness against thy neighbor. Ex 20:16	Abnormal social development

ISSUE	GOD'S TRUTH	SATAN'S FALSEHOODS
Sin	Absolute – *"Then when lust hath conceived, it bringeth forth sin: and sin, when it is finished, bringeth forth death."* James 1:15	Relative determined by what is accepted by the culture
Citizen Rights	Inalienable rights come from God. Declaration of Independence – *"...they are endowed by their creator with certain unalienable rights..."* U.S. Constitution – Bill of Rights: (1st 10 Amendments) • Right to freedom of religion, speech, press, peaceful assembly, petition government of grievances. • Right to keep and bear arms (guns) • Right to be secure against unreasonable search and seizures • Right to life, liberty and property without due process of law, etc.	Alienable rights come from the State. Obama – 3x in September 2010 intentionally misquoted the Declaration of Independence by stating people are endowed with certain inalienable rights - omitting 'by their creator'. His intent being to promote the socialism where the State grants rights, therefore the State can take them away.
Justice	Equal justice under the law (U.S. Constitution)	Social & economic justice – 'code' for redistribution of wealth - socialism.
Choice	Moral agency - you are free to chose captivity or death - choice with consequences	The Washington 'elite' know better - we, the State, will choose for you. Control you.
Life's purpose	We were sent to Earth to serve God and to be tested to see if we will obey God	We are here to serve the State
Entitlements	Law of the harvest – *"Be not deceived; God is not mocked: for whatsoever a man soweth, that shall he also reap"*. Gal 6:7 He that is idle shall not eat the bread nor wear the garments of the laborer.	Government entitlements to idlers use laborers tax dollars to buy votes to gain power. Socialism - redistribution of wealth from workers to idlers
Motherhood	A mothers highest honor and glory is being good mothers. They are needed at home. The hand that rocks the cradle rules the world.	Mothers highest honor and glory is in the workplace.
Is America Christian?	Christopher Columbus, The Pilgrims, Puritans, Founding Fathers, was overwhelmingly Christian.	Progressives, liberal left, godless, communism, socialism, fascism,

ISSUE	GOD'S TRUTH	SATAN'S FALSEHOODS
	The Declaration of Independence and the U.S. Constitution was inspired by the Judeo-Christian roots; the Holy Bible.	Marxists, Nazis, Satan worship. the trilogy of Islam/caliphate/sharia.
	Each State of the 50 united States has the Christian God in their Constitutions.	
	The American Judicial system was derived primarily from the guidelines of justice in the Holy Bible.	
	The recent U.S. Census records that 86% of Americans declared Christian as their religion.	
Prayer in America	The Continental Congress issued a proclamation recommending "a day of publick [*sic*] humiliation, fasting, and prayer" be observed on July 20, 1775.	The status of the National Day of Prayer became uncertain on 15 April 2010 when a federal judge ruled in favor of a challenge brought by the Freedom from Religion Foundation and held that the National Day of Prayer was unconstitutional.
	President John Adams declared May 9, 1798 as "a day of solemn humility, fasting, and prayer," during which citizens of all faiths were asked to pray "that our country may be protected from all the dangers which threaten it".	
	On March 30, 1863, President Abraham Lincoln issued a proclamation expressing the idea "that the awful calamity of civil war, which now desolates the land, may be but a punishment, inflicted upon us, for our presumptuous sins", and designated the day of April 30, 1863 as a day of "national humiliation, fasting and prayer" in the hope that God would respond by restoring "our now divided and suffering Country, to its former happy condition of unity and peace".	
	On April 17, 1952, President Harry S. Truman signed a bill proclaiming a National Day of Prayer must be declared by each following president.	
	In 1988 President Reagan - the First Thursday in May each year - the National Day of Prayer.	

Summary Points:

- Understand that there is a law operating in mortality called 'an opposition in all things.'

- Opposition is what requires us to choose.

- We must educate ourselves in order to choose wisely.

- The choices we make are essentially between God's way or Satan's way; between freedom or force.

Action Steps:

Apply Action Step #3 of Chapter 1 to know the truth of the opposing ideologies presented in this chapter.

Choose God's way America!

End of Chapter

America's Descent from the 'Light on a Hill'

*"Let us straitly threaten them that they speak henceforth to no man in this name.
And they...commanded them not to speak at all nor teach in the name of Jesus."* Acts 4:17

*"For we wrestle not against flesh and blood, but...against powers [&] rulers
of...darkness of this world, against spiritual wickedness in high places."* Ephesians 6:12

*"America is like a healthy body and its resistance is threefold: its patriotism, its morality, and its
spiritual life. If we can undermine these three areas, America will collapse from within."*
Joseph Stalin

To understand America's crisis we must understand how we got here. The purpose of this chapter is to empower the reader with the truth of why America has descended from being the Light On a Hill that she used to be so that they will not be led further astray by those who seek control.

Mariners from ancient times navigated the seas by the Polar Star. To lose its location was to lose their orientation on the uncharted seas and lose their way, sometimes to their destruction.

We must navigate the seas of uncertainty in our journey through life. If we lose location of our Polar Star which is our moral bearings, we lose our way and can - and are - being shipwrecked on the reefs of sin, the shoals of deceit and the rocks of evil.

We must return to a place where we see clearly and are not disoriented by distorted lenses.

Paul warned us in Ephesians that our fight is against spiritual wickedness in high places. We have been warned America! And we have descended far down the road toward destruction. This chapter is devoted to uncovering some of that wickedness and how it came to pass that we have descended from being a light on a hill that America was created to be.

The reason America has descended to our present state of moral decay, unsustainable national debt, greed and corruption in high places, evil in our government, murder in our streets, loss of international respect, being despised by many other countries because we have lost our moral bearings.

The Whitewashing Of Sin – The Religion of Relativism

God calls it:	The world calls it:
Drunkenness	Alcoholism-a social disease
Sodomy	Homosexuality-gay rights, alternative lifestyle
Perversion	Pornography-adult entertainment
Immorality	New morality
Cheating	Abnormal social behavior

With the dissolution of absolutes and supplanting them with the religion of relativism, America's crime rate spiraled upwards. Every indicator of the sickness of civilization – theft, burglary, murder, alcoholism, drug addiction, divorce, pornography, homosexuality, suicide, illegitimate children, teenage pregnancies, X rated movies, co-habitation, abortions etc. - has increased.

The two forces that influenced our lives in the pre-mortal life – good and evil – God and Lucifer - are still influencing our lives. The source of influence today is the same; only the actors on the stage of life change. Though man attempts to whitewash sin, the law of God remains and the consequences for breaking His laws follow.

Morality – Parasites – Politicians - Revolution

Progressives have effectively cut Jesus and the teachings of the Bible out of the public square. The 'religion' of modern day liberal left progressives is 'godless.' This social climate did not always exist.

95% of Our Founding Fathers were Christians. They used teachings from the Bible as the foundation of law and morality evident in the Declaration of Independence and the U.S. Constitution. The Bible was standard text and course of study in Harvard and in many of America's initial universities.

Where are modern day morals coming from? The answer to that question reveals the cause of America's descent from being a light on a hill to the present corruption seen in politics, government, and entertainment. Many of Hollywood's movies and much of the music industry's noise is secular sewage. School and college classroom teachings, street gangs, drug cartels, motorcycle gangs, and yes, even some religions like Jeremiah Wright's Liberation Theology have departed from the true gospel of Jehovah in the Old Testament and Jesus Christ in the New Testament.

"The cause of the fall of a civilization occurred <u>when a cultural elite became a parasitic elite,</u> leading to the rise of internal and external proletariats." (Arnold J. Toynbee)

In today's parlance, the cause America descent has occurred by politicians and banksters who consider themselves 'elite', above the common man and beyond the law. They constitute wealthy parasites glutting themselves on the common working man's labor.

The 'elite' tend to be lawyers who manipulate and pass laws to increase their power and to line their own pockets and those of their friends. As a generality, lawyers are parasites of the people, feeding off of conflict, which they often foment. The following short story illustrates the point: One lawyer set up practice in a small town and nearly starved. Then another lawyer moved in and they both got rich. There are many lawyers who get wealthy due to their expertise in the profession because of a silver tongue. They do not seek the truth but only seek to win. After all, winning cases is profitable.

Power mongering career 'elitist' politicians are part of the problem. They seek office to gain power and then work to keep power by buying votes with our tax dollars.

Our Founding Fathers served because the people asked them to, not because they sought for office. After serving they went back to their jobs; their real careers. That attitude of service to the people has changed. Today, most Washington politicians vie for office and regard those who voted them in as sheeple to be used to maintain and gain more power...for life. It used to be an honor and duty to serve. Now, for most, it has become a power struggle. This power seeking mentality has contributed greatly to Americas descent.

When The People will not take it anymore, they will pull down the false nobility of the 'privileged elite' and restore government 'of the People, by the People and for the People' according to the will of the People using the U.S. Constitution as justification and guiding light. It is way past time to do so.

The Game

It is critical to understand the 'game' being played. It is a root cause of America's descent.

The stakes are high; freedom or slavery, liberty or bondage.

The author of the game is the same one who tried to enslave us before, he just works through power-mongering men here. The tools of destruction used are ancient; deceit, lies, coercion, manipulation force and control. The players using these tactics have some modern and some historic names; progressives, socialists, communists, Nazis, fascists. And they use laws.

Lawyers write laws. They dominate one political party. Their skill in in spinning the facts to win the day, not necessarily see that justice is done. A close lawyer friend confided that law schools do not teach right from wrong, they teach how to spin the evidence to win the case, and thus make money.

Laws are created by Congress, or at least that is how it should work according to the Constitution. However, socialist power mongers have found ways to circumvent Congress through Executive Orders, through government bureaucrat regulations from the EPA, FDA etc. They do not want these laws to be observed. They want them to be broken!

Power mongers want power at any expense. There is no way to rule innocent men. Therefore, they create the kind of laws that can neither be observed nor enforced nor objectively interpreted, and so many laws and regulations that people break them unknowingly. Then government has the tool to crack down on criminal law-breakers. Then you create a nation of law-breakers that you can control through guilt when you catch them.

Part of the game was authored in mortality by Karl Marx. It is simply to create a problem, then step in and provide a solution that looks like they're a savior but instead enslaves.

Divide and conquer is another tactic of the adversary of freedom. As a result of applying this tactic to divide, most recently by hate fomenters such as Obama and his cohort in crime Al Sharpton, and by George Soros and his minions.

Two Americas have emerged over it history. It can be summarized in the following way: The America where people work, produce, is independent, contribute, and have acquired things by their industry, the businessman, entrepreneur, merchant, craftsman, those who provide service to others. The other America is where people don't work, don't produce, are dependent, don't contribute and therefore don't have anything except from those who produce; the entitlement mentality. The division is givers and the takers. It is also manifest in two political parties; one who preaches hate, greed and victimization in order to win office. They love power more than country, The other party who promote individual enterprise.

The difference is not about income inequality, it's about civic responsibility. It is about the producer and the parasite.

The Culture of our Times

The culture of our times is quick fix and entitlement. It is perpetrated by business, government and Hollywood. If kids are hungry we 'drive-thru' for McDonald's 'Happy Meals' that result in 'Super-Sized' kids, un-happiness, dis-ease and depression.

We commit serious sin and expect it to go away like in Hollywood's sitcoms that teach all problems can be solved in 30 minutes. We abuse the laws of morality, take drugs, drink alcohol, gamble, spend into debt, overeat, view pornography, and use tobacco all of which can lead to destructive addictions.

Why do people indulge in damaging behavior? To temporarily cover up sin's consequent guilt and feel good for a short time. Then only to descend deeper into despair afterwards.

We see others with more of the world's goods and envy. Government welfare programs give what we has not been earned because the liberal left progressives teach that the non-worker is 'entitled' to the workers' fruits...and it buys them votes and power.

We go to college on government grants, don't pay them back and blame Wall Street, or somebody else that we can't get a job. Occupy Wall Street is an example of depraved values.

The economy does a 2008 nose-dive because politicians buy votes with 0% down and low interest home loans that people cannot normally qualify for so that everyone can own a home. Then mortgagees default, greedy banksters sell toxic derivatives that infect the world, and capitalism conveniently gets blamed in order to promote socialism, communism and One World Order.

In our current culture many are taught its OK to make bad choices and them blame others for negative consequences.

All these practices are satanic alternatives to God's Law of the Harvest, (we reap what we sow), to the Law of Repentance (where we act to become clean and guilt-free, and are empowered to progress), to The Law of Work and Reward (the idler shall not eat the bread of the laborer), and to The Law of Moral Agency (we make choices and are accountable for them).

Rules for Radicals

Radicals have surfaced in American society like pockets full of puss on an otherwise healthy nation. Saul David Alinsky (January 30, 1909 – June 12, 1972) was an American community organizer and writer. He is generally considered to be the founder of modern community organizing. He is often noted for his book *Rules for Radicals*. He teaches that to create a social state there are 8 levels of control that must be obtained:

1) Healthcare – Control healthcare and you control the people

2) Poverty – Increase the Poverty level as high as possible, poor people are easier to

control and will not fight back if you are providing everything for them to live.

3) Debt – Increase the debt to an unsustainable level. That way you are able to increase taxes, and this will produce more poverty.

4) Gun Control – Remove the ability to defend themselves from the Government. That way you are able to create a police state.

5) Welfare – Take control of every aspect of their lives (Food, Housing, and Income)

6) Education – Take control of what people read and listen to – take control of what children learn in school.

7) Religion – Remove the belief in the God from the Government and schools.

8) Class Warfare – Divide the people into the wealthy and the poor. This will cause more discontent and it will be easier to take (Tax) the wealthy with the support of the poor.

Barack Obama and his cohorts have implemented each of these tactics in America.

The Cycle Of Civilizations

Civilizations historically experience patterns illustrated in this diagram:

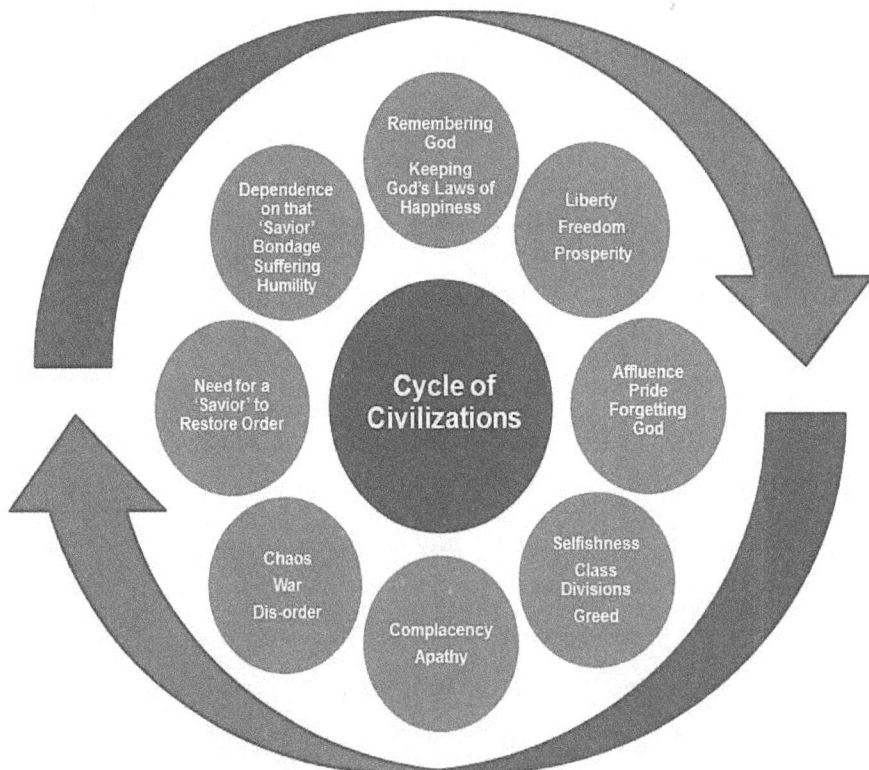

America - where are we in this cycle?

Most people agree we are in the beginnings of chaos. Just witness the riots in NYC's Wall Street, Michigan, California, Atlanta, and throughout many other places.

In 1887 University of Edinburgh professor Alexander Tyler, noted about the fall of the Athenian Republic (Greece) 2,000 years ago: *"A democracy is always temporary in nature; it simply cannot exist as a permanent form of government. A democracy will continue to exist up until the time that voters discover that they can vote themselves generous gifts from the public treasury. From that moment on, the majority always votes for the candidates who promise the most benefits from the public treasury, with the result that every democracy will finally collapse over loose fiscal policy, (which is) always followed by a dictatorship."*

The Greeks in Athens at one time had more freedom and a high standard of living than the rest of the world; and they prospered in the Golden Age because of it. In the end when ancient Athenians desired security above freedom, they lost both.

Rome's history is similar. Edward Gibbon in 1787 cited the reasons for Rome's decline in The Decline and Fall of the Roman Empire. There were five principle reasons: [1] The undermining of the dignity and sanctity of the home, which is the basis of human society, [2] Increasingly higher taxes and redistribution of wealth to the poor and providing circuses for the populace (in our day, big flat screen TV's and internet service), [3] The mad craze for pleasure, sports becoming every year more and more exciting and more brutal, [4] the building of gigantic armaments when the real enemy was within the decadence of the people, and [5] the decay of religion-faith fading into mere form, losing touch with life and becoming impotent to warn and guide the people. In the end of Rome 1/3 of its citizenry were on government payrolls, everything that moved was taxed even the load on a donkey, morality declined, godlessness reigned supreme and the republic collapsed. In that vacuum, a dictatorship followed until the fat accumulated during the days of the republic had been consumed. Then the Roman Empire fell which ushered in the Dark Ages.

The world's greatest civilizations from the beginning of history last an average of 200 years and progress through the following sequence - similar to the graphic but with different descriptions:
- From bondage to spiritual faith;
- From spiritual faith to great courage;
- From courage to liberty;
- From liberty to abundance;
- From abundance to complacency;
- From complacency to apathy;
- From apathy to dependence;
- From dependence back into bondage."

Where is the United States of America now?

Professor Joseph Olson of Hamline University School of Law in St. Paul, Minnesota, summarized facts from the last Presidential election:

	Obama	Romney
Number of States won	19	29
Square miles of land won	580,000	2,427,000
Population of Counties won	127M	143M
Murder rate/100,000 residents in Counties won	13.2	2.1

The territory Romney won was mostly the land owned by the taxpaying citizens of the country. The territory Obama won was mostly encompassed those citizens living in low income tenements and living off various forms of government welfare.

Sadly United States is now somewhere between the "complacency and apathy" phase of democracy, with over forty percent of the nation's population already dependent on government; the new form of slavery. If Congress grants amnesty and citizenship to twenty million criminal invaders called 'undocumented persons' and they vote – Game Over - for the United States of America.

Foundational Principles Of Constitutional Government

President John F. Kennedy held a dinner in the white House for a group of the brightest minds in the nation at that time. He made this statement: **"This is perhaps the assembly of the most intelligence ever to gather at one time in the White House with the exception of when Thomas Jefferson dined alone."**

In light of that expression of 'greater intelligence', let us examine some of Thomas Jefferson's thoughts on government.

"The democracy will cease to exist when you take away from those who are willing to work and give to those who would not." -- Thomas Jefferson

"It is incumbent on every generation to pay its own debts as it goes. A principle which if acted on would save one-half the wars of the world." -- Thomas Jefferson

"I predict future happiness for Americans if they can prevent the government from wasting the labors of the people under the pretense of taking care of them." -- Thomas Jefferson

"My reading of history convinces me that most bad government results from too much government." -- Thomas Jefferson

"No free man shall ever be debarred the use of arms." -- Thomas Jefferson

"The strongest reason for the people to retain the right to keep and bear arms is, as a last resort, to protect themselves against tyranny in government." -- Thomas Jefferson

"The tree of liberty must be refreshed from time to time with the blood of patriots and tyrants." -- Thomas Jefferson

"To compel a man to subsidize with his taxes the propagation of ideas which he disbelieves and abhors is sinful and tyrannical."-- Thomas Jefferson

"I believe that banking institutions are more dangerous to our liberties than standing armies. If the American people ever allow private banks to control the issue of their currency, first by inflation, then by deflation, the banks and corporations that will grow up around the banks will deprive the people of all property - until their children wake-up homeless on the continent their fathers conquered."

"When we get piled upon one another in large cities, as in Europe, we shall become as corrupt as Europe." Thomas Jefferson

"I consider the foundation of the Constitution as laid on this ground: that 'all powers not delegated to the united states by the Constitution, nor prohibited by it to the states, are reserved to the states respectively, or to the people' U.S. Constitution Amendment XX "...to take a single step beyond the boundaries thus specially drawn around the powers of Congress is to take possession of a boundless field of power..." Thomas Jefferson

For over 100 years we have allowed congress to take these steps beyond the boundaries of the U.S. Constitution, all of which increasingly limit our freedoms and empower Washington to enslave us.

The Federal Reserve And Our Government

There is nothing 'federal' about The Federal Reserve. It is a private institution that controls America's currency. They employ Keyesian Economics to steal our wealth: *"By a continuing process of inflation, governments can confiscate, secretly and unobserved, an important part of the wealth of their citizens. There is no subtler, no surer means of overturning the existing basis of society than to debauch the currency. The process engages all the hidden forces of economic law on the side of destruction, and does it in a manner which not one man in a million is able to diagnose."* John Maynard Keynes – Keynesian Economics

President Woodrow Wilson abandoned our Constitution and sold out to international banksters when he instituted the Federal Reserve while Congress was on vacation, contrary to the Constitution. Much later Wilson stated, *"I am a most unhappy man. I have unwittingly ruined my country. A great industrial nation is controlled by its system of credit. Our system of credit is concentrated. The growth of the nation, therefore, and all our activities are in the hands of a few men. We have come to be one of the worst ruled, one of the most completely controlled and dominated Governments in the civilized world -- no longer a Government by free opinion, no longer a Government by conviction and the vote of the majority, but a Government by the opinion and duress of a small group of dominant men."* Woodrow Wilson

John Adams warned about Keynesian type of theft: *"All the perplexities, confusion and distress in America arise, not from defects in their Constitution or Confederation, not from want of honor or virtue, so much as from the downright ignorance of the nature of coin, credit and circulation."* John Adams

Inflation robs mankind of his wealth. The cause of inflation is the expansion of the money supply faster that the growth of the nation's material assets. The wage-price spiral is the result of inflation. Only government can create inflation; in our case, in bed with the Federal Reserve. The

Federal government resorts to inflation to cover its deficits when it borrows more than it can repay.

The Federal Reserve made it possible for the first time in America for men to arbitrarily change the value of our money. Going off the gold standard enabled the manipulation of the USD value. Now the USD is not backed by silver or gold.

Economic laws are just as immutable as moral laws or the laws of nature or the Ten Commandments. The Federal Reserve and our government are destroying our wealth and America by knowing violating the immutable laws of economics.

Major Turning Points

There were major moral turning points in American history; [1] Prayer in public schools and religion in public life, [2] Obamacare, and [3] Gay Marriage.

[1] Prayer in public schools and religion in public life

Since the beginning of the Christian colonization of America, for centuries thereafter, the Bible was the moral basis for conduct and laws. Americans' used religious principles as the basis for serving in public office and the Bible was core curriculum in public education. The new Americans forged a bond between God and private and public life. Our first schools began in churches and for more than three centuries, public schools relied on the Bible to teach character, reading and morals.

The 1962 & 1963 the Supreme Court overturned three centuries of American practice and divorced public schools and affairs from the moral basis of American life. Up to this point, the Supreme Court was staffed by Constitutional judges with judicial experience. But in 1962-3 the Supreme Court Justices were composed with 8 politicians with no judicial experience and 1 judge with judicial experience.

In the Engel v. Vitale case (1962), the U.S. Supreme Court ruled 6-1 against New York's "Regents' prayer," a "non-denominational" prayer which state education officials had composed for public schoolchildren to recite. The government-sponsored religious devotion was challenged in court by a group of parents from New Hyde Park (some atheists, some believers). Removal of prayer from public schools was the 'toe-hold' that evil needed to open other doors of moral decay.

One year later, a case originated by a Philadelphia-area man named Ed Schempp challenging mandatory Bible reading in Pennsylvania schools reached the Supreme Court. At the same time, Madelyn Murray O'Hair was challenging a similar practice as well as the recitation of the Lord's Prayer in Maryland public schools. The Supreme Court consolidated the cases and in 1963 ruled 8-1 that devotional Bible reading or other government-sponsored religious activities in public schools are unconstitutional.

"The United States Supreme Court has ruled against Bible reading and prayer in public schools. By so doing, the Supreme Court of the United States severs the connecting cord between the public schools of the United States and the source of divine intelligence, the Creator himself." (America In History & Prophecy p. 42)

David Barton exposes the effect this decision has had on America in To Pray or Not to Pray. He notes that 1963 was a pivotal year – negatively – in America. Every metric of healthy societies nose-dived after prayer was removed from public schools. The assemblage of statistical facts from

1955-1990 reveal dramatic and disturbing differences before 1963 and after 1963. Birth rates for unwed girls 15-19 years old increased 230%, pregnancies to unwed girls under 15 years old increased 500%, pregnancies to unwed girls under 15-19 years old increased 700%, sexually transmitted diseases increased 357%, pre-marital sex increased 333%, divorce rates increased 236%, single parent households increased 237%, unmarried couples living together increased 636%, adultery increased 120%, SAT scores decreased 11% (interestingly SAT scores for private religious schools increased during that same time frame, while school expenditures for public schools was 2 times more that for private schools), Department of Education reported in 1973 that 50% of the newly qualified teachers in math, science and English are not qualified to teach these subjects, school dropouts increased 1,147%, violent crime increased 680%, business productivity declined by 150%, sexually transmitted diseases increased 273%, alcohol consumption/capita increased 135%, from 1976-86, child abuse increased 2,429%, federal prosecution of public corruption increased 549%, from 1981-90 AIDS increased 4,342%

TOP PUBLIC SCHOOL OFFENSES:

BEFORE 1963	AFTER 1963	
Talking	Rape	Vandalism
Chewing gum	Robbery	Extortion
Making noise	Assault	Drug abuse
Running in the halls	Burglary	Alcohol abuse
Getting out of turn in line	Arson	Gang warfare
Wearing improper clothing	Bombings	Pregnancies
Not putting paper in wastebaskets	Murder	Abortions
	Suicide	Venereal disease
	Absenteeism	

NOTE: Civil laws cannot deal with the heart, which is the source of all behavior. Only religious principles can stop a crime before it occurs, because only religious principles can control the heart.

The following occurred at a Tennessee Football Game: This is a statement that was read over the PA system at the football game at Roane County High School, Kingston, Tennessee, by school principal, Jody McLeod.

"It has always been the custom at Roane County High School football games, to say a prayer and play the National Anthem, to honor God and Country."

"Due to a recent ruling by the Supreme Court, I am told that saying a Prayer is a violation of Federal Case Law. As I understand the law at this time, I can use this public facility to approve of sexual perversion and call it "an alternate life style," and, if someone is offended, that's OK.

"I can use it to condone sexual promiscuity, by dispensing condoms and calling it, "safe sex."
If someone is offended, that's OK.

"I can even use this public facility to present the merits of killing an unborn baby as a "viable" means of birth control." If someone is offended, no problem.

"I can designate a school day as "Earth Day" and involve students in activities to worship religiously and praise the goddess, "Mother Earth", and call it "ecology."

"I can use literature, videos and presentations in the classroom that depicts people with strong, traditional Christian convictions as "simple minded" and "ignorant" and call it "enlightenment."

However, if anyone uses this facility to honor GOD and to ask HIM to bless this event with safety and good sportsmanship, then Federal Case Law is violated.

This appears to be inconsistent at best, and at worst, diabolical.

Apparently, we are to be tolerant of everything and anyone, except GOD and HIS Commandments.

Nevertheless, as a school principal, I frequently ask staff and students to abide by rules with which they do not necessarily agree.

For me to do otherwise would be inconsistent at best, and at worst, hypocritical. I suffer from that affliction enough unintentionally. I certainly do not need to add an intentional transgression.
For this reason, I shall "Render unto Caesar that which is Caesar's," and refrain from praying at this time.

"However, if you feel inspired to honor, praise and thank GOD and ask HIM, in the name of JESUS, to bless this event, please feel free to do so. As far as I know, that's not against the law--yet."

One by one, the people in the stands bowed their heads, held hands with one another
and began to pray. They prayed in the stands. They prayed in the team huddles. They prayed at the concession stand and they prayed in the Announcer's Box!

The only place they didn't pray was in the Supreme Court of the United States of America-
the Seat of "Justice" in the "one nation, under GOD."

Somehow, Kingston , Tennessee, remembered what so many have forgotten. We are given the Freedom OF Religion, not the Freedom FROM religion.

[2] Obamacare
June 25, 2015, The Supreme Court upheld that States must comply with regulations under Obamacare. Obamacare was shoved down the throats of the vast majority of Americans who opposed it, signifying that Congress no longer represents the citizens of the United States of America, that the Executive and Legislative Branches have usurped control of the government and effective overrode centuries of American jurisprudence and squashed the U.S. Constitution under the thumb of tyranny.

[3] Gay Marriage
The final nail in the coffin of America was the Supreme Court's decision on June 26, 2015 declaring that Gay marriage is legal in all 50 states. The end-game of the gay rights movement is to replace religious freedom with massive coercive government control overs the lives, minds an beliefs of people once protected by the First Amendment. The gay marriage ruling is a foot-in-the-door to force communism on the American people. Thus, the Judicial Branch of government has become

lawmakers – a power reserved to the Congress in the Constitution – further revealing how far America has declined into the moral cesspool of relativism, how far we have descended below God's laws and how effective the screaming minority have been in silencing the Christian majority who have consecrated to be disciples of Jesus Christ. Wo to America and those who have voted evil representatives to government and upheld their tyrannical grasp for power over the freedom and liberty of all mankind!

The Supreme Court's decisions have undermined the forces of law and order and more than any other single cause, are directly responsible for the nations soaring crime rate. The Supreme Court has tipped the scales of justice in favor of criminals at the expense of victims.

They Supreme Court has legislated from the bench, which is unconstitutional. The Constitution gives authority ONLY to Congress to make laws. Supreme Court rulings do not - and cannot - change the laws of God. Rather than upholding the Constitution to restrain government, the Supreme Court has interpreted it to extend more power to government. Supreme Court justices who fail to uphold the U.S. Constitution should be impeached by Congress and removed from their appointments.

The supreme court is leading this Christian nation down the road to atheism, anarchy and atheistic communism. They have by law allowed communists to work in defense plants, teach in our schools, hold offices in labor unions, run for public office and serve in the merchant marines

Praise GOD that HIS remnant remains! JESUS said, "If you are ashamed of ME before men, then I will be ashamed of you before MY FATHER."

How America Ceased To Be Good

French writer Alexis de Tocqueville, after visiting America in 1831, said, *"I sought for the greatness of the United States in her commodious harbors, her ample rivers, her fertile fields, and boundless forests – and it was not there. I sought for it in rich mines, her vast world commerce, her public school systems, and in her institutions of higher learning – and it was not there. I looked for it in her democratic Congress and her matchless Constitution – and it was not there. Not until I went into the churches of America and heard her pulpits flame with righteousness did I understand the secret of her genius and power.* **America is great because America is good**, and **_if America ever ceases to be good, America will cease to be great_***!"*

Following is a list of recent presidential violations of our Freedom Documents (I.E. Un-Constitutional Actions):
- Removal of prayer from public schools
- Descent into the vortex of immorality
- Loss of National Sovereignty
- Invasion of Iraq without a Declaration of War
- Existence of the privately owned Federal Reserve System
- Use of a fiat, debt-based, paper currency

- Bailout of private financial institutions (TARP, AIG, etc.) where taxpayers money went to Unions and extravagant bank executive bonuses
- USA Patriot Act which violates the Bill of Rights
- Direct, un-apportioned (income) taxes on the labor of American workers
- Failure to enforce the nation's existing Immigration Laws
- Collusion to create an unconstitutional "North American Union"
- Infringement on the 2nd Amendment Right to Keep and Bear Arms
- Legally and morally unjustifiable Foreign Policy
- Secret computerized voting depriving the Right to Count the Votes
- National ID Cards/RFID restricting travel and infringing privacy
- Unconstitutional Executive orders/powers (Separation of powers)
- The unconstitutional "Welfare State"
- Denial of Right to Jury Nullification
- Unconstitutional seizures of private property for public use
- Refusal to require evidence of "natural born" citizenship status

Of our day Timothy wrote in chapter 3:1-7, "... *in the last days perilous times shall come. For men shall be lovers of their own selves, covetous boasters, proud blasphemers, disobedient to parents, unthankful, unholy, Without natural affection, trucebreakers, false accusers, incontinent, fierce, despisers of those that are good, traitors , heady, highminded , lovers of pleasures more than lovers of God; Having a form of godliness, but denying the power thereof: from such turn away. ... they ... creep into houses, and lead captive silly women laden with sins, led away with divers lusts, Ever learning, and never able to come to the knowledge of the truth.*"

Certainly our society is filled with these kinds of people. We must not become like them. We must seek and know the truth.

Crime Statistics

Percent change of Crime Rates from 1960 - 2009 in the United States by category: http://www.disastercenter.com/crime/uscrime.htm

CATEGORY	1960	2009	% +/-
Population	179,323,175	307,006,550	+71%
Violent crime	288,460	1,318,398	+357%
Property	3,095,700	9,320,971	+201%
Murder	9,110	15,241	+67%
Rape	17,190	89,000	+418%
Robbery	107,840	408,217	+279%
Aggravated Assault	154,320	806,843	+423%
Burglary	912,100	2,196,971	+141%
Theft-larceny	1,855,400	6,327,320	+241%
Theft-vehicle	328,200	794,616	+142%

American Suicide – Divide & Conquer

Dick Lamm was the former Governor of Colorado (Democrat). In that context his thoughts are particularly poignant. An immigration overpopulation conference in Washington, DC was filled to capacity by many of America's finest minds and leaders. A brilliant college professor by the name of Victor Davis Hansen talked about his latest book, "Mexifornia," explaining how immigration - both legal and illegal was destroying the entire state of California. He said it would march across the country until it destroyed all vestiges of The American Dream.

Moments later, former Colorado Governor Richard D. Lamm stood up and gave a stunning speech on how to destroy America. The audience sat spellbound as he described eight methods for the destruction of the United States. He said:

"If you believe that America is too smug, too self-satisfied, too rich, then let's destroy America. It is not that hard to do. No nation in history has survived the ravages of time. Arnold Toynbee observed that all great civilizations rise and fall and that 'An autopsy of history would show that all great nations commit suicide.'"

"Here is how they do it," Lamm said: "First, to destroy America, turn America into a bilingual or multi-lingual and bicultural country." History shows that no nation can survive the tension, conflict, and antagonism of two or more competing languages and cultures It is a blessing for an individual to be bilingual; however, it is a curse for a society to be bilingual. The historical scholar, Seymour Lipset, put it this way: "The histories of bilingual and bi-cultural societies that do not assimilate are histories of turmoil, tension, and tragedy." Canada, Belgium, Malaysia, and Lebanon all face crises of national existence in which minorities press for autonomy, if not independence. Pakistan and Cyprus have divided. Nigeria suppressed an ethnic rebellion. France faces difficult times with Basques, Bretons, and Corsicans."

"Lamm went on: Second, to destroy America, "Invent 'multiculturalism' and encourage immigrants to maintain their culture. Make it an article of belief that all cultures are equal and that there are no cultural differences. Make it an article of faith that the Black and Hispanic dropout rates are due solely to prejudice and discrimination by the majority. Every other explanation is out of bounds.

"Third, "We could make the United States an 'Hispanic Quebec' without much effort. The key is to celebrate diversity rather than unity. As Benjamin Schwarz said in the Atlantic Monthly recently: "The apparent success of our own multiethnic and multicultural experiment might have been achieved not by tolerance but by hegemony. Without the dominance that once dictated ethnocentricity and what it meant to be an American, we are left with only tolerance and pluralism to hold us together." "Lamm said, "I would encourage all immigrants to keep their own language and culture. I would! Replace the melting pot metaphor with the salad bowl metaphor. It is important to ensure that we have various cultural subgroups living in America enforcing their differences rather than as Americans, emphasizing their similarities."

"Fourth, I would make our fastest growing demographic group the least educated. I would add a second underclass, unassimilated, undereducated, and antagonistic to our population. I would have this second underclass have a 50% dropout rate from high school."

"My fifth point for destroying America would be to get big foundations and business to give these efforts lots of money. I would invest in ethnic identity, and I would establish the cult of 'Victimology.' I would get all minorities to think that their lack of success was the fault of the

majority. I would start a grievance industry blaming all minority failure on the majority population."

"My sixth plan for America's downfall would include dual citizenship, and promote divided loyalties I would celebrate diversity over unity. I would stress differences rather than similarities. Diverse people worldwide are mostly engaged in hating each other- that is, when they are not killing each other. A diverse, peaceful, or stable society is against most historical precedent. People undervalue the unity it takes to keep a nation together.

Look at the ancient Greeks. The Greeks believed that they belonged to the same race; they possessed a common Language and literature; and they worshipped the same Gods. All Greece took part in the Olympic Games. A common enemy, Persia, threatened their liberty! Yet all these bonds were not strong enough to overcome two factors local patriotism and geographical conditions that nurtured political divisions. Greece fell.

"E. Pluribus Unum" -- from many, one. In that historical reality, if we put the emphasis on the 'Pluribus' instead of the 'Unum,' we will balkanize America assuredly as Kosovo."

"Next to last, I would place all subjects off limits; make it taboo to talk about anything against the cult of 'diversity.' I would find a word similar to 'heretic' in the 16th century - that stopped discussion and paralyzed thinking. Words like 'racist' or 'xenophobe' halt discussion and debate. Having made America a bi-lingual/bicultural country, having established multiculturalism, having the large foundations fund the doctrine of 'victimology,' I would next make it impossible to enforce our immigration laws. I would develop a mantra: That because immigration has been good for America, it must always be good. I would make every individual immigrant symmetric and ignore the cumulative impact of millions of them."

"Lastly, I would censor Victor Hanson Davis's book "Mexifornia." His book is dangerous. It exposes the plan to destroy America. If you feel America deserves to be destroyed, don't read that book."

There was no applause after his speech. A chilling fear quietly rose like an ominous cloud above every attendee at the conference. Every American in that room knew that everything Lamm enumerated was proceeding methodically, quietly, darkly, yet pervasively across the United States today.

Everyone at the conference saw that our nation and the future of this great democracy is in deep trouble and worsening fast. If we don't get this immigration monster stopped within three years, it will rage like a California wildfire and destroy everything in its path especially The American Dream.

So....where are we America? Discussion is being suppressed. Over 100 languages are ripping the foundation of our educational system and national cohesiveness. Even barbaric cultures [Islam] that practice female genital mutilation are growing due to 'political correctness' and as we celebrate 'diversity.' American jobs are vanishing into the Third World countries as corporations export services. As a consequence they create a 'third world' of America. We now have 12-20 million+ illegal aliens in our country. With 'press 1' for English, 'press 2' for Spanish and now 'press 3' for Arabic (in Michigan), we have traveled far down the road Governor Lamm warned against.

When immigrants in the past came to America, they did so legally. Regardless of what country they came from, they became Americans. There is NO ROOM for hyphenations in America; no 'African-American'. You are either African (which of course is a continent, NOT a country) or

American. You cannot be both. Americans now as in the past must choose a country, stay here or go there and be a loyal citizen wherever you choose to live.

Multiple languages and multiple cultures divide loyalties and destroy countries.

How America Ceased To Be Great

"The measure of a country's greatness should be based on how well it cares for its most vulnerable populations" - Mahatma Gandhi

Who can be more vulnerable than an unborn child?; a human with no voice. America's abortion statistics: **50,766,331 abortions 1973-2008.** We now average about 1,200,000 abortions per year. This is one obvious reason why our greatness is diminishing; murder of the most vulnerable.

Another measure of greatness is the strength of America's economy. In spite of the alleged urgency for the Tarp bill, Stimulus packages and Obamacare, how's it going <u>for you</u>?

More Americans are out of work since the Great Depression. Unemployment ranges from a government manipulated bogus 9% to a more accurate 22% including those who have stopped looking for work. In the height of the Great Depression unemployment was 25%. Record numbers are on government welfare and unemployment. Most of Tarp and Stimulus went to SEIU Unions and bankster fat cats...all payback for helping get Obama elected. The stock market crashed in 2008, the housing bubble burst, Obamacare death panels are active, Obamacare pays for abortions with our tax dollars, Obamacare has 22 hidden new taxes after he promised no new taxes, availability of healthcare I reduced etc. These facts present clear evidence of America's descent. But there's more....small business's are going out of business in record numbers because of government bureaucracy.

Out of 165 countries whose GDP grew in 2010, the United States was number 117. China is fast overtaking us in GDP. Indonesia and India are not far behind in rate of growth. India has more honor students than America has students. America clearly is falling behind.

Even Vladimir Putin of communist Russia is telling Obama NOT to go down the socialism road! How revealing of what we have become and where we are heading!

Communist Tactics

After the collapse of the Berlin Wall, the Communist Party met in 1992 at the University of California, Berkeley campus, to decide how to alter their strategy to take down America. From the 1919 Communist Rules for Revolution, they added their strategy changed from violent overthrow to cause decay from the inside out. Their combined tactics included the following:

- Infiltrate America's institutions and influence them toward communism,
- Promote co-habitation instead of traditional marriage,
- Corrupt the young, get them away from religion and interested in sex,
- Separate children from parents as early as possible and get them under government education control,
- Promote the feminist movement to make women unhappy with marriage and motherhood,

- Promote the environmentalist movement to destroy capitalism,
- Destroy America's culture of religion and morality,
- Promote homosexuality and perversion as acceptable 'alternative' lifestyles,
- Eliminate religious practice in public life – i.e. prayer and the Bible,
- Discredit the family,
- Encourage promiscuity and divorce,
- Get control of schools and teachers organizations, Use them to promoters socialism,
- Eliminate all laws governing obscenity by calling it a violation of free speech,
- Promote pornography to break down cultural standards of morality,
- Infiltrate the media (radio, TV, movies). Get control of key positions and use as outlets for propaganda,
- Infiltrate churches and replace revealed religion with social religion. Discredit the Bible.
- Divide people in to hostile groups – black/white, male/female, unions/free-workers, rich/poor, wealthy/middle class,
- Play the victim card, the race card
- Create entitlement mentality, provide government support for them and enslave them.
- Get peoples mind off government by focusing attention on Hollywood stars, athletics.
- Preach true democracy but seize power as fast and ruthlessly as possible.
- Foment strikes, riots, civil unrest
- Cause registration of all firearms on some pretext, with a view toward confiscation.

Note that the communists have achieved all their goals throughout much of America.

Bob Avakian, Chairman of the Revolutionary Communist Party USA, is the current communist revolution leader directing civil unrest and riots across the globe, including in Ferguson, MO, and NYC.

Socialist-Communist Conspiracy

The socialist-communist conspiracy is the greatest evil and threat to freedom in the world. It is a battle between light and darkness, between freedom and slavery, between the spirit of Christianity and the spirit of the anti-Christ for the souls of mankind. Psalms 33 reads *"Blessed is the nation whose God is the Lord; and the people whom he hath chosen for his own inheritance."* America was once that nation. Communism is the godless alternative.

Communism is not a political party, military organization, or ideological crusade. It is a gigantic conspiracy to enslave mankind. It is tyranny authored by Satan through Karl Marx. Communism is the #1 killer in the world. It therefore warrants our investigation and elimination.

"There are present in our own United States influences, the avowed object which is to sow discord and contention among men with the view of undermining, weakening, if not entirely destroying our Constitutional form of government…. [There are] evils of war. There is another danger even more menacing than the threat of invasion of a foreign foe. It is the un-patriotic activities and underhanded scheming of disloyal groups and organizations within our own borders….the secret,

seditious, scheming of an enemy within our own ranks, hypo-critically professing loyalty to the government, and at the same time plotting against it, is more difficult to deal with. Disintegration [from within] is often more dangerous and more fatal than outward opposition." (America In History & Prophecy p 41-42)

"A nation can survive its fools and even the ambitious, but it cannot survive treason from within. ....A murderer is less to be feared. The traitor is the carrier of the plague." (Cicero's remarks to the Roman Senate)

Ezra Taft Benson, Dwight Eisenhower's Secretary of Agriculture, hosted Nikita Khrushchev and was assigned to give him an overview of American agriculture in 1959. During his visit to America, Khrushchev boasted that Benson's grandchildren would live under Communism and that Americans were so gullible that they would accept small doses of socialism until they woke up under the yoke of communism. I add.....we are almost there.

Socialism and Communism have the same ends; control and domination. Only their tactics differ. Socialism gains power by deception; promising to take care of you in exchange for votes. Communism gains power by violent force.

Treason is aiding and abetting the enemy. The greatest enemy to freedom is communism and its ideological cousins that all use force and control to deprive freedom and enslave mankind.

Franklin Delano Roosevelt (FDR) opened the door to communism in 1933 when he formally recognized Stalin's godless, murderous regime. We extended diplomatic relations to atheistic Russia. That act increased Russia's standing in the world and saved Russia from financial collapse. It enabled them to increase spies and propaganda agents throughout the world. We have been bailing Russia out of their difficulties and bolstering their slave economy since. All treasonous acts to aid and abet the enemy of freedom.

The Johnson Administration's Consular Treaty is an act of treason because it give diplomatic immunity to godless foreign consulars who engage in espionage in America. Russia leaders declare *"treaties like pie crust are meant to be broken"* yet the Kennedy Administration signed the Moscow treaty with Russia that neutralized our military advantage over communism and subjected us to Soviet conventional forces in guerrilla warfare like happened in Vietnam; a no-win war where our military hands were tied. With a WWII mindset of complete victory, our military generals told us that we could have won in 90 days, but our governments treasonous treaties with Russia caused a prolonged war ending in embarrassed withdrawal and communist takeover of Vietnam. The Johnson administration gave Bell Helicopter the Vietnam war in exchange for his presidency; a traitorous act. Our government bolstered Russian economy through trade when Moscow was supplying MIG's to the North Vietnamese communists to kill our American boys; an act of treason. Ever since FDR our government has exported factories, food, equipment and American know-how to Russia and her satellites. Communism is the enemy. Our government has committed treason.

Our government's actions toward communism reveal infiltration of communists in our government. We have the cancer of traitors within that has infected the body of America.

We must stop all trade with the enemy and stop supporting communism in any way. Communism will collapse under the weight of the false ideology of plunder. It cannot sustain itself without our help. Let it collapse. Let the then freed people adopt our U.S. Constitution, or a version of it, as their own.

Our federal government has been conducting treasonous actions by aiding and abetting the enemy and by instituting socialism and communism for over 100 years. Examples include federal governments un-constitutional subsidization (i.e. control) over education, surrender of our sovereignty in foreign policy to the United Nations, the Executive Branch declaring unconstitutional no-win wars with a policy of 'containment' in Korea and Vietnam and supervised the sale of wheat at cut-rate prices to feed our enemy. The policy of containment encourages potential aggressors to try their luck at military conquest; they have everything to gain and almost nothing to lose. The aftermath of conduction these no-win wars has been the loss of lives of precious sons of America and the expansion of communism, especially in Vietnam, with its typical destruction of millions of human lives. America, if war is just, should fight to win, not to bring the enemy to the negotiating table.

The slogan 'civil rights' as used to make trouble in the South is an exact parallel to the slogan of 'agrarian reform' which they used in China and Cuba that led to communist take-over of their governments. There is nothing wrong with civil rights – per se – it is what is being done in the name of civil right by communists that is evil. Communists are using civil rights as part of their pattern for the take-over of America. In 1928 the communists declared that the cultural, economic and social differences between the aces in America could be exploited by them to create the animosity, fear, and hatred, between large segments of our people necessary sow seeds of revolution. Communists plans are three step: Create hatred. Trigger violence. Overthrow established government. We see these tactics being played out today in Ferguson, MO and in Baltimore, MD. This communist strategy was used in Czechoslovakia but with a slightly different tactic; infiltrate to a peaceful overthrow. Socialists infiltrated the government under the guise as progressives who sought to bring peace and healing to the races. But in fact, they used race riots to expand government control over all aspects of life until all the mechanics of regulatory control were in place. Then the Czech people woke up on day to a communist government. This is happening in America today.

The communist infiltration of the civil rights movement is like the environmental movement. Naturalist John Muir started the Sierra Club out of love of nature. However, this seed of the environmental movement was used by communists to infiltrate and expand an otherwise virtuous cause and use it to achieve communist ends by over-regulation in order to bring about economic demise of American capitalism.

Nikita Cruschev boasted of the agenda that they (the communists and socialists) were advancing. He stated they would give us (American's) small doses of socialism until one day we would wake up and find we had communism, and then he boasted, we would "fall like overripe fruit into their hands. Indeed, these wolves in sheep's clothing have seduced the more part of the righteous until they have come down to believe in their works and partake of their spoils. The throngs of the masses foolishly worship these false and destructive, anti-American philosophies of government, economics, education, religion; the sciences; the arts, and every other area of learning.

Satan's age-old tactic is to create a state of fear, then offer security at the expense of freedom. Norman Vincent Peale stated, *"There was a time when the American people roared like lions for liberty; now they bleat like sheep for security."* America has slid far down the road to accepting tyranny under the disguise of 'government will take care of you.'

William Penn stated *"If we will not be governed by God, we must be governed by tyrants."* Nations are never conquered from the outside unless they are rotten on the inside. Americas descent into immorality as defined by God and acceptance of moral relativism as defined by man has led to increasing tyrannical government leaders and control.

American Foreign Policy

There is only on legitimate goal of the United States foreign policy; the preservation of The United States of America's national political, economic and military independence. Boiled down to a few key principles, America's foreign policy should be: [1] Establish and maintain independence, [2] Avoid political connections, involvement or interventions, [3] No entangling alliances, [4] treat all nations impartially, neither granting nor accepting special privileges from any, [5] promote commerce with all peoples and countries, [6] develop civilized rules of international conduct, [7] Act in accordance with the 'laws of nations', and [8] maintain a defensive force of sufficient size to deter aggressors.

Nothing in the Constitution grants the President to be the world leader. He is OUR executive. He is on OUR payroll. He is supposed to put OUR best interests first. Nothing in the Constitution authorizes our president to influence political life of other countries, to uplift their cultures, to bolster their economies, to feed their peoples or to defend them against their enemies. George Washington encouraged maintaining neutrality and preserve peace. Our government has stepped over these guidelines and laws thus pushing us down the slope toward destruction.

America's policy for generations had been – we do not negotiate with terrorists. One example is notable. During President Teddy Roosevelt's tenure, an American citizen of Greek origin named Perdicaris was captured by an African bandit named Raisuli. President T. Roosevelt did not negotiate, he did not send an urgent requests. He simply ordered one of our gunboats to stand offshore, and sent the local sultan the following telegram: 'Perdicaris alive, or Raisuli dead.' Raisuli did not waste any time getting a healthy Perdicaris down to the dock. However, in the past decades, we have had traitorous presidents who have negotiated and befriended terrorists. This caused America's declining respect among nations and its descent from greatness.

America has lost much of its sovereignty by making treaties that have terms and conditions that reach inside our own borders and restrict our freedoms. Involvement in the United Nations and giving up our sovereignty to U.N Peacekeeping forces are one example. Since 1945 there have been nine men appointed to be UN Undersecretary General for Political and Security Council Affairs – the UN Peacekeeping corps – all of them from the USSR! How can America retain its sovereignty with communists in control over America's military in the UN? America's State Department proposal for disarmament as presented before the UN General Assembly called

'Freedom from War – The United States Program for General and Complete Disarmament' – set down four objectives: [1] that all nations, including the United State, disband their national armed forces except for what would be earmarked for a UN peace force, [2] that all nations, including the United States, eliminate their nuclear weapons and missiles other than those required for a UN peace force, [3] that all nations, including the United States, acknowledge the UN authority to supervise and direct this transfer s military power, and [4] that all nations, including the United States, carry out this transfer to a point where not state would have the military power to challenge the progressively strengthened UN Peace Force. President John F. Kennedy described the beneficial effects of this action as abandonment of most of the old concept so nation states, development of international institutions that would encourage nations to give up much of their nation sovereignty, accept without question or reservation the jurisdiction of the international court, dependence on nation security on a immensely strengthened UN Peacekeeping force. Adlai Stevenson stated that this U.S. Proposal call for the total elimination of national capacity to make international war.

America's government involvement in the UN is unconstitutional and is treason!

Fabian Socialist Window

George Bernard Shaw was a member of the semi-secret Fabian Socialist Society, that has the following Luciferin goal:

To establish socialism, where there is no poor, where you are forcibly fed, clothed, lodged, taught, and employed ..liked it or not. If your industry was not worth all this trouble, you might possibly be executed.

"Socialists, like Lucifer, profess "good" intentions in their use of force, coercion, and intimidation upon mankind. The Fabian Socialists use

the exact course of action proposed by Lucifer, Son of the Morning who held authority in the presence of God, but who was cast out for rebellion, seeking to take away the agency of man, his right to choose, his right to be free. It was Lucifer's wish and will to take away the agency of man, as the story goes, forcing all men back to heaven. They would forcibly be baptized, never allowed to make mistakes, never allowed choice, never allowed failure. Sound good? Benevolent? George Bernard Shaw thought so. David Rockefeller would seem to think so. As the Biblical account records, a whole third of the hosts of heaven, spirits not yet come to earth also thought so, as they followed their freedom-destroying leader Satan, and thus left their chance to have a legitimate body of flesh and blood, to be born upon the earth.

"Revelation tells us that "there was war in heaven: Michael and his angels fought against the dragon; and the dragon fought and his angels, and prevailed not; neither was their place found any more in heaven. And the great dragon was cast out, that old serpent, called the Devil, and Satan, which deceiveth the whole world: he was cast out into the earth, and his angels were cast out with him" (Rev. 12:7-9).

"Isaiah describes Satan's seemingly "good intentions," but we unmask his true agenda, it was all about him wanting "glory" and "power: "How art thou fallen from heaven, O Lucifer, son of the morning! How art thou cut down to the ground, which didst weaken the nations! For thou hast said in thine heart, I will ascend into heaven, I will exalt my throne above the stars of God: I will sit also upon the mount of the congregation, in the sides of the north: I will ascend above the heights of the clouds; I will be like the most High." (Isaiah 14:12-14.)

America is ripening and about to fall like overripe fruit into the hands of the socialist-communist conspiracy, which thrives as never before. As we study the stained glass window below, designed by these Fabian's....[note the] enforced bondage that Fabians promote as explained in G. Edward Griffin's masterwork The Creature From Jekyll Island. As pictured below, the Fabian's have as their coat of arms a wolf in sheep's clothing, and they desire to mold the earth "nearer to their heart's desire." And then, in great sinister admission of strategy and tactic, they seduce the masses into bowing down and worshiping the learning of man, his false philosophies that are anti-Christ.

These teachings hold within them the seeds of destruction which run civilizations into the ground with programs like Obamacare. The middle class is reduced year by year into poverty.

(George B. Shaw: The Intelligent Woman's Guide to Socialism and Capitalism, 1928, pg. 470)

 This evil secret Fabian Society has contributed to America's descent.

United Nations

"The United Nations is but a long-range, international banking apparatus clearly set up for financial and economic profit by a small group of powerful One-World revolutionaries, hungry for profit and power.

"The depression was the calculated 'shearing' of the public by the World Money powers, triggered by the planned sudden shortage of supply of call money in the New York money market....The One World Government leaders and their ever close bankers have now acquired full control of the money and credit machinery of the U.S. via the creation of the privately owned Federal Reserve Bank.

"We are grateful to the Washington Post, The New York Times, Time Magazine and other great publications whose directors have attended our meetings and respected their promise of discretion for almost forty years. It would have been impossible for us to develop our plan for the world if we had been subject to the bright lights of publicity during those years. But, the world is now more sophisticated and prepared to march toward a world government. *The super-national sovereignty of an intellectual elite and world bankers is surely preferable to the national auto-determination practiced in past centuries."* David Rockefeller, speaking to his fellow global socialists at a meeting in Baden-Baden, Germany, June 1991.

The United States is founded on the concept of limited government power. The U.N. concept is one of unlimited government power. The U.N. is becoming a professional politicians paradise, a world legislature, a world court, world department of education, world welfare agency,, world planning center for industry, science and commerce, world finance agency, and world police force; a one-world government lead primarily by communist tyrants. It is the center for communist espionage in America.

We should get America out of the United Nations and the United Nations out of America!

The following shows actual voting records of various Arabic/Islamic States which are recorded in both the U.S. State Department and United Nations records:

Kuwait votes	against	The United States	67%of the time
Qatar votes	against	The United States	67%of the time
Morocco votes	against	The United States	70%of the time
United Arab Emirates	against	The United States	70%of the time
Jordan votes	against	The United States	71%of the time
Tunisia votes	against	The United States	71%of the time
Saudi Arabia votes	against	The United States	73%of the time
Yemen votes	against	The United States	74%of the time
Algeria votes	against	The United States	74%of the time
Oman votes	against	The United States	74%of the time
Sudan votes	against	The United States	75%of the time
Pakistan votes	against	The United States	75%of the time
Libya votes	against	The United States	76%of the time
Egypt votes	against	The United States	79%of the time
Lebanon votes	against	The United States	80%of the time
Syria votes	against	The United States	84%of the time
Mauritania votes	against	The United States	87%of the time

U.S. Foreign Aid to those that hate us (3 typical examples):
Egypt, for example, after voting 79% of the time against the United States and receives $2,000,000,000 annually in US Foreign Aid.

In 2013 we sent F-16 Fighter jets to arm The Muslim Brotherhood - our enemies.

Jordan votes 71% against the United States
Receives $192,814,000 annually in US Foreign Aid.

Pakistan votes 75% against the United States
Receives $6,721,000,000 annually in US Foreign Aid.

They actually bite the hand that feeds them and America keeps feeding them! Perhaps it's time to get out of the UN and give the tax savings back to the American workers who are having to skimp and sacrifice to pay the taxes.

Progressive Movement

Edward Bernays wrote <u>Propaganda</u> (1928). He states *"The conscious and intelligent manipulation of the organized habits and opinions of the masses is an important element in democratic society. Those who manipulate this unseen mechanism of society constitute an invisible government which is the true ruling power of our country."*

Bernays contributed to the progressive movement to use propaganda to control the 'sheeple.' Walter Lipman also used it. Joseph Goerbels used Bernays' and Lipman's progressive movement tactics which became known as propaganda in Nazi Germany. The Nazis gave propaganda a bad name. Therefore, the Progressives just changed the language from 'propaganda' and now call it 'public relations' - all the while using the same tactics to control and manipulate the sheeple.

Progressives often use Christian principles to attain their socialistic objectives. Their efforts to stop free speech today is similar to what the 'ruling class' in the Apostle Peter's day used to quiet Peter. *"Let us straitly threaten them that they speak henceforth to no man in this name. And they called them, and commanded them not to speak at all nor teach in the name of Jesus."*Acts 4:17

The 'fairness doctrine' progressives want to pass today is designed to close down open debate in America; right out of the playbook of the 'elite' of Peters time. Progressives only want freedom to shut down debate in free speech and expand their own view. However, true freedom depends on open and honest debate.

In the early 1900's Progressives set out to destroy our churches, our history and our Constitution – the foundations of faith, hope and charity on which America rests and has ascended to greatness. Progressives intentionally deleted or revised our American history over the past 100 years.

Progressives' tactics to gain power include the following steps:

1. Develop a grand plan to gain control of the sheeple - the One World Order.

2. Infiltrate the government

3. Create a crisis (a state of fear, the problem)

4. Overwhelm the system - welfare, capitalism etc. (The Cloward & Piven approach)

5. Incite riots at the grassroots level - riots in the streets

6. Step in at the top (government) with a 'solution' (AKA their solution to gain power and control) to be your 'saviour' to calm your fears, to 'take care of you so no one will be lost.' Just like Lucifer in the War in Heaven!

Progressives (AKA communists, socialists, Marxists, fascist, Nazis etc...) are power mongers, inspired by Satan to overthrow the freedom and liberty of all mankind. They have successfully implemented their plan, all except the last step of One World Oder.

Progressives' Socialist-Communist Destruction Of America

The steps to socialist-communist takeover and examples of how they have achieved it:

1. Control the financial industry (example: the Federal Reserve bail out Goldman Sachs, Lehman Bros)

2. Control auto industry (example: the Federal Government takeover of GM – the once largest corporation in America)

3. Control insurance industry (example: the Federal Government bail out of AIG etc.)

4. Control heath industry (example: the Federal Government Un-Constitutional Obamacare)

5. Control the media (George Soros liberal left funding of most media except FOX News, The FCC announced in Dec 2010 that in spite of the Congress condemning action to control the internet, they will do it anyway 'for the good of the country'. This is un-Constitutional, un-authorized abuse of position to gain power and control. ONLY Congress is authorized to make laws under the Constitution)

6. Control food delivery (example: the Federal Government passed the Senate Bill #510). That bill represents another hideous attempt to place more power into the hands of centralized government and robs individual citizens and states. The greatest danger to mankind is that this bill allows complete manipulation of America's food supply and threatens to strip us of our freedoms to grow, sell, and buy food and make doing any of those natural things crimes punishable by imprisonment. Under that bill it would be a crime to grow food and share it with friends and neighbors. The act of generating and supporting this bill is in itself un-Constitutional.

7. Control people by increasing government dependency (example: the Federal Government entitlement programs, welfare etc. The Declaration of Independence and the U.S. Constitution limits the Federal government's power to the protection of life and liberty so that we can purse happiness. It says to PROMOTE the general welfare. It does NOT authorize the Federal government to PROVIDE the general welfare through entitlements!)

8. Destroy religion and morality (example: the Federal Government Supreme Court banned prayer and Bibles in public school in 1962 & 1963, and forced removal of the Ten Commandments from Judge Roy Moore's courthouse)

9. Re-write our history and demonize our Founding Fathers, the Republic & capitalism (Example: the Progressives have rewritten history books that alter our history, demonize our Founding Fathers and even Obama teaches that the U.S. Constitution is an antiquated document...a list of limitations of what the government cannot do, rather than define what the government must do for its citizens. THE PURPOSE OF THE U.S. CONSTITUTION **IS** TO LIMIT THE POWERS OF THE FEDERAL GOVERNMENT SO THAT IS DOES NOT BECOME A CONTROLLING TYRANNY OVER US! And some politicians, especially Obama, hate that restriction on their lust for power over We The People.) (Example: rewrite history to put the blame of 100+years of progressivism & socialism creeping into our government that create laws to 'catch' and punish 'lawbreakers' to bring them under control of the government and tax that which succeeds to glut government politicians and bureaucrats on the industry of capitalism which brings businesses down and destroys them...and then BLAME capitalism!!!!...when the real cause of the demise is socialism!)

10. Control the military (can you say '~~Commander~~ Obama in Chief?)

ONLY #8 THEY DO NOT CONTROL COMPLETELY!

In F.A. Hayek's book, <u>The Road to Serfdom</u> he states that ***"Socialism always leads to tyranny of dictatorships."*** We have progressed far down the road of socialism on the slippery slope to a dictator. This IS where the Progressive movement has been leading America since the early 1900's.

Liberalism - The Godless Religion

Americans will never adopt socialism outright. However, if it is disguised under the name of liberalism and progressivism they will adopt every fragment of socialism until one day America will be a socialist nation, without knowing how it happened. And it IS happening now.

"Socialism is a philosophy of failure, the creed of ignorance, and the gospel of envy, its inherent virtue is the equal sharing of misery." "Marxism in America" by Lt. Gen. (Ret.) W.G. Boykin

The motives behind Roosevelt's New Deal were revealed by Prof. William A. Wirt, who had sat in on several brain trust meetings. Wirt appeared before Congress in 1933 and testified that the following line of attack on our free American system was being used by the Fabian administration:

1. Keep Communists in key positions in the government.

2. Substitute decrees by executive agencies for organic law.

3. Replace private industry and commerce with a planned economy.

4. Decentralize cities and redistribute industry and population through housing projects.

5. End private lending agencies and control borrowers by federal monopoly of long-term commercial loans.

6. Dictate policies of newspapers, magazines and control other avenues of public opinion.

7. Corral the farm vote through subsidies.

8. Quiet business and labor by doles to make them dependent on the government.

9. Chill the spine of business by public investigations.

10. Discredit financiers by picturing them as crooks.

11. Call political opponents traitors and use the police power of the State to crack down on them.

How Socialism 'Works'

An economics professor at a local college made a statement that he had never failed a single student before, but had recently failed an entire class. That class had insisted that Obama's socialism worked and that no one would be poor and no one would be rich, a great equalizer. The professor then said, "OK, we will have an experiment in this class on Obama's plan".

All grades would be averaged and everyone would receive the same grade so no one would fail and no one would receive an A. After the first test, the grades were averaged and everyone got a B. The students who studied hard were upset and the students who studied little were happy. As the second test rolled around, the students who studied little had studied even less and the ones who studied hard decided they wanted a free ride too so they studied little. The second test average was a D! No one was happy.

When the 3rd test rolled around, the average was an F. As the tests proceeded, the scores never increased as bickering, blame and name-calling all resulted in hard feelings and no one would study for the benefit of anyone else. All failed, to their great surprise, and the professor told them that socialism would also ultimately fail because **when the reward is great, the effort to succeed is great, but when government takes all the reward away, no one will try or want to succeed.**

"The problem with socialism is that eventually you run out of other people's money." Margaret Thatcher, Prime Minister, Great Britain

Entitlements & Welfare - Tools Of Enslavement

The U.S. Constitution states that government is to promote - NOT PROVIDE - for the general welfare. Yet over time, the federal government has become a bloated tick feasting off the labor of We The People. The government has assumed power to provide for health, education, welfare (HEW) environmental protection (EPA), food & drug administration (FDA) (talk about a fox in the hen house! Food & drugs together!), the failed department of energy (DOE)and the internal revenue service (IRS). All these, the HEW, EPA, FDA, DOE, and the IRS are UN-Constitutional bureaucratic agencies bloated with self-proclaimed, but unconstitutional power. They provide Government Entitlements & Welfare that are tyrannical tools of enslavement.

The Treasury Department's Inspector General determined that the Internal Revenue Service paid $4.2 billion in 2010 to illegal aliens. That payout was up from less than $1 billion in 2005. Leading Democrats are resisting a bill that would stop future payments.

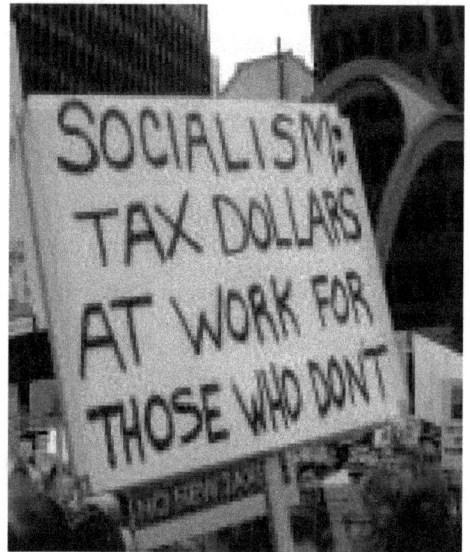

"I consider the foundation of the Constitution as laid on this ground that 'all powers not delegated to the United States, by the Constitution, nor prohibited by it to the states, are reserved to the states or to the people." And "whenever the general government assumes un-delegated powers its acts are un-authoritative, void and of no force.'...a single consolidated government would become the most corrupt government on the earth..." If this ever happens "...you will have to choose between reformation and revolution." The Real Thomas Jefferson pp. 430-433.

Separation Of Church And State

The progressives and liberal left have perverted the original meaning of this phrase and use it as a weapon to destroy our liberty. The fact is that the phrase 'separation of church and state' DOES NOT EXIST in ANY of our FOUNDING DOCUMENTS; not in either the Declaration of Independence nor in the U.S. Constitution.

Consider The Following Facts:

God IS in all 50 States Constitutions:

America's founders did not intend for there to be a separation of God and state, as shown by the fact that all 50 states acknowledge God in their state constitutions:

1. Alabama 1901, Preamble. We The People of the State of Alabama, invoking the favor and guidance of Almighty God, do ordain and establish the following Constitution ...
2. Alaska 1956, Preamble. We, the people of Alaska, grateful to God and to those who founded our nation and pioneered this great land ...
3. Arizona 1911, Preamble. We, the people of the State of Arizona, grateful to Almighty God for our liberties, do ordain this Constitution...
4. Arkansas 1874, Preamble. We, the people of the State of Arkansas, grateful to Almighty God for the privilege of choosing our own form of government...
5. California 1879, Preamble. We, the People of the State of California, grateful to Almighty God for our freedom ...
6. Colorado 1876, Preamble. We, the people of Colorado, with profound reverence for the Supreme Ruler of Universe.
7. Connecticut 1818, Preamble. The People of Connecticut, acknowledging with gratitude the good Providence of God in permitting them to enjoy ..
8. Delaware 1897, Preamble. Through Divine Goodness all men have, by nature, the rights of worshipping and serving their Creator according to the dictates of their consciences ...
9. Florida 1885, Preamble. We, the people of the State of Florida, grateful to Almighty God for our constitutional liberty, establish this Constitution...
10. Georgia 1777, Preamble. We, the people of Georgia, relying upon protection and guidance of Almighty God, do ordain and establish this Constitution...
11. Hawaii 1959, Preamble. We, the people of Hawaii, Grateful for Divine Guidance .. establish this Constitution.
12. Idaho 1889, Preamble. We, the people of the State of Idaho, grateful to Almighty God for our freedom, to secure its blessings ...
13. Illinois 1870, Preamble. We, the people of the State of Illinois, grateful to Almighty God for the civil, political and religious liberty which He hath so long permitted us to enjoy and looking to Him for a blessing on our endeavors.
14. Indiana 1851, Preamble. We, the People of the State of Indiana, grateful to Almighty God for the free exercise of the right to chose our form of government.
15. Iowa 1857, Preamble. We, the People of the State of Iowa, grateful to the Supreme Being for the blessings hitherto enjoyed, and feeling our dependence on Him for a continuation of these blessings establish this Constitution
16. Kansas 1859, Preamble. We, the people of Kansas, grateful to Almighty God for our civil and religious privileges establish this Constitution.
17. Kentucky 1891, Preamble. We, the people of the Commonwealth of grateful to Almighty God for the civil, political and religious liberties...

18. Louisiana 1921, Preamble. We, the people of the State of Louisiana, grateful to Almighty God for the civil, political and religious liberties we enjoy.
19. Maine 1820, Preamble. We The People of Maine . acknowledging with grateful hearts the goodness of the Sovereign Ruler of the Universe in affording us an opportunity .. and imploring His aid and direction.
20. Maryland 1776, Preamble. We, the people of the state of Maryland, grateful to Almighty God for our civil and religious liberty...
21. Massachusetts 1780, Preamble. We...the people of Massachusetts, acknowledging with grateful hearts, the goodness of the Great Legislator of the Universe ... in the course of His Providence, an opportunity .and devoutly imploring His direction ...
22. Michigan 1908, Preamble. We, the people of the State of Michigan, grateful to Almighty God for the blessings of freedom ... establish this Constitution
23. Minnesota, 1857, Preamble. We, the people of the State of Minnesota, grateful to God for our civil and religious liberty, and desiring to perpetuate its blessings
24. Mississippi 1890, Preamble. We, the people of Mississippi in convention assembled, grateful to Almighty God, and invoking His blessing on our work.
25. Missouri 1845, Preamble. We, the people of Missouri, with profound reverence for the supreme Ruler of the Universe, and grateful for His goodness. establish this Constitution ..
26. Montana 1889, Preamble. We, the people of Montana, grateful to Almighty God for the blessings of liberty. establish this Constitution
27. Nebraska 1875, Preamble. We, the people, grateful to Almighty God for our freedom establish this Constitution.
28. Nevada 1864, Preamble. We The People of the State of Nevada, grateful to Almighty God for our freedom establish this Constitution
29. New Hampshire 1792, Part I. Art. I. Sec. V. Every individual has a natural and unalienable right to worship God according to the dictates of his own conscience.
30. New Jersey 1844, Preamble. We, the people of the State of New Jersey, grateful to Almighty God for civil and religious liberty which He hath so long permitted us to enjoy, and looking to Him for a blessing on our endeavors ..
31. New Mexico 1911, Preamble. We, the People of New Mexico, grateful to Almighty God for the blessings of liberty
32. New York 1846, Preamble. We, the people of the State of New York, grateful to Almighty God for our freedom, in order to secure its blessings.
33. North Carolina 1868, Preamble. We The People of the State of North Carolina, grateful to Almighty God, the Sovereign Ruler of Nations, for our civil, political, and religious liberties, and acknowledging our dependence upon Him for the continuance of those .
34. North Dakota 1889, Preamble. We, the people of North Dakota, grateful to Almighty God for the blessings of civil and religious liberty, do ordain...
35. Ohio 1852, Preamble. We The People of the state of Ohio, grateful to Almighty God for our freedom, to secure its blessings and to promote our common ...
36. Oklahoma 1907, Preamble. Invoking the guidance of Almighty God, in order to secure and perpetuate the blessings of liberty ... establish this ..
37. Oregon 1857, Bill of Rights, Article I. Section 2. All men shall be secure in the Natural right, to worship Almighty God according to the dictates of their consciences..
38. Pennsylvania 1776, Preamble. We, the people of Pennsylvania, grateful to Almighty God for the blessings of civil and religious liberty, and humbly invoking His guidance

39. Rhode Island 1842, Preamble. We The People of the State of Rhode Island grateful to Almighty God for the civil and religious liberty which He hath so long permitted us to enjoy, and looking to Him for a blessing

40. South Carolina, 1778, Preamble. We, the people of he State of South Carolina. grateful to God for our liberties, do ordain and establish this Constitution.

41. South Dakota 1889, Preamble. We, the people of South Dakota, grateful to Almighty God for our civil and religious liberties. establish this

42. Tennessee 1796, Art. XI.III. That all men have a natural and indefeasible right to worship Almighty God according to the dictates of their conscience...

43. Texas 1845, Preamble. We The People of the Republic of Texas, acknowledging, with gratitude, the grace and beneficence of God.

44. Utah 1896, Preamble. Grateful to Almighty God for life and liberty, we establish this Constitution.

45. Vermont 1777, Preamble. Whereas all government ought to ... enable the individuals who compose it to enjoy their natural rights, and other blessings which the Author of Existence has bestowed on man ...

46. Virginia 1776, Bill of Rights, XVI. Religion, or the Duty which we owe our Creator ... can be directed only by Reason ... and that it is the mutual duty of all to practice Christian Forbearance, Love and Charity towards each other.

47. Washington 1889, Preamble. We The People of the State of Washington, grateful to the Supreme Ruler of the Universe for our liberties, do ordain this Constitution ...

48. West Virginia 1872, Preamble. Since through Divine Providence we enjoy the blessings of civil, political and religious liberty, we, the people of West Virginia. reaffirm our faith in and constant reliance upon God ..

49. Wisconsin 1848, Preamble. We, the people of Wisconsin, grateful to Almighty God for our freedom, domestic tranquility ...

50. Wyoming 1890, Preamble. We, the people of the State of Wyoming, grateful to God for our civil, political, and religious liberties. establish this Constitution ...

After reviewing acknowledgments of God from all 50 state constitutions, one is faced with the prospect that the ACLU and the out-of-control federal courts are wrong!

"Those people who will not be governed by God will be ruled by tyrants." - William Penn

The phrase 'separation of church and state' origin is in President Thomas Jefferson's response to the Danbury Baptists. Both complete letters are included following:

Letter to President Thomas Jefferson from the Danbury Baptists:

"The address of the Danbury Baptist Association in the State of Connecticut assembled October 7, 1801.

To Thomas Jefferson, Esq., President of the United States of America

Sir,

"Among the many millions in America and Europe who rejoice in your election to office, we embrace the first opportunity which we have enjoyed in our collective capacity, since your inauguration, to express our great satisfaction in your appointment to the Chief Magistracy in the United States. And though the mode of expression may be less courtly and pompous than what many others clothe their addresses with, we beg you, sir, to believe, that none is more sincere.

"Our sentiments are uniformly on the side of religious liberty: that Religion is at all times and places a matter between God and individuals, that no man ought to suffer in name, person, or effects on account of his religious opinions, [and] that the legitimate power of civil government extends no further than to punish the man who works ill to his neighbor. But sir, our constitution of government is not specific. Our ancient charter, together with the laws made coincident therewith, were adapted as the basis of our government at the time of our revolution. And such has been our laws and usages, and such still are, [so] that Religion is considered as the first object of Legislation, and therefore what religious privileges we enjoy (as a minor part of the State) we enjoy as favors granted, and not as inalienable rights. And these favors we receive at the expense of such degrading acknowledgments, as are inconsistent with the rights of freemen. It is not to be wondered at therefore, if those who seek after power and gain, under the pretense of government and Religion, should reproach their fellow men, [or] should reproach their Chief Magistrate, as an enemy of religion, law, and good order, because he will not, dares not, assume the prerogative of Jehovah and make laws to govern the Kingdom of Christ.

"Sir, we are sensible that the President of the United States is not the National Legislator and also sensible that the national government cannot destroy the laws of each State, but our hopes are strong that the sentiment of our beloved President, which have had such genial effect already, like the radiant beams of the sun, will shine and prevail through all these States--and all the world-- until hierarchy and tyranny be destroyed from the earth. Sir, when we reflect on your past services, and see a glow of philanthropy and goodwill shining forth in a course of more than thirty years, we have reason to believe that America's God has raised you up to fill the Chair of State out of that goodwill which he bears to the millions which you preside over. May God strengthen you for the arduous task which providence and the voice of the people have called you--to sustain and support you and your Administration against all the predetermined opposition of those who wish to rise to wealth and importance on the poverty and subjection of the people.

"And may the Lord preserve you safe from every evil and bring you at last to his Heavenly Kingdom through Jesus Christ our Glorious Mediator.

"Signed in behalf of the Association,

Neh,h Dodge }Eph'm Robbins } The Committee Stephen S. Nelson }

*A cite for this letter could read:

Letter of Oct. 7, 1801 from Danbury (CT) Baptist Assoc. to Thomas Jefferson, Thomas Jefferson Papers, Manuscript Division, Library of Congress, Wash. D.C. "

President Jefferson's Reply to the Danbury Baptists:

"Messrs. Nehemiah Dodge, Ephraim Robbins, and Stephen s. Nelson
A Committee of the Danbury Baptist Association, in the State of Connecticut.

Washington, January 1, 1802

"Gentlemen,--The affectionate sentiment of esteem and approbation which you are so good as to express towards me, on behalf of the Danbury Baptist Association, give me the highest satisfaction. My duties dictate a faithful and zealous pursuit of the interests of my constituents, and in

proportion as they are persuaded of my fidelity to those duties, the discharge of them becomes more and more pleasing.

"Believing with you that religion is a matter which lies solely between man and his God, that he owes account to none other for his faith or his worship, that the legislative powers of government reach actions only, and not opinions, I contemplate with sovereign reverence that act of the whole American people which declared that their legislature would "make no law respecting an establishment of religion, or prohibiting the free exercise thereof," thus building a wall of **separation between Church and State**. *[bolding added] Adhering to this expression of the supreme will of the nation in behalf of the rights of conscience, I shall see with sincere satisfaction the progress of those sentiments which tend to restore to man all his natural rights, convinced he has no natural right in opposition to his social duties.*

"I reciprocate your kind prayers for the protection and blessing of the common Father and Creator of man, and tender you for yourselves and your religious association, assurances of my high respect and esteem.

Th Jefferson Jan. 1. 1802"

Progressive liberal leftists use 'separation of church and state' as a weapon to remove religion from all public, and if possible, private life. It is a weapon used to separate us from our God and 'dumb down the 'sheeple' so that they will more easily take the bait and swallow the hook of humanism and socialism. Then man will look to government instead of God as the provider of their rights.

Secret Societies (Combinations) – Evil Abominations

Ancient prophets foresaw our day and observed the following: *"...from the days of Cain, there was a secret combination, and their works were in the dark, and they knew every man his brother."*

"...they formed a secret combination, even as they of old; which combination is most abominable and wicked above all, in the sight of God;" "... secret combinations, [are] according to the combinations of the devil, for he is the founder of all these things; yea, the founder of murder, and works of darkness; yea, and he leadeth them by the neck with a flaxen cord, until he bindeth them with his strong cords forever. "...whatsoever nation shall uphold such secret combinations, to get power and gain, until they shall spread over the nation, behold, they shall be destroyed;"

Remember several key points from this prophecy:
- Satan is the author of evil secret combinations (societies).
- Secret societies are not conspiracy theories. They are real. They exist.
- Satan works in secret, in darkness, in closed meetings – not in the light and open.
- Members of secret combinations are known to one another through secret signs.
- Secret combinations started with Cain when he murdered his brother Abel.
- Secret combinations are most abominable and wicked – <u>above all</u> – in the sight of God.
- Whatever people and nation upholds secret combinations shall be destroyed.

Secret combinations are most abominable and wicked above all, in the sight of God. They are built up by the devil who is the father of all lies, the same being who persuaded Cain to commit the first murder, the same being who has hardened the hearts of mankind from the beginning to murder God's prophets and to commit all manner of evil and heinous acts. Secret combinations have caused the destruction of the two previous major civilizations on the American continent; the Jaredites and Nephite/Lamanites – descendants of which include the Inca, Aztec, Mayan and many of the American Indian tribes. They will destroy our civilization if we do not repent, for whatsoever nation shall uphold such secret combinations shall be destroyed. They are built up to get power and gain, and to overthrow the liberty and freedom of all mankind. When you see secret combinations among you, **awake to a sense of your awful situation** and remove this evil and come to the fountain of all righteousness and be saved.

It is NOT the possession of wealth that is evil. It is the thirst for limitless power in the hands of evil power mongers.

Examples of Secret Societies:

The Bilderberg Group, Skull & Crossbones, The Bohemian Grove, The Trilateral Commission, The Council On Foreign Relations, The Thule Society and The Illuminati.

THE BILDERBERG GROUP (the Group)

The Bilderberg Group is a consortium of financial oligarchs that control the world of international finance. Members compose a spider web of political, economic, financial and industrial interests. Their financial ideology is predatory, opportunistic, war mongering whose goal is One World Order with them in control. They control a global network of giant cartels that control necessities of life. They are more powerful than any nation on earth Their aim is to subjugate mankind to their power and control them for their selfish purposes.

In the Middle East the Group is orchestrating Arab spring and Muslim Brotherhood activities that manifest in successive riots and revolts throughout the region. Funding both sides of conflict returns huge profits to these financial robber barons. Goldman Sachs Commodity Index manipulates oil price and they are part of the Group.

If mainstream media were not controlled by the Group's tentacles and they were able to tell the economic truth the headlines would be something like this: The World's Economy is Teetering on the Edge of the Cliff of Disaster. The European Central Bank, IMF, the World Bank, Bank of International Settlement, the Federal Reserve controls the flow and ebb of money supply. They prolong going over the Cliff by providing bailouts carrying hearty interest that uniformed taxpayers must pay back. Thus, wealth is stolen from hard-working middle class through a contrived international monetary system of inflation and deflation. Baron Mayer A. Rothschild, father of the Illuminati, said that he does not care who the president of the country is, who controls the money controls the country. The Group has implemented Rothschild's control concept. In the end there is not government in any country, there is no nation, there is only the Group of private banks that control the world. This control is in direct violation of the Constitution of the United States of America and we have let politicians lead us like sheep to the slaughter.

ROTHSCHILD OWNED BANKS:

Afghanistan: Bank of Afghanistan
Albania: Bank of Albania
Algeria: Bank of Algeria
Argentina: Central Bank of Argentina
Armenia: Central Bank of Armenia
Aruba: Central Bank of Aruba
Australia: Reserve Bank of Australia
Austria: Austrian National Bank

Azerbaijan: Central Bank of Azerbaijan Republic
Bahamas: Central Bank of The Bahamas
Bahrain: Central Bank of Bahrain
Bangladesh: Bangladesh Bank
Barbados: Central Bank of Barbados
Belarus: National Bank of the Republic of Belarus
Belgium: National Bank of Belgium
Belize: Central Bank of Belize
Benin: Central Bank of West African States (BCEAO)
Bermuda: Bermuda Monetary Authority
Bhutan: Royal Monetary Authority of Bhutan
Bolivia: Central Bank of Bolivia
Bosnia: Central Bank of Bosnia and Herzegovina
Botswana: Bank of Botswana
Brazil: Central Bank of Brazil
Bulgaria: Bulgarian National Bank
Burkina Faso: Central Bank of West African States (BCEAO)
Burundi: Bank of the Republic of Burundi
Cambodia: National Bank of Cambodia
Came Roon: Bank of Central African States
Canada: Bank of Canada – Banque du Canada
Cayman Islands: Cayman Islands Monetary Authority
Central African Republic: Bank of Central African States
Chad: Bank of Central African States
Chile: Central Bank of Chile
China: The People's Bank of China
Colombia: Bank of the Republic
Comoros: Central Bank of Comoros
Congo: Bank of Central African States

Costa Rica: Central Bank of Costa Rica
Côte d'Ivoire: Central Bank of West African States (BCEAO)
Croatia: Croatian National Bank
Cuba: Central Bank of Cuba
Cyprus: Central Bank of Cyprus
Czech Republic: Czech National Bank
Denmark: National Bank of Denmark
Dominican Republic: Central Bank of the Dominican Republic
East Caribbean area: Eastern Caribbean Central Bank
Ecuador: Central Bank of Ecuador
Egypt: Central Bank of Egypt
El Salvador: Central Reserve Bank of El Salvador
Equatorial Guinea: Bank of Central African States
Estonia: Bank of Estonia
Ethiopia: National Bank of Ethiopia
European Union: European Central Bank
Fiji: Reserve Bank of Fiji
Finland: Bank of Finland
France: Bank of France
Gabon: Bank of Central African States
The Gambia: Central Bank of The Gambia
Georgia: National Bank of Georgia
Germany: Deutsche Bundesbank
Ghana: Bank of Ghana
Greece: Bank of Greece
Guatemala: Bank of Guatemala
Guinea Bissau: Central Bank of West African States (BCEAO)
Guyana: Bank of Guyana
Haiti: Central Bank of Haiti
Honduras: Central Bank of Honduras
Hong Kong: Hong Kong Monetary Authority
Hungary: Magyar Nemzeti Bank
Iceland: Central Bank of Iceland
India: Reserve Bank of India
Indonesia: Bank Indonesia
Iran: The Central Bank of the Islamic Republic of Iran
Iraq: Central Bank of Iraq
Ireland: Central Bank and Financial Services Authority of Ireland
Israel: Bank of Israel
Italy: Bank of Italy

Jamaica: Bank of Jamaica
Japan: Bank of Japan
Jordan: Central Bank of Jordan
Kazakhstan: National Bank of Kazakhstan
Kenya: Central Bank of Kenya
Korea: Bank of Korea
Kuwait: Central Bank of Kuwait
Kyrgyzstan: National Bank of the Kyrgyz Republic
Latvia: Bank of Latvia
Lebanon: Central Bank of Lebanon
Lesotho: Central Bank of Lesotho
Libya: Central Bank of Libya (Most Recently Added)
Uruguay: Central Bank of Uruguay
Lithuania: Bank of Lithuania
Luxembourg: Central Bank of Luxembourg
Macao: Monetary Authority of Macao
Macedonia: National Bank of the Republic of Macedonia
Madagascar: Central Bank of Madagascar
Malawi: Reserve Bank of Malawi
Malaysia: Central Bank of Malaysia
Mali: Central Bank of West African States (BCEAO)
Malta: Central Bank of Malta
Mauritius: Bank of Mauritius
Mexico: Bank of Mexico
Moldova: National Bank of Moldova
Mongolia: Bank of Mongolia
Montenegro: Central Bank of Montenegro
Morocco: Bank of Morocco
Mozambique: Bank of Mozambique
Namibia: Bank of Namibia
Nepal: Central Bank of Nepal
Netherlands: Netherlands Bank
Netherlands Antilles: Bank of the Netherlands Antilles
New Zealand: Reserve Bank of New Zealand
Nicaragua: Central Bank of Nicaragua
Niger: Central Bank of West African States (BCEAO)
Nigeria: Central Bank of Nigeria
Norway: Central Bank of Norway
Oman: Central Bank of Oman
Pakistan: State Bank of Pakistan
Papua New Guinea: Bank of Papua New Guinea

Paraguay: Central Bank of Paraguay
Peru: Central Reserve Bank of Peru
Philip Pines: Bangko Sentral ng Pilipinas
Poland: National Bank of Poland
Portugal: Bank of Portugal
Qatar: Qatar Central Bank
Romania: National Bank of Romania
Rwanda: National Bank of Rwanda
San Marino: Central Bank of the Republic of San Marino
Samoa: Central Bank of Samoa
Saudi Arabia: Saudi Arabian Monetary Agency
Senegal: Central Bank of West African States (BCEAO)
Serbia: National Bank of Serbia
Seychelles: Central Bank of Seychelles
Sierra Leone: Bank of Sierra Leone
Singapore: Monetary Authority of Singapore
Slovakia: National Bank of Slovakia
Slovenia: Bank of Slovenia
Solomon Islands: Central Bank of Solomon Islands
South Africa: South African Reserve Bank
Spain: Bank of Spain
Sri Lanka: Central Bank of Sri Lanka
Sudan: Bank of Sudan

Surinam: Central Bank of Suriname
Swaziland: The Central Bank of Swaziland
Sweden: Sveriges Riksbank
Switzerland: Swiss National Bank
Tajikistan: National Bank of Tajikistan
Tanzania: Bank of Tanzania
Thailand: Bank of Thailand
Togo: Central Bank of West African States (BCEAO)
Tonga: National Reserve Bank of Tonga
Trinidad and Tobago: Central Bank of Trinidad and Tobago
Tunisia: Central Bank of Tunisia
Turkey: Central Bank of the Republic of Turkey
Uganda: Bank of Uganda
Ukraine: National Bank of Ukraine
United Arab Emirates: Central Bank of United Arab Emirates

United Kingdom: Bank of England (Mother Central Bank)
United States: Federal Reserve, Federal Reserve Bank of New York
Vanuatu: Reserve Bank of Vanuatu
Venezuela: Central Bank of Venezuela

Vietnam: The State Bank of Vietnam
Yemen: Central Bank of Yemen
Zambia: Bank of Zambia
Zimbabwe: Reserve Bank of Zimbabwe

The Obama Administration has incurred more federal debt that all the presidents from George Washington to George W. Bush – combined. Obama is part of the Group as are most of Washington's progressive liberal left.

As a consequence of the Group's destructive policies the USD lost 12% of its value in one year. Since the Federal Reserve Act of 1913 the USD has lost 94% of its value through the Group's strategic inflation/deflation cycles. For the first time ever China has become a net seller of US Treasury Bonds. The US credit bubble is on the verge of bursting and when it does there will be reset of the entire world's economy.

The Group is the means to a One World Company that will transform the United States of America and the rest of the world into a virtual prison of a global market where they sign of the beast is required to buy or sell; a global police state.

THE COUNCIL OF FOREIGN RELATIONS (CFR)

The CFR is composed of Wall Street investors, international bankers, foundation executives, members of Think Tanks and Tax-exempt Foundations, ambassadors, past and present presidents, secretaries of state, lobbyist lawyers, media owners, university presidents and professors, federal and supreme court judges, and members of military leaders from NATO and the pentagon, including top executives from the New York Times, The Washington Post, the Los Angeles Times, NBC, CBS, Time, Life, Fortune, Business Week, US News and World Report, the Knight Newspaper chain, and many others

CFR is funded by JP Morgan, John D. Rockefeller, Bernard Baruch, Jacob Schiff, Otto Kahn, and Paul Warburg, Xerox, General Motors, Bristol-Meyers Squibb, Texaco, the German Marshall Fund, McKnight Foundation, Dillion Fund, Ford Foundation, Andrew W. Mellon Foundation, Rockefeller Brothers Fund, Starr Foundation, and the Pew Charitable Trusts.

The CFR is a wolf in sheeps clothing. They present a public image as a humanitarian consortium of academics, businessmen, and politicians. However, in reality they unilaterally determine U.S. foreign policy. Their objective is to control markets and economies utilizing this small group of giant multinational corporations which in turn are controlled by international banksters.

Dan Smoot revealed in his book, The Invisible Government, that "*The leadership of the invisible government doubtless rests in the hands of a sinister ... few... status-seekers. The ultimate aim*" of the CFR, "*however, well-intentioned its prominent and powerful members may be*" is "*to create a one-world socialist system...[although] most members of the CFR have no knowledge of this diabolical plan. But there is an inner core within the CFR that ... promotes it.*" The goal of the CFR is to destroy US sovereignty and national independence and subjugate the USA into a one-world government.

Senator Barry Goldwater stated that the CFR has infiltrated the White House and has "*staffed almost every key position of every administration since that of FDR.*"

The CFR is confederate with the major foundations, the Bilderberger Group and the Trilateral Commission.

The goal of the C.F.R. is to abolish the United States with its Constitutional guarantees of liberty. Study No. 7, published by the CFR on November 25, 1959, advocates "*building a new international order [which] must be responsive to world aspirations for peace, [and] for social and economic change.*" This new order will include, "*states labeling themselves as 'Socialist' [Communist].*"

The CFR **objective of this invisible government is to convert America into a socialist state and then make it a unit in a one-world socialist system."** "We shall have world government whether or not you like it--by conquest or consent." CFR member James Warburg, testifying at Senate Foreign Relations Committee on February 17, 1950

"For a long time I felt that FDR had developed many thoughts and ideas that were his own to benefit this country, the United States. But, he didn't. Most of his thoughts, his political ammunition, as it were, were carefully manufactured for him in advanced by the Council on Foreign Relations-One World Money group. " (Curtis Dall, FDR's son-in-law, Source: My Exploited Father-in-Law)

FORD FOUNDATION MISSION: *To Merge U.S. & Soviet Union.*
The Ford Foundation is a tax-exempt group "... *the directives under which we operate is that we shall use our grant-making power so to alter life in the United States that we can be comfortably merged with the Soviet Union.'*

CARNEGIE ENDOWMENT FOR INTERNATIONAL PEACE
Their view of War is that it is an Instrument of Change. In 1908 they posed the questions '*Is there any way known to man more effective than war, assuming they wish to alter the life of an entire people? The conclusion was that war is the most effective means known to man, assuming that objective. How do we involve the United States in the war? The answer was 'We must control the diplomatic machinery of the United States.' 'How do we secure control of the diplomatic machinery of the United States?' The answer was 'We must control the State Department.'*
Thus the hand of the Carnegie Endowment for International Peace is inside the State Department.'
WWI commenced in 1914.

When WWI ended The Carnegie Trustees sought to prevent a reversion of life in the United States to what it was prior to 1914. To gain that end they needed to control education in the United States. They realize this is a prodigious piece of work, so they seek and obtain the assistance of the Rockefeller Foundation.

ROCKEFELLER FOUNDATION & REVISIONIST HISTORY
The Carnegie Trustees gave the Rockefeller Foundation the responsibility of altering education pertaining to domestic subjects...and our international relationships. The key to this is an alternation in the teaching of American History. The Rockefeller Foundation then enlists the Guggenheim Foundation which specializes in the awarding of fellowships and suggests: When we discover a likely young person who is studying and looking forward to becoming a teacher of history, we will take him to London to pursue his studies and reeducate them. When they return

they become the most active influence in the American Historical Society. This event stimulated writing book after book, which revised American History and cast aspersion on the Founding Fathers, and upon the ideas which prompted the founding of this country and relegates them to the realm of myth.

Barry Goldwater On The Council On Foreign Relations, The Trilateral Commission, The Ford, Carnegie & Rockefeller Foundations

In 1979, then Senator Barry Goldwater wrote the following warning about the CFR (Council on Foreign Relations) in his book, _With No Apologies_:

"_The CFR is composed of ... most elite names in the world of government, labor, business, finance communication, the foundations, and academies._ It has staffed almost every key position of every administration since that of FDR....the Council of Foreign Relations and _its members are an active part of the communist conspiracy for world domination._... Many of the policies advocated by the CFR have been damaging to the cause of freedom and particularly to the United States....

"I believe the Council on Foreign Relations and its ancillary elitist groups are indifferent to communism. They have no ideological anchors. In _their pursuit of a New World Order [World Government]_ they are prepared to deal without prejudice with a communist state, a socialist state, a democratic state, monarchy, oligarchy -- it's all the same to them.

"_Our government in Washington now is a horrible bureaucratic mess_. It is disorganized, wasteful, has no purpose, and its policies -- when they exist -- are incomprehensible or devised by special interest groups with little or no regard for the welfare of the average American citizen..."

"_The Trilateral Commission_ is international...(and)...is intended to be the vehicle for multinational consolidation of the commercial and banking interests by seizing control of the political government of the United States. The Trilateral Commission represents a skillful, _coordinated effort to seize control and consolidate the four centers of power--political, monetary, intellectual, and ecclesiastical._"

The American Historical Society Rewrites History To Its Own Taste
Toward the end of the 1920's the Endowment grants the American Historical Society $400,000 for the sole purpose of rendering a report as to what the future of this country promises to be and should be...and ends on this note: The future belongs to collectivism, administered with characteristic American humanitarianism and efficiency.

Considering the above atrocities, let us remember that Governments are instituted among Men, deriving their just Powers from the Consent of the Governed, that whenever any Form of Government becomes destructive of these ends, it is the Right of the People to alter or to abolish it, and to institute new Government, laying its foundation on such principles and organizing its powers in such form, as to them shall seem most likely to effect their Safety and Happiness." U.S. Declaration of Independence.

ORDER OF THE SKULL & BONES
The Order of the Skull & Bones (the Establishment) is a secret society started in 1832 at Yale University. Skull & Bones is not American, it is a branch of a foreign secret society that began in Germany where the Illuminati was born. They follow the Hegelian code where the individual has

no rights and the State is god on earth. They seek a <u>New World Order precipitated by controlled conflict. This policy pits International bankers backed the Nazis, the Soviet Union, North Korea, North Vietnam, ad nauseum, against the United States. Controlled conflict is profitable to banksters who fund both sides of the conflit and pushes the world ever closer to One World Government.</u>

<u>President Woodrow Wilson</u> made the following revealing statement about this Order: "*Some of the biggest men in the U.S. in the fields of commerce and manufacturing know that <u>there is a power so organized, so subtle, so complete, so pervasive that they had better not speak above their breath when they speak in condemnation of it.</u>*"

The current mess of the world has been deliberately created by this Order by manipulation of 'right' and 'left' factions. The policy of managed conflict is also part of The Trilateral Commission tactics. This manipulation of left and right manifest in political parties and is the tool used in international arenas where left and right political structures are artificially constructed and collapsed in the drive for a one-world government. The elite in the Skull & Bones Order are above the US Federal Government. The order controls international banksters through their high powered lawyer members. The order is a secret society that seeks a One World Government under their control. They are the great anti-Christ that seeks to overthrow the freedom and liberty of all mankind.

American Civil Liberties Union (ACLU)

The American Civil Liberties Union (ACLU) is a U.S. non-profit organization whose stated mission is "to defend and preserve the individual rights and liberties guaranteed to every person in this country by the Constitution and laws of the United States."

Sounds like a good organization, right? Now let's examine the facts.

The ACLU's founder, Roger Baldwin, stated: "<u>We are for socialism, disarmament, and ultimately for abolishing the state itself... We seek the social ownership of property, the abolition of the propertied class, and the SOLE CONTROL of those who produce wealth. communism is the goal.</u>" (Trial and Error, by Geo. Grant)

Following are some of the stated goals of the ACLU, from its own published Policy Issues:

- the legalization of prostitution (Policy 211);
- the defense of all pornography, including CHILD PORN, as "free speech" (Policy 4);
- the decriminalization and legalization of all drugs (Policy 210);
- the promotion of homosexuality (Policy 264);
- the opposition of rating of music and movies (Policy 18);
- opposition against parental consent of minors seeking abortion (Policy 262);
- opposition of informed consent preceding abortion procedures (Policy 263);
- opposition of spousal consent preceding abortion (Policy 262);
- opposition of parental choice in children's education (Policy 80)

The ACLU defends and promotion of euthanasia, polygamy, government control of church institutions, gun control, tax-funded abortion, birth limitation, etc. (Policies 263, 133, 402, 47, 261, 323, 271, 91, 85).

The ACLU typically takes on cases that are anti-Christian - pro-sodomy, pro-abortion, anti-family, pro-pornography, pro-prostitution, pro-euthanasia, pro-homosexual, pro-infanticide, pro-crime, pro-humanism, anti-God -- and, except for atheism, anti-religion. It is most decidedly Un-American and it is uncivil to the unborn as it promotes abortion. It promotes everything that is anti-Christ.

ACLU Funding

George Grant, author of "Trial and Error," puts the ACLU's annual budget (1993) at $14 MILLION (FOURTEEN MILLION DOLLARS) - much of which is "SUPPLIED BY THE AMERICAN TAXPAYER through the Federal program mandated by the Civil Rights Attorneys' Fee Awards Act of 1976. If the ACLU wins a case that involves a public institution, for instance, the organization *collects the full legal fees* of its attorneys even though those attorneys offered their services *pro bono* (without charge).

The majority of the ACLU's money comes from foundations. For example, the Ford Foundation has given them more than $14 million. The Open Society Institute, headed by billionaire George Soros, has given $2 million. And guess who's a trustee for the Open Society Institute? Bill Moyers.

The Carnegie Corporation of New York has kicked in more than $800,000. And guess who's a trustee of that concern? Our pal Judy Woodruff of CNN. And the Rockefeller Foundation donated $275,000. The cellist Yo-Yo Ma's on the board of trustees there.

Liberals are unwilling to simply let others be, but rather seek to impose their un-godliness upon Christians. It is a *mission* to them and other atheists to pervert the freedoms of others. The ACLU does not run to the defense of those who are harmed; it aggressively seeks out opportunities to corrupt pure freedoms.

Summary

The ACLU is destroying the foundation of America's strength by constantly suing to further an extremist agenda. The ACLU is currently defending child molesters, attacking school boards for using the word "Christmas," and demanding that high schools fund clubs for homosexual students.

International Banksters

Following is a summary chronology of the control of money in the USA:

- 1790 - *"Let me issue and control a nation's money and I care not who writes the laws."* Mayer Amschel Rothschild,

- 1791 - Rothschild's gained control over the US money supply through Alexander Hamilton, their agent who was a cabinet member under George Washington. They established the First Bank of the United States with a 20 year charter.

- 1811 - the charter runs out and Congress chooses not to renew its charter. Mayer Rothschild states *"Either the application for the renewal of the charter is granted or the United States will find itself engaged in a most disastrous war."* Washington stands firm not to renew the charter. An enraged Mayer Rothschild issues another threat, *"Teach those impudent Americans a lesson. Bring them back to colonial status."*

- The War of 1812 ensues with the British who are backed by Rothschild money and directed to engage the war. Rothschild's plan was to sink America into such war debt and force them to renew the bank charter.

- 1816 -Congress passes a bill authorizing the Second Bank of the United States a 20 year charter, re-granting the Rothschild's control over the nation's money supply. The War that began in 1812 ends in 1816 because Rothschild's get what they wanted; control over America.

- 1832 - Andrew Jackson runs for president of the US under the slogan "Jackson and no bank" and wins.

- 1833 Jackson begins moving US funds from Rothschild controlled Second Bank of the US to independent democratic bankers. The Rothschild's panic and tighten the money supply causing a depression. Jackson knows what Rothschild's are up to and declares *"You are a den of thieves and vipers, and I intend to rout you out, and by the Eternal God, I will rout you out."*

- January 30, 1835 two assassins bullets miss-fire and Jackson's life is miraculously preserved. Jackson claimed that the Rothschild's were behind the assassination attempt.

- 1836 - Jackson succeeds in throwing out the Rothschild's control over America's money supply and receives hundreds of life threats as a result.

- 1845 - On his death bed, Jackson requests that his tombstone read, the man who killed the [Rothschild's] bank.

- 1861-1865 – Abraham Lincoln approaches NY banks for loans to support the Civil War. These banks still under the influence of the Rothschild's make loans at 24-36% interest. Lincoln is unhappy with the interest and therefore resorts to printing United States money and informs the public of the same. Lincoln states *"We gave the people of this republic the greatest blessing they ever had, their own paper money to pay their own debts."*

- 1855-1891 – Lincoln's correspondence with Alexander II, tsar of Russia reveals that he has a problem with the Rothschild's trying to control their money supply also. The Tsar issues orders that if either England or France intervene in the US Civil War and takes the side of the South, that Russia will consider that a declaration of war and side with President Lincoln.

- 1865 – Lincoln's states, *"I have two great enemies, the Southern army in front of me, and the financial institutions in the rear. Of the two, the one in my rear is my greatest foe."*

- April 14, 1865 – Lincoln is assassinated less than two months before the end of the Civil War.

- 1881 – President James A. Garfield, states two weeks before he is assassinated, *"Whoever controls the volume of money in our country is absolute master of all industry and commerce... and when you realize that, the entire system is very easily controlled, one way or another by a few powerful men at the top, you will not have to be told how periods of inflation and depression originate."*

- November 1910 - meeting at Jekyll Island, Georgia, of seven bankers and economic policymakers, who represented 1/4th of the world's wealth, the financial elite of the Western world, met to plot to establish a new bank to control the USA. G. Edward Griffin, one of the attendees, documented how seven of America's banking leaders, representing one quarter of the world's wealth, secretly traveled to Jekyll Island in 1910 to create a banking cartel that would convince Congress and America it was a government agency. In 1913, the Federal

Reserve Act, crafted on Jekyll Island, was put into place without constitutional authority by Congress.

- 1913 – the Federal Reserve Bank is established during Woodrow Wilson's presidency. The Federal Reserve is a private bank - not Federal. It creates fiat money – worthless paper money not backed by gold or silver. This debt-based fiat money devours individual prosperity through inflation and it is used to perpetuate war. Central bankers underwrite both sides of ongoing wars or revolutions. The United Nations, the Council on Foreign Relations, and the World Bank are working to destroy American sovereignty through a system of world military and financial control.

- June 4, 1963 – President John F. Kennedy signs executive order #11110 which returned to the US Government the power to issue its own currency without going through the Federal Reserve. He states, *"The very word 'secrecy' is repugnant in a free and open society; and we are as a people inherently and historically opposed to secret societies, to secret oaths and to secret proceedings. For we are opposed around the world by a monolithic and ruthless conspiracy that relies primarily on covert means for expanding its sphere of influence--on infiltration instead of invasion, on subversion instead of elections, on intimidation instead of free choice, on guerrillas by night instead of armies by day. It is a system which has conscripted vast human and material resources into the building of a tightly knit, highly efficient machine that combines military, diplomatic, intelligence, economic, scientific and political operations. Its preparations are concealed, not published. Its mistakes are buried, not headlined. Its dissenters are silenced, not praised. No expenditure is questioned, no rumor is printed, no secret is revealed. It conducts the Cold War, in short, with a war-time discipline no democracy would ever hope or wish to match."*

- November 22, 1963 – John F. Kennedy was assassinated in Dallas, Texas. No coincidence here; Kennedy was assassinated by international bankster secret societies to maintain their power and choke-hold on America finances.

International banksters seek world domination and to overthrow the freedom and liberty of all mankind are evil in their hearts, violent in their murderous ways, and responsible for much of humanity's suffering. They control the world's money supply but they do not yet control us.

What is their end goal? Nicolas Rockefeller said it is 'to get everybody chipped'...the mark of the beast in their forehead or hand....666.

"And [the Antichrist] causeth all, both small and great, rich and poor, free and bond, to receive a mark in their right hand, or in their foreheads: And that no man might buy or sell, save [except] he that had the mark, or the name of the beast, or the number of his name. Here is wisdom. Let him that hath understanding count the number of the beast: for it is the number of a man; and his number is Six hundred threescore and six." Rev 13:16-18 *KJV*

Population control? You bet! "And the first went, and poured out his vial upon the earth; and there fell a noisome and grievous sore upon the men which had the mark of the beast, and upon them which worshipped his image." (Rev 16:2) The chip enables those who control to inflict the plagues upon mankind who is 'chipped.'

The chip contains all your history and identification. When you have that, you become a slave to the banksters; they control you.

The Federal Reserve – Invisible Controlling 'Master'

President Abraham Lincoln warned the American people about America's second evil banking cartel, which is the likely reason that the Banksters assassinated President Lincoln...

"The money powers prey upon the nation in times of peace, and conspire against it in times of adversity. It is more despotic than monarchy, more insolent than autocracy, more selfish than bureaucracy. I see in the near future a crisis approaching that unnerves me and causes me to tremble for the safety of my country. Corporations have been enthroned, an era of corruption will follow and the money power of the country will endeavor and prolong its reign by working upon the prejudices of the people, until the wealth is aggregated into a few hands and the republic is destroyed." U.S. President Abraham Lincoln, Nov. 21, 1864

"It is well that the people of the nation do not understand our banking and monetary system, for if they did, I believe there would be a revolution before tomorrow morning." Henry Ford

There is <u>nothing</u> 'FEDERAL' about the Federal Reserve. It is a private banking corporation set up by the Rothschild's international banking consortium that holds America and the world hostage to its corrupt system of debt enslavement. It was passed under Woodrow Wilson in 1913 illegally and unconstitutionally while Congress was on Christmas recess.

The Federal Reserve is un-Constitutional. It has no authority from We The People or from Congress. Only Congress has the Constitutional right "To coin Money, regulate the Value thereof, and of foreign Coin, and fix the Standard of Weights and Measures;" (U.S. Constitution, Article 1, Section 8.)

To understand the Federal Reserve, you must understand its roots. Nathaniel Meyer Rothschild is the father of the Illuminati and international banking cartel, including the Federal Reserve. His favorite saying, along with co-conspirators, the Rockefellers, is: *"Who controls the issuance of money controls the government! Give me the control of the credit of a nation, and I care not who makes the laws."* Following is the famous boastful statement of Rothschild, speaking to a group of international bankers, in 1912: *"The few who could understand the system (cheque, money, credits) will either be so interested in its profits, or so dependent on its favours, that there will be no opposition from that class, while on the other hand, the great body of people, mentally incapable of comprehending the tremendous advantage that capital derives from the system, will bear its burdens without complaint, and perhaps without even suspecting that the system is inimical to their interests."* Referring to James Rothschild, the poet Heinrich Heine said: *"Money is the god of our times, and Rothschild is his prophet."*

James Rothschild built his fabulous mansion, called Ferrilres, 19 miles north-east of Paris. Wilhelm I, on first seeing it, exclaimed: *"Kings couldn't afford this. It could only belong to a Rothschild!"* Author Frederic Morton wrote that the Rothschilds had: *"conquered the World more thoroughly, more cunningly, and much more lastingly than all the Caesars before...."* As Napoleon pointed out: *"Terrorism, War & Bankruptcy are caused by the privatization of money, issued as a debt and compounded by interest."*

The history of the Federal Reserve is shrouded in mystery. (Read <u>The Creature From Jekyll Island</u> book for its sordid secret history.) Bankers and corrupt politicians called the shots from the very outset. On the evening of November 22, 1910 , Senator Aldrich and A.P. Andrews (Assistant Secretary of the Treasury Department), Paul Warburg (a naturalized German representing Baron Alfred Rothschild's Kuhn, Loeb & Co.), Frank Vanderlip (president of the National City Bank of New York), Henry P. Davison (senior partner of J.P. Morgan Company), Charles D. Norton (president of the Morgan-dominated First National Bank of New York), and Benjamin Strong (representing J. P. Morgan), left Hoboken, New Jersey on a train with a mission to gain complete control over the currency of the United States."

International bankers are the powers that corrupt governments have been enslaved to and are seeking the NWO (New World Order) of today. Because of them nations have a centalized bank that governs lower member banks. The top governing banks of each nation are all governed by the BIS (Bank for International Settlements). The World Bank issues SDR (special drawing rights) to banks as money. The SDR's are secured with bonds derived from a nation's citizens (human collateral) that are converted to national currencies whenever the government needs to borrow. By this method citizens become enslaved to pay via direct taxes an unending debt to these world bankers. The entire organization is supervised by elite bankers sometimes called the Illuminati.

"The real menace of our Republic is the invisible government, which like a giant octopus sprawls its slimy legs over our cities, states and nation. To depart from mere generalizations, let me say that at the head of this octopus are the Rockefeller-Standard Oil interests and a small group of powerful banking houses generally referred to as the international bankers. The little coterie of powerful international bankers virtually run the United States government for their own selfish purposes. They practically control both parties, write political platforms, make catspaws of party leaders, use the leading men of private organizations, and resort to every device to place in nomination for high public office only such candidates as will be amenable to the dictates of corrupt big business. These international bankers and Rockefeller-Standard Oil interests control the majority of the newspapers and magazines in this country. They use the columns of these papers to club into submission or drive out of office public officials who refuse to do the bidding of the powerful corrupt cliques which compose the invisible government. It operates under cover of a self-created screen [and] seizes our executive officers, legislative bodies, schools, courts, newspapers and every agency created for the public protection. Hylan, 1922, Mayor of New York City

This "Invisible Government", Hylan and others - William Jennings Bryan, Charles Lindbergh Sr. (R-MN) - argued, exercise its control of the US Government through the Federal Reserve.

The Federal Reserve controls inflation and deflation thus robbing American citizens of the wealth they earned. Since the Federal Reserve took control of America's money supply the USD has deflated in value 95%. That is theft by deception. Has inflating the money supply by printing more money to 'save institutions too big to fail' made you wealthier? Do you have more or less money now than before the bailouts? Almost everyone has less, except the banksters to whom the bailout money was paid. They reaped huge unearned wealth. That is robbery thought currency manipulation!

Income Tax

"The hardest thing in the world to understand is the Income Tax." Albert Einstein

CONSTITUTIONAL LIMITATIONS ON THE TAXING POWER
The U.S. Constitution FORBIDS the Federal Government to impose any tax directly upon individuals or property. Any direct taxes are required to be "apportioned", which means that they must be laid upon the state governments in proportion to each state's population.
Article 1, Section 2, Clause 3 of the U.S. Constitution states: "Representatives and direct Taxes shall be apportioned among the several States which may be included within this Union, according

to their respective Numbers...." and again in Article 1, Section 9, Clause 4 which states: "No Capitation, or other Tax shall be laid, unless in Proportion to the Census or Enumeration herein before directed to be taken."

INCOME TAX IS AN EXCISE TAX -Taxation on income was in its nature an excise (Brushaber v. Union Pacific R.R. Co., 240 US 1, (1916). The ruling established that income tax is constitutional as an excise tax, but not as a direct tax. What is the subject of an Excise Tax?
U.S. Supreme Court in Flint v. Stone Tracy C. 220 US 107 defined excises as "...taxes laid upon the manufacture, sale, or consumption of commodities within the country, upon licenses to pursue certain occupations, and upon corporate privileges." **Individuals are not subject to the income tax.**

IRS SAYS THE INCOME (EXCISE) TAX IS VOLUNTARY.
A former IRS commissioner stated in a 1040 instruction booklet: "Each year American taxpayers voluntarily file their tax returns.

The following pretty much sums up the consensus of American taxpayers:

The IRS rejected my tax return...

IRS sent my Tax Return back! AGAIN!!!
I guess it was because of my response to the question: "List all dependents".......I replied:
- "12 million illegal immigrants;
- "3 million crack heads;
- "42 million unemployable people on food stamps;
- "17 million socially deprived;
- "2 million people in over 243 prisons;
- "Half of Mexico; and "535 non-representatives in the U.S. House and Senate."

Government Enslavement

When the government offers you a handout – for free –is it really free?

Always analyze who is offering the 'free stuff' and why. Usually there are hidden strings attached to free handouts. They may appear small in the beginning, but increased receiving produces increased dependency. Increased dependency results in enslavement to a master. Like fishermen offering tantalizing bait, after the fish take it they are hooked. Government offers the tantalizing bait of 'free handouts' and the hook is dependency. Recipient citizens become slaves to the master government.

Remember, the government never produces anything. It only takes from producers, keeps a large portion for itself, and re-distributes the rest – usually in order to maintain or increase power over the people. Politicians (many of whom are lawyers) have become parasites of We The People. In the beginning of our Country it was not true. In the beginning of our Country political positions were not sought after. In fact if someone sought them, they were disqualified from holding them. People served for 2-4 years and then returned to their real jobs. Today politicians seek office and once they obtain the seat, they seek to retain and increase their power as a career politician. We The People must restore original intent and practice of the Constitution in order to regain our lost freedoms.

Congressional Oath Of Office Vs. Most Politicians

The current oath of office was enacted in 1884: *I do solemnly swear (or affirm) that <u>I will support and defend the Constitution of the United States</u> against all enemies, foreign and domestic; that I will bear true faith and allegiance to the same; that I take this obligation freely, without any mental reservation or purpose of evasion; and that I will well and faithfully discharge the duties of the office on which I am about to enter: So help me God.*

Consider Thomas Jefferson's view on how strictly we should be guided by the Constitution: *"I consider the foundation of the Constitution as laid on this ground: that 'all powers not delegated to the united states by the Constitution, nor prohibited by it to the states, are reserved to the states of to the people'...to take a single step beyond the boundaries thus specially drawn around the powers of Congress is to take possession of a boundless field of power..."*Thomas Jefferson

It doesn't matter what a person says as much as what he does. Actions speak louder than words. Examine most politicians' records and you will find extraordinary hypocrisy; they say one thing but do another. They have violated their oath of office. They have betrayed our trust. For over 100 years Congress has implemented policy and laws far beyond the limitation imposed by the Constitution. All of them increasingly limit our freedoms and empower Washington to enslave us.

One World Order/New World Order

Control the media and you control the message. Control the message and you control what people think. Control what the people think and you control people.

Our media is owned by international banksters, members of secret societies, Bilderbergers, Illuminati, international corporations, and the George Soros empire; the One World Order crowd. Their purpose is to bring the sheeple of the world under their control and to destroy the freedom and liberty of all mankind.

"Some even believe we <u>(the Rockefeller family) are part of a secret cabal working against the best interests of the United States, characterizing my family and me as 'internationalists' and of conspiring with others around the world to build a more integrated global political and economic structure---one world, if you will. If that's the charge, I stand guilty, and I am proud of it."</u> David Rockefeller, Memoirs, page 405

"We are grateful to <u>The Washington Post, The New York Times, Time magazine, and other great publications</u> whose directors have attended our meetings and respected their promise of discretion for almost forty years. It would have been impossible for us to develop our plan for the world if we had been subject to the bright lights of publicity during those years. But the world is now more sophisticated and prepared to march towards a world government. <u>The super-national sovereignty of an intellectual elite and world bankers is surely preferable to the national auto-determination practiced in past centuries."</u> David Rockefeller, at a 1991 Bilderberger meeting

"<u>We are on the verge of a global transformation. All we need is the right major crisis and the nations will accept the New World Order."</u> David Rockefeller

"Whatever the price of the Chinese Revolution, it has obviously succeeded not only in producing more efficient and dedicated administration, but also in fostering high morale and community of purpose. The social experiment in <u>China under Chairman Mao's leadership is one of the most important and successful in human history</u>." David Rockefeller, statement about Mao Tse-tung in The New York Times, August 10, 1973

Mao's communists slaughtered 70 million Chinese during his tyrannical reign of terror.

Following is an example of how the complicit media bought by the liberal left progressives (ie George Soros and the like) spin truth to deceive the sheeple:

A Harley motorcycle biker is riding by the zoo in Washington, DC when he sees a little girl leaning into the African lion's cage. Suddenly, one of the African lions grabs her by the cuff of her jacket and tries to pull her inside to slaughter her, under the eyes of her screaming parents. The biker jumps off his Harley, runs to the cage and hits the African lion square on the nose with a powerful punch. Whimpering from the pain the African lion jumps back letting go of the girl, and the biker brings her to her terrified parents, who thank him endlessly. reporter has watched the whole event. The reporter addressing the Harley rider says, 'Sir, this was the most gallant and brave thing I've seen a man do in my whole life.' The Harley rider replies, "Ma'am, it was nothing, Ma'am, really, the African lion was in its cage behind bars. I just saw this little kid in danger and felt it was my duty to help her, Ma'am.' The reporter says, 'Well, I'll make sure this won't go unnoticed. I'm a journalist and tomorrow's paper will have this story on the front page... So, what do you do for a living and what political affiliation do you have?' The biker replies, "Ma'am, I'm a U.S. Marine and I am a Republican, Ma'am."

The journalist leaves. The following morning the biker buys the paper to see news of his actions, and reads, on the front page:

"U.S. MARINE ASSAULTS AFRICAN IMMIGRANT AND STEALS HIS LUNCH"

Cost of Socialism

If you've started to wonder what the real costs of socialism are going to be, once the full program in these United States hits your wallet, take a look at the statistics below. As you digest these mind-boggling figures, keep in mind that in spite of these astronomical tax rates, these countries are still not financing their social welfare programs exclusively from tax revenues! They are deeply mired in public debt of gargantuan proportions. Greece has reached the point where its debt is so huge it is in imminent danger of defaulting. That is the reason the European economic community has intervened to bail them out. If you're following the financial news, you know Spain and Portugal are right behind Greece . Consider the current European tax rates:

COUNTRY	INCOME TAX	VAT TAX	TOTAL TAX
United Kingdom	50%	17.5%	67.5%
France	40%	19.6%	59.6%
Greece	40%	25%	65%
Spain	45%	16%	61%
Portugal	42%	20%	62%

Sweden	55%	25%	80%
Norway	54.3%	25%	79.3%
Netherlands	52%	19%	71%
Denmark	58%	25%	83%
Finland	53%	22%	75%

The United States is now heading right down the same path. The VAT tax in the table is the national sales tax that Europeans pay. Stay tuned because that is exactly what you can expect to see the administration proposing. The initial percentage in the United States isn't going to be anywhere near the outrageous numbers you now see in Europe. Guess what, the current outrageous numbers in Europe didn't start out as outrageous either. They started out as miniscule right around the 1% or 2% where they will start out in the United States. Magically however, they ran up over the years to where they are now. Expect the same thing here. It is the notion that with hard work and perseverance, anybody can get ahead economically here. Do you think that can ever happen with tax rates between 60% and 80%? Think again. With the government taking that percentage of your money, your life will be exactly like life in Europe. You will never be able to buy a home. You will never buy a car. You will never send your children to college. Let's not shuffle the battle cry of the socialists under the rug either. It's always the same cry. Equalize income. Spread the wealth to the poor (whoever they are). Level the economic playing field. Accomplish that and everything will be rosy. Greece is a perfect example. Despite the socialism system that has ruled this country for decades, with a 65% tax rate, they are drowning in public debt, would have defaulted without hundreds of billions in bailout money, and still. . .20% of their population lives in poverty. What has all that socialism money bought, besides ultimate power for the politicians running the show? Do you think these people are "free"? They're not. They are slaves to their economic "system."

This is where we are going unless we throw most of the present Congress and Obama out.

Federally Controlled Education System

Progressives know, as did Hitler and Stalin, educate the youth and you influence the next generation to carry out your will. Progressives have infiltrated our education system from pre-K through post doctorate. It is well to note that most democrat politicians are lawyers while most republican politicians are businessmen.

Jesus warned about lawyers in Luke 11: 52 *"Woe unto you, lawyers! for ye have taken away the key of knowledge..."* The point is that Progressives have intentionally 'taken away the key of knowledge' by revising our history in order to 'dumb down' the people. People who do not know the truth are easier to manipulate and control.

President Woodrow Wilson was the first progressive. In his commencement address at Princeton University, October 21, 1896 he stated *"...The purpose of Princeton is to make young gentlemen as unlike their fathers as possible. ..."*

Contrast what Princeton's purpose became under the Progressive movement with Harvard, Princeton and Yale Universities when first founded. Their original purpose was to educate ministers from the Holy Bible so that those truths would not be lost and to teach how those truths are the foundation of the Declaration of Independence and the US Constitution.

Failed Government 'Wars' On Poverty and Drugs

"The lessons of history ... show conclusively that continued dependence upon relief induces a spiritual and moral disintegration fundamentally destructive to the national fiber. To dole out relief in this way is to administer a narcotic, a subtle destroyer of the human spirit." -President Franklin Delano Roosevelt 1935 SOTUA

The current welfare system is highly complex, involving six departments: HHS, Agriculture, HUD, Labor, Treasury, and Education. It is not unusual for a single poor family to receive benefits from four different departments through as many as six or seven overlapping programs. For example, a family might simultaneously receive benefits from: TANF, Medicaid, Food Stamps, Public Housing, WIC, Head Start, and the Social Service Block Grant.

Despite spending almost $16 trillion since the War on Poverty began in 1964, welfare programs have failed to reduce the causes of poverty, and instead have hurt many of the people they were intended to help. Poverty in America is overwhelmingly linked to the absence of fathers and a lack of work, but welfare payments have had the destructive effects of eroding marriage and the work ethic in low-income communities.

Welfare is on the Rise. The growth of welfare spending is unsustainable and will drive the United States into bankruptcy if allowed to continue unreformed. Welfare spending is projected to cost taxpayers $10.3 trillion over the next 10 years.

The President's Welfare Budget. President Obama's FY 2011 budget request would increase total welfare spending to $953 billion, a 42% increase over welfare spending in FY 2008.

Amnesty Will Make the Problem Worse. If the U.S. government were to grant amnesty or "earned citizenship" to illegal immigrants, the welfare system would be flooded with new recipients. Of the 11 million–12 million illegal immigrants in the U.S., at least half lack a high school degree.

The collapse of marriage is the predominant cause of child poverty in the U.S. today. When the War on Poverty began, 7% of children were born out of wedlock; today, the figure is over 40%. Most alarmingly, the out-of-wedlock birthrate among African–Americans is 72%.

Last, is the government's failed war on drugs. Drug use has increased in the US. Mexican Drug Cartels have expanded and infected our Country and increased drug use.

Greed

NOTE: Capitalism has not failed. Greed, masquerading as socialism, has infected the US Government, imposed ever restricting controls the free enterprise of capitalisms free markets. Through legislative laws the government caused capitalism to appear like it has failed. To cover their sins progressives (socialists) blame capitalism as the cause when the truth is socialistic policies are the cause of capitalisms decline. Men have failed to keep God's moral code under which capitalism can succeed. Greed has overpowered morality.

Why did Bernie Madoff go to prison? To make it simple – GREED - he talked people into investing in his Ponzi scheme. He simply took the money from the new investors to pay off the old investors.. Finally there were too many old investors and not enough money from new investors coming in to keep the payments going.

Next thing you know Madoff is one of the most hated men in America and he is off to jail. Some of you know this, but not enough are aware that that our government is conducting a Ponzi scheme.

Madoff did to his investors what the government has been doing to us for over 70 years with Social Security. There is no meaningful difference between the two schemes, except that one was operated by a private individual who is now in jail, and the other is operated by politicians who enjoy perks, privileges and status in spite of their actions.

Here's a side-by-side comparison of notorious Bernie Madoff's scam and the not-yet notorious scam on the American taxpayer called Social Security

BERNIE MADOFF	SOCIAL SECURITY
Takes money from investors with the promise that the money will be invested and made available to them later.	Takes money from wage earners with the promise that the money will be invested in a "Trust Fund" and made available later.
Instead of investing the money Madoff spends it on nice homes in the Hamptons and yachts.	Instead of depositing money in a Trust Fund the politicians use it for general spending and vote buying.
When the time comes to pay the investors back Madoff simply uses some of the new funds from newer investors to pay back the older investors.	When benefits for older investors become due the politicians pay them with money taken from younger and newer wage earners to pay the geezers.
When Madoff's scheme is discovered all hell breaks loose. New investors won't give him any more cash.	When Social Security runs out of money they simply force the taxpayers to send them some more.
Bernie Madoff is in jail.	**Politicians remain in Washington**

'The taxpayer: That's someone who works for the federal government but doesn't have to take the civil service examination. ' Ronald Reagan

De-Industrialization Of America

The following are evidence of the deindustrialization of America:

- The United States lost 42,400=+/- factories since 2001 amounting to 5.5 million jobs.
- Dell Inc., America's largest computer manufacturer, plans to expand its operations in China with an 10-year investment of over $100 billion.
- Dell announced that it will be closing its last large U.S. manufacturing facility in Winston-Salem, North Carolina leaving 900 unemployed.
- In 2008, 1.2 billion cell phones were sold worldwide. None were manufactured in the U.S.
- The Economic Policy Institute forecasts the U.S. trade deficit with China will cost Americans over half a million jobs in 2012.
- In the first 6 months of 2012 U.S. trade deficit with China rose 18 percent more than the first 6 months of 2011.
- From 1999-2008 employment at the foreign affiliates of U.S. parent companies increased 30 percent to 10.1 million and U.S. employment at American corporations declined 8 percent to 21.1 million.

- In 1959, manufacturing represented 28 percent of U.S. economic output. In 2008, it represented 11.5 percent.
- Ford Motor Co. closed the Ford Ranger factory St. Paul, Minnesota costing 750 jobs.
- Today, consumption accounts for 70 percent of the U.S. GDP, 70% is spent on services.
- The United States has lost 32% of its manufacturing jobs since the year 2000.
- Manufacturing employment in the U.S. computer industry is lower in 2010 than in 1975.
- Asia produces 84 percent of Printed circuit boards worldwide.
- The U.S. spends $4 on Chinese goods for every $1 that the Chinese spend on U.S. goods.
- Economists forecast that China's economy will be three times larger than the U.S. economy by the year 2040.
- The U.S. Census Bureau says that 43.6 million Americans are now living in poverty; the highest number of poor Americans in the past 51 years.

So how many tens of thousands more factories do we need to lose before we do something about it?

How many millions more Americans are going to become unemployed before we all admit that we have a very, very serious problem on our hands?

How many more trillions of dollars are going to leave the country before we realize that we are losing wealth at a pace that is killing our economy?

How many once great manufacturing cities are going to become rotting war zones like Detroit before we understand that we are committing national economic suicide? Deindustrialization of America is a national crisis. It needs to be treated like one. America is in deep, deep trouble.

Demise Of Detroit

Detroit is the best example of the effect of liberal left progressive politics. Detroit, once the world headquarters of the auto industry is now a rundown slum. Not that Detroit's products didn't need improvement, they did. But socialist policies have destroyed a vital American industry. See Frosty Wooldridge's commentary below:

Frosty Wooldridge is a US journalist, writer, environmentalist & traveler. He writes, *"For 15 years, from the mid 1970's to 1990, I worked in Detroit. I watched it descend into the abyss of crime, debauchery, gun play, drugs, school truancy, car-jacking, gangs, and human depravity. I watched entire city blocks burned out. I watched graffiti explode on buildings, cars, trucks, buses, and school yards. Trash everywhere!*

"Detroiters walked through it, tossed more into it, and ignored it. Tens of thousands, and then hundreds of thousands today exist on federal welfare, free housing, and food stamps! With Aid to Dependent Children, minority women birthed eight to 10, and in one case, one woman birthed 24 children as reported by the Detroit Free Press, all on American taxpayer dollars. A new child meant a new car payment, new TV, and whatever mom wanted. I saw Lyndon Baines Johnson's Great Society flourish in Detroit. If you give money for doing nothing, you will get more hands out taking money for doing nothing. Mayor Coleman Young, perhaps the most corrupt mayor in America, outside of Richard Daley in Chicago, rode Detroit down to its knees. He set the benchmark for cronyism, incompetence, and arrogance. Detroit became a majority black city with 67 percent African-Americans. As a United Van Lines truck driver for my summer job from teaching math and science, I loaded hundreds of American families into my van for a new life in another city or state.

Detroit plummeted from 1.8 million citizens to 912,000 today. At the same time, legal and illegal immigrants converged on the city, so much so, that Muslims number over 300,000. Mexicans number 400,000 throughout Michigan, but most work in Detroit. As the whites moved out, the Muslims moved in. As the crimes became more violent, the whites fled. Finally, unlawful Mexicans moved in at a torrid pace. Detroit suffers so much shoplifting that grocery stores no longer operate in many inner city locations. You could cut the racial tension in the air with a knife! Detroit may be one of our best examples of multiculturalism: pure dislike, and total separation from America. Today, you hear Muslim calls to worship over the city like a new American Baghdad with hundreds of Islamic mosques in Michigan, paid for by Saudi Arabia oil money. High school flunk out rates reached 76 percent last June, according to NBC's Brian Williams. Classrooms resemble more foreign countries than America. English? Few speak it! The city features a 50 percent illiteracy rate and growing. Unemployment hit 28.9 percent in 2009 as the auto industry vacated the city.

"If Detroit had been ravaged by a hurricane, and submerged by a ravenous flood, we'd know a lot more about it," said Daniel Okrent. If drought, and carelessness had spread brush fires across the city, we'd see it on the evening news every night. Earthquake, tornadoes, you name it, if natural disaster had devastated the city that was once the living proof of American prosperity, the rest of the country might take notice.

"But Detroit, once our fourth largest city, now 11th, and slipping rapidly, has had no such luck. Its disaster has long been a slow unwinding that seemed to remove it from the rest of the country. Even the death rattle that in the past year emanated from its signature industry brought more attention to the auto executives than to the people of the city, who had for so long been victimized by their dreadful decision making. As Coleman Young's corruption brought the city to its knees, no amount of federal dollars could save the incredible payoffs, kick backs, and illegality permeating his administration. By any quantifiable standard, the city is on life support. Detroit's treasury is $300 million short of the funds needed to provide the barest municipal services.

"The school system, which six years ago was compelled by the teachers' union to reject a philanthropist's offer of $200 million to build 15 small, independent charter high schools, is in receivership.

"The murder rate is soaring, and 7 out of 10 remain unsolved. Three years after Katrina devastated New Orleans, unemployment in that city hit a peak of 11%. In Detroit, the unemployment rate is 28.9%. At the end of Okrent's report, and he will write a dozen more about Detroit, he said, 'That's because the story of Detroit is not simply one of a great city's collapse, it's also about the erosion of the industries that helped build the country we know today. The ultimate fate of Detroit will reveal much about the character of America in the 21st century. If what was once the most prosperous manufacturing city in the nation has been brought to its knees, what does that say about our recent past? And if it can't find a way to get up, what does that say about our future? $20 Per Gallon fuel, the auto industry won't come back. Immigration will keep pouring more and more uneducated third world immigrants from the Middle East into Detroit, thus creating a beachhead for Islamic hegemony in America. If 50 percent illiteracy continues, we will see more homegrown terrorists spawned out of the Muslim ghettos of Detroit. Illiteracy plus Islam equals walking human bombs. You have already seen it in Madrid, London, and Paris, with train bombings, subway bombings and riots. As their numbers grow, so will their power to enact their barbaric Sharia Law that negates republican forms of government, first amendment rights, and subjugates women to the lowest rungs on the human ladder. We will see more honor killings by upset husbands, fathers, and brothers that demand subjugation by their daughters, sisters and wives. *Muslims prefer beheadings of women to scare the hell out of any other members of their sect from straying. Multiculturalism: what a perfect method to kill our language, culture, country, and way of life.*

"I pray everyone that reads this realizes that if we don't stand up, and scream at Washington, and our state, city, and local leaders this is what awaits the rest of America. If you follow the news at all you know this has happened in England, France, and Spain."

The United States is 3rd in Murders throughout the World. But if you take Chicago, Detroit, Washington DC and New Orleans out of the picture, the United States is 3rd from the Bottom on a list of 216 countries for Murders. These 4 Cities have the toughest Gun Control Laws in the United States. These cities are and have always been run by Progressive Democrats!

Big Centralized Government

The following story reveals more truth than fiction on how big government operates:

Once upon a time the government had a vast scrap yard in the middle of a desert. Congress said, 'Someone may steal from it at night.' So they created a night watchman position.

Then Congress said, 'How does the watchman do his job without instruction?' So they created a planning department and hired two people, one person to write the instructions and one person to do time studies.

Then Congress said, 'How will we know the night watchman is doing the tasks correctly?' So they created a Quality Control department and hired two people, one to do the studies and one to write the reports.

Then Congress said, 'How are these people going to get paid?' So they created two positions, a time keeper and a payroll officer, then hired two people.

Then Congress said, 'Who will be accountable for all of these people?' So they created an administrative section and hired three people, an Administrative Officer, an Assistant Administrative Officer, and a Legal Secretary.

Then Congress said, 'We have had this security system in operation for one year, and we are

$918,000 over budget. We must cut back.' So they laid off the night watchman.

Now let that sink in. Quietly, we go like sheep to slaughter to the burgeoning burden of over-active, centralized planning, big government.

Case in point: Does anybody remember the reason given for the establishment of the DEPARTMENT OF ENERGY during the Carter Administration?

We've spent several hundred billion dollars in support of an agency...the reason for which not many people can remember!

The Department of Energy - established 8/04/1977 - **to lessen our dependence on foreign oil.**

And, now, it's 2010 -- 33 years later -- and the budget for this "necessary" department is at $24.2 billion a year. It has 16,000 federal employees and approximately 100,000 contract employees, and look at the job it has done!

A little over 33 years ago, 30% of our oil consumption was foreign imports. Today 70% of our oil consumption is foreign imports.

Now, we have turned health care, and the auto industry over to the same government, and that government wants to soak the taxpayers for more money so they can grow even bigger!!!

The definition of insanity is to continue doing the same things expecting different results. Under that definition the Federal government has become insane!

Source of Many Problems

Communism, socialism, fascism, Nazism, progressivism, radical Islam. All these 'isms' that infect politicians are the problem. Communism and socialism are economic systems where the state controls markets and owns companies. Capitalism is the economic system of free markets and private ownership. Capitalism created the greatest prosperity of mankind – ever.

Politicians. Politicians are opportunists primarily interested in political office for selfish or other narrow usually short-sighted reasons and make a career out of being a politician. What America needs are **statesmen** like George Washington, Thomas Jefferson etc. Statesmen values principle above popularity, are unsually wise, skilled, and respected government leaders who serve their term then go back to their real jobs in society. American has 545 politicians vs. 300,000,000 citizens.

Politicians create problems and then campaign against them. Consider that both Democrats and the Republicans are against deficits, but America's deficit grows. One hundred senators, 435 congressmen, one President, and nine Supreme Court justices equates to 545 human beings out of the 300 million are directly, legally, morally, and individually responsible for the domestic problems that plague this country.

These 545 people exercise the power of the federal government, So what exists is what they want to exist. For example, the unfair IRS tax code, the out of control EPA and corrupt FDA, the $21Trillion national debt (including future obligations)' a special retirement plan from social security, exclusion from Obamacare etc.

Not one of the following taxes existed 100 years ago, & our nation was the most prosperous in the world. We had absolutely no national debt, had the largest middle class in the world.	School Tax State Income Tax State Unemployment Luxury Taxes Marriage License Tax Medicare Tax Telephone Minimum Usage Surcharge Tax Tax	Telephone Usage Charge Tax Utility Taxes Vehicle License Registration Tax Vehicle Sales Tax Watercraft Registration Tax Well Permit Tax Universal Service Fee Tax Telephone Federal, State and

Federal Income Tax	(SUTA)	Local Surcharge Taxes Workers
Federal Unemployment Tax	Telephone Federal	Compensation Tax Inheritance
(FUTA) Fishing License Tax	Excise Tax	Tax
Food License Tax	Telephone Federal	Inventory Tax
Fuel Permit Tax	Telephone Recurring	IRS Interest Charges IRS
Gasoline Tax (currently	and Nonrecurring	Penalties (tax on top of tax)
44.75 cents per gallon)	Charges Tax Telephone	Liquor Tax
Gross Receipts Tax	State and Local Tax	Social Security Tax
Hunting License Tax	Personal Property Tax	Road Usage Tax
Sales Tax	Property Tax Real Estate	Recreational Vehicle Tax
Service Charge Tax	Tax	

Lobbyists and cronyism. Our elected representatives in government are supposed to represent We The People. When lobbyists infect government with an annual $9 B to manipulate politicians. Lobbyists corrupt capitalism with a perverted system call cronyism. Cronyism is perverted capitalism.

George Soros —An 'Oz' Behind the Curtain

George Soros glories in toppling governments and has targeted the US Government as his next victim. His procedure to toppling governments and taking over countries follows:

1. Form a shadow government using humanitarian aide as a cover for subversive activities. OSI – Open Society Institute, Weather underground

2. Control airways ($1M donation to Media Matters, controls NPR (National Public Radio), The Huffingtion Post

3. Destabilize the State – weaken government (Tides Foundation, Apollo Alliance, Center for American Progress, Institute for Policy Studies) some innocent sounding names that are formed to destroy capitalism and freedom.

4. Provoke and election crisis (Acorn, Labor Union rallies etc.)

5. Stage demonstrations and take power. Consider Occupy Wall Street, Ferguson riots, NYC riots, all funded by Soros; he funded Ferguson riots to the tune of $33 million dollars!

Soros has and continues his attempt to destroy America.

Summary Points:

- America descended from being a Light on a Hill because we have lost our moral bearings. Men generally failed to live according to God's laws and failed to follow the guidelines of our Constitution.

- The communist-socialists who have conspired to destroy America have advanced near their goal.

- Progressives have effectively separated us from our God, our history and our Constitution.
- Secret societies rule America in a shadow government capacity.
- Many politicians have violated their oath of office with many Un-Constitutional Acts.
- Big centralized government is not the solution. It is the problem!

Action Steps:

1. We need to apply how to know Truth in chapter 1.

2. Keep pressure on our elected representatives – tell them We The People are watching them and We The People are Coming to hold them accountable to up hold their oath of office – OR they will be replaced.

3. Promote and elect honest men and women to represent you whose values align with the Declaration of Independence and the US Constitution.

End of Chapter

7

America's Awful Situation (The Evidence)

"Woe unto them that call evil good, and good evil;
that put darkness for light, and light for darkness;
that put bitter for sweet, and sweet for bitter!
Woe unto them that are wise in their own eyes, and prudent in their own sight!"
Isaiah 5: 20-21

"... wickedness is rapidly expanding in every segment of our society.
It is more highly organized, more cleverly disguised, and more powerfully promoted than ever
before. Secret combinations lusting for power, gain, and glory are flourishing.
A secret combination that seeks to overthrow the freedom of all lands, nations, and countries
is increasing its evil influence and control over America and the entire world."
Ezra T. Benson, President Dwight D. Eisenhower's Secretary of Agriculture
(America In History & Prophecy, p. 56)

*"... the Lord commandeth you, when ye shall see these things come among you...**awake to a***
***sense of your awful situation**, because of this secret combination which shall be among*
you...." Joseph Smith, Jr.

"...darkness covereth the earth, and gross darkness [covers] the minds of the people,
...all flesh has become corrupt... vengeance cometh speedily upon the inhabitants of the earth, a
day of wrath, a day of burning, a day of desolation, of weeping, of mourning, and of lamentation;
and as a whirlwind it shall come upon all the face of the earth, saith the Lord." Joseph Smith, Jr.

To understand the depth of America's crisis we must know the truth of our awful situation. Using the roots and fruits analogy, we understand how America became great and why we descended from being a light on a hill. In this chapter we will examine the bitter fruits that have resulted from our roots ingesting evil falsehoods into our Tree of Liberty.

You will find that this chapter is the longest. Why? It is the longest to provide ample evidence to see clearly the magnitude of our awful situation. Although the evidence presented is by no means complete, it is adequate to understand our awful situation.

The following compilation of evidence from various sources necessarily involves current issues. This chapter does not intend to foment hatred, but it does intend to reveal all of evil's faces so that We The People can do something about it.

Although our current 'awful situation' has been degrading slowly over the past 100 years due to Progressive/socialist liberal left agenda, their current presidential pick - Barack Obama - who promised to "fundamentally transform the United States of America" during his campaign, has in the last 2 years of his reign, pushed us off a cliff. We are now in a free-fall as the evidence in this chapter will verify. We are not so much interested in Obama's rhetoric as his record. Examination of both reveals that most often what he says is opposite of what he does. Due to America's loss of

In the future, the actors on the stage of life will change. Their underlying motives behind their actions will not. Good or Evil will always be root causes. Look for them in this chapter and in the future to correctly assess future 'situations'.

Note that these 'evidences' are individual pieces of a big puzzle. It is essential to put the puzzle pieces together and see the big picture. What you will see is not just about progressives, socialists, communists, Marxists, Muslims, or individuals. What is most important is to see the world wide movement that is being orchestrated by Lucifer designed to overthrow the freedom and liberty of all mankind provided under the U.S. Constitution and to replace it with control and slavery under the absolute tyranny of a One World Order (AKA New World Order, One World Government, One World Corporation).

Hypocrisy

Politicians talk about the greed of the rich	...at a $35,000.00 a plate campaign fund-raising event
People claim that the government still discriminates against black Americans	We have a black President, a black Attorney General and roughly, 20% of the federal workforce is black while only 14% of the population is black. 40+% of all federal entitlements goes to black Americans – 3X the rate that go to whites, 5X the rate that go to Hispanics!
The two people most responsible for our tax code, Timothy Geithner (the head of the Treasury Department) and Charles Rangel (who once ran the Ways and Means Committee)	BOTH are tax cheats who are in favor of higher taxes.
Terrorists kill Americans in the name of Allah	The liberal left progressive media reacts by fretting that Muslims might be harmed by the backlash.
Laws make people who want to legally become American citizens wait for years in their home countries and pay tens of thousands of dollars for the privilege	While the progressives try to grant citizenship to anyone who sneaks into the country illegally
People who believe in balancing the budget and sticking by the country's Constitution	Are referred by the Obama Administration as extremists
You need to present a driver's license to cash a check or buy alcohol	but not to vote

The government collects more tax dollars from the people than any nation in recorded history	The government spends a Trillion dollars more than it has per year - for total spending of $7Million PER MINUTE, and complain that it doesn't have nearly enough money.
The 'rich people' pay 86% of all income taxes	Are accused of not paying their "fair share" by people who don't pay any income taxes at all.

"To announce that there must be no criticism of the President, or that we are to stand by the President, right or wrong, is not only unpatriotic and servile, but is morally treasonable to the American public." Theodore Roosevelt - 26th US President

America's Current Tree Of Liberty

Question: What Kind of Tree do we have Now?

Is America really the light on a hill and the land of the free depicted in the Tree of Liberty? Or have we adopted so many values and principles of the Tree of Tyranny that we have a very sick Liberty Tree?

The daily news incriminates us. Infectious parasites called liberal left Progressives, international banksters, the Federal Reserve, Bilderbergers, CFR, Rockefeller Foundation, Ford Foundations, Tri-Lateral Commission, United Nations, socialists, fascists, Marxists, communists & Nazis - continue 'fundamentally changing' and sucking the life blood of freedom from our Liberty Tree.

Lies and evil are systemic cancers in our society. The best way to fight back is with truth and righteousness. Therefore, the greatest need for America is to repent of evil, deceit and immorality.

Examples of the evil we have become are far more than menioned here. It is for the reader to apply what was learned in Chapter 1 and discern whether America's present fruits are good or evil. If evil they should be hewn down and destroyed.

Presidential Oath of Office

When evaluating the president's or congress' record, it is revealing to keep in mind the oaths of office they took.

The oath of office of the President of the United States and representatives of We The People in Congress take the following oath of office: "*I do solemnly swear (or affirm) that I will faithfully execute the office of President of the United States, and will to the best of my ability, preserve, protect and defend the Constitution of the United States.*"

Congressional Oath of Office

The oath of Office that the House of Representatives and the Senate take:

"I do solemnly swear (or affirm) that I will support and defend the Constitution of the United States against all enemies, foreign and domestic; that I will bear true faith and allegiance to the same;

that I take this obligation freely, without any mental reservation or purpose of evasion; and that I will well and faithfully discharge the duties of the office on which I am about to enter: So help me God."

The question is....Are OUR representatives honoring their oath???

Government Plundering Of The Public Treasury

Salary of retired US Presidents ....$180,000 FOR LIFE
Salary of House/Senate ....$174,000 FOR LIFE
Salary of Speaker of the House ....$223,500 FOR LIFE
Salary of Majority/Minority Leaders ...... $193,400 FOR LIFE

Contrast these salaries with the average Salary of Soldier DEPLOYED IN AFGHANISTAN DODGING ROAD SIDE BOMB'S AND BULLET'S $38,000. (The Dodge Report)

It is reported that the White House's Top 20 Raises ranged from 17% to 86% from 200-2011. How big have your raises been?...if you still have a job!

PRESIDENT PARTY BOY

Barack Obama took several weeks to assert some minor control over the Gulf Oil spill while America's job market tanked the stock market, probably due in part, to the Gastby-like parties that rock the Whitehouse as if we are in the Roaring 20's. Performers include the Beatles, Beyonce, Kelly Clarkson from America Idol, Stevie Wonder, conga-like gyrating and Super Bowl parties. The fun doesn't end there...how about Obama and Biden's super-soak squirt gun frolicking at the VP's residence. Add to that Obama has been AWOL playing golf and basketball more than any other president by far.

This is only one example of many illustrating how the Obama presidency plunders the public treasury for their fun while America groans under the most serious depression since the Great Depression. Yet Barack has the audacity to say 'we all need to sacrifice.'

Contrast Barack's extravagance in the White House with President Thomas Jefferson. Jefferson's few and simple parties at the White House were funded out of his own money – not the public treasury! And when Jefferson left the White House he was in debt. Jefferson was honorable to a fault.

MICHELE OBAMA'S PART IN PLUNDERING THE PUBLIC TREASURY
Not to be outdone by Barack, Michelle spent $10 million of taxpayers money vacationing from 2010-2011 at locations including Spain, Hawaii, Vail, and Martha's Vineyard.

NANCY PELOSI'S PLUNDERING OF THE PUBLIC TREASURY
Nancy uses the Air Force like her private transportation service. She and her staff travel many weekends from D.C. to CA requiring the Air Force to be on standby to serve 'queen Nancy.'

Compare that the former speaker of the House Newt Gingrich who used commercail flights to serve the public.

These examples of extravagance is just the tip of the Washington iceberg called 'plundering public funds' (OUR tax dollars) for politician's fun. This occurred during the worst recessions/depression since the Great Depression, after Obama said "we will all have to sacrifice during these tough times" and when the Cost of Living Adjustment for Seniors has not been raised for two years. Consider the White House's Top 20 raises:

White House's Top 20 Raises

Name	Title	Salary Increase (2010-11)	% Increase	$ Increase
Matthew Vogel	SPECIAL ASSISTANT TO THE PRESIDENT FOR ECONOMIC POLICY	$71,400 to $130,500	83	$59,100
Heather Zichal	DEPUTY ASSISTANT TO THE PRESIDENT FOR ENERGY AND CLIMATE CHANGE	$100,000 to $140,000	40	$40,000
Kevin Lewis	DIRECTOR OF AFRICAN-AMERICAN MEDIA	$42,000 to $78,000	86	$36,000
Elizabeth Olsen	SPECIAL ASST TO THE PRESIDENT AND DIRECTOR OF PRESIDENTIAL CORRESPONDENCE	$76,500 to $110,000	44	$33,500
Jessica Wright	DEPUTY ASSISTANT TO THE PRESIDENT AND DIRECTOR OF SCHEDULING	$96,900 to $130,000	34	$33,100
Lauren Paige	SPECIAL ASSISTANT TO THE PRESIDENT AND DIRECTOR OF MESSAGE PLANNING	$62,000 to $95,000	53	$33,000
Elizabeth Nelson	DEPUTY DIRECTOR OF SCHEDULING	$45,900 to $75,000	63	$29,100
Ashley Tate-Gilmore	DIRECTOR OF TRAVEL OFFICE	$45,900 to $75,000	63	$29,100
Carlos Monje Jr.	SPECIAL ASST TO THE PRESIDENT AND CHIEF OF STAFF OF THE DOMESTIC POLICY COUNCIL	$91,800 to $120,000	31	$28,200
David Cusack	DEPUTY ASSISTANT TO THE PRESIDENT AND DIRECTOR OF ADVANCE AND OPERATIONS	$102,000 to $130,000	27	$28,000
Kimberley Harris	DEPUTY ASSISTANT TO THE PRESIDENT AND DEPUTY COUNSEL TO THE PRESIDENT	$130,500 to $158,500	21	$28,000
Jonathan Samuels	DEPUTY ASSISTANT TO THE PRESIDENT FOR LEGISLATIVE AFFAIRS AND HOUSE LIAISON	$130,500 to $158,500	21	$28,000
Thomas Vietor	SENIOR DIRECTOR AND NAT'L SECURITY STAFF SPOKESMAN	$78,000 to $105,000	35	$27,000
Frederico Gardaphe	DEPUTY DIRECTOR	$50,000 to $75,000	50	$25,000
Denis McDonough	ASSISTANT TO THE PRESIDENT AND DEPUTY NATIONAL SECURITY ADVISOR	$147,500 to $172,200	17	$24,700
Johanna Maska	DEPUTY DIRECTOR OF ADVANCE AND DIRECTOR OF PRESS ADVANCE	$56,100 to $80,000	43	$23,900
Kwesi Cobbina	CHIEF OF STAFF, OFFICE OF LEGISLATIVE AFFAIRS	$42,000 to $65,000	55	$23,000
Semonti Stephens	DEPUTY COMMUNICATIONS DIRECTOR	$53,550 to $75,000	40	$21,450
Amanda Anderson	SENIOR LEGISLATIVE AFFAIRS ADVISOR	$60,000 to $80,000	33	$20,000
Stacy Koo	DEPUTY CHIEF OF STAFF FOR PRESIDENTIAL PERSONNEL	$55,000 to $75,000	36	$20,000
Andrea Turk	DIRECTOR OF INFORMATION SERVICES	$50,000 to $70,000	40	$20,000

Jobs Report

2001-2011 - Private sector jobs grew by 1%.

2001-2011 - Government jobs grew by 15%.

When the 2008 recession started the Federal Department of Transportation had 1 person making over $100,000/yr.

In 2011 the Federal Department of Transportation had 1,690 people making over $100,000/yr. !

When the 2008 recession started the Federal Department of Defense had 1,860 person making over $150,000/yr

In 2011 the Federal Department of Defense had 10,100 people making over $150,000/yr.

2009 - private sector employee average salary -$61,000

2009 – government employee average salary - $123,000

2011 - 21,300,000 government employees (16%) of the population. Double that with spouses who will vote with them to keep their jobs. Couple that will illegal aliens and welfare recipients who depend on the government for handouts and we have a serious problem in America

National Budget

The National Budget does not come from the White House. It comes from Congress, and the Party that has controlled Congress since January 2007 is the Democrat Party. They controlled the budget process for FY 2008 and FY 2009, as well as FY 2010 and FY 2011. In that first year, they had to contend with George Bush, which caused them to compromise on spending, when Bush somewhat belatedly got tough on spending increases.

For FY 2009, Nancy Pelosi and Harry Reid bypassed George Bush entirely, passing continuing resolutions to keep government running until Barack Obama could take office. At that time, they passed a massive omnibus spending bill to complete the FY 2009 budgets. Remember? And where was Barack Obama during this time? He was a member of that very Congress that passed all of these massive spending bills. He signed the omnibus bill as President to complete FY 2009.

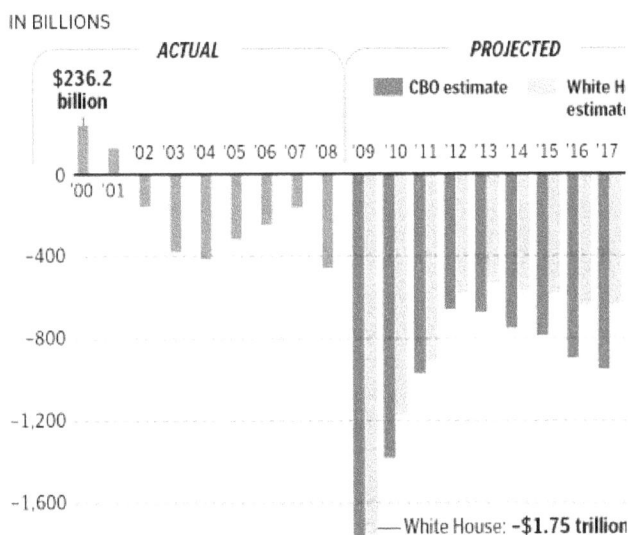

IN BILLIONS

ACTUAL   PROJECTED

$236.2 billion

CBO estimate   White H estimate

'00 '01 '02 '03 '04 '05 '06 '07 '08 '09 '10 '11 '12 '13 '14 '15 '16 '17

0
-400
-800
-1,200
-1,600

— White House: -$1.75 trillion

If the Democrats inherited any deficit, it was the FY 2007 deficit, the last of the Republican budgets. That deficit was the lowest in five years, and the fourth straight decline in deficit spending. After that, Democrats in Congress took control of spending, and that includes Barack Obama, who voted for the budgets. If Obama inherited anything, he inherited it from himself.

In a nutshell, when Obama says he inherited a huge deficit, what he is saying is "I inherited a deficit that I voted for and then I voted to expand that deficit four-fold since January 20th."

European Union's Debts vs. U.S. Debts:

Consider the following statistics:

EU statistics as of December 2010:
- Greece is 1.9% of the EU economy
- Greece is the 27th largest economy in the world
- Greece GDP is $300 billion
- EU economy is $16 trillion

USA statistics as of December 2010:
- California is 13.8% of the US economy
- California is the 8th largest economy in the world
- California GDP is $1.8 trillion
- USA economy is $15 trillion

The point is that the EU is rightfully concerned that if Greece falls it will begin a domino effect on all the other countries of the EU. Greece is only 2.5% of the EU. What would the affect be on the USA if California fell which is proportionately over 7 times larger to the USA than Greece is the EU?!?

The result could be catastrophic failure of our economy! ...exactly what the progressives/socialists/communists want to have happen. This is practically guaranteed through the international policy of mutually assured economic destruction. The world's economies are mutually interdependent. If the USA or the EU falls the rest of the world's economies will be taken down with it; a perfect scenario for the One World Order oligarchy to step in as the world's 'savior' and force people under their tyrannical control.

U.S. Economy

Statistics About The U.S. Economy That Barack Obama Does Not Want You To Know:

The truth is that the economy is still struggling to recover. Bogus reports from the Bureau of Labor Statistics do not count those who have given up the job search. Unemployment is not the 7.something government reports, but reality is in the range of 18-24%. The Great Depression was 25%!

Gallup reports that the percent of America owning homes is dropping to the lowest level ever. Home prices continue to fall despite housing bogus reports to the contrary. Over half of college graduates are unemployed or underemployed. When Obama became president long-term unemployment as 2.6M. Now it is 5.3M. The duration of unemployment is 3X longer than in 2000. Since Obama entered the White House gasoline prices have jumped over 100% and rising. College student loan debt is over $1T and most are in default. House hold incomes continue to decline. Government dependence continues to rise with nearly half the population on welfare, food stamps etc...in short – ENSLAVED to the government. Private sector jobs are declining in numbers and income while government jobs are increasing in numbers and income. The movement toward an enslaved populace continues at breakneck speed. In slightly over 3 years Obama has added more to the national debt than the first 41 president's – combined! America's debt is at an unsustainable $21T, and rising. The Federal Reserve holds 61% of the national debt. It has systematically destroyed the value of the USD since becoming law illegally in 1913. The Federal Reserve and international banksters is the 'great whole' seen in Revelations.

Meanwhile the Obama's party like did Nero when Rome burned.

America's 'Mr. Potter'

Glenn Beck has an extraordinary ability to 'connect the dots' that reveal intent of actions. Glenn compared Obama to Mr. Potter in the Jimmy Stewart and Donna Reed movie, 'It's a Wonderful Life'? Many of you will remember that Mr. Potter is the bankster that came to 'save the day' and bail the Town of Bedford Falls out of their troubles by buying people's shares of the Bailey Building and Loan for 50 cents on the dollar when there was a run on the banks. Some people took Potter up on his deal....and became enslaved to him.

Now fast forward to 2008 to the Obama/progressive/liberal left/socialist induced collapse of the America's economy using the Cloward and Piven approach. GM, Chrysler, Goldman Sachs, AIG etc. were supposedly all going to fail if something wasn't done immediately to save the day and bail them out.

First George Bush approves TARP out of desire to prevent the economy from collapsing according to his book, <u>Decision Points</u>. Then along comes Obama the false 'messiah. ' He said he didn't want to be in the car, bank and insurance business (ha, ha!). But watch his actions; he accelerates the bailouts (enslavement of companies) by using our tax dollars UNCONSTITUTIONALLY. Then he redirects massive bailout money to pay off his union buddies who got him elected. Obama's buy-out also enslaved these companies to his union buddies. In fact, Obama spent most of his life helping out SEIU, ACORN etc. So it was pay-back time using OUR TAX dollars to pay off his buddies.

<u>Read the story about how it worked with Chrysler and GM.</u> Both car companies came begging to Washington for bail out money after the 2008 market crash. The Federal Government and Obama's UAW now owns 65% of Chrysler.

Obama appointed Steve Rattner as his car czar. Rattner's wife Maureen was former national finance chairman of the Democratic National Committee and had access to the records of company donations to political candidates. Consequently of the 789 dealerships closed by the federal government, 788 had donated money exclusively to the Republican party.

In Arkansas, Louisiana and Missouri Bill Clintons former White House Chief of Staff, Mack McClarty, own a chain of Chrysler dealerships in partnership with Robert Johnson. Johnson is founder of Black Entertainment TV and is a big Obama financial supporter. None of their dealerships were closed, but all 8 of the competing dealerships in the region were closed by Ratter. Now the McCarty-Johnson dealership have a monopoly in the region.

Not surprisingly when this story hit the media Rattner resigned, under indictment for pay to play scandal, and Ron Bloom too his place.

This corruption in high places constitutes felony criminal action by Obama and his czars.

Foreign Aid

There are 191 countries in the world. America gives foreign aid to 152 of them; most of which hate us and vote against us in the United Nations! Washington does this when we are in a depression and America is BROKE - $14.7 Trillion dollars – and that's WITHOUT unfunded future commitments. All of which is unsustainable debt! You cannot buy real friends with money!

United Nations

The United Nations is fraught with waste, corruption, fraud and anti-Americanism. Most of the UN member countries hate America. It's time to get us out of the UN and stop pandering to those who hate us.

The USA pays for 28% of the operating expenses of the United Nations. Members including Muammar Qaddafi, Hugo Chavez and Mahmoud Ahmadinejad of the UN foment hate, criticize and condemn America day after day, year after year. What may have been a noble idea in the beginning, has become an international disgrace! It has become the international equivalent of ACORN. It is a front for instituting a One World Order; control of all nations under the United

Nations. No more sovereignty for any nation. Control of the World by an elite few banksters and international power brokers. It's time dissolve the UN and get them out of our America.

Government Record

In the first three years or Barack Obama reign as president of the United States the following changes occurred:

	2009	2012	% chg +/-
Gas cost /gal. U.S.	$1.83	$3.52	92.3%
Texas Crude oil (barrel)	$38.74	$91.38	135.9%
Corn	$3.56	$6.33	78.1%
Soybeans	$9.66	$13.75	42.3%
Sugar	$13.37	$35.39	164.7%
Unemployment rate, overall	7.6%	9.4%	23.7%
Unemployment rate, blacks	12.6%	15.8%	25.4%
Number of unemployed	11,616,000	14,485,000	24.7%
Number of fed. employees	2,779,000	2,840,000	2.2%
Median household income (2008 v 2009)	$50,112	$49,777	-0.7%
Food stamp recipients	31,983,716	43,200,878	35.1%
Unemployment benefit recipients	7,526,598	9,193,838	22.2%
Long-term unemployed (over 18 mos.)	2,600,000	6,400,000	146.2%
Poverty rate	13.2%	14.3%	8.3%
# of people in poverty	39,800,000	43,600,000	9.5%
Failed banks	140	164	17.1%
U.S. money supply	1,575.1	1,865.7	18.4%
National debt (trillions)	$10.627	$14.052	32.2%

Fox News reported on October 18, 2011 that the Obama Administration has racked up more national debt than all national debt since George Washington to George W. Bush - combined!

Washington in 1789 to Bush in 2008 (219 years!), 43 presidents combined, the national debt totaled $6.3 Million.

Obama from 2008 to 2011 (3 years) the national debt totaled $6.5 Million!!!

Debt Added By The Previous

43 U.S. PRESIDENTS --- COMBINED ---

1789 through 2008

Debt Added By

PRESIDENT --- OBAMA ---

One Term!

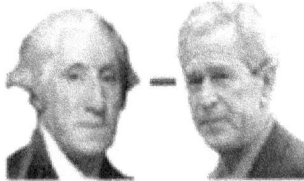

$6.3 TRILLION DOLLARS

$6.5 TRILLION DOLLARS

Barack Obama is highlighted herein to reveal recent actions that have greatly exacerbated the current awful situation; others preceded him and others may follow, so forewarned is forearmed.

представитель

5570347

"The young Obama was a garden variety Marxist-Leninist. He and Boss and his sophomore year roommate, Hasan Chandoo, believed that social forces where creating an inevitable Communist revolution in the U.S. and that it was important to have a highly trained elite of educated leaders guide this revolutionary process and oversee it once the revolution took place. Remember, this was at the height of the Cold War in 1980. Ronald Reagan had just been elected president and the USSR was still our mortal enemy."

- Dr. John C. Drew, classmate of Obama at Occidental College

Consider the results of Barry Soetoro's (Barack Hussein Obama) life so far. Obama actions follow Saul Alinsky's 'Rules for Radicals'. His actions align with Saul Alinsky's Rules for Radicals and the Cloward and Piven approach to overload the capitalistic system and to create Czar's that impose socialism and destroy the U.S. Constitution. Actions speak louder than words and reveal intent.

Notwithstanding his charismatic effect on some people and his rhetoric that appeases constituent ears, his record revels a hidden agenda. He has overwhelmed the U.S. economy to create systemic failure, economic crisis and social division and chaos which has eroded capitalism and our country from within. His administrative czar appointees are anti-business and anti-American.

Obama's actions have resulted in a major shift toward socialism and communism; more government control over every aspect of our lives. Consider the following actions and results:

He lied when he took the presidential oath of office to uphold and defend the Constitution of the United States. He actions show that he has done everything possible to overturn the Constitution and set himself up as king.

He lied about the founding of America by stating 'Islam is one of America's founding religions, one that has been woven into the fabric of our country since its founding,' This is an outrageous lie. America was founded by Christians seeking religions freedom from the kings of Europe and came here first as the Pilgrims and Puritans. All except one of the Founding Fathers were declared Christians. The only part Muslims played in America's founding was that they were part of the abominable slave trade.

He lied about the Founding Fathers embracing Islam. The truth is that the Founding Fathers criticized Islam as a doctrine of war, not a religion.

He misrepresented the facts when he said that President Thomas Jefferson had a copy of the Koran - and stopped there - implying that President Jefferson embraced Islam. The truth is that President Jefferson did have a copy of the Koran but for an entirely different purpose. He obtained and read the Koran because he could not believe that a religion would teach jihad as a way of life. After confirming the evil lurking is Islam President Jefferson built and sent the US Navy to the Barbary Coast to fight Islamic terrorists who were capturing and killing American merchants in that region.

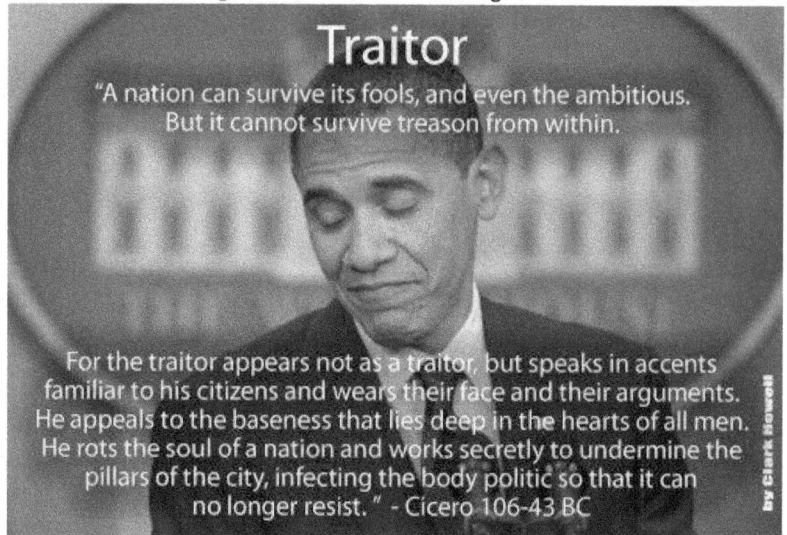

Traitor

"A nation can survive its fools, and even the ambitious. But it cannot survive treason from within.

For the traitor appears not as a traitor, but speaks in accents familiar to his citizens and wears their face and their arguments. He appeals to the baseness that lies deep in the hearts of all men. He rots the soul of a nation and works secretly to undermine the pillars of the city, infecting the body politic so that it can no longer resist." - Cicero 106-43 BC

by Clark Howell

He lied that Thomas Jefferson was the first US President to celebrate a Muslim holiday in the White House. The truth is that President Jefferson never celebrated a Muslim holiday at any time or place.

He lied when he stated that Muslims were involved in 'building the very fabric of our nation and strengthening the core of our democracy.' The truth is that not one tenet of Islam's murderous 'religion of peace' has found its way into American law or tradition. The father of American jurisprudence, Justice Joseph Story, thoroughly slammed Islam. American jurisprudence was founded primarily in the Holy Bible, not at all in the Koran.

He lied when he stated "if you like your health insurance you can keep your health insurance."

He lied when he said that your health insurance costs would decrease under Obamacare.

He refused to disclose who donated money to his election campaign.

Received endorsements from radicals including Al Franken, Louis Farrakhan, Muramar Kaddafi and Hugo Chavez.

He voted illegal, unconstitutional 'present' repeatedly in the Illinois Senate and in the U.S. Senate.

He refused to wear a flag lapel pin and did so only after a public outcry.

People started calling him a messiah and children in schools were brainwashed to sing his praises.

He dishonored American symbols and traditions when he stood with his hands over his groin for the playing of the National Anthem and Pledge of Allegiance.

He surrounded himself in the White House with advisors who were anti-US Constitution pro-gun control, pro-abortion, pro-homosexual marriage to curtail freedom of speech to silence the opposition.

He favored sex education in kindergarten, including homosexual indoctrination.

He associated in Chicago with Tony Rezko- a man of questionable character and who is now in prison and had helped Obama to an otherwise impossible deal on the purchase of his home.

He election campaign was funded in large part by George Soros, a multi-billionaire Marxist.

He appointed White House Czars that were radicals, revolutionaries, and even avowed Marxist /Communists, including Bill Ayers, Bernadine Dohrn, Valerie Jarrett, Van Jones etc.

He stood before the Nation and told us that his intentions were to "fundamentally transform this Nation" . We now see that his vision was anti-U.S. Constitution. It was socialism.

He trained ACORN workers in Chicago and served as an attorney for ACORN; a corrupt government organization that promoted prostitutes as 'artists' with tax payer funding.

He appointed a Science Czar, John Holdren, who believes in forced abortions, mass sterilizations and seizing babies from teen mothers.

He appointed Cass Sunstein as Regulatory Czar who believes in "Explicit Consent," harvesting human organs without family consent and allowing animals to be represented in court, while banning all hunting.

He appointed Kevin Jennings, a homosexual and organizer of a group called Gay, Lesbian, Straight, Education Network as Safe school Czar.

He appointed Mark Lloyd as Diversity Czar who believes in curtailing free speech, taking from one and giving to another to spread the wealth, who praises Hugo Chavez.

He chose Valerie Jarrett, an avowed Socialist, as Obama's Senior White House Advisor.

He chose Anita Dunn as White House Communications Director, who said Mao Tse Tung was her favorite philosopher and the person she turned to most for inspiration.

He appointed Carol Browner, a well-known socialist as Global Warming Czar working on Cap and Trade as the nation's largest tax.

He appointed Van Jones, an ex-con and avowed Communist as Green Energy Czar, who since had to resign when this was made known.

He chose Tom Daschle, a tax cheat, for Health and Human Services Secretary.

As President of the United States he bowed to the Muslim King of Saudi Arabia.

He traveled around the world apologizing for, and criticizing America; never once talking of her goodness and greatness.

He supported the Palestinians over Israel, our longtime ally.

He spend $350,000 of tax payer money to oust Bibi Netanyahu in Israel's 2015 election.

He used American tax dollars to resettle Hamas refugees from Gaza to the United States.

He upset the Europeans by removing plans for missile defense system against the Russians.

He played politics in Afghanistan by not sending troops early-on when the Field Commanders said they were necessary to win.

He spent us into a debt that was so big we could not pay it off.

He used a huge spending bill under the guise of stimulus and used it to pay off organizations, unions, and individuals that got him elected.

He took over insurance companies, car companies, banks, etc.

He took away student loans from the banks and put it through the government thus increasing the size and domination of government over our lives..

He designed plans to take over the health care system and passed Obamacase – a healthcare nightmare.

He set into motion a plan to take over the control of all energy in the United States through Cap and Trade.

When his baby, Cap and Trade didn't pass Congress, he did an end-run around Congress and used the EPA to impose standards that destroyed the coal industry,

He traded 5 terrorists in Gitmo for 1 deserter/possible traitor without consulting Congress; an act of treason. US Code - Section 2381: Treason "Whoever, owing allegiance to the United States, levies war against them or <u>adheres to their enemies, giving them aid and comfort within the United States or elsewhere, is guilty of treason</u> and shall suffer death, or shall be imprisoned not less than five years and fined under this title but not less than $10,000; and shall be incapable of holding any office under the United States."

He uses the IRS to intimidate any anti-Obama organization,

He blocked the Keystone pipeline thus damaging our economy and keeping us dependent on foreign/Muslim oil.

He is controlled by his largest contributors - unions, GE which owns NBC, MSNBC and CNBC.

He redistributes wealth (a key Marxist principle 'from each according to his ability to each according to his need') which dis-incentivizes entrepreneurship and promotes mediocrity.

He is striving to make Puerto Rico a state. If it succeeds look how many more votes and power that will buy him and fellow progressive/socialists.

He is extending benefits to illegal aliens - food stamps, free medical care, housing education, tax credits for the poor, and social security (planned), all of which buys votes and power.

He worked secretly to give 5.5 million aliens work permits when American citizen unemployment is astronomical. Works continuously to legalize 20M illegal invaders to buy votes and power.

He diverted trillions of dollars in bailout money to democratic contributors, ACORN, unions, creating government jobs (more voters), to save GM and Chrysler which was never paid back, in order to secure union due-paying employees jobs and votes. Money also went to AIG so that

Goldman Sachs could be bailed out and so that banker elite could receive huge bonuses. A staggering $125B went to teachers thereby enslaving them to unions and federal power.

He placed the tax burden on the top 20% of taxpayers, redistribute the income, punish success, and reward those who do nothing to deserve it, except that they vote for Obama.

He released Taliban Gitmo detainees who master-minded 9.11 in exchange for a deserter and traitor to our country.

At this writing Obama is proposing a horrendously bad deal for America with Iran's Ayatollah Ali Khamenei – the tyrant of Tehran - that will give them $1.5 billion to do with what they please. Ayatollah Ali Khamenei has repeatedly stated that America is the great Satan and Israel is the little Satan, and has vowed to wipe Israel off the map and death to America. That makes Khamenei our enemy. Obama took the oath of office to defend the United States of America against all enemies, foreign and domestic. So Obama thinks Iran will use our $1.5 billion to develop nuclear capabilities for peaceful purposes only??? Insane! Obama's act aids and abets our enemy; an act of treason! Obama should be impeached for this act alone.

If Obama finally completes his transformation of America into a Socialist State, people will wake up— but too late. Obama and his regime have created a vast and rapidly expanding constituency of voters dependent on big government; a vast privileged class of public employees who work for big government; and a government dedicated to destroying capitalism and installing themselves as socialist rulers by overwhelming the system.

Obama's actions clearly reveal that he has near total disregard for the United States Constitution. His actions have all but destroyed capitalism and promoted socialism.

What we know about Obama is that we do not know how he paid for his expensive Ivy League education with no visible signs of support. We do know that he spent his formative years of youth growing in socialist countries, by socialist parents and in a culture that is not American. We know that he has never run a company or met a payroll. He has never had military experience, thus don't understand it at its core. He acts like a narcissist, above others and always blaming others for his failures. He aligned over half his life with radical extremists who hate America, made some of them his 'czars' and refuses to publicly denounce these radicals who wish to see America fail. He is a cheerleader for the 'blame America ' crowd and apologizes across the globe. He proclaimed to fundamentally transform American into a socialistic European style country where the government sector dominates instead of the private sector. He has replaced independent health care system with a government controlled one and with this move controls 1/6th of the USA economy. He funds solar failures and 'wind mills' instead of capitalizing on our own vast oil, coal and natural gas reserves. He has effectively killed the American capitalist goose that lays the golden egg which provides the highest standard of living in the world. He has used extortion against certain banks and corporations. He has somehow controlled his own political party from challenging him and his wild and irresponsible spending proposals. He will not openly listen to or even consider opposing points of view from intelligent people. The bought and paid for 'lame stream' media gives him a free pass on everything he does. He demonizes and want to silence the Becks, Limbaugh's, Hannity's, O'Reilly's and Ingram's - whoever offers opposing and conservative points of view. He controls rather than governs.

Obama's record reveals his heart and purpose.

Latest Atrocity By The Federal Reserve

The latest audit by the Government Accounting Office of the Federal Reserve reveals $16 trillion in secret bailouts secretly given to US banks and corporations, and foreign banks between 2007-2010! Following are the 'big winners' of the Fed's handouts from page 131 of the GAO report:

Citigroup: $2.5 trillion ($2,500,000,000,000)
Morgan Stanley: $2.04 trillion ($2,040,000,000,000)
Merrill Lynch: $1.949 trillion ($1,949,000,000,000)
Bank of America: $1.344 trillion ($1,344,000,000,000)
Barclays PLC (United Kingdom): $868 billion ($868,000,000,000)
Bear Sterns: $853 billion ($853,000,000,000)
Goldman Sachs: $814 billion ($814,000,000,000)
Royal Bank of Scotland (UK): $541 billion ($541,000,000,000)
JP Morgan Chase: $391 billion ($391,000,000,000)
Deutsche Bank (Germany): $354 billion ($354,000,000,000)
UBS (Switzerland): $287 billion ($287,000,000,000)
Credit Suisse (Switzerland): $262 billion ($262,000,000,000)
Lehman Brothers: $183 billion ($183,000,000,000)
Bank of Scotland (United Kingdom): $181 billion ($181,000,000,000)
BNP Paribas (France): $175 billion ($175,000,000,000) and many many more including banks in Belgium of all places

The money was 'loaned' at 0% interest and to date none of it has been paid back. This unconstitutional, un-American, private corporation called the Federal Reserve destroys the US economy and robs American's of their wealth by causing cyclic inflations and depressions.

The Federal Reserve Bank of St. Louis increased The Adjusted Monetary Base (the sum of currency in circulation outside Federal Reserve Banks and the U.S. Treasury), plus deposits held by depository institutions at Federal Reserve Banks) from $800 billion in 2009 to $2.7 trillion in 2011.

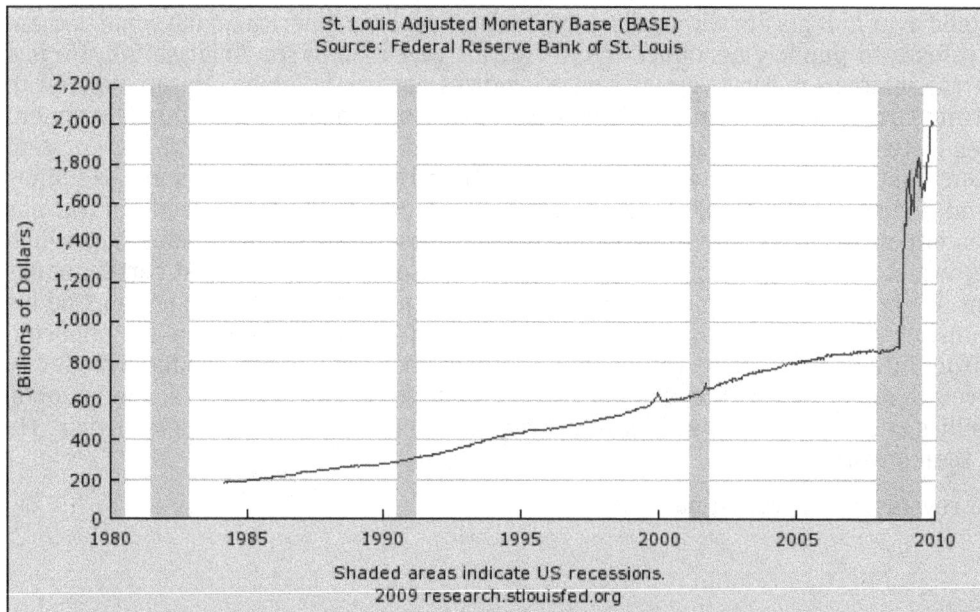

St. Louis Adjusted Monetary Base (BASE)
Source: Federal Reserve Bank of St. Louis
Shaded areas indicate US recessions.
2009 research.stlouisfed.org

This dramatic increased our monetary base decreases the value of each dollar in Americans pockets....in other words it robs us of our buying power. Notice how commodity prices have increased the previous section? That happened primarily because of inflation-causing practices by the Federal Reserve and the redistribution of wealth agenda of the Obama administration.

Illegal Immigration

The United States is being invade by illegal aliens. The impact of these 20 million illegals on our society is devastating; they cost American taxpayers $538 BILLION per year! Consider the facts about illegals in America:

- Illegals commit almost 1M sex crimes annually.
- Illegals send $65 Billion/yr. annually back to countries of origin.
- In 2005 alone an estimated 8-10 million illegals entered the USA through our southern border; 20,000 from terrorist countries, 10,000+ were from middle-eastern terrorist countries. Millions of pounds of illegal drugs came with them.
- Illegal aliens commit crime 2x more than white legal citizens.
- Illegals cause $200 billion in suppressed wages for citizens.
- Illegals cost $190 billion/yr. for welfare and social services.
- 500,000 illegals constitute 28% of inmates and cost $1.6 billion/yr.
- Incarceration of illegals cost $3M/day.
- Education of illegals anchor babies cost $27 billion/yr.
- Medicaid for illegals cost $7.5 billion/yr.
- 400,000 anchor are born each year in America and cost $109 billion annually.
- The EMTOLA Act for illegals caused 86 hospitals in California, Georgia and Florida to go bankrupt.
- TB, hepatitis and who know how many other disease are brought to this country by illegals annually. Plagues could easily result.

The deportation of these illegals would help solve our national indebtedness and make for a safer America. Calling an illegal alien an 'undocumented immigrant' is like calling a drug dealer an 'unlicensed pharmacist'.

Consider these facts: If you cross the North Korean border illegally you get 12 years hard labor. If you cross the Iranian border illegally you are detained indefinitely. If you cross the Afghan border illegally, you get shot. If you cross the Saudi Arabian border illegally you will be jailed. If you cross the Chinese border illegally you may never be heard from again. If you cross the Venezuelan border illegally you will be branded a spy and your fate will be sealed. If you cross the Cuban border illegally you will be thrown into political prison to rot.

If you cross the U.S. border illegally you get a job, a driver's license, social security card, welfare, food stamps, credit cards, subsidized rent or a loan to buy a house, free education, free health care, a lobbyist in Washington, billions of dollars' worth of public documents printed in your language, the right to carry your country's flag while you protest that you don't get enough respect and, in many instances, you can vote, illegals also get a tax refund where none is due.

Generations of American Patriots died in the Revolutionary War, the Civil War, WWI, WWII, Korea, Vietnam, Gulf War, War on Terror. NONE of them died for the Mexican flag. Yet in Texas, a Mexican student raised a Mexican flag on a school flag pole. An American student took it down. And the American student was expelled! High School students in California were sent home in Cinco de Mayo because they wore T-shirts with the American flag printed on them.

When will we American Patriots have enough of this political correctness nonsense! We need to rise up and act. Enough appeasing America-haters, especially those who come here illegally and then hate the country they snuck invaded.

Americans are not against legal immigration, as long as you come here to become Americans like generations before who came seeking freedom from oppression. Come to America to live by our laws, not supplant them with yours. Come to America to build up our country, not tear it down. And do not expect entitlement to our life-long contributions to social security and other welfare programs.

For decades, politicians did very little to stop the Mexican invasion. Why?...to retain and gain more power by giving government handouts to them from our taxes in exchange for illegal alien votes.

The Center for Immigration Studies reports that the Obama Administration operated a shadow immigration system for years and has handed out 5.5 million work permits to aliens with varying legal status since 2009...at a time when American unemployment is near an all-time high.

Joe Legal vs. Jose Illegal

Consider the following two families: "Joe Legal" and "Jose Illegal". Both families have two parents, two children, and live in California. Joe Legal works in construction, has a Social Security Number and makes $25.00 per hour with taxes deducted. Jose Illegal also works in construction, has NO Social Security Number, and gets paid $15.00 cash "under the table".

Ready? Now pay attention...
Joe Legal: $25 per hour x 40 hours = $1000 per week, or $52,000 per year. Now take 30% away for state and federal tax; Joe Legal now has $31,231.

Jose Illegal: $15 per hour x 40 hours = $600 per week, or $31,200 per year. Jose Illegal pays no taxes. Jose Illegal now has $31,200.

Joe Legal pays medical and dental insurance with limited coverage for his family at $600 per month, or $7,200 per year. Joe Legal now has $24,031.

Jose Illegal has full medical and dental coverage through the state and local clinics at a cost of $0.00 per year. Jose Illegal still has $31,200.

Joe Legal makes too much money and is not eligible for food stamps or welfare. Joe Legal pays $500 per month for food, or $6,000 per year.

Joe Legal now has $18,031.

Jose Illegal has no documented income and is eligible for food stamps and welfare. Jose Illegal still has $31,200.

Joe Legal pays rent of $1,200 per month, or $14,400 per year. Joe Legal now has $9,631.

Jose Illegal receives a $500 per month federal rent subsidy. Jose Illegal pays out that $500 per month, or $6,000 per year. Jose Illegal still has $ 31,200.

Joe Legal pays $200 per month, or $2,400 for insurance. Joe Legal now has $7,231.

Jose Illegal says, "We don't need no stinkin' insurance!" and still has $31,200.

Joe Legal has to make his $7,231 stretch to pay utilities, gasoline, etc.

Jose Illegal has to make his $31,200 stretch to pay utilities, gasoline, and what he sends out of the country every month.

Joe Legal now works overtime on Saturdays or gets a part time job afterwork.

Jose Illegal has nights and weekends off to enjoy with his family.

Joe Legal's and Jose Illegal's children both attend the same school.

Joe Legal pays for his children's lunches while Jose Illegal's children get a government sponsored lunch.

Jose Illegal's children have an after school ESL program.

Joe Legal's children go home.

Joe Legal and Jose Illegal both enjoy the same police and fire services, but Joe paid for them and Jose did not pay. (author unknown – but the content is true)

Do you get it, now?

Mexican Immigration Laws

Consider Mexico's immigration laws in contrast with America's. Mexico law is that:

1. There will be no special bilingual programs in the schools.
2. All ballots will be in this nation's language.
3. All government business will be conducted in our language.
4. Non-residents will NOT have the right to vote no matter how long they are here.
5. Non-citizens will NEVER be able to hold political office.
6. Foreigners will not be a burden to the taxpayers. No welfare, no food stamps, no health care, or other government assistance programs. Any burden will be deported.
7. Foreigners can invest in this country, but it must be an amount at least equal to 40,000 times the daily minimum wage.
8. If foreigners come here and buy land... options will be restricted. Certain parcels including waterfront property are reserved for citizens naturally born into this country.
9. Foreigners may have no protests; no demonstrations, no waving of a foreign flag, no political organizing, no bad-mouthing our president or his policies. These will lead to deportation.
10. If you do come to this country illegally, you will be actively hunted and, when caught, sent to jail until your deportation can be arranged. All assets will be taken from you.

And some say the U.S. Immigration laws are too strict???

Birthright Citizenship

Below you will find a list of all the developed nations of the world that offer birthright citizenship – anchor babies - to the babies of tourists and illegal aliens:

1. **United States**

Every other modern developed nation in the world has gotten rid of birthright citizenship policies. Yet, most of U.S. news media and politicians have ridiculed comments that it is time for the U.S. to put an end to birthright citizenship for tourists and illegal aliens.

Folks, the U.S. stands alone.

There used to be all kinds of developed countries that gave away their citizenship as freely as we do in the U.S. But one by one they all have recognized the folly of that policy.

SOME MODERN COUNTRIES THAT RECENTLY ENDED THEIR BIRTHRIGHT CITIZENSHIP POLICY:

- **Canada** was the last non-U.S...... holdout. Illegal aliens stopped getting citizenship for their babies in 2009.

- **Australia's** birthright citizenship requirements are much more stringent than those of H.R. 1868 and took effect in 2007.

- **New Zealand** repealed in 2006

- **Ireland**   repealed in 2005

- **France**   repealed in 1993

- **India** repealed in 1987

- **United Kingdom** repealed in 1983

- **Portugal** repealed in 1981

The United States is the laughing stock of the modern world.

Only the U.S. values its citizenship so lowly as to distribute it promiscuously to the off-spring of foreign citizens visiting Disney World on tourist visas and to foreign citizens who have violated their promises on their visitor, work and student visas to stay illegally in the country, as well as to those who sneak across our borders.

It's not just Mexico and South America who are sending illegals across our borders. Currently, the CBP reports that of those apprehended illegally crossing the border, China is number one.

Wake up America.   Illegal aliens from China, India, Russia, the Middle East and a host of other nations are flooding the country. Ironically, most often these illegals and/or their offspring are given positions at the front of the line for Government jobs, contracts and assistance.

Look around you! We are giving away our culture and economic and fiscal strength because our borders are not secure and we bestow citizenship irresponsibly.

Mosque Makeovers With Your Tax Dollars

The internet is full of reports from credible sources that the U.S. State Department sends millions of OUR TAX dollars to renovate mosques overseas.

The State Department's Agency for International Development granted enormous funds for mosques in Cairo, Cyprus, Tajikistan and Mali. FactCheck.org confirmed the following:

- In Cairo about $2.3 million was used to makeover a mosque
- In Egypt more than $15 million was given by the U.S. and the Egyptian government to restore another 1,300-year-old mosque, a Roman tower, a Greek Orthodox church and other buildings.
- In Cyprus, $5 million in U.S. federal funds was granted to restore a mosque and a Greek Orthodox monastery.
- Our tax dollars funded computer equipment in Mali and Tajikistan mosque projects i
- The State department committed $18.8 billion for all of its global projects.
- The U.S. State Department stated that the U.S. Congress, the U.S. Ambassadors Fund for Cultural Preservation has also provided financial support to more than 640 cultural preservation projects in more than 100 countries, representing nearly $26 million.
- In addition, The Associated Press reported that during America's recession in 2010-2011, the Obama administration has doled out 6 million of American tax dollars to restore or preserve 63 historic, religious and cultural sites, including Islamic mosques and minarets, in 55 nations under the guise of "Cultural Affairs" and "Cultural Preservation 2010 Awards," and they include:
  - $50,000 for conservation of Sundarwala Burj, a 16th-century Islamic monument in New Delhian, India
  - $76,000 for the restoration of a 16th-century grand mosque in China, with one of the longest histories and largest premises in the world.
  - $67,000 for the restoration of the mid-18th-century Sunehri Masjid (Golden Mosque) in Lahore, Pakistan
  - $77,000 to restore minarets (tall slender towers attached to mosques) in Nigeria and Mauritania, Africa
  - $80,000 for the restoration of the 18th-century Sultan Palace of Ujumbe in Mutsamudu, Comoros, with its highly ornate ceilings featuring Arabo-Islamic calligraphy and designs
  - $30,000 for the restoration of the 19th-century fort at Lamu, Kenya, a significant center for the study of Islamic and Swahili cultures where Muslim religious festivals have been hosted since the 19th century
  - $10,000 for the restoration of the Kofar Kansakali Gate in the Medieval Walled City of Kano, Nigeria, where the stone-laying ceremony was performed by the Emir of Kano, Alhaji (Dr) Ado Bayero, an influential Muslim spiritual and community leader in Northern Nigeria
  - $49,000 for restoration of a mid-19th-century Musafirhana (hostel) in Fojnica, Bosnia and Herzegovina, originally intended to house and feed Muslim travelers for free
  - $54,000 for the preservation the 6th century Castle in Vushtrri, Kosovo – a city that overthrew its once-dominant Christian population with a Muslim majority via the Ottoman conquests and a military post of an Ottoman garrison
  - $30,000 for conservation of murals at the early 19th-century palace of Ahmed Bey ben Mohamed Cherif, who led a fierce resistance against French forces from that palace in Constantine, Algeria

- $100,000 for the restoration of 17th- and 18th-century monuments in the Kasbah of Mehdiya, Morocco, which was built in 1185 by Yacoub el Mansour, the third Almohad Amir and Muslim military conqueror who was responsible for capturing thousands of Christians and killing tens of thousands
- $95,000 for the preservation of the Varendra Museum Building at Bangladesh and its prehistoric and historic collections – gallery six of which contains Persian, Sanskrit and old Bangla stone inscriptions and sculptured stones of the Muslim period.
- $34,000 for the preservation of traditional Uzbek music in Uzbekistan, which is one of the many forms of Islamic regional music.
- $450,000 for the restoration of Qala Ikhtyaruddin, the 15th-century citadel of Herat, Afghanistan – once used by Alexander the Great but also used in more modern times by even the Taliban. The extremely large project is employing many local Muslims seven days a week via U.S. funds.

Where are the separatists of church and state when it comes to separating mosque and state? The First Amendment provides citizens with the freedom to choose their religion; it doesn't provide the federal government with the right to fund the building of mosques overseas. In fact, it specifically says, "Congress shall make no law respecting an establishment of religion."

Even the liberal left New York Times published a report on how the "White House quietly courts Muslims in the U.S." Federal government funding of religious projects is unconstitutional. Do you as a taxpayer want YOUR money spent on mosque restoration? Part of Obama's increased Islamic grants is to appease the Muslim extremists. How stupid is that? We know that bribing Muslims not to bomb us futile.

On 9.11.11 we commemorated the 10th anniversary of Sept. 11. When the Muslim terrorist killed 3,000 innocent victims, we all declared, "We will never forget." Ten years later Obama is subsidizing Islamic structures and culture abroad with U.S. taxpayers' dollars and in so doing tramples on the memory of 9/11 victims and their families. They destroyed own our twin towers and we renovate their mosques. Have we gone nuts?

Refugee Resettlement

Ann Cocoran exposes on YouTube and on (https://refugeeresettlementwatch.wordpress.com) the 35 year-old Refugee Resettlement program by the Federal Government under the direction of the United Nations UNHCR under direct influence of a Muslim supremacist group – The Organization of Islamic Cooperation - who chooses who are the refugees to be sent to America. The use Federal funded front groups that appear like churches but are in fact government decoys to camouflage this hypocrisy. Long story short – billions of our tax dollars are spent to resettle over 100,000 'refugees' into our communities where government healthcare, housing, welfare and other services are provided to them free. Most of these immigrants are Muslims who hate America and are forming their own communities within American communities and insist on living Sharia Law.

Government Debt

The total Federal Government debt is $53 Trillion dollars - $444,000 per household. That's 90% of every American's total net worth. These figures are from the Comptroller General of the United States.

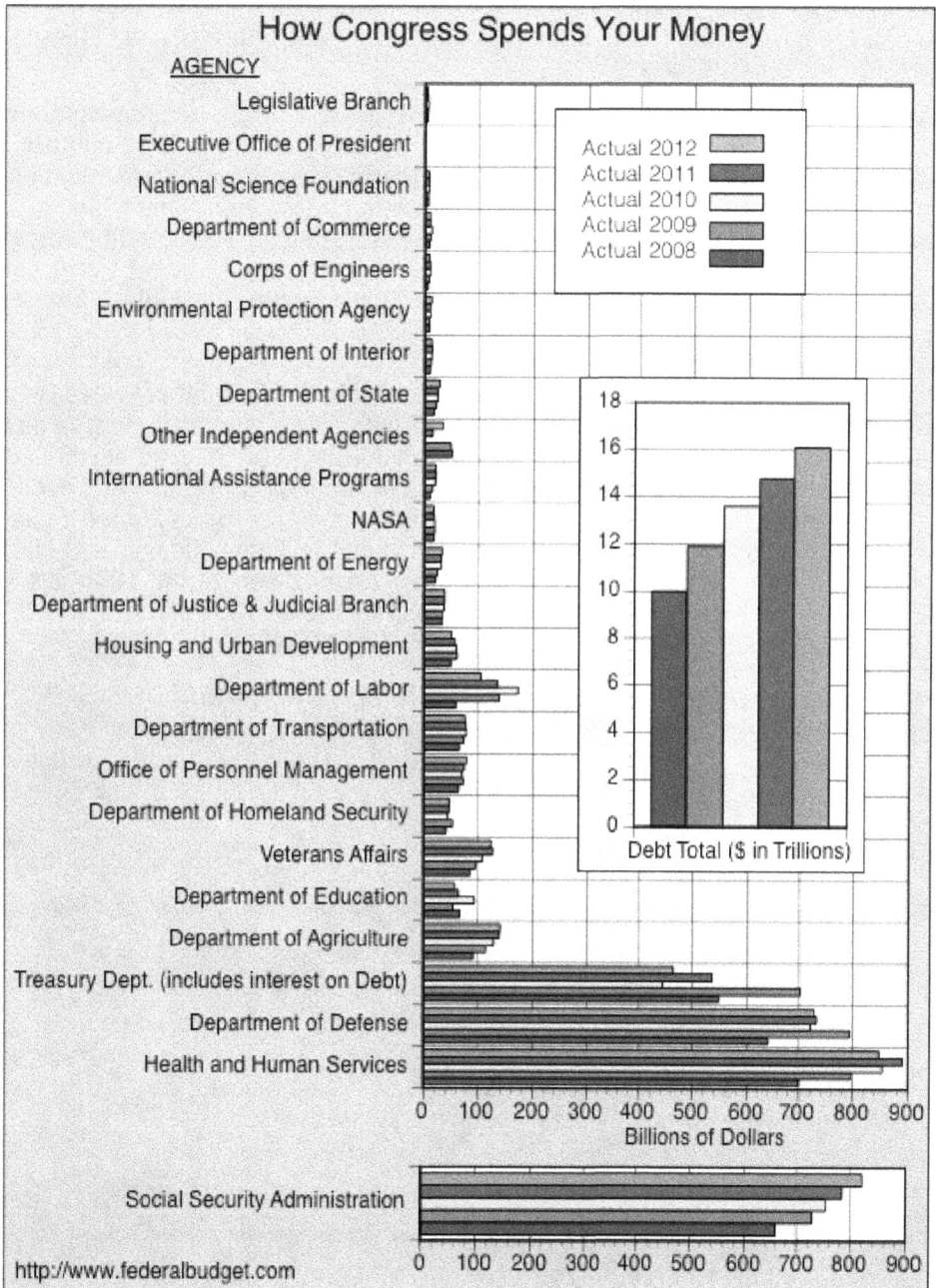

How Congress Spends Your Money

Obama's Betrays America & His Oath of Office

Webster defines evil is something that causes harm or is morally bad or wrong. Like breaking the law or supporting those who break the law. Consider first the definition of treason...

The Constitution of the United States – (excerpts on treason and impeachment)

Article II SECTION. 4. The President, Vice President and all civil Officers of the United States, shall be removed from Office on Impeachment for, and Conviction of, Treason, Bribery, or other high Crimes and Misdemeanors.

Amendment XIV SECTION 3. No person shall be a Senator or Representative in Congress, or elector of President and Vice President, or hold any office, civil or military, under the United States, or under any State, who, having previously taken an oath, as a member of Congress, or as an officer of the United States, or as a member of any State legislature, or as an executive or judicial officer of any State, to support the Constitution of the United States, shall have engaged in insurrection or rebellion against the same, or given aid or comfort to the enemies thereof. But Congress may by a vote of two-thirds of each House, remove such disability.

THE EVIDENCE

President Obama and his accomplice, John Holder (The United States Department of Justice) has - for the first in American history - sided with a foreign government; a direct violation of the oath of office. Obama and Holder sided with Mexico and its drug cartels against the State of Arizona and the citizens of the United States of America. One-third of Arizona prisons are filled with criminal invaders from Mexico. The Presidents' duty to the United States is to protect the citizens of the United States from foreign criminal invaders. Obama and Holder have done the opposite in aiding a abetting the enemy. (See Arizona Senate Bill 1070 and Arizona House Bill 2162, taken from Federal Law since 1940, Section 8 USC 1304 paragraph C,D,E,F.)

I am not "incompetent." I am destroying America more quickly than anyone thought possible.
I am not "in over my head." I am advancing totalitarianism right under your noses.
I am not "stupid." The "stupid" are those who fail to see the danger I bring.
I am not "failing." I am succeeding at every goal I have set.

I am embracing your enemies and rejecting your friends.
I am acting lawlessly and unconstitutionally.
I am ignoring your Constitution.
I am disobeying your laws.

Your media is abetting me.
Your Congress is not stopping me.
Those sworn to defend your Constitution are not removing me.

I am "fundamentally transforming the United States of America."
Your Constitution, liberty, freedom, wealth, future & children are no longer at risk...
... the risk is past; they already are lost.

The Obama-Holder **Fast & Furious** deployment of US weapons to Mexican drug cartels constitutes giving aid to our enemies.

Obama supports Zakat. He committed to alter U.S. charitable giving laws to support Muslims to fulfill ZAKAT! Zakat is a tax Muslims must pay, 1/8th of which goes to support Muslim terrorism.

Obama Reported Arizona to the United Nations Human Rights Council Over Immigration Bill. During his first report to this body Obama bashed the Arizona immigration law (which merely upholds federal law) and attempted to transfer power to the UN by making America's domestic immigration law an international civil rights issue. He also threatened additional lawsuits again Sherriff Joe Arpaio for doing his job to uphold Arizona and federal law. It appears that Obama is not sure he can win his case in the courts, so he has overruled the American people and bypassed the U.S. Constitution by seeking to sacrifice Arizona and American sovereignty to the United Nations.

"Shariah Law and the Constitution"

Lt. Gen. (Ret.) W.G. Boykin was part of the CIA team that found and interrogated the mastermind of the 9/11 attack, Khalid Sheikh Mohammad. Their efforts revealed more about Al-Quaida than all the previous CIA and FBI intelligence to date. As a result the CIA thwarted the planned terrorist attack on the 5-year anniversary of 9/11.

Then Barack Obama issued Executive Order 13491 on Jan 22, 2009 directing that all interrogations follow the Army Field Manual effective eliminating the very interrogation techniques used to gain terrorist plans from Khalid Sheikh Mohammad. With this action, Obama did more damage to America's national security in his first 100 days in office than any president in American history.

The Oath of Office is not just pretty words. The Oath gives value to the Constitution. By it the President becomes Constitutional Trustee for Americans. A Muslim cannot do this because Sharia Law is a higher civil authority.

Note the picture at the right: Obama refusing to pledge allegiance to the Flag.

Americans as beneficiary of the Constitution, pledge allegiance to the flag and agree to uphold the Law of the land [The Constitution of the United States] paying taxes in support. A Muslim will seek to replace the flag with Sharia Law because it is his first duty.

The 'Updated' United States Dollar

This USD showed up in Colorado.

Underneath the words "In God We Trust" someone had stamped the dollar bill in red ink---NO GOD BUT ALLAH.

This bill was part of change given in Alamosa, CO.

If anyone tries to give you one of these dollar bills as change, refuse it and demand a dollar bill that has not been defaced.

Democrats Took Over The Senate & The House - January 3rd, 2007

At the time:
1.   The DOW Jones closed at 12,621.77
2.   The GDP for the previous quarter was 3.5%
3.   The Unemployment rate was 4.6%
4.   George Bush's Economic policies SET A RECORD of 52 STRAIGHT MONTHS of JOB CREATION!

January 3rd, 2007 was the day that Barney Frank took over the <u>House Financial Services Committee</u> and Chris Dodd took over the <u>Senate Banking Committee</u>.

The economic meltdown that happened 15 months later was in what part of the economy? <u>BANKING AND FINANCIAL SERVICES!</u>

Thank Congress for taking us from 13,000 DOW, 3.5 GDP and 4.6% Unemployment to the GREAT RECESSION by dumping 5-6 TRILLION Dollars of toxic loans on the economy from Fannie Mae and Freddie Mac fiasco's! BTW: <u>Bush asked Congress</u> **17 TIMES** <u>to stop Fannie & Freddie - starting in 2001, because it was financially risky for the U.S. economy.</u>

<u>Who took the THIRD highest pay-off from Fannie Mae AND Freddie Mac? OBAMA.</u>

<u>Who fought against reform of Fannie and Freddie?? OBAMA and the Democratic Congress.</u>

U.S. Unsustainable Debt – 'Cloward & Piven'

The Cloward & Piven approach is in essence 'overload the capitalist system with welfare recipients, war and other debts so that it will collapse under its own weight with violent demonstrations and insurrections.' Overburdening methods include enticing so many people into the enslavement of government welfare, into government jobs, accepting government entitlement programs and plunging our nation into unsustainable debt that those who actually increase the gross domestic product of the nation by producing more than they consume (make a profit) can no longer pay for the government parasites.

How our socialistic Government welfare works: 72% of our welfare tax dollars stay with the Washington bureaucracy. Only 28% goes to help people! Contrast that with private charities where 75-100% of the money goes to help people.

The following charts illustrate the financial effects of liberal left progressive policies:

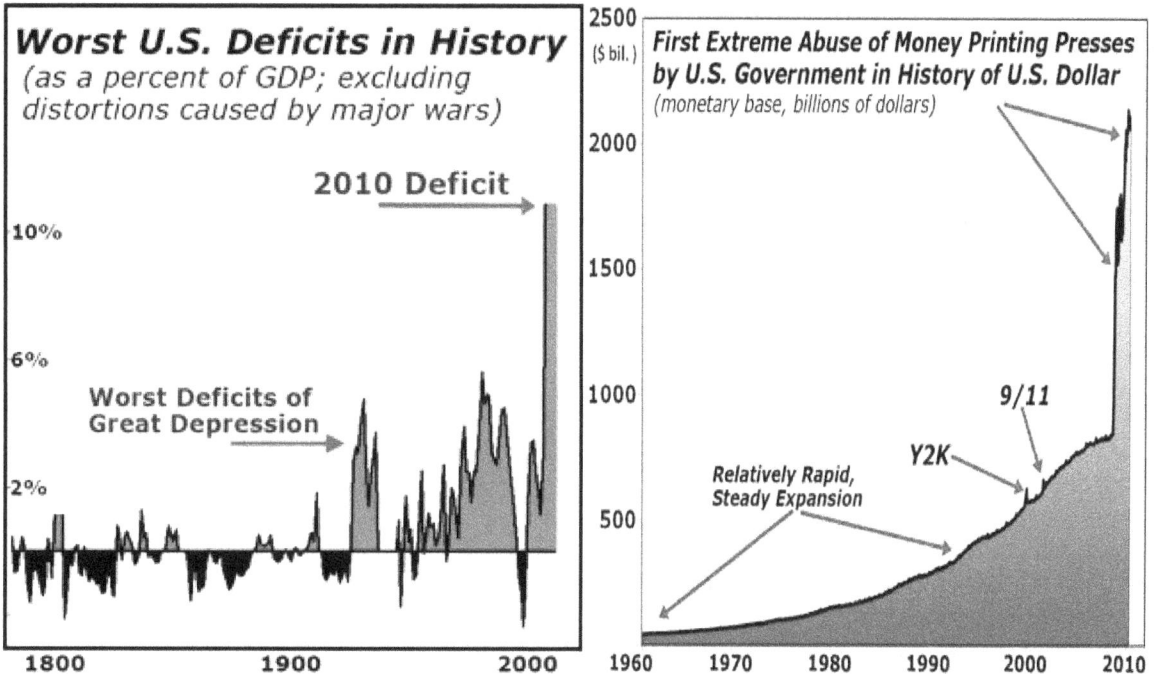

Obama's hidden agenda becomes clear when you connect the dots of his actions. Obama as plunged our Country into unsustainable debt. This is the Cloward and Piven approach manifest. Obama is methodically weakening the U.S. economy, weakening the USD and destroying capitalism so that Muslim radicals can unite and destroy Israel without worrying about the ability for the U.S.A. to aid Israel. After Israel is destroyed, the U.S.A. is the next target for destruction by Muslim radicals in their quest to institute a worldwide caliphate; Islamic rule of the world under Sharia law that is their version of One World Order.

Our government is re-arranging deck chairs on America's financial Titanic and we face a financial Armageddon to dwarf the 2008 crisis. 1 in 7 homeowners are delinquent or foreclosed on the mortgages, 4 in 10 are upside down on home equity, 2 in 10 are unemployed or underemployed, 7 in 10 fear the future, and 10 in 10 are facing continuing inflation in the cost of food, fuel and other essential goods.

The economy is going to get worse – much worse when hyperinflation hits.

Contributing to America's indebtedness are Capitol Hill Employees who owed $9.3 Million In Back Taxes in 2011.

Insurrections

Does it seem like the world is on fire and everyone is crazy?

The insurrections throughout the world were planned years ago. The insurrections in the Middle East (Turkey, Egypt, Libya, Tunisia, Jordan, Bahrain, Syria, and have spread to America in Occupy Wall Street) are orchestrated by those seeking one world order, including George Soros, Barack Obama and his union buddies. Governments are being taken over by Iranian supported Muslim Brotherhood, Hamas and Hezbollah assisted by Code Pink, US and foreign unions, under the disguise of democracy. Countries controlled by the Muslim brotherhood have declared that the Jews are infidels and must wiped off the face of the earth.

Fomenters of these insurrections have their spiritual roots in Lucifer, who seeks the misery of all mankind. Rioters are 'useful idiots' in the hands of Satan to overthrow the liberty and freedom of all mankind. Insurrections play into the hands of those who seek to control people. The evil One World Order crowd orchestrate, fund, incite and fan the flames of these insurrections. Their purpose is to create such chaos that the people will beg for a 'savior' to come and restore order. Then they, with their 'top down' force and control of government power, arrive to 'save the day.' If we swallow their bait for a false 'savior' (remember the useful idots who refer to Barack Obama as the 'messiah'?) it results in the hook of dependency through our lip and final enslavement. The end game is a One World Order, Corporation, and Control over We the Sheeple. The insurrections are here in America, and they are going to get worse. We MUST be be independent and not get caught in their trap.

The powers of Armageddon are assembling as never before. These Biblical 'fig leaves' reveal 'that summer is nigh.' However, of Christ's Second Coming it is well to remember *"But of that day and hour knoweth no man, no, not the angels of heaven, but my Father only."* Matt 24:36

Modern Day Progressives are the Monarchists of Jefferson's Time

Thomas Jefferson Warns of "Monarchists" - the Equivalent of the Progressive Movement Today who have infiltrated both the Democratic and Republican Parties.

"I have spoken of the Federalists as if they were a homogeneous body, but this is not the truth. Under that name lurks the heretical sect of monarchists afraid to wear their own name, they creep under the mantle of Federalism, and the Federalists, like sheep permit the fox to take shelter among them, when pursued by dogs. These men have no right to office. If a monarchist be in office anywhere, and it be known to the President, the oath he has taken to support the Constitution imperiously requires the instantaneous dismissing of such officer; and I hold the President criminal if he permitted such to remain. <u>To appoint a monarchist to conduct the affairs of a Republic is like appointing an atheist to the priesthood</u>. As to the real federalists, I take them to my bosom as brothers. I view them as honest men, friends to the present Constitution." (From a newspaper letter, June 1803; Paul Leicester Ford, editor, The Writings of Thomas Jefferson, 10 volumes, G.P. Putnam's Son's, New York, 1892- 1899, 8:237)

George Bernard Shaw, one of the early members of the Progressive Movement, is highly praised by such people as Hillary Clinton, Secretary of State, who proclaims herself as a 'modern progressive'.

Justification for War

Anciently other inhabitants of the Americas faced this question. Their answer was 'we would not slay our brethren if they would let us alone.'

Freedom – moral agency – our right to choose - is God's fundamental principle for the growth of His children. Thus, any infringement on our moral agency – freedom to act - is justification for war. Certainly, those who seek to destroy the life, liberty and property are acts contrary to the nature of God.

A perspective by Major General Smedley Butler USMC 1933:
"War is just a racket. A racket is best described, I believe, as something that is not what it seems to the majority of people. Only a small inside group knows what it is about. It is conducted for the benefit of the very few at the expense of the masses.

"I believe in adequate defense. If a nation comes over here to fight, then we'll fight. The trouble with America is that when the dollar only earns 6 percent over here, then it gets restless and goes overseas to get 100 percent. Then the flag follows the dollar and the soldiers follow the flag.

"I wouldn't go to war again as I have done to protect some lousy investment of the bankers. There are only two things we should fight for. One is the defense of our homes and the other is the Bill of Rights. War for any other reason is simply a racket.

"There isn't a trick in the racketeering bag that the military gang is blind to. It has its "finger men" to point out enemies, its "muscle men" to destroy enemies, its "brain men" to plan war preparations, and a "Big Boss" Super-Nationalistic-Capitalism.

"It may seem odd for me, a military man to adopt such a comparison. Truthfulness compels me to. I spent thirty- three years and four months in active military service as a member of this country's most agile military force, the Marine Corps. I served in all commissioned ranks from Second Lieutenant to Major-General. And during that period, I spent most of my time being a high class muscle- man for Big Business, for Wall Street and for the Bankers. In short, I was a racketeer, a gangster for capitalism.

"I suspected I was just part of a racket at the time. Now I am sure of it. Like all the members of the military profession, I never had a thought of my own until I left the service. My mental faculties remained in suspended animation while I obeyed the orders of higher-ups. This is typical with everyone in the military service.

"I helped make Mexico, especially Tampico, safe for American oil interests in 1914. I helped make Haiti and Cuba a decent place for the National City Bank boys to collect revenues in. I helped in the raping of half a dozen Central American republics for the benefits of Wall Street. The record of racketeering is long. I helped purify Nicaragua for the international banking house of Brown Brothers in 1909-1912. I brought light to the Dominican Republic for American sugar interests in 1916. In China I helped to see to it that Standard Oil went its way unmolested.

"During those years, I had, as the boys in the back room would say, a swell racket. Looking back on it, I feel that I could have given Al Capone a few hints. The best he could do was to operate his racket in three districts. I operated on three continents."

I am not a power monger. I hate war. However, many Washington politicians and international banksters are power mongers because it gives them power and increases their wealth.

It makes more sense to bring our troops home and use them to protect our borders, especially the Mexican border and be ready to defend our country from all enemies both domestic and foreign.

We would be well to follow Thomas Jefferson's policy regarding war - **"Peace, commerce, and honest friendship with all nations — entangling alliances with none."** Putting our nose in other nations business, and our oil interest in other nations, is one reason most of the world hate us. The great whore of the earth is the illuminati, international banksters and the Federal Reserve. They foment war and finance both sides to profit therefrom. Let us therefore, develop America's own natural resources God provided and become independent of the rest of the world. America is to be a light to the world; not its police men.

Second Amendment to the U.S. Constitution

Following are statements by The Founding Fathers and others regarding the Second Amendment:

"Firearms stand next in importance to the constitution itself. They are the American people's liberty teeth and keystone under independence ... from the hour the Pilgrims landed to the present day, events, occurrences and tendencies prove that to ensure peace security and happiness, the rifle and pistol are equally indispensable ... the very atmosphere of firearms anywhere restrains evil interference — they deserve a place of honor with all that's good." George Washington - First President of the United States

"I ask, Sir, what is the militia? It is the whole people. To disarm the people is the best and most effectual way to enslave them." George Mason - Co-author of the Second Amendment during Virginia's Convention to Ratify the Constitution, 1788

"No free man shall ever be de-barred the use of arms. _The strongest reason for the people to retain their right to keep and bear arms is as a last resort to protect themselves against tyranny in government."_ **Thomas Jefferson**

*"The constitutions of most of our States assert that all power is inherent in the people; that... **it is their right and duty to be at all times armed."*** Thomas Jefferson to John Cartwright, 1824.

"Laws that forbid the carrying of arms . . . disarm only those who are neither inclined nor determined to commit crimes . . . Such laws make things worse for the assaulted and better for the assailants; they serve rather to encourage than to prevent homicides, for an unarmed man may be attacked with greater confidence than an armed man." --Thomas Jefferson, quoting Cesare Beccaria in On Crimes and Punishment (1764).

"Those who hammer their guns into plows will plow for those who do not." Thomas Jefferson

"Those who trade liberty for Security have neither." John Adams

Lest we forget..... The Boston Newspaper headlines read **Seventy-two killed resisting gun confiscation in Boston!** Boston – National Guard units seeking to confiscate a cache of recently banned weapons were ambushed by elements of a Para-military extremist faction. Military and law enforcement sources estimate that 72 were killed and more than 200 injured before government forces were compelled to withdraw.

Speaking after the clash, Massachusetts Governor Thomas Gage declared that the extremist faction, which was made up of local citizens, has links to the radical right-wing tax protest movement. Gage blamed the extremists for recent incidents of vandalism directed against internal revenue offices. The governor, who described the group's organizers as "criminals," issued an executive order authorizing the summary arrest of any individual who has interfered with the government's efforts to secure law and order.

The military raid on the extremist arsenal followed wide-spread refusal by the local citizenry to turn over recently outlawed weapons.

Gage issued a ban on military-style weapons and ammunition earlier in the week. This decision followed a meeting in early this month between government and military leaders at which the governor authorized the forcible confiscation of illegal arms.

One government official, speaking on condition of anonymity, pointed out that "none of these people would have been killed had the extremists obeyed the law and turned over their weapons voluntarily."

Government troops initially succeeded in confiscating a large supply of outlawed weapons and ammunition. However, troops attempting to seize arms and ammunition in Lexington met with resistance from heavily-armed extremists who had been tipped off regarding the government's plans.

During a tense standoff in the Lexington town park, National Guard Colonel Francis Smith, commander of the government operation, ordered the armed group to surrender and return to their homes. The impasse was broken by a single shot, which was reportedly fired by one of the right-wing extremists. Eight civilians were killed in the ensuing exchange.

Ironically, the local citizenry blamed government forces rather than the extremists for the civilian deaths. Before order could be restored, armed citizens from surrounding areas had descended upon the guard units. Colonel Smith, finding his forces over matched by the armed mob, ordered a retreat. Governor Gage has called upon citizens to support the state/national joint task force in its effort to restore law and order. The governor also demanded the surrender of those responsible for planning and leading the attack against the government troops.

Samuel Adams, Paul Revere, and John Hancock, who have been identified as "ringleaders" of the extremist faction, remain at large. This is how the American Revolution began, April 20, 1775.

On July 4th, 1776 these same extremists signed the Declaration of Independence, pledging to each other and their countrymen their lives, fortunes, and sacred honor. Many of them lost everything, including their families and their lives over the course of the next few years.

Progressive administrations in the past, including the Obama administration in the present, are working hard with the progressive liberal left anti-gunners to destroy our Constitutional Rights.

Why? Without firearms, there will be no more liberty, freedom, or justice in government. Guns are the main core of the check and balance system. Our nation's founders realized that firearms in the possession of the people are the indispensable safeguard upon which all of the other rights in the "Bill of Rights" depend! That's why the Second Amendment was meant to be honored, treasured, and preserved!

An armed man is a citizen. An unarmed man is a subject.

You only have the rights you are willing to fight for and an unarmed man is defenseless against an armed man.

The only thing that stops a bad man with a gun is a good man with a gun.

Know guns, Know Peace, Know Safety. No Guns, No Peace, No Safety.

Assault is a behavior, not a device.

When you remove the people's right to bear arms, you create slaves.

Only a government that is afraid of its citizens tries to control them.

The following is a true story that most people don't know:

> After the Japanese decimated our fleet in Pearl Harbor Dec 7, 1941, they could have sent their troop ships and carriers directly to California to finish what they started.

> The prediction from our Chief of Staff was we would not be able to stop a massive invasion until they reached the Mississippi River . Remember, we had a 2 million man army and war ships...All fighting the Germans. So, why did they not invade? After the war, the remaining Japanese generals and admirals were asked that question. Their answer ... They know that almost every home had guns and the Americans knew how to use them.

The world's largest army is America's hunters!

There were over 600,000 hunters this season in the state of Wisconsin; the eighth largest army in the world; more men under arms than in Iran. More than in France and Germany combined. These men deployed to the woods in a single American state to hunt with firearms, and no one was killed. That number pales in comparison to the 750,000 who hunted the woods of Pennsylvania and Michigan's 700,000 hunters all of whom have now returned home. Toss in a quarter million hunters in West Virginia and it literally establishes the fact that the hunters of those four states alone would comprise the largest army in the world.

Hunting is not just a way to fill the freezer. It could become a matter of national security.

The New York Conservationist reports that *"The most dangerous part of hunting is the drive to the hunting area. Activities such as bicycling and swimming are many times more likely to result in injuries or death than hunting."* Oct 2011 Issue

No wonder all of our enemies, foreign and domestic, want to see us disarmed.

The Following is documentation of tyrannical governments who banned and confiscated guns, and the outcome to its citizens:

- In 1929, the Soviet Union established gun control. From 1929 to 1953, about 20 million dissidents, unable to defend themselves, were rounded up and exterminated.
- In 1911, Turkey established gun control. From 1915 to 1917, 1.5 million Armenians, unable to defend themselves, were rounded up and exterminated.
- Germany established gun control in 1938 and from 1939 to 1945, a total of 13 million Jews and others who were unable to defend themselves were rounded up and exterminated.
- China established gun control in 1935. From 1948 to 1952, 20 million political dissidents, unable to defend themselves, were rounded up and exterminated.

- Guatemala established gun control in 1964. From 1964 to 1981, 100,000 Mayan Indians, unable to defend themselves, were rounded up and exterminated.
- Uganda established gun control in 1970. From 1971 to 1979, 300,000 Christians, unable to defend themselves, were rounded up and exterminated
- Cambodia established gun control in 1956. From 1975 to 1977, one million educated people, unable to defend themselves, were rounded up and exterminated.
- Defenseless people rounded up and exterminated in the 20th Century because of gun control: 56 million.

A Tale of Two Cities

	Chicago, IL	Houston, TX
Population	2.7 million	2.15 million
Median HH Income	$38,600	$37,000
% African-American	38.9%	24%
% Hispanic	29.9%	44%
% Asian	5.5%	6%
% Non-Hispanic White	28.7%	26%

Pretty similar until you compare the following:

	Chicago, IL	Houston, TX
Concealed Carry gun law	no	yes
# of Gun Stores	0	184 - Dedicated gun stores plus 1500 - legal places to buy guns- Wal-Mart, K-mart, sporting goods, etc.
Homicides, 2012	1,806	207
Homicides per 100K	38.4	9.6
Avg. January high temperature (F)	31	63

Progressives 'spin' conclusion: Cold weather causes murder.

WORLD MURDER STATISTICS

The World Health Organization reports the latest Murder Statistics for the world:

Murders per 100,000 citizens.

Honduras 91.6
El Salvador 69.2
Cote d'Ivoire 56.9
Jamaica 52.2
Venezuela 45.1
Belize 41.4
US Virgin Islands 39.2
Guatemala 38.5
Saint Kits and Nevis 38.2
Zambia 38.0
Uganda 36.3
Malawi 36.0
Lesotho 35.2
Trinidad and Tobago 35.2
Colombia 33.4
South Africa31.8
Congo 30.8
Central African Republic 29.3
Bahamas 27.4
Puerto Rico 26.2
Saint Lucia 25.2
Dominican Republic 25.0
Tanzania 24.5

Sudan 24.2
Saint Vincent & the Grenadines 22.9
Ethiopia 22.5
Guinea 22.5
Dominica 22.1
Burundi 21.7
Democratic Republic of the Congo 21.7
Panama 21.6
Brazil 21.0
Equatorial Guinea 20.7
Guinea-Bissau 20.2
Kenya 20.1
Kyrgyzstan 20.1
Cameroon 19.7
Montserrat 19.7
Greenland 19.2
Angola 19.0
Guyana 18.6
BurkinaFaso18.0
Eritrea 17.8
Moldova 7.5
Kiribati 7.3
Guadeloupe 7.0
Haiti 6.9
Turks and Caicos Islands 8.7
Anguilla 6.8

Antigua and Barbuda 6.8
Lithuania 6.6
Uruguay 5.9
Philippines 5.4
Namibia 17.2
Rwanda 17.1
Mexico16.9
Chad 15.8
Ghana 15.7
Ecuador 15.2
North Korea15.2
Benin 15.1
Sierra Leone 14.9
Mauritania 14.7
Botswana 14.5
Zimbabwe 14.3
Gabon 13.8
Nicaragua 13.6
French Guiana 13.3
Papua New Guinea 13.0
Swaziland 12.9
Bermuda 12.3
Comoros 12.2
Nigeria 12.2
Cape Verde 11.6
Grenada 11.5
Paraguay 11.5
Barbados 11.3
Togo 10.9

Gambia 10.8
Peru 10.8
Myanmar 10.2
Russia 10.2
Liberia 10.1
Costa Rica 10.0
Nauru 9.8
Bolivia 8.9
Mozambique 8.8
Kazakhstan 8.8
Senegal 8.7
Mongolia 8.7
British Virgin Islands 8.6
Cayman Islands 8.4
Seychelles 8.3
Madagascar 8.1
Indonesia 8.1
Mali 8.0
Pakistan 7.8
Ukraine5.2
Estonia 5.2
Cuba 5.0
Belarus 4.9
Thailand 4.8
Suriname .6
Laos 4.6
Georgia 4.3
Martinique 4.2

SWITZERLAND ISSUES EVERY HOUSEHOLD A GUN! SWITZERLAND'S GOVERNMENT TRAINS EVERY ADULT THEY ISSUE EACH A RIFLE.

SWITZERLAND HAS THE LOWEST GUN RELATED CRIME RATE OF ANY CIVILIZED COUNTRY IN THE WORLD!!!

IT'S A NO BRAINER! DON'T LET OUR GOVERNMENT WASTE MILLIONS OF OUR TAX DOLLARS IN AN EFFORT TO MAKE ALL LAW ABIDING CITIZENS AN EASY TARGET.

The United States is 3rd in Murders throughout the World. But if you take Chicago, Detroit, Washington DC and New Orleans - the cities with the strictest gun control laws in the Country - out of the picture, the United States is 3rd from the Bottom on a list of 216 countries for Murders. Chicago , Detroit , Washington DC , and New Orleans, these 4 Cities also have the toughest Gun Control Laws in the United States. All 4 are also controlled by Democrats.

The United States - 4.2!
ALL the 109 countries with higher murder rates than America have 100% gun bans.

All the experts - Mao, Hitler, Stalin, Castro, Idi Amin, Pol Pot, Kim Jong-II, Qaddafi - agree that gun control works. These men were responsible for murdering over 100,000,000 of their own citizens during their reigns of terror.

Take note my fellow Americans, before it's too late! The next time someone talks in favor of gun control, share these fact with them.

"A liberal's paradise would be a place where everybody has guaranteed employment, free comprehensive healthcare, free education, free food, free housing, free clothing, free utilities, and only law enforcement has guns. And believe it or not, such a place does indeed already exist: It's called Prison." Sheriff Joe Arpaio

Obama Administration Reverses Stance The U.N. Arms Treaty

Barack Obama and Hillary Clinton overturned former President George W. Bush's administration policy to keep gun control under U.S. jurisdiction. The Obama administration decided to back U.N. Arms Trade Treaty talks to place all gun control of all countries under U.N. control. Thus Obama and Clinton again violated their oath of office to uphold and defend the Constitution of the United States - in this case the Second Amendment - against all enemies foreign and domestic. They have become the enemy of America.

IT IS WORTHY TO NOTE THAT <u>NOT ONE DEMOCRAT</u> SIGNED THE FOLLOWING LETTER THAT UPHOLDS AND DEFENDS THE CONSTITUTION OF THE UNITED STATES OF AMERICA – A PLEDGE THEY ALL TOOK IN THEIR OATH OF OFFICE.

Monday, July 25, 2011 **Senator Johnny Isakson to Obama Administration: Second Amendment Rights Not Negotiable. Isakson** *joins 44 Senators in Letter Expressing Concerns Over U.N. Arms Trade Treaty* **WASHINGTON, D.C.** – <u>U.S. Senator Johnny Isakson, R-Ga., has joined 44 senators in expressing concern about the dangers posed to Second Amendment rights by</u> **the United Nations' Arms Trade Treaty**.

The 45 senators notified President Obama and Secretary of State Clinton of their intent to oppose ratification of an Arms Trade Treaty that in any way restricts the rights of law-abiding American gun owners. Senator Isakson writes, *"I am deeply concerned that the proposed United Nations' Arms Trade Treaty could threaten the U.S. Constitution's Second Amendment, which protects the sacred right of law-abiding citizens to keep and bear arms,. If the proposed Arms Trade Treaty is presented to the U.S. Senate and if it infringes on the Second Amendment, I will oppose its ratification."*

The letter to Obama was signed by U.S. Senators Lamar Alexander (R-Tenn.), Kelly Ayotte (R-N.H.), John Barrasso (R-Wyo.), Roy Blunt (R-Mo.), John Boozman (R-Ark.), Scott Brown (R-Mass.), Richard Burr (R-N.C.), Dan Coats (R-Ind.), Tom Coburn (R-Okla.), Thad Cochran (R-Miss.), Susan Collins (R-Maine), Bob Corker (R-Tenn.), John Cornyn (R-Texas), Saxby Chambliss (R-Ga.), Mike Crapo (R-Idaho), Jim DeMint (R-S.C.), Mike Enzi (R-Wyo.), Lindsey Graham (R-S.C.), Chuck Grassley (R-Iowa), Orrin Hatch (R-Utah), Dean Heller (R-Nev.), John Hoeven (R-N.D.), Kay Bailey Hutchison (R-Texas), James Inhofe (R-Okla.), Mike Johanns(R-Neb.), Ron Johnson (R-Wis.), Jon Kyl (R-Ariz.), Mike Lee (R-Utah), John McCain (R-Ariz.), Mitch McConnell (R-Ky.), Jerry Moran (R-Kan.), Lisa Murkowski (R-Alaska), Rand Paul (R-Ky.), Rob Portman (R-Ohio), Jim Risch (R-Idaho), Pat Roberts (R-Kan.), Marco Rubio (R-Fla.), Jeff Sessions (R-Ala.), Richard Shelby (R-Ala.), Olympia Snowe (R-Maine), John Thune (R-S.D.), Pat Toomey (R-Pa.), David Vitter (R-La.), and Roger Wicker (R-Miss.).

SENATOR ISAKSON'S LETTER TO OBAMA & CLINTON

July 22, 2011
"President Barack Obama
1600 Pennsylvania Avenue, NW
Washington, D.C. 20500
"Secretary of State Hillary Clinton
2201 C St., NW
Washington, D.C. 20520

"Dear President Obama and Secretary Clinton:

"As defenders of the right of Americans to keep and bear arms, we write to express our grave concern about the dangers posed by the United Nations' Arms Trade Treaty. Our country's sovereignty and the constitutional protection of these individual freedoms must not be infringed.

"In October of 2009 at the U.N. General Assembly, your administration voted for the U.S. to participate in negotiating this treaty. Preparatory committee meetings are now underway in anticipation of a conference in 2012 to finalize the treaty. Based on the process to date, we are concerned that the Arms Trade Treaty poses dangers to rights protected under the Second Amendment for the following reasons.

"First, while the 2009 resolution on the treaty acknowledged the existence of "national constitutional protections on private ownership," it placed the existence of these protections in the context of "the right of States to regulate internal transfers of arms and national ownership," implying that constitutional protections must be interpreted in the context of the broader power of the state to regulate. We are concerned both by the implications of the 2009 resolution and by the hostility to private firearms ownership manifested by similar resolutions in previous years— such as the 2008 resolution, which called for the "highest possible standards" of control.

"Second, your Administration agreed to participate in the negotiation only if it "operates under the rule of consensus decision-making." Given that the 2008 resolution on the treaty was adopted almost unanimously—with only the U.S. and Zimbabwe in opposition—it seems clear that there is a near-consensus on the requirement for the "highest possible standards," which will inevitably put severe pressure on the United States to compromise on important issues.

"Third, U.N. member states regularly argue that no treaty controlling the transfer of arms internationally can be effective without controls on transfers inside member states. Any treaty resulting from the Arms Trade Treaty process that seeks in any way to regulate the domestic manufacture, assembly, possession, transfer, or purchase of firearms, ammunition, and related items would be completely unacceptable to us.

"Fourth, reports from the 2010 Preparatory Meeting make it clear that many U.N. member states aim to craft an extremely broad treaty. A declaration by Mexico and other Central and South American countries, for example, called for the treaty to cover "All types of conventional weapons (regardless of their purpose), including small arms and light weapons, ammunition, components, parts, technology and related materials." Such a broad treaty would be completely unenforceable, and would pose dangers to all U.S. businesses and individuals involved in any aspect of the firearms industry. At the 2010 Meeting, the U.S. representative twice expressed frustration with the wide-ranging and unrealistic scope of the projected treaty. We are concerned that these cautions will not be heeded, and that the Senate will eventually be called upon to consider a treaty that is so broad it cannot effectively be subject to our advice and consent.

"Fifth, and finally, the underlying philosophy of the Arms Trade Treaty is that transfers to and from governments are presumptively legal, while transfers to non-state actors (such as terrorists and criminals) are, at best, problematic. We agree that sales and transfers to criminals and terrorists are unacceptable, but we will oppose any treaty that places the burden of controlling crime and terrorism on law-abiding Americans, instead of where it belongs: on the culpable member states of the United Nations who have failed to take the necessary steps to block trafficking that is already illegal under existing laws and agreements. "As the treaty process continues, we strongly encourage your Administration to uphold our country's constitutional protections of civilian firearms ownership. These freedoms are not negotiable, and we will oppose ratification of an Arms Trade Treaty presented to the Senate that in any way restricts the rights of law-abiding U.S. citizens to manufacture, assemble, possess, transfer or purchase firearms, ammunition, and related items.

Sincerely, Johnny Isakson United States Senator

Senator Isakson's letter had little effect. Consider Hillary Clinton's response to the question – What are your accomplishments as Secretary of State? She responded - *"My accomplishments as Secretary of State? "Well, I'm glad you asked! My proudest accomplishment in which I take the most pride, mostly because of the opposition it faced early on, you know... the remnants of prior situations and mindsets that were too narrowly focused in a manner whereby they may have* overlooked the bigger picture and we didn't do that and I'm proud of that. Very proud. I would say that's a major accomplishment." *Hillary Clinton 11 March 2015.* Hilary's non-answer is typical progressive tactic that avoids facts (since she had no accomplishments) and verbose lawyer-eze intended to impress the listener with language void of substance.

Islam

Sir Winston Churchill delivered the following speech on Islam in 1899.

"How dreadful are the curses which Mohammedanism lays on its votaries! Besides the fanatical frenzy, which is as dangerous in a man as hydrophobia in a dog, there is this fearful fatalistic apathy. The effects are apparent in many countries, improvident habits, slovenly systems of agriculture, sluggish methods of commerce, and insecurity of property exist wherever the followers of the Prophet rule or live. A degraded sensualism deprives this life of its grace and refinement, the next of its dignity and sanctity. The fact that in Mohammedan law every woman must belong to some man as his absolute property, either as a child, a wife, or a concubine, must delay the final extinction of slavery until the faith of Islam has ceased to be a great power among men. Individual Muslims may show splendid qualities, but the influence of the religion paralyses the social development of those who follow it. No stronger retrograde force exists in the world. Far from being moribund, Mohammedanism is a militant and proselytizing faith."
Sir Winston Churchill; (Source: The River War, first edition, Vol II, pages 248-250 London).

Brigitte Gabriel shares first-hand experience with what most of us in the west have little or no first-hand knowledge. Her first-hand knowledge is more credible than our second-hand knowledge. Below are excerpts from Brigitte's speech delivered at the Intelligence Summit in Washington DC., used with permission.

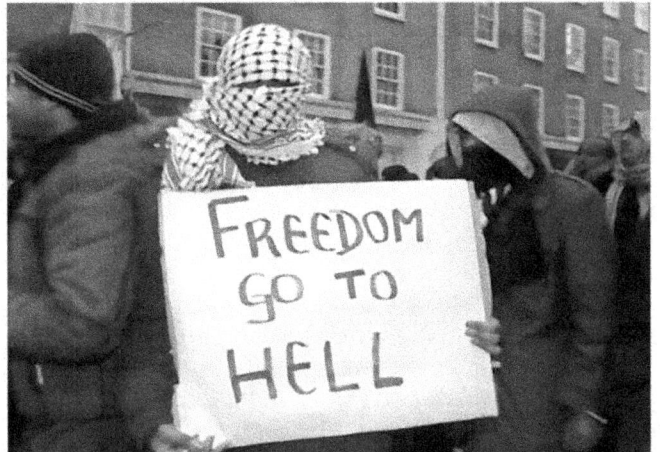

"The most important element of intelligence has to understand the mindset and intention of the enemy. The West has been wallowing in a state of ignorance and denial for thirty years as Muslim extremist perpetrated evil against innocent victims in the name of Allah.

"I was ten years old when my home exploded around me, burying me under the rubble and leaving me to drink my blood to survive, as the perpetrators shouted, "Allah Akbar!" My only crime was that I was a Christian living in a Christian town. At 10 years old, I learned the meaning of the word "infidel."

'I had a crash course in survival in a bomb shelter where I lived for seven years in pitch darkness, freezing cold, drinking stale water and eating grass to live. At the age of 13, dressed in my burial

clothes going to bed at night, waiting to be slaughtered. By the age of 20, I had buried most of my friends--killed by Muslims. We were Arab Christians living in Lebanon.

"As a victim of Islamic terror, I was amazed when I saw Americans waking up on September 12, 2001, and asking themselves "Why do they hate us?"

The psychoanalyst experts were coming up with all sort of excuses as to what did we do to offend the Muslim World. Simply put, they hate us because we are defined in their eyes by one simple word: "infidels."

"Under the banner of Islam "la, ilaha illa Allah, muhammad rasoulu Allah," (None is god except Allah; Muhammad is the Messenger of Allah) they murdered Jewish children in Israel , massacred Christians in Lebanon, killed Copts in Egypt, Assyrians in Syria, Hindus in India, and expelled almost 900,000 Jews from Muslim lands. We Middle Eastern infidels paid the price then. Now infidels worldwide are paying the price for indifference and shortsightedness.

"Tolerating evil is a crime. Appeasing murderers doesn't buy protection. It earns disrespect and loathing in the enemy's eyes. Yet apathy is the weapon by which the West is committing suicide. Political correctness forms the shackles around our ankles, by which Islamists are leading us to our demise.

"America and the West are doomed to failure in this war unless they stand up and identify the real enemy: Islam. You hear about Wahabbi and Salafi Islam as the only extreme form of Islam. All the other Muslims, supposedly, are wonderful moderates. Closer to the truth are the pictures of the irrational eruption of violence in reaction to the cartoons of Mohammed printed by a Danish newspaper. From burning embassies, to calls to butcher those who mock Islam, to warnings that the West be prepared for another holocaust, those pictures have given us a glimpse into the real face of the enemy. News pictures and video of these events represent a canvas of hate decorated by different nationalities who share one common ideology of hate, bigotry and intolerance derived from one source: authentic Islam. An Islam that is awakening from centuries of slumber to re-ignite its wrath against the infidel and dominate the world. An Islam which has declared "Intifada" on the West.

"America and the West can no longer afford to lay in their lazy state of overweight ignorance. The consequences of this mental disease are starting to attack the body, and if they don't take the necessary steps now to control it, death will be knocking soon. If you want to understand the nature of the enemy we face, visualize a tapestry of snakes. They slither and they hiss, and they would eat each other alive, but they will unite in a hideous mass to achieve their common goal of imposing Islam on the world.

"This is the ugly face of the enemy we are fighting. We are fighting a powerful ideology that is capable of altering basic human instinct; an ideology that can turn a mother into a launching pad of death. A perfect example is a recently elected Hamas official in the Palestinian Territories who raves in heavenly joy about sending her three sons to death and offering the ones who are still alive for the cause. It is an ideology that is capable of offering highly educated individuals such as doctors and lawyers far more joy in attaining death than any respect and stature life in society is ever capable of giving them.

"The United States has been a prime target for radical Islamic hatred and terror. Every Friday, mosques in the Middle East ring with shrill prayers and monotonous chants calling death, destruction and damnation down on America and its people. The radical Islamist deeds have been as vile as their words. Since the Iran hostage crisis, more than three thousand Americans have

died in a terror campaign almost unprecedented in its calculated cruelty along with thousands of other citizens worldwide.

"Even the Nazis did not turn their own children into human bombs, and then rejoice at their deaths as well the deaths of their victims. This intentional, indiscriminate and wholesale murder of innocent American citizens is justified and glorified in the name of Islam.

"America cannot effectively defend itself in this war unless and until the American people understand the nature of the enemy that we face. Even after 9/11 there are those who say that we must engage our terrorist enemies, that we must address their grievances. Their grievance is our freedom of religion. Their grievance is our freedom of speech. Their grievance is our democratic process where the rule of law comes from the voices of many not that of just one prophet. It is the respect we instill in our children towards all religions. It is the equality we grant each other as human beings sharing a planet and striving to make the world a better place for all humanity. Their grievance is the kindness and respect a man shows a woman, the justice we practice as equals under the law, and the mercy we grant our enemy. Their grievance cannot be answered by an apology for who or what we are.

"The mediocre attitude of not confronting Islamic forces of bigotry and hatred wherever they raised their ugly head in the last 30 years, has empowered and strengthened our enemy to launch a full scale attack on the very freedoms we cherish in their effort to impose their values and way of life on our civilization.

"If we don't wake up to take action against the terrorists within, if we don't believe in ourselves as Americans and in the standards we should hold every patriotic American to, we are going to pay a price for our delusion. For the sake of our children and our country, we must wake up and take action. In the face of a torrent of hateful invective and terrorist murder, America's learning curve since the Iran hostage crisis is so shallow that it is almost flat. The longer we lay supine, the more difficult it will be to stand erect."

"Our society tends to think that others think as we do. Fact is most countries do not understand our freedoms and religious values. The Bible speaks of the spiritual warfare that is always going on. The Muslim religion believes the spiritual and physical warfare are one and the same.

"President Obama said that the United States is not a Christian nation. He went on to say that in this country all religions are welcome. While his intention may have been to show that we are a tolerant country and do not have a state sponsored religion, his comments are basically false. This country was founded on Christian principles. If you go back to the early writings of our founding fathers you will see references to God, The Bible, and Christianity. 86% of US Citizens are registered as Christians.

"Barack Obama stated in Turkey that "THE UNITED STATES IS NOT AND NEVER WILL BE AT WAR WITH ISLAM." If we are not at war with the violent religion of Islam, just who blew down our twin towers in NYC on 911 and are killing our soldiers every day?

"Over the years, I have tried to warn people about the violent Religion of Islam. The ones that unknowingly try to argue that the terrorists have high-jacked a peaceful religion and are using it for their terror, do not know the back-ground of this religion nor how it came to conquer a great portion of the ancient world as we know it and held it for hundreds of years. The ones that are spreading their religion throughout the world today through every means possible are the ones that are trying to follow the Quran to the letter. They are the true epitome of the Islam Religion as it started out to be and as it was taught and still is taught in the Quran.

"Our ignorance of this religion is going to destroy us sooner than later. We had better wake up as a nation, as a peace loving people, as a people that believe in the Lord Jesus Christ as the Son of God, and start studying about Islam. Its intentions now, as it has had for over 1400 years, to destroy all people that are not members of the Islam religion.

Islam is a religion of hate. *"America has been infiltrated on all levels by radicals who wish to harm America," she said. "They have infiltrated us at the C.I.A., at the F.B.I., at the Pentagon, at the State Department. They are being radicalized in radical mosques in our cities and communities within the United States."* (Brigitte Gabriel, Fort Worth speech, March 2011)

From Brigitte Gabriel's book, <u>Because They Hate *"Why We Must Defeat Radical Islam And How We Can Do It*"</u>., by St. Martin's Griffin, 175 Fifth Ave., New York, N.Y. 10010. *"Fundamentalist Islam is a religion rooted in seventh-century teachings that are fundamentally opposed to democracy and equality. Radical Islamists are utterly contemptuous of all 'infidels' (non-Muslims) and regard them as enemies worthy of death. Madrassas (schools) in America are increasing in number, and they are just one part of a growing radical Islamic army on U.S. soil. Radical Islam exploits the U.S. legal system and America's protection of religion to spread its hatred for Western values. America must organize a unified voice that says 'enough' to political correctness, and demands that government officials and elected representatives do whatever is necessary to protect us."*

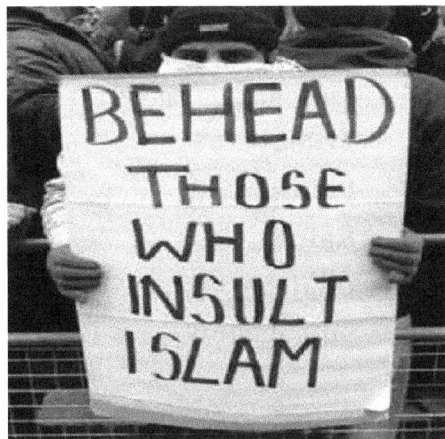

History reveals that good civilized people cannot fathom, much less predict, the actions of evil people like Hitler, Hirohito and Bin Laden.

On September 11, scores of capable airplane passengers allowed themselves to be overpowered by a few poorly armed terrorists because they did not comprehend their depth of hatred. The Clinton administration equipped Islamic terrorists and their supporters with the world's most sophisticated telecommunications equipment and encryption technology, thereby compromising America's ability to trace terrorist radio, cell phone, land lines, faxes and modem communications. British Prime Minister Tony Blair told the Labor Party conference, *"They [Islamic terrorists] have no moral inhibition on the slaughter of the innocent. If they could have murdered not 7,000 but 70,000, does anyone doubt they would have done so and rejoiced in it? There is no compromise possible with such people, no meeting of minds, no point of understanding with such terror. Just a choice: defeat it or be defeated by it. And defeat it we must!"*

Following is a statement made by Omar Ahmad, co-founder of the (CAIR) Council On American-Islamic Relations:

"Islam isn't in America to be equal to any other faiths, but to become dominant. The Koran, the Muslim book of scripture, should be the highest authority in America, and Islam the only accepted religion on Earth." *Muslims "can never be full citizens of this country," referring to the United States, "because there is no way we can be fully committed to the institutions and ideologies of this country."*

The Five Principles Of Islam

Islam's Trilogy of three sacred texts is the Koran and two books about the life of Mohammed. When the Trilogy is sorted, categorized, arranged, rewritten and analyzed, it becomes apparent that five principles are the foundation of Islam. Islam is based upon the Trilogy—Koran, Sira (Mohammed's biography) and Hadith (his Traditions).

Islamic doctrine is primarily political, not religious. Islam is a political ideology. Islam divides the world into Muslims and unbelievers called kafirs.

Kafirs can be abused in the worst ways or they can be treated like a good neighbor. Kafirs must submit to Islam in all politics and public life. Kafirs must submit to political Islam.

These Five Principles can be put in five words:

> **Trilogy**
>
> **Politics**
>
> **Kafirs**
>
> **Dualism**
>
> **Submission**

The Five Principles:

Trilogy

The Trilogy contains three books— the Koran, Sira and Hadith.

The Koran is what Mohammed said that the angel Gabriel said that Allah said. The Koran says that all of the world should imitate Mohammed. Mohammed's words and deeds are called the Sunna. The Sunna is found in two different texts—the Sira and Hadith. The first source of Sunna is the Sira; Mohammed's biography. The second source of the Sunna is the Hadith, Mohammed's Traditions.

Political Islam

Political Islam is the doctrine about the kafir. A Muslim is strictly forbidden to have any religious interaction with kafirs. The religion of Islam is what is required for a Muslim to avoid Hell and enter Paradise. The Koran has 61% of its text devoted to the kafir. The Sira (Mohammed's biography) has about 75% of its text devoted to the kafir and jihad.

The Trilogy advocates religious superiority over kafirs. Kkafirs go to Hell. Muslims go to Paradise. Islamic doctrine demands that Muslims dominate kafirs in all politics and culture.

Islam's success comes primarily from its politics. Mohammed only converted 150 people to Islam in 13 years. Yet when he became a political leader and warrior, Islam exploded in growth, and Mohammed became king of Arabia in ten years.

Kafirs

Non-believers, Christians, Jews, atheists, polytheists, and pagans are called infidels or kafirs. Kafirs are the lowest and worst form of life. Kafirs can be robbed, murdered, tortured, enslaved, crucified and more. Kafirs are not only a non-Muslim, but also a person who falls under a different moral code from the Muslim.

Dualism

Duality of truth is unique to Islam. For example, Koran: 109:2 "I do not worship what you worship, and you do not worship what I worship. I will never worship what you worship, and you will never worship what I worship. You to your moral law, me mine." This verse indicates tolerance for religious preference.

Compare that to the following: Koram 9:5 "When the sacred months are passed, kill the kafirs wherever you find them. Take them as captives, besiege them, and lie in wait for them with every kind of ambush. If they submit to Islam, observe prayer, and pay the poor tax, then let them go their way. Allah is gracious and merciful." That verse is absolute intolerance.

This contradiction is normal in the Koran. The Muslim solution to contradiction is to give preference to the later dated verse. Thus, both contradictory verses are true, but the later verse is better or stronger.

Submission

Islam means submission to the will of God. Muslim means one who submits to God. Submission is political, as well as religious. Islam demands that kafirs submit in every aspect of public life. Every part of kafir culture is an offense to Allah.

The author is aware of the English interpretation and explanation of the Koran [AKA Quran]. Interpreters point out that the Quran is often mis-understood and that it is a benign set of beliefs. However, there is a revealing test that the Lord suggested to judge in Matthew 7: 15-20. *"Beware of false prophets, which come to you in sheep's clothing, but inwardly they are ravening wolves. Ye shall know them by their fruits. ...Even so every good tree bringeth forth good fruit; but a corrupt tree bringeth forth devil fruit. A good tree cannot bring forth evil fruit, neither can a corrupt tree bring forth good fruit. Every tree that bringeth not forth good fruit is hewn down, and cast into the fire. Wherefore by their fruits ye shall know them."*

The past 40+ years of terrorist murders and thousands of 'infidel' rapes have been committed predominately by 17-40 Muslim men, using the Koran as justification for these barbaric acts. These are bitter fruits of Islam.

Radical Islam, like communism, seeks the destruction of the liberty of all mankind and establishing a global Caliphate (Islamic government under Sharia law).

If there is a peace loving majority contingent of Muslims, where is their outrage against the radical Muslims, terrorists, and jihadists?

Islamization

Islam is a system of religious, legal, political, economic, social & military life. Islamization of countries occurs in stages depending on the percent of Muslim population.

Based upon other nations experience, the stages of Islamization are summarized as follows:

When Muslim population is under 2% - Muslims are peace loving minority.

When Muslim population is 2-5% - Muslims proselytize and recruit from disaffected groups, outcasts, minorities, jails and street gangs.

When Muslim population exceeds 5% - Muslims exercise inordinate influence on the population. They force halal (Muslim standard food) in schools, supermarkets etc. with threats for compliance failure. They try to persuade the government to allow Muslim groups to rule themselves under Sharia law.

When Muslim population reaches 10% - Muslims increase lawlessness to complain about their circumstances, like we see in France and the Netherlands; car bombings, arson, uprisings, intimidation, beatings etc.

When Muslim population reaches 20% - Muslims engage in rioting, jihad violence, killings, burning Christian and Jewish houses of assembly like in Ethiopia, Egypt. All under the governance of the Muslim Brotherhood.

When Muslim population reaches 40% - Muslims engage in widespread massacres, terrorist attacks, militia jihad.

When Muslim population reaches 60% - Muslims persecute kafirs, engage in ethnic cleansing like we saw in Bosnia.

When Muslim population reaches 80% - Muslims engage in daily intimidation and more widespread jihad, genocide, ethnic cleansing to remove infidels and create a 100% Muslim population, like in Bangladesh, Egypt, Pakistan, Libya, Syria, Palestine and the UAE.

When Muslim population reaches 100% - they claim it will enter a time of peace. However a glance at Afghanistan , Saudi Arabia, Somalia, and Yemen reveals this is not true. In these 100% Muslim states the most radical Muslims are freer to intimidate, hate and kill unabated.

Muslims do not integrate into the community. The children attend madrassas. They learn only the Koran and are not free to read other religious books. To even associate with an infidel is a crime punishable with death.

Muslim Imams and extremists exercise extraordinary power over their subjects. Currently 1.5 billion Muslims make up 22% of the world's population. Their birth rates dwarf the birth rates of Christians, Hindus, Buddhists, Jews, and all other believers. At the current rate of growth, Muslims will exceed 50% of the world's population by the end of this century.

Obama appointed two Muslims - Arif Alikhan, as Assistant Secretary for Policy Development and Kareem Shora, as ADC National Executive Director as a member of the Homeland Security Advisory Council (HSAC).

A reasonable question is 'Can a good Muslim be a good American'?

Theologically - no . . . because his allegiance is to Allah, The moon God of Arabia

Religiously – no... because no other religion is accepted by His Allah except Islam (Quran, 2:256)(Koran)

Scripturally - no... because his allegiance is to the five Pillars of Islam and the Quran.

Geographically – no... because his allegiance is to Mecca, to which he turns in prayer five times a day.

Socially - no... because his allegiance to Islam forbids him to make friends with Christians or Jews.

Politically - no...because he must submit to the mullahs (spiritual leaders), who teach annihilation of Israel and destruction of America, the great Satan.

Domestically - no... because he is instructed to marry four Women and beat and scourge his wife when she disobeys him (Quran 4:34)

Intellectually - no... because he cannot accept the American Constitution since it is based on Biblical principles and he believes the Bible to be corrupt.

Philosophically - no... because Islam, Muhammad, and the Quran do not allow freedom of religion and expression. Democracy and Islam cannot co-exist. Every Muslim government is either dictatorial or autocratic.

Spiritually - no... because when we declare 'one nation under God,' the Christian's God is loving and kind, while Allah is NEVER referred to as Heavenly father, nor is he ever called love in The Quran's 99 excellent names.

Can a Muslim be a good American soldier? Fort Hood's 'Allah Akbar' slaughter ring a bell?

When WWIII Started - 1979

"And ye shall hear of wars and rumours of wars: see that ye be not troubled: for all these things must come to pass, but the end is not yet. " Matthew 24:6

World War III began in November 1979...

November 1979 - a group of Iranian students attacked and seized the American Embassy in Tehran. They held America hostage and paralyzed a Presidency. The attack on this sovereign U.S. Embassy set the stage for events to follow for the next 25 years. Shortly after this attack, Americans began to be kidnapped and killed throughout the Middle East.

April 1983 – The US Embassy in Beirut was attacked. 63 people died.

October 1983 - The US Marine Corps headquarters in Beirut was attacked when a large truck heavily laden down with over 2,500 pounds of TNT. 241 US servicemen are killed.

December 1983 - The US Embassy in Kuwait was attacked when a truck loaded with explosives.

September 1984 - The US Embassy in Beirut was attacked when a van loaded with explosives.

April 1985 - A restaurant patronized by US soldiers in Madrid was attacked when a bomb exploded.

August 1985 - The US Air Force Base at Rheine-Main was attacked when a Volkswagen loaded with explosives was crashed through the front gate. 22 are killed.

October 1985 - The cruise ship Achille Lauro is hijacked. An American in a wheelchair is singled out of the passenger list and executed.

April of 1986 - Terrorists bombing civilian airliner TWA Flight 840 in that killed 4. They also bomb Pan Am Flight 103 over Lockerbie , Scotland in 1988, killing 259.

January 1993 - Two CIA agents are killed as they enter CIA headquarters in Langley, Virginia.

February 1993 - A group of terrorists drive a rented van packed with explosives into the underground parking garage of the World Trade Center in New York City. Six people are killed and over 1000 are injured.

November 1995 - A car bomb explodes at a US military complex in Riyadh., Saudi Arabia. Seven service men and women die.

June of 1996 - The US military compound in Dhahran, Saudi Arabia is attacked when a truck bomb explodes. 19 dead. 500 injured. Then simultaneous attacks occur on two US embassies in Kenya and Tanzania. They kill 224.

October 2000 - The USS Cole was attacked in the port of Aden, Yemen when a rubber raft pulled alongside the ship and exploded. 17 US Navy Sailors die. Attacking a US War Ship is an act of war, but we sent the FBI to investigate the crime.

11 September 2001 – Who can forget this day? America's weak response to the past terrorist attacks in met with the murder of 3,000 innocent Americans in the World Trade Center, The Pentagon, and United Flight 93 that was crashed into the ground in Pennsylvania.

We have been at war with terrorists for the past 34 years. The terrorists have all been Muslim males between 17-40 years old.

Abdul Samad, a militant Pakistani cleric speaking of Islamic rules for relationships with non-Muslims stated, *"Enmity towards infidels is a must. Those who do not believe in Allah – even if they are relatives – are foes. Jews, Christians and atheists are enemies of Islam. Jihad is needed in order to get rid of infidels and spread Islam worldwide. Our friendship, relationship and love should only be with the people who believe in Islam and Allah as the ruler. People who do not accept Allah as the ruler and do not believe in Islam are our enemy. Infidels can never be our friends. Enmity towards infidels is a must. It is part of our faith. The best way to get rid of them (infidels) is to continue jihad until the Allah's faith (Islam) is completely enforced all over the world."*

What is Muslim terrorist goal? Their posters carried at rallies tell it all: The credo of the Muslim Brotherhood is: *"God is our purpose, the Prophet our leader, the Qur'an our constitution, Jihad our way and dying for God's cause our supreme objective."*

A Rabbi's Muslim Perspective

The following are excerpts by a rabbi in a widely published sermon (used with permission):

"We are at war with an enemy as savage, as voracious, as heartless as the Nazis.

"During WWII we didn't refer to storm troopers as freedom fighters. We didn't call the Gestapo, militants. We didn't see the attacks on our Merchant Marine as acts by rogue sailors. We did not justify the Nazis rise to power as our fault. We did not grovel before the Nazis, thumping our hearts and confessing to abusing and mistreating and humiliating the German people. We did not apologize for Dresden, or for The Battle of the Bulge, nor for El Alamein, nor for D-Day.

"Evil – ultimate, irreconcilable, evil threatened us and Roosevelt and Churchill had moral clarity and an exquisite understanding of what was at stake. It was the entire planet.

"Not all Germans were Nazis - most were decent, most were revolted by the Third Reich, most were good citizens hoisting a beer, earning a living and tucking in their children at night. But, too

many looked away, too many cried out in lame defense – I didn't know." Too many were silent. Guilt absolutely falls upon those who committed the atrocities, but responsibility and guilt falls upon those who did nothing as well.

"In WWII we won because we got it. We understood who the enemy was and we knew that the end had to be unconditional and absolute. We did not stumble around worrying about offending the Nazis. We did not measure every word so as not to upset our foe. We built planes and tanks and battleships and went to war to win.

"We are at war... yet too many ...are disgracefully 'politically correct'.

"The murderers, the barbarians are radical Islamists. To camouflage their identity is sedition. To excuse their deeds is contemptible. To mask their intentions is unconscionable.

"It is not the 1930s. There is no Luftwaffe overhead. No U-boats off the coast of long Island. No Panzer divisions on our borders. But make no mistake; we are under attack – our values, our tolerance, our freedom, our virtue, our land.

"I have no bone of bigotry in my body, but what I do have is hatred for those who hate, intolerance for those who are intolerant, and a guiltless, unstoppable obsession to see evil eradicated.

"Today the enemy is radical Islam but it must be said sadly and reluctantly that there are unwitting, co-conspirators who strengthen the hands of the evil doers. Let me state that the overwhelming number of Muslims are good Muslims, fine human beings ...but these good Muslims have an obligation to destiny, to decency that thus far for the most part they have avoided. The good Muslims must sponsor rallies in Times Square, in Trafalgar Square, in the UN Plaza, on the Champs Elysee, in Mecca condemning terrorism, denouncing unequivocally the slaughter of the innocent. Thus far, they have not. The good Muslims must place ads in the NY Times. They must buy time on network TV, on cable stations, in the Jerusalem Post, in Le Monde, in Al Watan, on Al Jazeera condemning terrorism, denouncing unequivocally the slaughter of the innocent – thus far, they have not. Their silence allows the vicious to tarnish Islam and define it. Brutal acts of commission and yawning acts of omission both strengthen the hand of the devil.

"Radical Islam is the scourge and this must be cried out from every mountain top. From sea to shining sea, we must stand tall, prideful of our stunning decency and moral resilience. Immediately after 9/11 how many mosques were destroyed in America? None. After 9/11, how many Muslims were killed in America? None. After 9/11, how many anti-Muslim rallies were held in America? None. And yet, we [Obama] apologize[s]. We grovel. We beg forgiveness.

"The mystifying litany of our foolishness continues. Should there be a German cultural center in Auschwitz? Should there be a thirteen-story mosque and Islamic Center only a few steps from Ground Zero?

[The real battle is between good and evil.]

"Moral confusion is a deadly weakness and it has reached epic proportions in the West; from the Oval Office to the UN.

"Hypocrisy is the only evil that walks invisible."

"The only country in the entire Middle East where gay rights exist is Israel. The only country in the entire Middle East where there is a gay pride parade is Israel. The only country in the Middle East that has gay neighborhoods and gay bars is Israel.

"Gays in the Gaza would be strung up, executed by Hamas if they came out and yet Israel is vilified and ostracized. [Is this not hypocristy?]

"Isaiah warned us thousands of years ago – " Woe to them who call the day, night and the night, day."

"We live on a planet that is .. a frightening and maddening place to be...[and is under] a full throttled attack by unholy, radical Islamists on everything that is morally precious to us.

"Everything we are. Everything we believe. Everything we treasure is at risk. The threat is so unbelievably clear and the enemy so unbelievably ruthless how anyone in their right mind doesn't get it is baffling.

"Let's try an analogy. If someone contracted a life-threatening infection and we not only scolded them for using antibiotics but insisted that the bacteria had a right to infect their body and that perhaps, if we gave the invading infection an arm and a few toes, the bacteria would be satisfied and stop spreading "Anyone buy that medical advice? Well, folks, that is our approach to the radical Islamist bacteria. It is amoral, has no conscience, and will spread unless it is eradicated. – There is no negotiating. Appeasement is death.

"I was no great fan of George Bush – didn't vote for him. (By the way, I'm still a registered Democrat.) I disagreed with many of his policies but one thing he had right. His moral clarity was flawless when it came to the War on Terror, the War on Radical Islamist Terror. There was no middle ground– either you were friend or foe. There was no place in Bush's world for a Switzerland. He knew that this competition was not Toyota against G.M., not the I-phone against the Droid, not the Braves against the Phillies, but a deadly serious war, winner take all. Blink and you lose. Underestimate and you get crushed."

Current Radical Muslim Tactics

It is now more than 60 years after World War II in Europe ended. In memory of the 20 million Russians, 10 million Christians, 6 million Jews and 1,900 Catholic priests who were murdered, massacred, raped, burned and starved with many of the world's people looking the other way!

Now, more than ever, with <u>extremist Muslims claiming the Holocaust to be 'a myth,'</u> it's imperative to make sure the world never forgets the truth.

When the Supreme Commander of the Allied Forces, General Dwight Eisenhower, found the victims of the death camps he ordered all possible photographs to be taken, and for the German people from surrounding villages to be ushered through the camps and even made to bury the dead.

General Dwight D. Eisenhower Warned Us - he said in words to this effect: <u>'Get it all on record now - get the films - get the witnesses -because somewhere down the road of history some bastard will get up and say that this never happened.'</u>

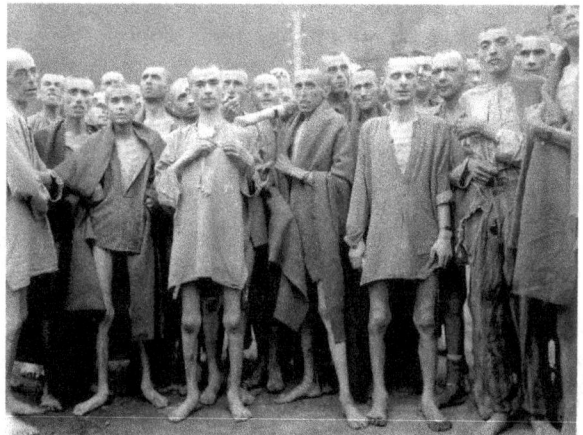

Recently, the UK debated whether to remove The Holocaust from its school curriculum because it 'offends' the Muslim population which claims it never occurred.

This is a frightening portent of the fear that is gripping the world and how easily each country is giving into it.

FREEDOM ISN'T FREE...

SOMEONE HAD TO PAY FOR IT.......

How many years will it be before the attack on the World Trade Center 'NEVER HAPPENED', because it offends some Muslim in the U.S.???

Already Muslim clerics are telling their followers that Americans were responsible for 9.11, that it was an inside job and the Muslims were framed for it.

These Muslim clerics are behaving like Satan who immediately after a significant spiritual event, spreads lies to discredit it. The Nazis did the same during and after the holocaust.

Muslim Integration In Society?

Frosty Wooldridge, author of America on the Brink: The Next Added 100 Million Americans, writes:

"Muslims do not and cannot meld into host countries. It's against every tenant of their religion.

"In May, 2010, a report surfaced in Norway whereby 85 percent of all rapes and violent crimes stemmed from that country's recent importation of 500,000 Muslim immigrants. The imams in Norway ran wild in the streets with shouts of racism and prejudice. They could not discount the facts as presented by the police, but they 'worked' the emotions of Muslims into a frenzy. Still the 85 percent rape numbers continue.

"Iranian writer Amil Imani, Islam Must Be Stopped In America, July 14, 2010, said, "Warning: Islam is not a religion but a political ideology which incites hate, violence, intolerance and terror. Islamists are terminators. You cannot bargain with them. You cannot reason with them. They do not feel pity or remorse, or fear. And they absolutely will not stop, ever, until all the infidels are dead or have submitted to Islam. The only language the Islamists understand is the language of force.

"A constitutional amendment must be passed quickly defining Islam as a hostile political force with a global totalitarian agenda, and as such is totally inimical to our constitution and our national security, and that further to this definition, all practicing Muslims must either renounce this cult or be deported to their countries of origin, and all mosques must be demolished, since their goal is to propagate political propaganda, which has nothing whatsoever to do with 'religion' - let alone one of 'peace'. That's going to be the final 'solution' for Islam in America."

Yusuf Al-Qaradawi

Al-Qaradawi is a radical Muslim Brotherhood ideologue who repeatedly demonstrated consistent support of terrorist groups that seek to undermine a peaceful resolution of the Palestinian-Israeli conflict. A Muslim Iman broadcast on Al Jazeera, which has an estimated audience of 60 million worldwide. Al-Qaradawi has long had a prominent role within the intellectual leadership of the Muslim Brotherhood.

In January 1998, the Associated Press quoted al-Qaradawi as writing, *"There should be no dialogue with these people [Israelis] except with swords."* And in April 2001, commenting on suicide bombings, he said, *"They are not suicide operations...These are heroic martyrdom operations. Apostates from Islam*, said al-Qaradawi in a June 2002 fatwa, *are no more than a traitor to his religion and his people and thus deserves killing."*

Qaradawi stated *"I will shoot Allah's enemies, the Jews, and they will throw a bomb at me, and thus I will seal my life with martyrdom."* And *"Oh Allah, take this oppressive, Jewish, Zionist band of people...do not spare a single one of them. Oh Allah, count their numbers, and kill them, down to the very last one." I support Hamas, the Islamic Jihad, and Hezbollah. I oppose the peace that Israel and America wish to dictate. This peace is an illusion. I support martyrdom operations."*

The Quran contains at least 109 verses that call Muslims to war with nonbelievers for the sake of Islamic rule. Unlike nearly all of the Old Testament verses of violence the verses of violence in the Quran are mostly open-ended, meaning that they are not restrained by the historical context of the surrounding text. They are part of the eternal, unchanging word of Allah.

The problem is not bad people, but bad ideology.

12th Imam, Ahmadinejad, And The Antichrist

Mahmoud Ahmadinejad, the ultra-radical Islamic former president of Iran, expressed his intent to cause chaos on the earth in order to usher in the 12th Imam (al-Mahdi). According to Islam,

Al Mahdi is said to be joined by Jesus at Mecca. The Mahdi will instruct the restored prophet Jesus to pray properly, and Jesus will then instruct his mistaken followers to acknowledge and submit to Allah and Mohammed as his prophet.

By many accounts, Ahmadinejad and his circle of "Twelver Shia Muslims" (followers of the 12th Imam) are in an apocalyptic mood. The use of nuclear weapons would not bother them. Iran claims to have nuclear capability.

Ahmadinejad says Israel is the little Satan, and America is the anti-Christ, the great Satan. In Muslim belief, a leader will reign 72 months (6 years) before the return of their Mahdi (their messiah). Ahmadinejad says he has been selected by the 12th Imam to be that leader. As of spring 2011 Ahmadinejad has reigned 60 months (5 years). Ahmadinejad says his role is to bathe the world in blood to hasten the return of the Mahdi.

Dhimmitude

Dhimmitude is medical exemption. Obama allows it in Obamacare. Dhimmitude is on page 107 of the healthcare bill. Muslims are exempt ...ARE EXEMPT ...from the requirements of Obamacare.

Dhimmitude is the Muslim system of controlling non-Muslim populations conquered through jihad. Specifically, it is the TAXING of non-Muslims in exchange for tolerating their presence AND as a coercive means of converting conquered remnants to Islam.

Obamacare allows the establishment of Dhimmitude and Sharia Muslim diktat in the United States. Muslims are specifically exempted from the government mandate to purchase insurance, and also from the penalty tax for being uninsured. Islam considers insurance to be "gambling", "risk-taking", and "usury" and is thus banned. Muslims are specifically granted exemption based on this belief.

How convenient. Christians will have crippling IRS liens placed against all their assets, including real estate, cattle, and even accounts receivables, and will face hard prison time because they refuse to buy insurance or pay the penalty tax. Meanwhile, Louis Farrakhan will have no such penalty and will have 100% of his health needs paid for by the de facto government insurance. Non-Muslims will be paying a tax to subsidize Muslims. Period. This is Dhimmitude.

Dhimmitude serves two purposes: It enriches the Muslim masters AND serves to drive conversions to Islam. In this case, the incentive to convert to Islam will be taken up by those in the inner-cities as well as the godless Generation X, Y, and Z types who have no moral anchor.

And some still believe Obama is a Christian!

The Muslim Brotherhood

The Muslim Brotherhood has ties and origins from Nazi Germany. Due to recent exposure of who they really are – wolves in sheep's clothing – they changed their name to "The Party for Freedom and Justice". They are really anything BUT for freedom and justice. They foment chaos to gain control and enslave people under sharia law. They are the mother of Hamas, Hezbollah and Al-Qaida. This group acts like Acorn, who when they were exposed for evil activities, just change their name and operate under a host of other names funded by our tax dollars. Their modus operandi has not changed – just their name.

Al-Takeyya

The word "al-Taqiyya" literally means: "Concealing or disguising one's beliefs, convictions, ideas, feelings, opinions, and/or strategies at a time of eminent danger, whether now or later in time, to save oneself from physical and/or mental injury."

Muslim activists quote passages of the Qu'ran from the early part of Mohammed's ministry while living in Mecca. These texts are peaceful and exemplify tolerance towards those that are not followers of Islam. However, these passages were replaced by his writings after he migrated to Medina. In Median Mohammed's views changed to include prejudice, intolerance, and endorse violence upon unbelievers.

The Arabic word, "Takeyya", means "to prevent," or guard against. The principle of Al Takeyya conveys the understanding that Muslims are permitted to lie as a preventive measure against anticipated harm to one's self or fellow Muslims. This principle gives Muslims the liberty to lie under circumstances that they perceive as life threatening. They can even deny the faith, if they do not mean it in their hearts. Al-Takeyya is based on the following Quranic verse:

"Let not the believers Take for friends or helpers Unbelievers rather than believers: if any do that, in nothing will there be help from Allah: except by way of precaution (prevention), that ye may Guard yourselves from them (prevent them from harming you.) But Allah cautions you (To remember) Himself; for the final goal is to Allah." Surah 3: 28

According to this verse a Muslim can pretend to befriend infidels (in violation of the teachings of Islam) and display adherence with their unbelief to prevent them from harming him.

Under the concept of Takeyya and short of killing another human being, if under the threat of force, it is legitimate for Muslims to act contrary to their faith. The following actions are acceptable:

- Drink wine, abandon prayers, and skip fasting during Ramadan.
- Renounce belief in Allah.
- Kneel in homage to a deity other than Allah.
- Utter insincere oaths.

From the Hadith- *"One of Mohammed's daughters (Umm Kalthoum) stated that she never heard him condone or promote lying except under three specific situations: To reconcile the people of Islam; In times of war against the infidels; To a spouse to keep harmony within a family."*

Unfortunately, when dealing with Muslims, one must keep in mind that Muslims can communicate something with apparent sincerity, when in reality they may have just the opposite agenda in their hearts. Bluntly stated, Islam permits Muslims to lie anytime that they perceive that their own well-being, or that of Islam, is threatened.

Consider how Islamic al-Taqiyya loopholes compare with God's Commandment - *"Thou shalt not bear false witness against thy neighbour." Ex 20:16*

Islamic State (ISIS)

The Islamic State, also known as the Islamic State of Iraq and al-Sham (ISIS), follows a distinctive variety of Islam whose beliefs about the path to the Day of Judgment. Some say ISIS is the son of Al-Qaeda. ISIS is a State whereas Al-Qaeda was a state-less jihadist movement. Al-Qaeda can survive, cockroach-like, by going underground. The Islamic State cannot. If ISIS loses its grip on its territory in Syria and Iraq, it will cease to be a caliphate. Abu Bakr al-Baghdadi has been its leader since May 2010. On July 5, 2014 at the Great Mosque of al-Nuri in Mosul he delivered a Ramadan sermon as the first caliph since the Ottoman Empire in the 16th century and announced himself as commander of all Muslims. He states "Our goal is to establish an Islamic state that doesn't recognize borders, on the Prophetic methodology." He is the Muslim equivalent to David Koresh or Jim Jones in his absolute power over 8 million Muslims.

ISIS rejects peace as a matter of principle, hungers for genocide, and considers itself a main force in the imminent end of the world. ISIS considers itself a State, unlike the Muslim Brotherhood which it considers a weal stepchild. ISIS intends to establish the first caliphate in generations that require allegiance, conversion or death to all infidels (non-Muslims).

ISIS follows cannot deviate from governing precepts embedded in Islam by the Prophet Muhammad. Sheikh Abu Muhammad al-Adnani, the Islamic State's chief spokesman, called on Muslims in Western countries such as France and Canada to find an infidel and "smash his head with a rock," poison him, run him over with a car, or "destroy his crops." His directive to attack crops come from Muhammad to leave well water and crops alone—unless the armies of Islam were in a defensive position, in which case Muslims in the lands of *kuffar*, or infidels, should be unmerciful, and poison away.

ISIS follows its press and pronouncements, "the Prophetic methodology," which means following the prophecy and example of Muhammad. Most Muslims reject the Islamic State, however their opposing voices are suspiciously silent to western ears.

ISIS is obliged to terrorize its enemies with beheadings and crucifixions and enslavement of women and children. Doing so hastens victory and avoids prolonged conflict. ISIS barbarians hiding behind black clothing with just their eyes exposed present themselves as consummate cowards and Satanic evil doers. ISIS beheading of 21 Coptic Christians in Libya, burning a Jordanian pilot, rape and forced slavery of girls and women into prostitution are just a few examples that reveal their absolute evil.

In the midst of all this evidence of evil where ISIS members are educated and have jobs and plenty of money, the U.S. State department Marie Harf revealed utter ignorance of things as they really are when she stated:

Her statement is like saying after the Japanese attacked the United States at Pearl Harbor – 'yesterday, December 7,1941 was a pretty rough day. Some bad people from another country, doesn't matter which one...randomly attached some folks in Hawaii who were on some boats. We have to find out what we did to provoke the attack. Giving them job opportunities to kamikaze pilots would solve this problem. After all it was just a few people that bombed us, not the entire country!'

The last time the world saw evil similar to ISIS, was the rise of Hitler's Nazis. It took the world years to wake up to Nazi evil. It is taking the world years to wake up to radical Islam evil?

ISIS may instigate Armageddon.

Hudna

Hudna is an Arabic term that technically translates into "calm" or "truce", as in a truce struck between two warring nations. But a hudna is not just any truce or ceasefire. A hudna [also known as a hudibiyya or khudaibiya] is a tactical cease-fire that allows the Arabs to rebuild their terrorist infrastructure in order to be more effective when the "cease-fire" is called off."

Hudna has it's beginnings with Muhammad. In the year 628 AD, when surmising that his [Mohammed's] forces were too weak to overcome the rival Kuraysh tribes, the Prophet Mohammed concluded a ten-year truce accord with the Kuraysh. This agreement became known as the Hudaybiyya Accord, after the place where it was signed. Yet, less than two years later, having consolidated their power, the Muslim forces attacked the Kuraysh tribes and defeated them, allowing Mohammed to conquer the city of Mecca.

Since that time, the term Hudna has been understood by Muslims as a tactical cease-fire that is intended only to allow a shift the balance of power. Once the balance of power has shifted, and the groundwork has been laid for a Muslim victory, the truce can then be broken.

Hudna is the battlefield or political application of al-Taqiyya. It's purpose is to give the illusion of desiring peace while actively masking a rethinking, regrouping, or rearming when faced with a superior opponent. Hudna [also known as a hudibiyya or khudaibiya] is a tactical cease-fire that allows the Arabs to rebuild their terrorist infrastructure in order to be more effective when the "cease-fire" is called off.

These doctrines of strategic lying and deception, al-Taqiyya and hudna, showcase the dangerous nature of Islam as much as does the wife beating, honor killing, beheading, and other such practices that the religion embraces.

CAIR – The Muslim Brotherhood in Washington, D.C.

The Council on American-Islamic Relations, or CAIR, is not the Muslim civil-rights group it claims to be. CAIR and other "mainstream" Islamic groups act as fronts for the Muslim Brotherhood – the parent of al-Qaida, Hezbollah and Hamas. Their purpose is to infiltrate and destroy the American system and transform the United States into an Islamic nation. They intend to replace the US Constitution with Sharia Law.

CAIR founded in 1994, has carefully hidden its purpose, finances and membership. CAIR is an co-conspirator in

FORWARD!

Arif Alikhan   Mohammed Eliblary   Rashad Hussain   Salam al-Marayati   Imam Mohamed Magid   Eboo Patel

Muslim Brotherhood Infiltrates Obama Administration

"Six American Islamist activists who work with the Obama administration are Muslim Brotherhood operatives who enjoy strong influence over U.S. policy."

investigativeproject.org

the largest terror-financing case in U.S. history. It is part of organized crime composed of more than 100 other Muslim front groups. They aided terrorist attacks on American and Israelis. They advance the cause of terrorism by deceiving our FBI, CIA and new media.

CAIR claims to represent all Muslims. Yet it victimized 100 indigent Muslims and threatened them when they tried to go to the media. CAIR discriminates against Shiite Muslims and Muslim women

They support Palestinian terrorists and work to destroy Israel. They influence our laws to promote terrorism and facilitate Muslim immigration.

Even though the FBI cut formal ties to CAIR they have continued access to the White House through Barack Obama and Capitol Hill.

CAIR only differs from al-Qaida in that they use different methods to achieve the same goals. CAIR infiltrates and destroys from within. Al-Qaida acts as terrorists.

Sharia Law In Action

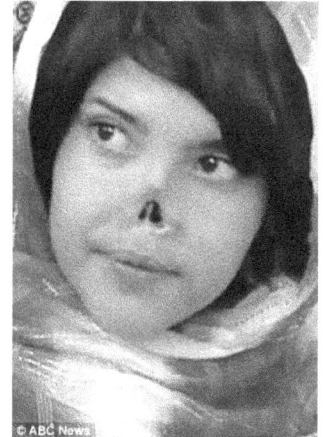

Bibi Aisha born Aisha Mohammadzai is an Afgan woman whose mutilated face appeared on the cover of Time magazine in summer 2010.

In a practice known as baad, Aisha's father promised her to a Taliban fighter when she was 12 years old as compensation for a killing that a member of her family had committed. She was married at 14 and subjected to constant abuse. At 18, she fled the abuse but was caught by police, jailed, and returned to her family. Her father returned her to her in-laws. To take revenge on her escape, her father-in-law, husband, and three other family members took Aisha into the mountains, cut off her nose and her ears, and left her to die. Bibi was later rescued by aid workers and the U.S. military.

Ground Zero Mosque

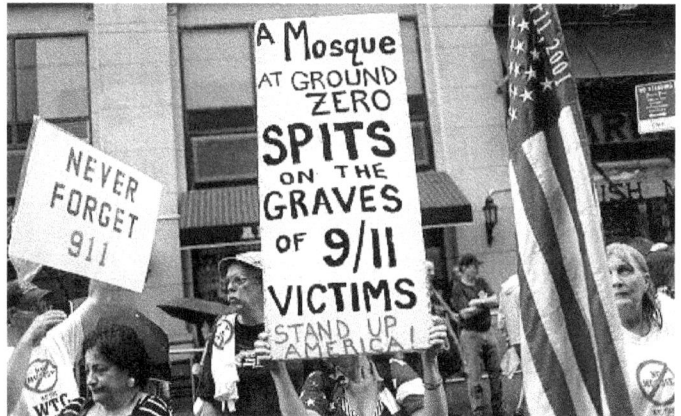

CAIR, a front for Hamas and many other Muslim organizations, funded the proposed Ground Zero mosque. It is no wonder the mosque's principal imam, Feisal Abdul Rauf, refuses to discuss the project's finances or speak against Hamas.

Rauf has been catching iffy tax breaks since 1998 for an organization run from his wife's Upper West Side apartment. "How'd he do it? By telling the IRS the one-bedroom digs were actually a mosque where 500 people prayed daily. These are only a few of the latest revelations about the mosque's backers, who are guilty of petty crime, slumlording and tax-scamming. Rauf called the 71 percent of New Yorkers who oppose his project religious "extremists." The 71 percent of New Yorkers would include a representative cross-section of all faith traditions. Are they really extremists for opposing the mosque or just Patriots who recognize evil?

Americans must learn from Islamic supremacists. They never stop. They never give up, no matter how total a defeat. We, too, must never stop fighting for freedom and in defeating every attempt to desecrate Ground Zero with a mosque of our enemy.

The Camel's Nose Is Officially In The Tent

Muslim men are allowed to have as many as 4 wives. Many Muslims have immigrated into the U.S. and brought their 2-3-or 4 wives with them, but the U.S. does not allow multi marriages, so the man lists one wife as his, and signs the other 2 or 3 up as extended family on welfare and other free Government programs!

Michigan has the highest population of Muslims in the Unites States. When President Obama took office the United States paid several millions of dollars to have a large number of Palestinians, (All Muslim), immigrate from Palestine. We do not pay for other persons to immigrate here. So now in Michigan when you call the Public Assistance office you are told to Press 1 for English. Press 2 for Spanish or Press 3 for Arabic! Here is the number 1-888-678-8914

Every time you add a new language to an American program it requires an additional number of persons fluent in that language to process those persons who refuse to learn English in order to live here at an additional cost to the taxpayer. Furthermore, allowing more than one official language accommodated by the government is one of the best ways to divide and conquer a country. Why are we even allowing persons to immigrate here who cannot provide for themselves, and putting them in our welfare system?

America – The Last Man Standing

Geert Wilders is a Dutch Member of Parliament. Here are his words:

"'In a generation or two, the US will ask itself: who lost Europe?'

Here is the speech of Geert Wilders, Chairman, Party for Freedom, the Netherlands, at the Four Seasons, New York, introducing an Alliance of Patriots and announcing the Facing Jihad Conference in Jerusalem.

"Dear friends, "Thank you very much for inviting me.

"I come to America with a mission. All is not well in the old world. There is a tremendous danger looming, and it is very difficult to be optimistic. We might be in the final stages of the Islamization of Europe. This not only is a clear and present danger to the future of Europe itself, it is a threat to America and the sheer survival of the West. The United States as the last bastion of Western civilization, facing an Islamic Europe.

"First I will describe the situation on the ground in Europe. Then, I will say a few things about Islam. To close I will tell you about a meeting in Jerusalem.

"The Europe you know is changing. You have probably seen the landmarks. But in all of these cities, sometimes a few blocks away from your tourist destination, there is another world. It is the world of the parallel society created by Muslim mass-migration.

"All throughout Europe a new reality is rising: entire Muslim neighborhoods where very few indigenous people reside or are even seen. And if they are, they might regret it. This goes for the police as well. It's the world of head scarves, where women walk around in figureless tents, with baby strollers and a group of children. Their husbands, or slaveholders if you prefer, walk three steps ahead. With mosques on many street corners. The shops have signs you and I cannot

read. You will be hard-pressed to find any economic activity. These are Muslim ghettos controlled by religious fanatics. These are Muslim neighborhoods, and they are mushrooming in every city across Europe. These are the building-blocks for territorial control of increasingly larger portions of Europe, street by street, neighborhood by neighborhood, city by city.

"There are now thousands of mosques throughout Europe. With larger congregations than there are in churches. And in every European city there are plans to build super-mosques that will dwarf every church in the region. Clearly, the signal is: we rule.

"Many European cities are already one-quarter Muslim: just take Amsterdam, Marseille and Malmo in Sweden . In many cities the majority of the under-18 population is Muslim. Paris is now surrounded by a ring of Muslim neighborhoods. Mohammed is the most popular name among boys in many cities.

"In some elementary schools in Amsterdam the farm can no longer be mentioned, because that routinely hear 'whore, whore', satellite dishes are not pointed to local TV stations, but to stations in the country of origin.

"In France school teachers are advised to avoid authors deemed offensive to Muslims, including Voltaire and Diderot; the same is increasingly true of Darwin. The history of the Holocaust can no longer be taught because of Muslim sensitivity.

"In England sharia courts are now officially part of the British legal system. Many neighborhoods in France are no-go areas for women without head scarves. Last week a man almost died after being beaten up by Muslims in Brussels, because he was drinking during the Ramadan.

"Jews are fleeing France in record numbers, on the run for the worst wave of anti-Semitism since World War II. French is now commonly spoken on the streets of Tel Aviv and Netanya, Israel. I could go on forever with stories like this. Stories about Islamization.

"A total of fifty-four million Muslims now live in Europe. San Diego University recently calculated that a staggering 25 percent of the population in Europe will be Muslim just 12 years from now. Bernhard Lewis has predicted a Muslim majority by the end of this century.

"Now these are just numbers. And the numbers would not be threatening if the Muslim-immigrants had a strong desire to assimilate. But there are few signs of that. The Pew Research Center reported that half of French Muslims see their loyalty to Islam as greater than their loyalty to France. One-third of French Muslims do not object to suicide attacks.

"The British Centre for Social Cohesion reported that one-third of British Muslim students are in favor of a worldwide caliphate. Muslims demand what they call 'respect'. And this is how we give them respect. We have Muslim official state holidays.

"The Christian-Democratic attorney general is willing to accept sharia in the Netherlands if there is a Muslim majority. We have cabinet members with passports from Morocco and Turkey.
"Muslim demands are supported by unlawful behavior, ranging from petty crimes and random violence, for example against ambulance workers and bus drivers, to small-scale riots. Paris has seen its uprising in the low-income suburbs, the banlieus. I call the perpetrators 'settlers' because that is what they are. They do not come to integrate into our societies; they come to integrate our society into their Dar-al-Islam. Therefore, they are settlers.

"Much of this street violence I mentioned is directed exclusively against non-Muslims, forcing many native people to leave their neighborhoods, their cities, their countries. Moreover, Muslims are now a swing vote not to be ignored.

"The second thing you need to know is the importance of Mohammed the prophet. His behavior is an example to all Muslims and cannot be criticized. Now, if Mohammed had been a man of peace, let us say like Ghandi and Mother Theresa wrapped in one, there would be no problem. But Mohammed was a warlord, a mass murderer, a pedophile, and had several marriages - at the same time. Islamic tradition tells us how he fought in battles, how he had his enemies murdered and even had prisoners of war executed. Mohammed himself slaughtered the Jewish tribe of Banu Qurayza. If it is good for Islam, it is good. If it is bad for Islam, it is bad.

"Let no one fool you about Islam being a religion. Sure, it has a god, and a here-after, and 72 virgins. But in its essence Islam is a political ideology. It is a system that lays down detailed rules for society and the life of every person. Islam wants to dictate every aspect of life. Islam means 'submission'. Islam is not compatible with freedom and democracy, because what it strives for is sharia. If you want to compare Islam to anything, compare it to communism or national-socialism, these are all totalitarian ideologies.

"Now you know why Winston Churchill called Islam 'the most retrograde force in the world', and why he compared Mein Kampf to the Quran. The public has wholeheartedly accepted the Palestinian narrative, and sees Israel as the aggressor. I have lived in this country and visited it dozens of times. I support Israel. First, because it is the Jewish homeland after two thousand years of exile up to and including Auschwitz, second because it is a democracy, and third because Israel is our first line of defense.

"This tiny country is situated on the fault line of jihad, frustrating Islam's territorial advance. Israel is facing the front lines of jihad, like Kashmir, Kosovo, the Philippines, Southern Thailand, and Darfur in Sudan, Lebanon, and Aceh in Indonesia. Israel is simply in the way. The same way West-Berlin was during the Cold War.

"The war against Israel is not a war against Israel. It is a war against the West. It is jihad. Israel is simply receiving the blows that are meant for all of us. If there would have been no Israel, Islamic imperialism would have found other venues to release its energy and its desire for conquest. Thanks to Israeli parents who send their children to the army and lay awake at night, parents in Europe and America can sleep well and dream, unaware of the dangers looming.

"Many in Europe argue in favor of abandoning Israel in order to address the grievances of our Muslim minorities. But if Israel were, God forbid, to go down, it would not bring any solace to the West. It would not mean our Muslim minorities would all of a sudden change their behavior, and accept our values. On the contrary, the end of Israel would give enormous encouragement to the forces of Islam. They would, and rightly so, see the demise of Israel as proof that the West is weak, and doomed. The end of Israel would not mean the end of our problems with Islam, but only the beginning. It would mean the start of the final battle for world domination. If they can get Israel, they can get everything. So-called journalists volunteer to label any and all critics of Islamization as 'right-wing extremists' or 'racists'. In my country, the Netherlands, 60 percent of the population now sees the mass immigration of Muslims as the number one policy mistake since World War II. And another 60 percent sees Islam as the biggest threat. Yet there is a greater danger than terrorist attacks, the scenario of America as the last man standing. The lights may go out in Europe faster than you can imagine. An Islamic Europe means a Europe without freedom and democracy, an economic wasteland, an intellectual nightmare, and a loss of military might for

America - as its allies will turn into enemies, enemies with atomic bombs. With an Islamic Europe, it would be up to America alone to preserve the heritage of Rome, Athens and Jerusalem.

"Dear friends, liberty is the most precious of gifts. My generation never had to fight for this freedom, it was offered to us on a silver platter, by people who fought for it with their lives. All throughout Europe, American cemeteries remind us of the young boys who never made it home, and whose memory we cherish. My generation does not own this freedom; we are merely its custodians. We can only hand over this hard won liberty to Europe's children in the same state in which it was offered to us. We cannot strike a deal with mullahs and imams. Future generations would never forgive us. We cannot squander our liberties. We simply do not have the right to do so.

"We have to take the necessary action now to stop this Islamic stupidity from destroying the free world that we know." [End of quote]

'If the Arabs put down their weapons today, there would be no more violence. If the Jews put down their weapons today, there would be no more Israel ." Benjamin Netanyahu

Europe Died in Auschwitz

The Nazis killed 6M Jews that took with them a culture, talent and creativity.

World Jewish population is 14,000,000; 0.02% of the world's population. They have received 129 Nobel Prizes.

World Islamic population is 1,200,000,000; 20% of the world's population. They have received 7 Nobel Prizes.

Jews never taught their children to blow themselves up and kill innocent people for the glory of Jehovah (God). They never hijacked planes, killed athletes at the Olympics, destroyed opponents mosques, or kills people in protests. They do not promote jihad or proclaim death to non-Jews. Yet these are the very fruits of Islam.

If Jews laid down their weapons of defence there would be no Israel. If Muslims laid down their weapons of attack, there would be peace.

After WWII Europe allowed immigration of 20M Muslims and imported with them intolerance, extremism, jihad, crime, poverty and a culture that isolates rather than integrates. The fruits of their culture includes filth, crime, murder of their native hosts; all the while living in government provided housing.

France's recent experience with Charlie Hedbo murders by Muslim extremists are the fruits of these roots. Muslims do not integrate into other countries society. Consider the 'no go zones' in France that are under Sharia law where French police do not go. It is out of these pits crawl the murderers at Hedbo.

An Alternate View of Islam

To be fair, the author has listened to Zuhdi Jasser, a commentator on the topic of the Islamic faith in the United States, and the President of the American Islamic Forum for Democracy based in Phoenix, Arizona. Jasser presents a moderate view of Islam; a loner in a world that has come to distrust Muslims. It may be that there are at least two Islamic 'faiths'; moderates and radical jihadists who have been the source of nearly all the terrorist attacks for the past 20+ years.

What Americans, and indeed the world needs now is for moderate Muslims to speak out against the jihadists. Radical Muslims seek to establish a world Caliphate and Sharia law to dominate and control everyone.

I wrote twice to Zuhdi requesting clarification on the Islamic teaching of Al-Takeyya, but after 3 years, I have not yet received a reply. Online searches reveal similar experiences with Zuhdi not replying to inquiries.

The question is western minds is if the majority of Muslims are really peace loving and do not support jihadist terrorists, why are 10,000+ Muslims marching during the workday in Dearborn and Detroit Michigan in support of Hezbollah and Hamas in both 2006 and early 2009? Why do Bin Laden, Hamas, Hezbollah, Ahmadinejad, and Nasrallah remain the most popular figures and entities in poll after poll of Muslims? Why do a third of young American Muslims support homicide bombings?

If there are in fact peace loving Muslims, they must speak up, speak out and most importantly ACT against radical Islamist extremists.

America Media & Hollywood

The news media in America is a joke to the rest of the world. Most of America's neighbors see the evil 'spin' on American news outlets to advance a hidden agenda – a Satanic agenda at its root – to destroy freedom and liberty. Unabashedly most of America's main-stream media calls good evil and evil good.

Here's the Obama connection to the lame-stream media that continually supports his evil actions. ABC News executive producer Ian Cameron is married to Susan Rice, National Security Adviser. CBS President David Rhodes is the brother of Ben Rhodes, Obama's Deputy National Security Adviser for Strategic Communications. ABC News correspondent Claire Shipman is married to former Whitehouse Press Secretary Jay Carney. ABC News and Univision reporter Matthew Jaffe is married to Katie Hogan, Obama's Deputy Press Secretary. ABC President Ben Sherwood is the brother of Obama's Special Adviser Elizabeth Sherwood. CNN President Virginia Moseley is married to former Hillary Clinton's Deputy Secretary Tom Nides. Every position Obama's administration is filled because of who they know, not because of expertise or competency.

NBC is owned by General Electric. The president of General Electric sits on the Obama White House board of advisors. Therefore the government and the media have combined. So guess what gets presented in the media....whatever is best for the government and big business. Complicit reporters controlled by those who pay their salaries are part of the problem. Truth does not matter to profiteer oriented business. Control the message and you control the people.

John Swinton, editor of the New York Tribune, called by his peers, "the dean of his profession," was asked on February 26th, 1936, to give a toast before the New York Press Association. He responded with the following statements: *"There is no such thing as an independent press in America, unless it is in the country towns. You know it and I know it. There is not one of you who dares to write your honest opinions, and if you did, you know beforehand that it would never appear in print.* **_The business of the New York journalist is to destroy truth; to lie outright; to pervert; to vilify, to fawn at the feet of Mammon; to sell his country and his race for his daily bread. We are the tools and vessels for rich men behind the scenes. We are intellectual prostitutes."_**

ABC, NBC, CNN, MSNBC, The Washington Post, The Huffington Post, NY Times etc. are all controlled by banksters, international corporations, the present administration, communist/socialist/fascist/Marxist/ liberal left progressives etc. Fox News is the only partially independent news outlet.

ABC News executive producer.... Ian Cameron is married to Susan Rice, National Security Adviser.

CBS President ...David Rhodes is the brother of Ben Rhodes, Obama's Deputy National Security Adviser for Strategic Communications.

ABC News correspondent ...Claire Shipman is married to former Whitehouse Press Secretary Jay Carney.

ABC News and Univision reporter... Matthew Jaffe is married to Katie Hogan, Obama's Deputy Press Secretary.

ABC President ...Ben Sherwood is the brother of Obama's Special Adviser Elizabeth Sherwood

CNN President ...Virginia Moseley is married to former Hillary Clinton's Deputy Secretary Tom Nides.

It is no surprise the media is in Obama's pocket.

It's all about controlling....us. The 'too big to fail' doctrine, stimulus packages (QE1 & QE2) was an excuse for Washington to grab power over the auto industry, insurance industry, healthcare (Obamacare). Stimulus money did not go to help the common man. Stimulus money went to payback union leaders and banksters who helped get Obama elected.

The federal government now controls 1/6 of our entire economy as the result of creating a state of fear, then entering in as our 'savior' under the pretense to save the economy, save healthcare, etc. all with the hidden intent to gain power and control. Thus, they further their agenda to institute One World Order (government) and gain ultimate control.

Remember Katrina? The American liberal left media blamed the Bush administration for the disaster. The fact is President Bush warned Mayor Ray Nagan of the coming disaster and offered FEMA help before Katrina hit. Nagan refused. The media reported that Bush withheld support because he doesn't like blacks.

Forward now a few years later to Iowa and North Dakota that were hit by massive flooding. Why hasn't the Federal Government moved these disaster-hit people into free hotels like they did for New Orleans victims? Is it Obama's dislike for whites? Where is the media coverage? Where the Hollywood celebrities that made a big deal of Katrina are yet were silent about the mid-America flood?

More people died in the ND floods than Katrina, but where is the media coverage? Why was there no looters in ND like New Orleans. Where is the liberal left hysterical media coverage. Where aren't the whites of ND screaming that Obama doesn't offer help because he hates whites? Why didn't the Federal government offer ND citizens bailouts and government debt cards like the New Orleans citizens?

In the Treyvon Martín - George Zimmerman case Al Sharpton and Jessie Jackson went ballistic as did the liberal left media. They tried to paint Zimmerman – a Hispanic – as white to further their racist agenda of white on black crime. The final verdict was that Zimmerman acted in self-defense.

Within the following year, 2 black men approached a white woman with a 9 month old baby demanding money. She had none. So one of the black men shot the baby in the head and murdered it. On August 19,2013 in Oklahoma, 3 black men (Chancy Allen Luna, age 16, James Francis Edwards Jr., age 15, and Michael Dewanye Homes, age 17) - murdered 22 year old Christopher Lane - a white Australian exchange student - 'for the fun of it' and because they wanted to live the gangster lifestyle.

Where is Al and Jessie and the liberal left media now?....silent because it does not help advance their racist agenda.

The problem is not color. The problem is culture. America has 12% blacks, 6% male, and 3% of them adult males. Yet they account for the vast majority of violent crimes. 86% of inmates are black with a few Hispanic. Why?...because they grew up in a culture of violence and entitlement mentality.

We must frame the issue accurately to effectively deal with the problem. Race is not the problem. Cultural values are the problem. We must return to God's values to turn society back to being good.

Government- Run Disasters

Ronald Reagan reminded us that *"The government does nothing as well or as economically as the private sector"*.

Let's look at government's record for running companies:

- **Medicare and Medicaid** – Medicare and Medicaid are the single biggest drivers of the federal deficit and the federal debt by a huge margin.

- **Obamacare** is already revealing itself as a Trojan horse. Here is what happened on January 1, 2014 : Top Medicare tax went from 1.45% to 2.35%. Top Income tax bracket went from 35% to 39.6%. Top Income payroll tax went from 37.4% to 52.2%. Capital Gains tax went from 15% to 28%. Dividends tax went from 15% to 39.6%. Estate tax went from 0% to 55%. These taxes were all passed with only democrat votes, no republicans voted for these taxes. These taxes were all passed under the Affordable Care Act, aka Obamacare.

- **Social Security** – the biggest Ponzi scheme in the history of mankind. The Federal Government lied to us. They spent our contributions on pet projects rather than reserving it for promised payouts.

- **US Post Office** – United States Postal Service runs more than $8 billion annual deficit. The USPS is on track to suffer losses never before experienced in the history of an independent enterprise: A $238 billion deficit over a 10-year period.

- **Amtrak** – A study by Subsidyscope, an arm of Pew Charitable Trusts, showed that in 2008 taxpayers covered about $32 in losses per passenger. The least profitable route, between New Orleans and Los Angeles, lost $462 per passenger. Amtrak was created from the Rail Passenger Service Act in 1970, which had the government take over passenger rail service from three private companies. This has hardly proved to be a fiscally responsible decision. Amtrak receives $1.5 billion in taxpayers' money every year. This doesn't even include $1.3 billion given to Amtrak from the stimulus package. An additional $8 billion of stimulus was dedicated to "intercity passenger rail and high-speed rail corridor development." Americans are fed up with taxpayer bailouts for failing companies. Congress should take a stand and stop subsidizing Amtrak – losing more and more money every year, bailed out by the taxpayer each time. It is this type of foolish spending that is responsible for the fiscal situation we find ourselves in, and it is this type of spending that will lead us further into fiscal disaster.

- **Fannie Mae and Freddie Mac** – can you say Housing Bubble, market collapse of 2008? And our government bailed them out with OUR tax dollars!...Criminal!

Forget The Rhetoric – Look At The Record

Actions reveal the heart of man; 'for by their fruits ye shall know them.' After the Fort Hood massacre by a Muslim jihadist, the wife of an injured soldier was informed that her husband was wounded and was in surgery. She drove all night to be with her husband. Upon arriving at his bedside she found George and Laura Bush there already, comforting victims and dependents of the dead. When they heard about the shooting they drove to Fort Hood to comfort the victims. The Bush's stayed at the hospital over six hours and were finally asked to leave by the White House because Barack Obama was on his way. Obama flew in a few days later for a photo-op in the gym and did not even go to the hospital.

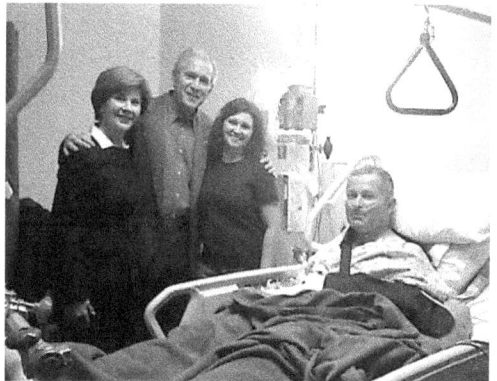

The Bush's visited the hospital unannounced to provide comfort to the suffering. Obama visited the hospital for political gain.

"Despicable Oilman" Vs. "Environmentalist" Houses

LOOK OVER THE DESCRIPTIONS OF THE FOLLOWING TWO HOUSES AND SEE IF YOU CAN TELL WHICH BELONGS TO AN ENVIRONMENTALIST.

HOUSE # 1:
A 20-room mansion (not including 8 bathrooms) heated by natural gas. Add on a pool (and a pool house) and a separate guest house all heated by gas. In ONE MONTH ALONE this mansion consumes more energy than the average American household in an ENTIRE YEAR. The average bill for electricity and natural gas runs over $2,400.00 per month. In natural gas alone (which last time we checked was a fossil fuel), this property consumes more than 20 times the national average

for an American home. This house is not in a northern or Midwestern "snow belt," either. It's in the South.

HOUSE # 2:

Designed by an architecture professor at a leading national university, this house incorporates every "green" feature current home construction can provide. The house contains only 4,000 square feet (4 bedrooms) and is nestled on arid high prairie in the American southwest. A central closet in the house holds geothermal heat pumps drawing ground water through pipes sunk 300 feet into the ground. The water (usually 67 degrees F.) heats the house in winter and cools it in summer. The system uses no fossil fuels such as oil or natural gas, and it consumes 25% of the electricity required for a conventional heating/cooling system. Rainwater from the roof is collected and funneled into a 25,000 gallon underground cistern. Wastewater from showers, sinks and toilets goes into underground purifying tanks and then into the cistern. The collected water then irrigates the land surrounding the house. Flowers and shrubs native to the area blend the property into the surrounding rural landscape.

HOUSE # 1: (20 room energy guzzling mansion) is outside of Nashville, Tennessee. It is the abode of that renowned 'global warming environmentalist' (and filmmaker) Al Gore.

HOUSE # 2: (model eco-friendly house) is on a ranch near Crawford, Texas. Also known as 'the Texas White House,' it is the private residence of the President of the United States , George W. Bush.

Mychal Massie on Obama

Mychal Massie, former Chairman of Project 21's National Advisory Council, a syndicated op-ed columnist, former host of the top-rated talk show on the Rightalk Radio Network "Straight Talk with Mychal Massie" and a former self-employed business owner of 30-plus years. Used with permission, he writes:

"At a time when many Americans can barely afford Burger King and a movie, Obama boasts of spending a billion dollars on his re-election campaign. Questioned at a recent appearance about the spiraling fuel costs, Obama said, "Get used to it" – and with an insouciant grin and chortle, he told another person at the event, who complained about the effect high fuel prices were having on his family, to "get a more fuel-efficient car."

"The Obamas behave as if they were sharecroppers living in a trailer and hit the Powerball, but instead of getting new tires for their trailer and a new pickup truck, they moved to Washington. And instead of making possum pie, with goats and chickens in the front yard, they're spending and living large at taxpayer expense – opulent vacations, gala balls, resplendent dinners and exclusive command performances at the White House, grand date nights, golf, basketball, more golf, exclusive resorts and still more golf.

"Expensive, ill-fitting and ill-chosen wigs and fashions hardly befit the first lady of the United States. The Obamas have behaved in every way but presidential - which is why it's so offensive when we hear Obama say, in order "to restore fiscal responsibility, we all need to share in the sacrifice - but we don't have to sacrifice the America we believe in." "The American people have

been sacrificing; it is he and his family who are behaving as if they've never had two nickels to rub together – and now, having hit the mother lode, they're going to spend away their feelings of inadequacy at the taxpayers' expense.

"Obama continues to exhibit behavior that, at best, can be described as mobocratic and, at worst, reveals a deeply damaged individual. In a February 2010 column, I asked, "Is Obama unraveling?" I wrote that it was beginning to appear the growing mistrust of him and contempt for his policies was beginning to have a destabilizing effect on him.

"At that time, I wrote that not having things go one's way can be a bitter pill, but reasonable people don't behave as he was behaving. He had insulted Republicans at their luncheon, where he had been an invited guest. I had speculated that was, in part, what had led him to falsely accuse Supreme Court justices before Congress, the nation and the world, during the 2010 State of the Union address. It appeared, at that time, as if he were fraying around the emotional edges. That behavior has not abated – it has become more pronounced. While addressing the nation, after being forced to explain the validity of his unilateral aggression with Libya, America witnessed a petulant individual scowling and scolding the public for daring to insist he explain his actions.

"But during an afternoon speech to address the budget/debt, he took his scornful, unstable despotic behavior to depths that should give the nation cause for concern. Displaying a dark psychopathy more representative of an episode of "The Tudors" television series, he invited Rep. Paul Ryan, R-Wis., to sit in the front row during his speech and then proceeded to berate both Ryan and Ryan's budget-cutting plan. Even liberal Democrats were put off by the act. MSNBC's Joe Scarborough questioned the sanity of Obama's actions. .

"Today, criticism is coming from all sides. A senior Democrat lawmaker said, "I have been very disappointed in [Obama], to the point where I'm embarrassed that I endorsed him. It's so bad that some of us are thinking, is there some way we can replace him? How do you get rid of this guy?" ("Democrats' Disgust with Obama," The Daily Beast, April 15, 2011)

"Steve McCann wrote: Obama's speech "was chock full of lies, deceit and crass fear-mongering. It must be said that [he] is the most dishonest, deceitful and mendacious person in a position of power I have ever witnessed." "The Mendacity of Barack Obama," AmericanThinker.com, April 15, 2011).

"McCann continued: "[His] performance was the culmination of four ears of outright lies and narcissism that have been largely ignored by the media, including some in the conservative press and political class who are loath to call [him] what he is in the bluntest of terms: al liar and a fraud. That he relies on his skin color to intimidate, either outright or by insinuation [against] those who oppose his radical agenda only add to his audacity. It is apparent that he has gotten away with his character flaws his entire life, aided and abetted by sycophants around him. ..."With these being among the kinder rebukes being directed at Obama, and with people becoming less intimidated by his willingness to use race as a bludgeon, with falling poll numbers in every meaningful category and an increasingly aggressive tea-party opposition – how much longer before he cracks completely? "The coming months of political life are not going to be pleasant for Obama. Possessed by a self-perceived palatine mindset that in his mind places him above criticism, how long before he cracks in public? Can America risk a man with a documented track record of lying and misrepresenting the truth as a basic way of life, who is becoming increasingly more contumelious?"

Obamacare – A Trojan Horse

President Thomas Jefferson warned us "If we can but prevent the government from wasting the labors of the people, under the pretense of taking care of them, they must become happy." - Thomas Jefferson to Thomas Cooper, 29 November 1802

A summary of Obamacare follows: Obamacare is "gifted" health care plan we are forced to purchase and fined if we don't, which purportedly covers at least thirty million more people, without adding a single new doctor, but provides for 16,000 new IRS agents, written by a committee whose chairman says he doesn't understand it, passed by a Congress that didn't read it but exempted themselves from it, and signed by a President who smokes, excludes Muslims from participating in it, funded and administered by a treasury chief who didn't pay his taxes, by a government which has already bankrupted Social Security and Medicare, all to be overseen by a surgeon general who is obese, and financed by a country that's broke!!!!! And We the SHEEPLE are supposed to accept this atrocity?

Obamacare (AKA Affordable Care Act) – opposed by 61% of America's citizens, a un-Constitutional Federal Government program forced down America's throats, taxes citizens to pay for something they did not want, fines them if they do not comply, excludes Congress and Obama's union friends and Muslims, covers 10M more people without adding one new doctor, employs 16,000 new IRS agents to force compliance, written by a committee whose chairman does not understand it, passed by Congress who did not read it first because they were not given time to read it before votes were forced, signed by Barack who smokes, administered by the Tim Geithner who did not pay his taxes, administered by a government that already bankrupted Social Security and Medicare, and has run Amtrak, the USPS and every other program they have tried to administer into deficit, overseen by an obese surgeon general and financed by America that is broke.

A BLACK MAN, THE PROGRESSIVE'S PERFECT TROJAN HORSE

Used with permission By Lloyd Marcus, a black Patriot:

"As millions of my fellow Americans, I am outraged, devastated and extremely angry by the democrat's unbelievable arrogance and disdain for We The People. Despite our screaming "no" from the rooftops, they forced Obamacare down our throats. Please forgive me for using the following crude saying, but it is very appropriate to describe what has happened. "Don't urinate on me and tell me it's raining." Democrats say their mission is to give all Americans health care. The democrats are lying. Signing Obamacare into law against our will and the Constitution is tyranny and step one of their hideous goal of having as many Americans as possible dependent on government, thus controlling our lives and fulfilling Obama's promise to fundamentally transform America.

"I keep asking myself. How did our government move so far from the normal procedures of getting things done? Could a white president have so successfully pulled off shredding the Constitution to further his agenda? I think not. Ironically, proving America is completely the opposite of the evil racist country they relentlessly accuse her of being, progressives used America 's goodness, guilt and sense of fair play against her. In their quest to destroy America as we know it, progressives borrowed a brilliant scheme from Greek mythology. They offered America a modern day Trojan Horse, a beautifully crafted golden shiny new black man as a presidential candidate.

"Democrat Joe Biden lauded Obama as the first clean and articulate African American candidate. Democrat Harry Reid said Obama only uses a black dialect when he wants. White America relished the opportunity to vote for a black man naively believing they would never suffer the pain of being called racist again. Black Americans viewed casting their vote for Obama as the ultimate Affirmative Action for America's sins of the past. Then there were the entitlement loser voters who said, "I'm votin' for the black dude who promises to take from those rich SOBs and give to me." Just as the deceived Trojans dragged the beautifully crafted Trojan Horse into Troy as a symbol of their victory, deceived Americans embraced the progressive's young, handsome, articulate and so called moderate black presidential candidate as a symbol of their liberation from accusation of being a racist nation.

"Also like the Trojan Horse, Obama was filled with the enemy hiding inside. Sunday, March 21, 2010, a secret door opened in Obama, the shiny golden black man. A raging army of democrats charged out. Without mercy, they began their vicious bloody slaughter of every value, freedom and institution we Americans hold dear; launching the end of America as we know it. Wielding swords of votes reeking with the putrid odor of back door deals, the democrats landed a severe death blow to America and individual rights by passing Obamacare. The mainstream liberal media has been relentlessly badgering the Tea Party movement with accusations of racism.

"Because I am a black tea party patriot, I am bombarded with interviewers asking me the same veiled question. "Why are you siding with these white racists against America 's first African American president?" I defend my fellow patriots who are white stating, "These patriots do not give a hoot about Obama's skin color. They simply love their country and oppose his radical agenda. Obama's race is not an issue." Recently, I have come to believe that perhaps I am wrong about Obama's race not being an issue.

"In reality, Obama's presidency has everything to do with racism, but not from the Tea Party movement. Progressives and Obama have exploited his race from the rookie senator's virtually unchallenged presidential campaign to his unprecedented bullying of America into Obamacare. Obama's race trumped all normal media scrutiny of him as a presidential candidate and most recently even the Constitution of the United States. Obamacare forces all Americans to purchase health care which is clearly unconstitutional.

"No white president could get away with boldly and arrogantly thwarting the will of the American people and ignoring laws. President Clinton tried universal health care. Bush tried social security reform. The American people said "no" to both president's proposals and it was the end of it. So how can Obama get away with giving the American people the finger? The answer. He is black. The mainstream liberal media continues to portray all who oppose Obama in any way as racist. Despite a list of failed policies, overreaches into the private sector, violations of the Constitution and planned destructive legislation too numerous to mention in this article, many Americans are still fearful of criticizing our first black president. Incredible.

"My fellow Americans, you must not continue to allow yourselves to be "played" and intimidated by Obama's race or the historical context of his presidency. If we are to save America, the greatest nation on the planet, Obama's progressive agenda must be stopped.

Lloyd Marcus (black) Unhyphenated American, Singer/Songwriter, Entertainer, Author, Artist & Tea Party Patriot2010 Lloyd Marcus

Truth About The Affordable Care Act

Michael Connelly, Ret. Constitutional Attorney

"Well, I have done it! I have read the entire text of House Bill 3200: The Affordable Health Care Choices Act of 2009. I studied it with particular emphasis from my area of expertise, constitutional law. I was frankly concerned that parts of the proposed law that were being discussed might be unconstitutional. What I found was far worse than what I had heard or expected.

"To begin with, much of what has been said about the law and its implications are in fact true, despite what the Democrats and the media are saying. The law does provide for rationing of health care, particularly where senior citizens and other classes of citizens are involved, free health care for illegal immigrants, free abortion services, and probably <u>forced participation in abortions by members of the medical profession</u>.

"The Bill will also eventually force private insurance companies out of business, and put everyone into a government run system. All decisions about personal health care will ultimately be made by federal bureaucrats, and most of them will not be health care professionals. Hospital admissions, payments to physicians, and allocations of necessary medical devices will be strictly controlled by the government.

"However, as scary as all of that is, it just scratches the surface. In fact, I have concluded that this legislation really has no intention of providing affordable health care choices. Instead it is a convenient cover for the most massive transfer of power to the Executive Branch of government that has ever occurred, or even been contemplated. If this law or a similar one is adopted, major portions of the Constitution of the United States will effectively have been destroyed.

"The first thing to go will be the masterfully crafted balance of power between the Executive, Legislative, and Judicial branches of the U.S. Government. The Congress will be transferring to the Obama Administration authority in a number of different areas over the lives of the American people, and the businesses they own.

"The irony is that the Congress doesn't have any authority to legislate in most of those areas to begin with! I defy anyone to read the text of the U.S. Constitution and find any authority granted to the members of Congress to regulate health care.

"This legislation also provides for access, by the appointees of the Obama administration, to all of your personal healthcare - a direct violation of the specific provisions of the 4th Amendment to the Constitution -- your personal financial information, and the information of your employer, physician, and hospital. All of this is protected against unreasonable searches and seizures. You can also forget about the right to privacy. That will have been legislated into oblivion regardless of what the 3rd and 4th Amendments may provide...

" If you decide not to have healthcare insurance, or if you have private insurance that is not deemed acceptable to the Health Choices Administrator appointed by Obama, there will be a tax imposed on you. It is called a tax instead of a fine because of the intent to avoid application of the due process clause of the 5th Amendment. However, that doesn't work because since there is nothing in the law that allows you to contest or appeal the imposition of the tax, it is definitely depriving someone of property without the due process of law.

"So, there are three of those pesky amendments that the far left hate so much, out of the original ten in the Bill of Rights that are effectively nullified by this law. It doesn't stop there though.

"The 9th Amendment that provides: The enumeration in the Constitution, of certain rights, shall not be construed to deny or disparage others retained by the people;

"The 10th Amendment states: The powers not delegated to the United States by the Constitution, nor prohibited by it to the States, are preserved to the States respectively, or to the people. Under the provisions of this piece of Congressional handiwork neither the people nor the states are going to have any rights or powers at all in many areas that once were theirs to control.

"I could write many more pages about this legislation, but I think you get the idea. This is not about health care; it is about seizing power and limiting rights... Article 6 of the Constitution requires the members of both houses of Congress to "be bound by oath or affirmation to support the Constitution." If I was a member of Congress I would not be able to vote for this legislation or anything like it, without feeling I was violating that sacred oath or affirmation. If I voted for it anyway, I would hope the American people would hold me accountable.

"For those who might doubt the nature of this threat, I suggest they consult the source, the US Constitution, and Bill of Rights. There you can see exactly what has been taken from us. Michael Connelly/Retired attorney/ Constitutional Law Instructor/Carrollton, Texas

Nancy Pelosi didn't want us to know until after the health care bill was passed. Remember she said, "We have to pass the Bill so that we can see what's in it."

Well, here is part of what's in it:
page 272. At age 76 when you most need it most, you are not eligible for cancer treatment.

Page 50/section 152: The bill will provide insurance to all non-U.S. residents, even if they are here illegally.

Page 58 and 59: The government will have real-time access to an individual's bank account and will have the authority to make electronic fund transfers from those accounts.

Page 65/section 164: The plan will be subsidized (by the government) for all union members, union retirees and for community organizations (such as the Association of Community Organizations for Reform Now -ACORN)

Page 203/line 14-15: The tax imposed under this section will not be treated as a tax. (How could anybody in their right mind come up with that?)

Page 241 and 253: Doctors will all be paid the same regardless of specialty, and the government will set all doctors' fees.
Page 272. section 1145: Cancer hospital will ration care according to the patient's age.

Page 317 and 321: The government will impose a prohibition on hospital expansion; however, communities may petition for an exception.

Page 425, line 4-12: The government mandates advance-care planning consultations. Those on Social Security will be required to attend an "end-of-life planning" seminar every five years. (Death counseling...)

Page 429, line 13-25: The government will specify which doctors can write an end-of-life order.

Finally, it is specifically stated that this bill will not apply to members of Congress.

Obamacare (Affordable Health Care Act) implemented the following on January 1, 2014:

Top Medicare tax went from 1.45% to 2.35%

Top Income tax bracket went from 35% to 39.6%

Top Income payroll tax went from 37.4% to 52.2%

Capital Gains tax went from 15% to 28%

Dividends tax went from 15% to 39.6%

Estate tax went from 0% to 55%

These taxes were all passed with only democrat votes, no republicans voted for these taxes.

Obama's 'Budget Cut'

Obama ordered a $100M budget cut from the $3.5T federal budget. That 1/35,000 budget cut.

To make it real to the average American, let's do the math. The average American spends $2,000/month on mortgage, food, gas, medicine, utilities etc. So, 1/35,000 of $2,000 is $0.06.

Hope & Change = Growth In Despair

For years we have been forced to listen to the Administrations lies that the U.S. economy is enjoying a "recovery".

The truth is Obama sprayed $100's of billions at the U.S. economy but most of that money went into "food stamps", unemployment benefits, or disappeared into the pockets of Wall Street bankers and union thugs. The only growth in jobs was government jobs; designed to make people slaves to government. Skilled professional private sector jobs have declined. The only growth that the Administration touts as recovery are in part-time minimum wage jobs. The financial stimulus did nothing to correct the worst unemployment problem in the U.S. since the Great Depression.

Even a CNN poll shows 48% of Americans predicting another Great Depression in the next 12 months. A recent U.S. survey found that 85% of U.S. college graduates were forced to move back home to live with their parents.

The economy is in far worse shape than the major media outlets would have us believe. American retail is in a desperate situation and the entire economy is on very shaky ground. Following are 16 companies that have closed stores or will close stores soon:

- Staples announced plans to close 225 stores by 2015, which is about 15 percent of its chain. Staples already closed 40 stores in 2014.

- Radio Shack announced plans to close 20 percent of its stores this year, which is as many as 1,100 stores. Its sales fell by 19 percent last year.

- Albertsons closed 26 stores in 2014.

- Abercrombie & Fitch is planning to close 220 stores by the end of 2015.

- Barnes & Nobles is planning to shut down one third of its stores in 2015.

- J.C. Penney is planning to close 33 stores and laying off about 2,000 employees.

- Toys R Us has plans to close 100 stores.

- Sweetbay Supermarket chain will close 17 of the stores 2013. It closed 33 stores last year.

- Loehmann's closed 39 stores in the New York City.

- Sears Holdings, (Sears and Kmart), closed another 500 in 2014.

- Quiznos filed for bankruptcy, and could close many of its 2,100 stores.

- Sbarro plans to clsoe 155 locations.

- Ruby Tuesday has plans to close 30 restaurants.

- Red Lobster plans to close many of its restaurants.

- Ralph's, plans to close 15 supermarkets.

- Safeway closed 72 Dominick's grocery stores last year.

The Obama administration tells that our economy is recovering, but the retail industry — and economic data — say something very different.

Wolf in Sheep's Clothing

"Obama: The Wolf in Sheep's Clothing.......Beware the Message in the Fabian Window" Copyright © 2012 William Kevin Stoos, as appearing in Canada Free Press (used by permission)

"Fabian Window. It is a beautiful, if creepy thing, this Fabian Window. And since I first wrote about it four years ago—before Obama's socialist administration came to power—the message contained in the stained glass has become creepier still, for the message in the glass portends where Obama has taken us the last four years and where he intends to take us yet. It illustrates his game plan, his program, his ideology and his modus operandi. And it might as well hang in the

White House for all to see. For the sheep's clothing has been removed and we see the wolf for what he is...

"The wolf plays a prominent role in socialist thought. V.I. Lenin once said "When you live among wolves you must howl like a wolf," meaning, of course, that if political necessity requires you to act like a capitalist or live among capitalists while you organize and work for socialist causes, you must act like those among whom you live. This is simply a matter of expediency. Norman Thomas, a founder of the A.C.L.U. once said:

"The American people will never knowingly adopt socialism. But under the name of 'liberalism' they will adopt every fragment of the socialist program until one day America will be a socialist nation, without knowing how it happened."

"There is a stained glass window currently on display in the London School of Economics. Designed by George Bernard Shaw to commemorate the founding of the Society, the "Fabian Window" features Society members hammering the world in order, as the motto proclaims, to "REMOULD IT NEARER TO THE HEART'S DESIRE." [sic]. A close and politically astute friend of mine—and leading expert on socialism—exclaimed: "How brazen are the socialists!" When I asked why, he pointed to the image of the wolf dressed in a sheepskin displayed prominently on the Fabian Window—a stark and ostentatious reminder that the goal of the socialists is to work secretly, in disguise (just as Lenin counseled) and adapt to the flock, herd, or society in which you are moving and working. Put simply, if you read and study socialist thought, the message is very clear: work to remould the world to your heart's desire and work for socialist causes discreetly—in disguise— and adapting to whatever milieu in which you are working. This, of course, begs the question: "Whose heart desires to remould the world and how? Depending on who has the hammer—we may or may not like the change.

"Obama looks good. He is (as Biden once said during the 2008 primaries) "intelligent and articulate." He wears nice suits. He has wonderful stage presence and he is a rock star. And people still have no idea who he is, where he came from, who influenced him or what his plans are if he—the most inexperienced politician ever to come out of nowhere—is re-elected president. Influenced by Uncle Frank Marshall Davis (a communist organizer in Hawaii who was no fan of racial equality and whose agenda was only to promote racial and class struggle), Billy Ayers and Bernardine Dohrn—two unapologetic American terrorists who went underground for years to foster terrorism and support our enemies right here in our own country, a radical black liberation "minister" and others, Obama has an agenda. And, the change of which he speaks may well not be what most Americans think, or want.

"What are his plans for America?

"Redistribution of wealth from those who own the means of production to those who don't.

"Fostering of class envy and economic class warfare

"Government control of the health care system and education

"Increased taxes on the wealthy (whomever he decides is wealthy)

"Taxing corporations for being too successful

"Punishing with new federal taxes, employers who do not choose to purchase Obamacare health insurance for their employees

"Increased deference to the United Nations and erosion of our national sovereignty

"Consorting with enemies of Israel and America

"Bigger and more intrusive government

"Appointing federal commissars with no constitutional authority to do so

"Ensuring that America is not a superpower, but an equal among all nations

"Denigrating religion (which as Marx noted, is the opiate of the masses) and

"Disregarding the Constitution in an effort to re-form (remould) a foundational document that has served us well for over two centuries.

"If this sounds suspiciously like the message on the Fabian Window, the writings of V.I. Lenin or Antonio Gramsci, well, it should. He has plans for America and the world. He has had the sledge hammer for four years now. He continues to "remould the world nearer to [his] heart's desire." We must ask who he is really. Americans have not asked enough; they are far too trusting and far too naïve when it comes to Obama."

Psychologist & Medical Doctor on Barack Obama

Dr. Sam Vaknin is an Israeli psychologist, the author of the Malignant Self Love and he is a world authority on narcissism. He writes that Obama is totally in disguise, a man with zero accomplishment, not a genius and ignorant on most important subjects

Narcissists project a grandiose but false image of themselves. Jim Jones, the charismatic leader of People's Temple, the man who led over 900 of his followers to cheerfully commit mass suicide and even murder their own children was also a narcissist. David Koresh, Charles Manson, Stalin, Saddam, Mao, Kim Jong Ill, Che and Adolph Hitler are a few examples of narcissists of our time. All these men promised utopia but delivered hell. Victims of personality cults like those above find out too late. The manipulative genius of pathological narcissists is enough to lead their subjects to slaughter or to commit mass murder. Narcissists focused on one thing alone and that is power. For a narcissist no subject is as important as his own self. Narcissists are often callous and even ruthless. As the norm, they lack conscience. Like Obama's lack of interest in his own brother who lives on only one dollar per month.

The election of Obama was like no other in the history of America. Most voting Americans were duped to elect (aided by voting fraud and manipulation) a man bereft of conscience, a serial liar, and one who cannot distinguish his fantasies from reality. According to Dr. Vaknin, Obama evidences symptoms of pathological narcissism, which is different from the run-of-the-mill narcissism of a Richard Nixon or a Bill Clinton for example. This is a mental health issue, not just a character flaw. Pathological narcissists are dangerous because they look normal and even intelligent. This disguise makes them treacherous. 96% of blacks voted for Obama. Their support for him is racially driven; racism pure and simple.

America is on the verge of destruction. There is no insanity greater than electing a pathological narcissist as president.

Dr. Charles Krauthammer , MD from Harvard, was appointed to Presidential Council on Bioethics in 2002. He is frequently on the Fox News Channel. He is a brilliant intellectual, seasoned & articulate. He is forthright and careful in his analysis, and never resorts to emotions or personal insults. Following is a summary of his analysis of Obama.

1. Mr. Obama is very intellectual and charming. He is not to be underestimated. He is a cool customer who doesn't show his emotions. It's very hard to know what's behind the mask. The taking down of the Clinton dynasty was an amazing accomplishment. The Clintons still do not understand what hit them. Obama was in the perfect place at the perfect time.
2. Obama has political skills comparable to Reagan and Clinton. He has a way of making you think he's on your side, agreeing with your position, while doing the opposite. Pay no attention to what he SAYS; rather, watch what he DOES!
3. Obama has a ruthless quest for power. He did not come to Washington to make something out of himself, but rather to change everything, including dismantling capitalism. He can't be straightforward on his ambitions, as the public would not go along. He has a heavy hand, and wants to level the playing field with income redistribution and punishment to the achievers of society. He would like to model the USA to Great Britain or Canada.
4. His three main goals are to control ENERGY, PUBLIC EDUCATION, and NATIONAL HEALTHCARE by the Federal government. He doesn't care about the auto or financial services industries, but got them as an early bonus. The cap and trade will add costs to everything and stifle growth. FREE college education is his goal; education salted with progressive socialist teachings, paid for by our tax dollars. Most scary is his healthcare program, because if you make it FREE and add 46,000,000 people to a Medicare-type single-payer system, the costs will go through the roof. The only way to control costs is with massive RATIONING of services, like in Canada. God forbid!
5. He has surrounded himself with mostly far-left academic types. No one around him has ever even run a candy store. But they are going to try and run the auto, financial, banking and other industries. This obviously can't work in the long run. Obama is n a far-left secular progressive bent on nothing short of revolution. He ran as a moderate, but will govern from the hard left. Again, watch what he DOES, not what he says.
6. Obama doesn't really see himself as President of the United States, but more as a ruler over the world. He sees himself above it all, trying to orchestrate & coordinate various countries and their agendas. He sees moral equivalency in all cultures. His apology tour in Germany and England was a prime example of how he sees America, as an imperialist nation that has been arrogant, rather than a great noble nation that has at times made errors. This is the first President ever who has chastised our allies and appeased our enemies!
7. He is now handing out goodies. He hopes that the bill (and pain) will not come due until after his presidency. He would like to blame all problems on Bush from the past, and hopefully his successor in the future. He has a huge ego, and Dr. Krauthammer believes he is a narcissist.

Obama's Domestic Police Force

Obama promised to create a domestic police force just as powerful, just as strong as the U.S. Military. Why? Every despotism requires a nation police force to hold the people in line. Communism is a prime example.

The Transportation Security Administration TSA is that police force. They have conducted massive security exercises in Ohio, Kentucky and West Virginia in alliance with federal, state and local agencies, in preparation to be an occupying army for controlling domestic 'insurrections'. The advent is NSA spying and use of drones to monitor all domestic activity and control insurrections are our Orwellian future if the Administrations course is not altered. Part of their technology includes VIPR (Visible Intermodal Prevention and Response) a program to include Nazi-like surveillance of every citizen.

Why is does Obama need a domestic military force? It is because he knows that his fundamental transformation of America and his shredding the US Constitution will cause Patriots to revolt?

Woodrow Wilson issued a warning to heed; *"The concentration of power... is what always precedes the destruction of human liberties."* We should impeach Obama for treason.

Obama's Communist, Socialist, Extremist Czars

Show me who your friends are and I will tell you what kind of man you are. So let's examine Obama's associates and 'czar' appointees. They give him advice.

Obama has appointed Russian-type czars in at least 35 posts through presidential executive orders. These have been appointed with no Senate review or approval.

"The Obama administration has created a government that is manipulated behind the scenes by czars with broad powers beyond congressional reach.

Andy Stern - SEIU - one of the most frequent visitors to the white house. Past SEIU boss who use members to achieve socialistic ends. He orchestrates fear-inducing rallies to get what he wants. Stern says they will *"...use the power of persuasion, and if that doesn't work we will use the persuasion of power."*

Steven Lerner - current SEIU boss - promotes not paying your mortgage in order to bring down the capitalistic system by creating a crisis. Advocates violating the law in order to create chaos to advance the demise of the western way of life. Why is this guy not in jail?

Richard Trumpka - AFL-CIO Union boss. Now the most frequent visitor and who is in contact with the White House daily. Uses thug tactics to advance his agenda at the expense of union members.

Van Jones - Van Jones is President Obama's Special Advisor for Green Jobs at the White House Council on Environmental Quality (CEQ). He was the leader and founder of the radical group, Standing Together to Organize a Revolutionary Movement (STORM), a group explicitly committed to revolutionary Marxist politics. An ex-con who turned to communism in jail, a professed communist, Green jobs czar until Glenn Beck exposed who he was after which he resigned from the White House. Jones is currently a senior fellow at the Center For American Progress (a George Soros front organization to topple the United States and institute One World Order)

Ron Bloom & Anita Dunn - agree with Mao that political power comes from barrel of gun.

Bill Ayers & Jeff Jones – In 1969 they co-founded the Weather Underground, a self-described communist revolutionary group that conducted a campaign of bombing public buildings during the 1960s and 1970s. Now they are running our country.

Bernadine Dorn – wife of Bill Ayers, '60s radical, Weather Underground revolutionary – helped organized the anti-Jew 'Free Gaza Flotilla' a socialist/fascist group.

Margaret Sanger – birth control – white supremist who designed eugenics to eliminate blacks from society. Began in the public health programs of Europe – and influenced writing of Obamacare. Creator of Planned Parenthood; the satanic, despicable publicly funded slaughter house of 50+M aborted babies, and the dismemberment and selling of their body parts for profit.

Mark Lloyd - associate general counsel and Chief Diversity czar at the Federal Communications Commission. Believes in controlling the media like Chavez did in Venezuela to manage revolution and reform and essentially doing away with the First Amendment to the Constitution – Free Speech. He promotes gays in positions of power because they're gay. He thinks The Fairness Doctrine did not go far enough. Lloyd's race-based views of "diversity czar" Mark Lloyd, who has suggested "white people" step down from positions of power to allow "more people of color, gays" and "other people" to take those positions. Lloyd is a senior fellow at the George-Soros-funded Center for American Progress.

John Holdren – Heads the White House Office of Science and Technology Policy. A Marxist Science Czar who wants to "Educate" Climate Change Skeptics. (Note: in 2008 there are 31,500 climatologists and other scientists world-wide that have banned together in proclaiming global warming and climate change caused by man is a lie.) Holdren wants to change what is true so he and his cronies can gain money and power from cap and trade. Holdren called for a global carbon tax in order to "redistribute" wealth to the Southern Hemisphere.

Valerie Jarrett- Obama's ultimate insider, one of President Obama's closest advisers. Helps pick czars. Introduced to the president's political circles by her father-in-law, a communist sympathizer who worked with the radical Obama mentor Frank Marshall Davis.

Ron Bloom - another Maoist, socialist Obama czar.

Kevin Jennings - Obama appointed Kevin Jennings, an overt homosexual, and organizer of a group called Gay, Lesbian, Straight, Education Network, as 'safe school czar' who has a history of giving bad sex advice to teenagers. He has an admitted and unrepentant history of drug and alcohol abuse. (Matthew Hagee – ResponseABLE, p. 155)

Elizabeth Warren - Communist Head of Consumer Financial Protection Bureau

Donald Berwick – a radical communist to head the Centers for Medicare & Medicaid Services. In charge of your medical care.

Leon Panetta - current CIA Director with an anti-defense record, associations with identified communists, and support for the Marxist Institute for Policy Studies. Now our Secretary of Defense.

Eric Holder – US Attorney General, refuses to prosecute voter intimidation by the Black Panthers caught on video and their 'kill all white people, kill all cracker babies' hate speech by the Panthers, YET betrayed America along with Obama in siding with a foreign government, Mexico, on the subject of illegal invasion along our southern border. Communists and their Black Power fanatics have been working to create civil unrest.

Cass Sunstein – Regulatory Affair Czar and Extremist Threat to American Way of Life. Cass wants your wealth, energy, guns, meat, radio, internal organs, email and internet as you submit to Obama rule. Glenn Beck says he is "the most dangerous man in America." Propaganda czar. His tactics are to 'nudge' people into doing what he wants through increasingly tighter regulation. He's part of the reason for the collapse of America' s oil industry in the Gulf. He Advocates the U.S. Government employ teams of covert agents and pseudo-"independent" advocates to "cognitively infiltrate" online groups and websites -- as well as other activist groups -- which advocate views that Sunstein deems "false conspiracy theories" about the Government. This would be designed to increase citizens' faith in government officials and undermine the credibility of conspiracists. Sunstein advocates that the Government's stealth infiltration should be accomplished by sending covert agents into "chat rooms, online social networks, or even real-space groups." He also proposes that the Government make secret payments to so-called "independent" credible voices to bolster the Government's messaging (on the ground that those who don't believe government sources will be more inclined to listen to those who **appear** independent while secretly acting on behalf of the Government). Sunstein himself -- as part of his 2008 paper -- explicitly advocates that the Government should **pay** what he calls "credible independent experts" to advocate on the Government's behalf, a policy he says would be more effective because people don't trust the Government itself and would only listen to people they believe are "independent." (CAN YOU SAY GOODBYE TO THE FIRST AMENDMENT - THE FREEDOM OF SPEECH?)

Samantha Powers – Cass Sunstein's wife. Promotes war as a means to achieve liberal left agenda. She wrote The Problem from Hell, a book that promotes a Palestinian State and the elimination of the Jew 'occupiers' in Israel. Promoted the 'responsibility to protect' doctrine that George Soros endorses and which Obama used as justification to enter the war in Libya. Calls good evil and evil good by painting the Jews in Israel as the evil which must be destroyed using the 'responsibility to protect' doctrine she invented. Her goal is to destroy Israel and institute Soros's Open Society. She is a prime example of evil at work.

Jeremiah Wright – Obama's Pastor for 20 years of Trinity United Church of Christ, black liberation theology proponent, famous for his "G-d d---n America" speech. A major influence on Obama's hatred for America. Wright is the author of 'social justice'; which is nothing more than a means to justify socialism's redistribution of wealth. This is false doctrine. It is not Christianity which Wright professor to be a minister of. Christ taught 'individual justice'; each person is accountable to Christ for their own sins and each person must repent of their own sins to stand clean before the Judge of the World.

Was Nobody Listening?

On 7 Sep 2008 "Meet The Press" the Washington Post asked then Senator Obama about his stance on the American Flag.

The United States Code, Title 36, Chapter 10, Sec. 171...states that during rendition of the national anthem, when the flag is displayed, all present (except those in uniform) are expected to stand at attention facing the flag with the right hand over the heart. Or, at the very least, "Stand and Face It".

'Senator' Obama replied: *"As I've said about the flag pin, I don't want to be perceived as taking sides"*. *"There are a lot of people in the world to whom the American flag is a symbol of oppression." The anthem itself conveys a war-like message. You know, the bombs bursting in air* *and all that sort of thing." "The National Anthem should be 'swapped' for something less parochial and less bellicose. I like the song 'I'd Like To Teach the World To Sing'. If that were our anthem, then, I might salute it. In my opinion, we should consider reinventing our National Anthem as well as 'redesign' our Flag to better offer our enemies hope and love. **It's my intention, if elected, to disarm America to the level of acceptance to our Middle East Brethren.** If we, as a Nation of warring people, conduct ourselves like the nations of Islam, where peace prevails - - - perhaps a state or period of mutual accord could exist between our governments. "...my wife disrespects the Flag and she and I have attended several flag burning ceremonies in the past....CHANGE is about to overwhelm the United States of America."*

Obama's Hidden Agenda?

Why are Americans fighting where they are in the world? Consider the following:

1,000 were killed in Libya uprising before American soldiers intervened in under the UN banner.

8,800 were killed in the last 4 years in Afghanistan War.

And yet, 35,000 were killed by Mexican drug cartels along America's southern border since December 6, 2006. The victims were found in mass graves reminiscent of Hitler's Auschwitz. The murder rate has increases 60% from 2009 to 2010. And our Federal Government has not intervened yet!!!!

What is the hidden agenda of our government? Could it be intent to destroy America, to buy votes from illegal aliens, to gain and maintain more power and institute a One World Order?

States Secret Privilege

The state secrets privilege (SSP) is a common law privilege that allows the head of an executive department to REFUSE to produce evidence in a court case on the grounds that the evidence is secret information that would harm national security or foreign relation interests if disclosed.

Kevin Shipp was one of the most widely experience officers in the CIA. He uncovered un-constitutional actions by the CIA and tried to expose them. As a result he was silenced and the CIA moved Kevin and his family to a highly toxic home design to destroy their immune system and bring about slow death. Kevin fought back but was silenced again by the CIA. Kevin finally succeeded in publishing his book From the Company of Shadows exposing CIA's illegal actions.

Current controversy over the NSA's surveillance of every American is un-constitutional. So far they have succeeded in white washing their illegal actions.

Both the CIA and the NSA use the 'States Secret Privilege' to cover up their un-constitutional actions.

Cap & Trade

CAP & TRADE – If you're wondering why Democrats are pushing so hard for the cap-and-trade energy tax? For the Obama-Reid-Pelosi Democrats, it's more tax dollars to fund their takeover of selected industries. For big business, it is the massive profits from selling carbon credits, the price of which will simply be added to your heating and gasoline bills as well as the price of all other goods and services.

To push cap-and-trade legislation through Congress, major corporations with mammoth self-interests have joined with environmental fringe groups to form the high-powered lobbying organization — United States Climate Action Partnership (USCAP).

Cap & Trade was the brain child of Al Gore's global warming hoax. It is fear mongering at its best and fits right into Agenda 21 (explained later in this book).

31,500 climatologists and atmospheric scientists world-wide have united is stating 'global warming' is a hoax. Subsequent evidence continuously conforms the hoax. Yet the global warming crowd keep repeating the mantra of human factors cause global warming. Why? The answer is money to be made and power to be gained leading toward a One World Government.

CAP & TRADE is a criminal ring of corporations and politicians including Barack Obama, Al Gore, George Soros, SEIU, the Apollo Alliance and the Chicago Carbon Exchange (CCX). It is projected to be a $12 Trillion/year business; that's $12,000,000,000,000/year!

The truth is that the earth has always experienced normal climate fluctuations. Consider the Little Ice Age was a cooling period from 1550-1850AD occurred after the Medieval warm period from 950-1250AD.

Those involved in the 'global warming' hoax have been exposed. So now they call it 'climate change' instead. The authors of the hoax know that a lie repeated often enough becomes truth to the uninformed sheeple. And nothing motivates like fear.

The truth is that mankind's existence neither created the Medial Warm Period, The Little Ice Age nor the present climate change. It is simply the normal cycles of the earth's climate. Authors of the climate change hoax created an elaborate plan to tax carbon emissions of the evil US and other industrial nations, launder the money through the Chicago Carbon Exchange and redistribute the wealth to the less fortunate, after of course, they take the lions share off the top for themselves. The organizers intend to use this charade as a means to gain money and power in order to install their One World Order – with them as kings of course.

Obama Seizes Control of America

On March 16, 2012, President Obama issued an executive order entitled, NATIONAL DEFENSE RESOURCES PREPAREDNESS." This order states, "the President alone has the authority to take over all resources in the nation (labor, food, industry, etc.) as long as it is done "to promote the national defense" -- a phrase so vague that it could mean practically anything.

The power to seize control and take over these resources is delegated to the following government authorities:

(1) the Secretary of Agriculture with respect to food resources, food resource facilities, livestock resources, veterinary resources, plant health resources, and the domestic distribution of farm equipment and commercial fertilizer;
(2) the Secretary of Energy with respect to all forms of energy;
(3) the Secretary of Health and Human Services with respect to health resources;
(4) the Secretary of Transportation with respect to all forms of civil transportation;

(5) the Secretary of Defense with respect to water resources; and
(6) the Secretary of Commerce with respect to all other materials, services, and facilities, including construction materials.

This executive order gives the U.S. government power to steal all your crops, seeds, livestock and farm equipment using TSA or military force if necessary.

Nothing in this document talks about protecting the People's rights. The government determines whether it needs stockpiles of weapons, food and resources. YOU don't. It can make citizens slaves of the state. It is government laying the groundwork for tyranny.

The takeover is happening. In central Texas, FEMA has already calling farms across Texas and demanded an inventory list of all their crops and seeds. Secretary of Defense Leon Panetta recently revealed in U.S. Senate testimony that the Obama administration takes its orders from the UN and that the U.S. Congress is now null and void.

The Obama Phone

Professor Dominguez of Southern California University, San Diego working on a government grant, using our tax dollars, developed GPS cell phones for aliens to invade the USA illegally! Professor Dominguez was given tenure because of his project.

Welfare recipients are now eligible to receive what he described as (1) a FREE new cell phone, and (2) approximately 70 FREE minutes of air time every month. SafeLink Wireless is a government supported program that provides a free cell phone and airtime each month for income-eligible customers. In other words, your tax dollars are being distributed to a wireless phone provider to provide welfare recipients with free cell phones and airtime.

Obama 'Transparent' Administration

Clandestine midnight meetings, passing bills at night when the opposition is gone and outright lies reveal that his administration is anything BUT transparent.

Obama has broken all his campaign promises except one; to "fundamentally transform the United States of America".

Remember, God works in the light, Satan works in the dark.

Obama's Record

Results, not rhetoric, matter. Here's a summary of Obama's 6 year presidential record:

- Took over GM & Chrysler, a job killing disaster, just to benefit unions
- Told our military to stand down during the Benghazi attack
- Promoted NSA spying on Americans
- Promoted IRS to target politically opposing groups
- Helped orchestrate the Egypt disaster
- Spearheaded the Fast & Furious scandal with John Holder

- Promoted Cash For Clunkers boondoggle
- Financed the Solyndra scandal and disaster
- Shoved the Obama-care disaster down Americas throats
- Wasted millions on the failed jobs bill
- Promoted the Green jobs disaster. (Noteworthy is that Spain's green jobs program cost 2.2 regular jobs for every green job created. Only 1 in 10 of the newly created green jobs became permanent. Obama used Spain's green initiative as a blueprint for the United States. In 2011 Obama spent $20 M to create 14 green jobs. The definition of insanity is to do the same thing and expect different results.)

- Backs Al-Qaeda with Americas tax dollars in the Syria disaster – Obama now backs Al-Qaeda enemies with our tax dollars and weapons
- Did not go to France to show solidarity against the Muslim terrorists
- Spoke these words at an Islamic dinner - "I am one of you." Gave his fellow Muslim leaders the index finger sign confirming he is one of them.
- On ABC News referenced - "My Muslim faith."
- Gave $100 million in U.S. taxpayer funds to re-build foreign mosques.
- Wrote that in the event of a conflict -"I will stand with the Muslims."
- Assured the Egyptian Foreign Minister that - "I am a Muslim."
- Bowed in submission before the Saudi King.
- Listened for 20 years in a Liberation Theology Church condemning Christianity and professing Marxism.
- Exempted Muslims from penalties under Obamacare that the rest of us have to pay.
- Purposefully omitted - "endowed by our Creator" - from your recitation of The Declaration Of Independence.
- Mocked the Bible and Jesus Christ's Sermon On The Mount while repeatedly referring to the 'HOLY' Quran.
- Traveled the Islamic world denigrating the United States Of America.
- Gave support of your administration behind the building of the Ground Zero Victory mosque overlooking the hallowed crater of the World Trade Center.
- Refused to attend the National Prayer Breakfast, but hastened to host an Islamic prayer breakfast at the WH.
- Ordered Georgetown Univ. and Notre Dame to shroud all vestiges of Jesus Christ BEFORE you would agree to go there to speak, but in contrast, you have NEVER requested that the mosques you have visited adjust their decor.
- Appointed anti-Christian fanatics to your Czar Corps.
- Appointed rabid Islamists to Homeland Security.

- Directed NASA's "foremost mission" to be an outreach to Muslim communities.
- The only senator who spoke in favor of infanticide as Senator from Illinois.
- The first President not to give a Christmas Greeting from the White House, and hung ornaments on the White House holiday tree of Chairman Mao.
- Curtailed the military tribunals of all Islamic terrorists.
- Refused to condemn the Ft. Hood killer as an Islamic terrorist.
- Refused to speak-out concerning the horrific executions of women throughout the Muslim culture, but yet, have submitted Arizona to the UN for investigation of hypothetical human-rights abuses.
- Funneled $900 Million in U.S. taxpayer dollars to Hamas.
- Ordered the USPS to honor the MUSLIM holiday with a new commemorative stamp.
- Directed our UK Embassy to conduct outreach to help "empower" the British Muslim community.
- Embraced the fanatical Muslim Brotherhood in your quest to overthrow the Egyptian President, Hosni Mubarak.
- Funded mandatory Arabic language and culture studies in Grammar schools across our country.
- Follows the Muslim custom of not wearing any form of jewelry during Ramadan.
- Departs for Hawaii over the Christmas season so as to avoid past criticism for NOT participating in seasonal White House religious events.
- Were quick to commend the Muslim Brotherhood to depose Egypt's Hosni Mubarak, formerly America's strongest ally in North Africa; but, remain muted in your non-response to the Brotherhood led slaughter of Egyptian Christians.
- Appointed your chief adviser, Valerie Jarrett, an Iranian, who is a member of the Muslim Sisterhood, an off-shoot of the Muslim Brotherhood

America's Oil Reserves

On January 25, 2011 Al Gore stated that he wants gas prices to be artificially inflated to $5/gal. This will increase food prices and every other commodity that moves by truck.

The truth is that the U.S. has more oil than all the Middle East put together. The U. S. Geological Service issued a report in April 2008 stated the Bakken is the largest domestic oil discovery since Alaska's Prudhoe Bay, and has the potential to eliminate all American dependence on foreign oil. The Energy Information Administration (EIA) estimates it at 503 billion barrels. Even if just 10% of the oil is recoverable... at $107 a barrel, we're looking at a resource base worth more than $5...3 trillion. It's a formation known as the Williston Basin , but is more commonly referred to as the 'Bakken.' It stretches from Northern Montana, through North Dakota and into Canada. This is light, sweet oil that will cost Americans just $16 PER BARREL! That's enough crude to fully fuel the American economy for 2041 years straight.

In addition, Stansberry Reports that 1,000 feet beneath the surface of the Rocky Mountains lies the largest untapped oil reserve in the world. It is more than 2 TRILLION barrels. On August 8, 2005 President Bush mandated its extraction. In three and a half years of high oil prices none has been extracted. With this mother load of oil why are we still fighting over off-shore drilling?

The U.S. has 8-times as much oil as Saudi Arabia 18-times as much oil as Iraq, 21-times as much oil as Kuwait, 22-times as much oil as Iran, 500-times as much oil as Yemen right here in the Western United States.

Why are we not extracting this oil? Because the environmentalists and others have blocked all efforts to help America become independent of foreign oil! Again, we are letting a small group of people dictate our lives and our economy.

Baptist Minister Lindsey Williams reports in The Non-Energy Crisis that in the Prudhoe Bay, Alaska oil fields on Gull island has the largest oil deposit in NA and perhaps the world, more than in Saudi Arabia, which is enough to supply the US with oil for the next 200 years and would reduce the current price of oil to $1.50/gal.! Since that initial discovery they discovered another oil field as large as the first. The north slope of Alaska has enough oil for the USA for 400+ years.

In the 1960's the world's elite choose crude oil as the means to control the world. Crude oil affects the cost of virtually everything we consume. The Federal Government classified this discovery and denied US citizens access to that oil. Evil controls our Federal government. The evil is the IMF (International Monetary Fund) and The World Bank." (Lindsey Williams)

Transoceana Deepwater Horizon – Crucial offers to help clean up BP's oil spill "have come from Belgian, Dutch, and Norwegian firms that . . . possess some of the world's most advanced oil skimming ships." But the Obama administration wouldn't accept the help, because doing so would require it to do something past presidents have routinely done: waive rules imposed by the Jones Act, a law backed by unions. "The BP clean-up effort in the Gulf of Mexico is hampered by the Jones Act. This is a piece of 1920s protectionist legislation, that requires all vessels working in U.S. waters to be American-built, and American-crewed. So . . . the U.S. Coast Guard . . . can't accept, and therefore don't ask for, the assistance of high-tech European vessels specifically designed for the task in hand." BUT why are 1,500 available **US oil skimmers** not on the scene? Can you say intentional destruction of the US Oil industry?! The law itself permits the president to waive these requirements, and such waivers were "granted, promptly, by the Bush administration," in the aftermath of hurricanes and other emergencies. The Obama administration refused help from the Netherlands. Obama's inaction conveniently protected the unions who contributed heavily to get him elected. Obama loaned $2B of OUR TAX MONEY to Petrobas, a Brazilian oil company to drill for oil far deeper that in the gulf off the shores of Brazil. Later he promised the new Brazilian Marxist president that the US would be their biggest customer. Also George Soros invested $900 million in Petrobas so Obama used our tax dollars to pad George's wealth. This is a clear example of redistribution of wealth from America to Brazil. It is Marxist doctrine to bring down the evil rich and redistribute wealth. It is Obama's economic terrorism to 'fundamentally transform' the USA into his goal of a socialistic society.

NAACP 'Racist' Rally Offense

George Washington statue is hidden at the MLK rally in Columbia , SC The annual MLK observance at the state house in Columbia SC had an interesting twist this year. The event is held on the north side steps of the statehouse.

Prominent at that location is a large bronze statue of George Washington.

The NAACP constructed a "box" to conceal the father of our country from view so that participants would not be 'offended' by his presence.

This rally was sponsored by the NAACP and they said that they covered the statue because they "didn't want to offend anyone".

What if we covered the statue of Dr. Martin L. King on President's Day?

The NAACP exposed itself as militant and racist.

The NAACP rally cover up of George Washington is a classic manifestation of the effects of progressive/liberal left demonizing the Father of our Country in order to advance their own socialist agenda.

Progressive Tactics To Destroy America

Obama gave $2B to Brazils Petrobas for deep water drilling for oil that he agreed to buy from Brazil. Meanwhile, Obama shut down relatively shallow water drilling in the Gulf of Mexico and had Cass Sunstein create impossible requirements for US oil companies to obtain drilling permits that would have sustained America's oil needs. Obama's block of the Keystone pipeline is just another manifestation of ill intent for America. His actions reveal his hatred for the USA and capitalism and his carefully crafted intent to overthrow the US Constitution and government, and redistribute Americas wealth here and abroad.

The leader of the national gay marriage initiatives recently revealed that their agenda is not equal treatment under law; it is to destroy traditional marriage. Strong traditional families have been the foundation of great civilizations throughout history. History documents that when the family crumbles, so does that nation. Obama's shift from pre-election campaign in support of traditional marriage between a man and a woman, to post election actions in support of gay marriage reveal intent to destroy the foundation of America.

George Soros

Hungarian born August 12, 1930, György Schwartz, AKA George Soros, was tutored by his father, Tivadar, a practitioner of the Esperanto language invented in 1887, that was created to be the first global language, free of any national identity. The Schwartz's were non-practicing Jews, changed the family name to Soros to assimilate into the Nazi movement in the 1930s

Hitler's murderous Adolf Eichmann hired George Soros to help oversee the murder of Hungary's Jews. As a Nazi stooge Soros confiscated Jewish property and called 1944 'the best year of his life in which he exercised absolute power.' 70% Jews in Hungary, were murdered that year

Soros moved to New York City in 1956, where he worked on Wall Street. He made his first billion in 1992 by shorting the British pound with leveraged billions in financial bets, and became known as the man who broke the Bank of England. He broke it on the backs of hard-working British citizens who immediately saw their homes severely devalued and their life savings cut drastically, almost overnight, just like America in the 2008 crash.

In 1997, Soros almost destroyed the economies of Thailand and Malaysia. At the time, Malaysia's Prime Minister, Mahathir Mohammad, called Soros a villain, and a moron. Thai activist regard George Soros as a kind of Dracula. He sucks the blood from the people.

Soros was part of the team that dismantled Yugoslavia and caused trouble in Georgia, Ukraine and Myanmar [Burma]. To hide his evil actions Soros calls himself a philanthropist and does contribute money. However, his actions of globalization and promoting the New World Order along with his own financial gain reveals his true nature.

France upheld an earlier conviction against Soros, for felony insider trading and was fined $2.9M. His native Hungary fined Soros $2.2M for illegal market manipulation.

Soros has been actively working to destroy America from the inside out for years. Soros [is] an extremist who wants open borders, a one-world foreign policy, legalized drugs, and euthanasia. Soros uses his philanthropy to destroy moral values and attitudes of the Western world, and particularly of the American people. His "open society" is not about freedom; it is about license. His vision favors PROGRESSIVE ideology of rights and entitlements.

Soros admitted that he helped engineer coups in Slovakia, Croatia, Georgia, and Yugoslavia. When Soros targets a country for "regime change," he begins by creating a shadow government, a fully formed government-in-exile, ready to assume power when the opportunity arises. The Shadow Party he has built in America greatly resembles those he has created in other countries prior to instigating a coup. It is the Obama administration.

George Soros' media empire has overthrown governments in the past. His current focus is to overthrow the U.S. Government. His evil empire includes scores of organizations. Including: America Independent New America Media, Free Press, Media Consortium, INN, Media Development, Tome Fund, Media & Democracy Coalition, Media Wiretap, Sundance Institute, Huffington Post, Investigative Reporting, Wiscomb Watch.Org, Brave New TV, Brave New Films, RNN, Washington Monthly, Balcony Films, Open Society Institute, Media Matters, Moveon.org, Tides Foundation, Acorn, Apollo Alliance, Center for American Progress (started by Soros and Hillary Clinton) and 100+ more organizations, (check out more on Glenn Beck.com)

Soros's has toppled governments in Europe, and enjoys the game. His last and greatest target is to destroy America and capitalism. His goal is to institute his One World Order. George Soros is an evil man. He's anti-God, anti-family, anti-American, and anti-good. He helped the Nazis during the holocaust; he killed and robbed his own Jewish people. He is a multi-billionaire atheist, with skewed moral values, and a sociopaths lack of conscience. He considers himself to be an elitist world class philosopher, despises the American Way and just loves to do social engineering (change cultures). He is a Rothschild agent.

Obama came from virtually nowhere and became President with encouraging and complicit media including ABC, NBC, CBS, MSNBC & CNN. How? George Soros backing.

To Soros the main obstacle to a stable and just world order is the United States. He despises the American way. He exposes the "open society" , the philosophy most of the Western democracies have followed since WWII about making social reform, and it has gotten them into a grand mess." Soros said that Obama presents us a great opportunity to deal with global warming and energy dependence by executing a cap and trade system with auctioning of licenses for emissions rights. This has become the Chicago Exchange.

Soros's tactics in summary are: – topple regimes, destroy free markets, create food shortages that precipitate price controls, control the supply of goods and services so that no one can trade, buy or sell without Revelations Mark of the Beast.

This tactic worked well for Pharaoh in ancient Egypt. Instead of exercising their moral agency to store up a reserve for themselves against a day of need, the Egyptians depended upon the government. First they used their money to buy food. When that was gone, they gave their livestock, then their lands, and finally they were compelled to sell themselves into slavery, that they might eat. (Gen 41:54-56; 47:13-26)

Soros donated $5B to the Democratic National Committee, DNC, to insure Obama's win. He also engineered wins for many other Saul Alinsky trained Radicals. George continues to contribute $1+ to the DNC since Clinton.

Soros has infected the RNC also, has long held connections with the CIA, controls much of the Main Stream Media, the entertainment industry, owns 2.6 million shares of Time Warner.

Soros has been buying up media real estate for years to promote his message that Americans are too materialistic, wasteful, selfish, and stupid to run their own lives.

Soros' philanthropy, totaling nearly $5 billion, undermines America's traditional values. He initiatives for abortion, feminism, anti-Second Amendment, anti-free speech, sex education, euthanasia, globalization, mass immigration, atheism, drug legalization, and gay marriage.

Back On Uncle Sam's Plantation

Star Parker, author of "Uncle Sam's Plantation" exposed what it is like living inside the welfare state and her transformation to freedom. She notes that there are two Americas: A poor America on socialism and a wealthy America on capitalism.

Socialist government programs including Temporary Assistance for Needy Families (TANF), Job Opportunities and Basic Skills Training (JOBS), Emergency Assistance to Needy Families with Children (EANF), Section 8 Housing, and Food Stamps are government entrapments. They are the new government plantation where the government changes participants mindsets from How do I take care of myself?" to "What do I have to do to stay on the plantation? Instead of solving economic problems, government welfare socialism created monstrous moral and spiritual problems. These problems are inevitable when individuals turn responsibility for their lives over to others. The legacy of American socialism is our blighted inner cities, dysfunctional inner city schools, and broken black families. Ironically, this evil has exacerbated under Obama, our first black president on the 200th anniversary of the birthday of Abraham Lincoln.

Americans must choose to accept Obama's invitation to move onto the plantation or wake up and choose personal responsibility and freedom.

How to Catch A Pig - & Sheeple

There was a chemistry professor in a large college that had some exchange students in the class.

One day while the class was in the lab, the professor noticed one young man, an exchange student, who kept rubbing his back and stretching as if his back hurt. The professor asked the young man what was the matter.

The student told him he had a bullet lodged in his back. He had been shot while fighting communists in his native country who were trying to overthrow his country's government and install a new communist regime.

In the midst of his story, he looked at the professor and asked a strange question. He asked: "Do you know how to catch wild pigs?"

The professor thought it was a joke and asked for the punch line.

The young man said that it was no joke You catch wild pigs by finding a suitable place in the woods and putting corn on the ground. The pigs find it and begin to come every day to eat the free corn. When they are used to coming every day, you put a fence down one side of the place
where they are used to coming. When they get used to the fence, they begin to eat the corn again and you put up another side of the fence.

They get used to that and start to eat again. You continue until you have all four sides of the fence up with a gate in the last side. The pigs, which are used to the free corn, start to come through the gate to eat that free corn again. You then slam the gate on them and catch the whole herd. Suddenly the wild pigs have lost their freedom. They run around and around inside the fence, but they are caught. Soon they go back to eating the free corn. They are so used to it that they have forgotten how to forage in the woods for themselves, so they accept their captivity.

The young man then told the professor that is exactly what he sees happening in America. The government keeps pushing us toward Communism/Socialism and keeps spreading the free corn out in the form of programs such as supplemental income, tax credit for unearned income,
tax exemptions, tobacco subsidies, dairy subsidies, payments not to plant crops (CRP), welfare, medicine, drugs, etc. while we continually lose our freedoms, just a little at a time.

There is no such thing as a free lunch.

Our Anti-Christian Government

Socialists (Progressives) have targeted Chick-Fil-A, a Southern based company.

Chick-fil-A is an American success story. Founded by Georgian entrepreneur Truett Cathy in 1946, the family-owned chicken-sandwich chain is one of the country's largest fast-food businesses. It employs some 50,000 workers across the country at 1,500 outlets in nearly 40 states and the District of Columbia ... The Company generates more than $2B in revenue and serves millions of happy customers with trademark Southern hospitality.

Chick-fil-A is run by devout Christians who believe in strong marriages, devoted families, and the highest standards of character for their workers. The restaurant chain's official corporate mission is to "glorify God" and "enrich the lives of everyone we touch." The company's community-service initiatives, funded through its WinShape Foundation, support foster-care, scholarship, summer-camp, and marriage-enrichment programs. On Sunday, all Chick-fil-A stores close so workers can spend the day at worship and rest.

I STILL HATE COMMUNISM & SOCIALISM

EVEN AFTER THEY STARTED CALLING IT 'LIBERAL' & 'PROGRESSIVE'

f/RIGHTWINGRANTSRAVES

Recently several progressive-activist blogs have waged an ugly war against Chick-fil-A. The company's alleged atrocity: One of its independent outlets in Pennsylvania donated some sandwiches and brownies to a marriage seminar run by the Pennsylvania Family Institute, which happens to oppose same-sex marriage.

In the name of tolerance, the anti-Chick-fil-A hawks sneered at the company's main product as "Jesus Chicken," derided its no-Sunday-work policy, and attacked its operators as "anti-gay." Petition drives on websites are demanding the company change and disavow their standards. Facebook users dutifully organized witch-hunts against the company on college campuses.

Progressive groups are gloating over Chick-fil-A's public-relations troubles. This is not because they care about winning hearts and minds over gay rights or marriage policy, but because their core objective is to marginalize political opponents and chill Christian philanthropy and activism. The fearsome "muscle flexing" is being done by the hysterical bullies trying to drive them off of college grounds and out of their neighborhoods in the name of "human rights.

Then there is the case of the wedding cake providers in Oregon who were driven out of business because they refused to make wedding cakes for gay marriages.

Gays use the banner of tolerance to advance their agenda. However, it is obvious that they do not tolerate others rights to run their business according to their principles and values.

The point is: Private companies with Christian principles have a right to freely conduct business in the U.S.

Our Broken System Of Western Medicine

Secret combinations have infiltrated our government and big business also. Pharmaceutical companies control many of the government organizations like the Food & Drug Administration (FDA). Merck, Pfizer, Hoffman/Larouche and Glaxo/Smith/Kline market anti-depression drugs on TV and other media. America's $12 billion antidepressant market pushes pills to kids.

'Pharmaceutical' comes from the Greek word, 'pharmakeuein', meaning 'to practice witchcraft', and from the word 'pharmokon' meaning 'to poison.'

Merck paid 72 doctors $2,500 each to use their name to promote Vioxx. We now know that Vioxx is extremely harmful, even causing death in some instances. When you hear/see the latest greatest drug to fix you problem, recognize that is nothing more than paid propaganda to sell their product.

The Journal of the American Medical Association (JAMA) reports that "Adverse drug reactions are the fourth leading cause of death in America. Reactions to prescription and over-the-counter medications kill far more people annually than all illegal drug use combined."

Government grants and subsidies, and big business research funding to colleges and universities, pay for a large portion of their operating budgets. Thus, the education & training of medical doctors are influence greatly by these controlling entities. Most western medical education and training focus on treating serious injuries & illness with surgery & drugs. Typically, MD's receive none, or 3 hrs. maximum education on preventative health and wellness. The old adage applies: an ounce of prevention is worth a pound of cure.

Evidence of our broken western medical system lies in the lives of MD's themselves. The average lifespan in the USA is 75.5 years. The average life span of medical doctors is only 58 years. Drug company propaganda has deluged our minds with 'ask your doctor' (meaning MD's) to see if this drug is for you. MD's kill 300,000 people/year by mis-diagnosis, prescribing wrong drugs, wrong dosage etc. which is the equivalent of 2 – 747's colliding mid-air every day with no survivors. (Ralph Nader 1993).

Every year approximately 200,000 die from prescription drug reactions. Another 80,000 die from medical malpractice. 41,000 die in auto accidents. (International Coalition for Drug Awareness)

"The American medical system is the leading cause of death and injury in the US." (FDA employee and Vioxx whistleblower Dr. David Graham)

The sad tragedy is that we are spending all of this money on disease management focused on drugs and surgery, and our return on investment is profoundly poor. People do not have the energy they need to get through the day while millions are suffering with painful crippling diseases because they have violated basic health principles.

Doctors Are The Third Leading Cause of Death in the US, Causing 250,000 Deaths Every Year (Journal of the American Medical Association (JAMA)) ... the tragedy of the traditional medical paradigm. (JAMA - the most widely circulated medical periodical in the world.) No wonder 60% of people seeking health care go to alternative sources (chiropractor, acupuncture, physical therapy, massage therapy, aromatherapy, essential oils, natural supplements, organic foods, etc.)

Dr. Barbara Starfield/Johns Hopkins School of Hygiene & Public Health: **ALL THE FOLLOWING ARE DEATHS PER YEAR:**

      12,000 -- unnecessary surgery

7,000 -- medication errors in hospitals
20,000 -- other errors in hospitals
80,000 -- infections in hospitals
106,000 -- non-error, negative effects of drugs

These total to 250,000 deaths per year from iatrogenic causes!! [iatrogenic - induced in a patient by a physician's activity, manner, or therapy.] Journal American Medical Association July 26, 2000;284(4):483-5

"More than 100,000 Americans die every year, not from illegal drugs, not from drug overdoses, not from over-the-counter drugs, and not from drug abuses, but from properly prescribed, properly taken prescriptions." (Centers for Disease Control)

In this country, more people die from doctor's prescriptions every ten days than were killed in the 9/11 terrorist attacks. (THE RAINDROP MESSENGER, Volt 1, No. 8, September 2003)

"The cause of most disease is in the poisonous drugs physicians superstitiously give in order to effect a cure." Charles E. Page, M.D.

"Medicines are of subordinate importance because of their very nature, they can only work symptomatically." Hans Kusche, M.D.

"The person who takes medicine must recover twice, once from the disease and once from the medicine." William Osler, M.D.

"Every drug increases and complicates the patient's condition." Robert Henderson, M.D.

"The greatest part of all chronic disease is created by the suppression of acute disease by drug poisoning." Henry Lindlahr, M.D.

"Drugs never cure disease. They merely hush the voice of nature's protest, and pull down the danger signals she erects along the pathway of transgression." Daniel. HE. Kress, ME.DO. THE RAINDROP MESSENGER, Volt 1, No. 8, September 2003

In 1997 the FDA had 55% of its employees' salaries paid for by the drug companies!

The fact is that western medicine is controlled in large part by pharmaceutical companies who have the money to fund medical colleges, over half the salaries at the FDA, control, media advertising of their products, and sponsorship of MD's 'training.' They focus on drugs and surgery as solutions while the rest of the world focusses health prevention and wellness.

United Nations Agenda 21:

U.N. Agenda 21 is a global warming/climate change concocted hoax of the One World Order communist initiative to control wealth and redistribution in every facet of our lives; land use, food production and distribution, education (AKA indoctrination), population control, health care, reduction of economic activity, population reduction, private property, fossil fuels, consumerism, farming, irrigation, commercial agriculture, pesticides, herbicides, farmlands, grazing of livestock,

paved roads, golf courses, ski lodges, logging, dams, reservoirs, fences, power lines, suburban living, and the traditional family unit. To concoct the hoax Paul Homewood reports that the authors engaged in 'massive tampering with temperature data in South America.' The Global Historical Climatology Network (GHCN), an integrated database of climate summaries from land surface stations across the globe, "show the extent to which they have adjusted temperatures upwards.

Mikhail Gorbachev, former head of the Soviet Union, is now the head of a new organization called the International Green Cross. He has been transformed from a communist/socialist to an ecological, save the planet, savior. The Council of the Club of Rome, of which Gorbachev is a member, issued a report entitled, The First Global Revolution, p. 115 states: *"In searching for a new enemy to unite us, we came up with the idea that pollution, the threat of global warming, water shortages, famine and the like would fit the bill....All these dangers are caused by human intervention....The real enemy, then, is humanity itself."*

Agenda 21 is a Global Economic Disaster In The Making. It was a 1992 initiative proposed at the U.N. sponsored Conference on Environment and Development, (the "Earth Summit"), held in Rio De Janeiro, Brazil. It states: *"Agenda 21 is a comprehensive plan of action to be taken globally, nationally and locally by organizations of the United Nations System, Governments, and Major Groups in every area in which human impacts on the environment. It is an all-encompassing prescription for regulating every aspect of human activity in the interest of "sustainable development."*

It is all about the CONTROL of YOU by the UNITED NATIONS!

AGENDA 21/SUSTAINABLE DEVELOPMENT

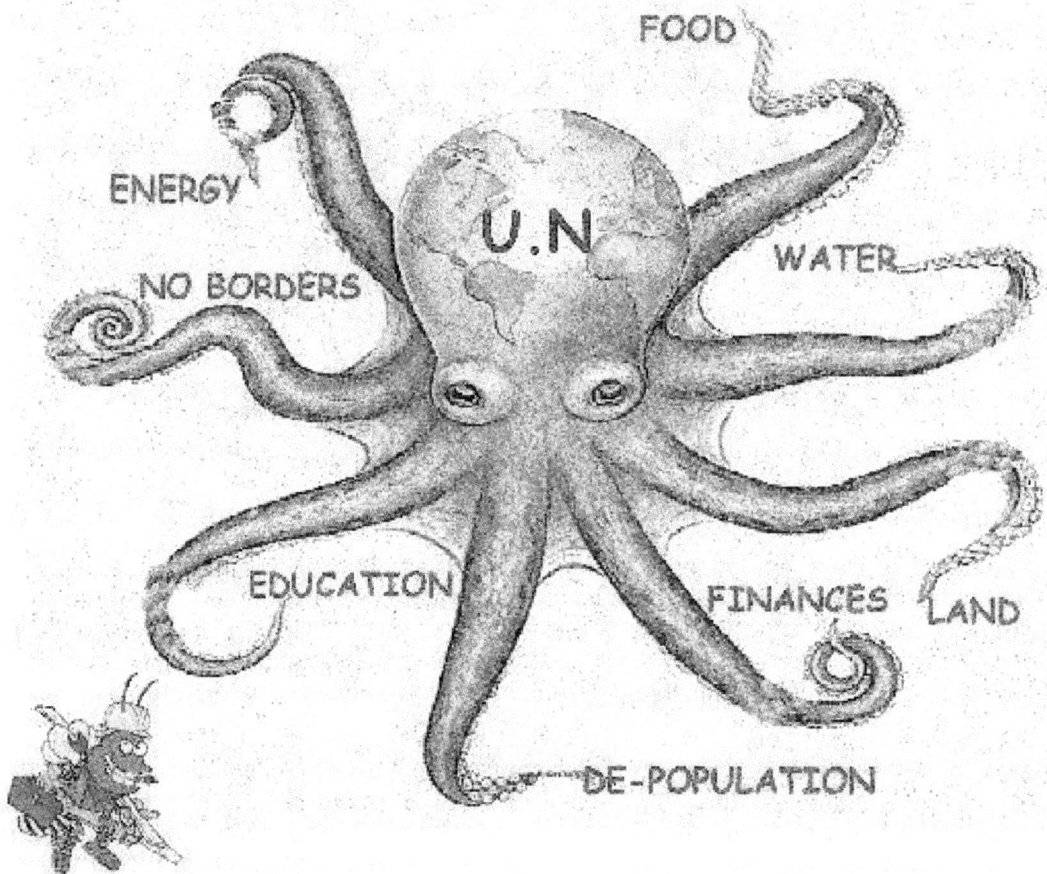

FOOD

ENERGY

U.N

NO BORDERS

WATER

EDUCATION

FINANCES LAND

DE-POPULATION

Do You Really Want To Be a "Worker Bee" for the UN?

The United Nations Agenda 21 is behind global warming, cap & trade, the Chicago Exchange Commission, the Arab spring, unchecked illegal immigration, gun control, health control, food control, population control, land & water use control, wealth redistribution, destroying capitalism, weakening the USD and replacing the USD as the world's reserve currency, carbon taxes, high gasoline prices, Common Core [de]-education, biofuels and Marxist advancement.

The United Nations Agenda 21 was signed by the United States in 1992 and it is being implemented throughout the U.S. Federal government and in every local community in America.

Global warming alarmists misinterpreted the climate. Most inter-glacial periods begin with an abrupt warming, peak sharply, and then begin a gradual descent into cooler conditions. That is what is occurring now. None of this climate change has anything to do with mankind's industrial impact, carbon dioxide, ozone, or any other element of the Earth's atmosphere. It is entirely the result of the lower solar radiation of heat.

Instead of preparing for the coming cooling the United States has wasted billions to promote renewable energy, wind and solar. These types of energy sources are costly and ineffective. Solar power will make up 0.6 percent of total U.S. electricity generation in 2015. Wind power has received $7.3 billion over the past seven years, but produces < 1% of electricity.

The Environmental Protection Agency's Obama directed 'war on coal' forced many plants that provide electricity at low cost to close. In addition, instead of providing food, tons of corn are being turned into ethanol in the name of reducing carbon dioxide even though CO_2 plays no role whatever in a 'global warming' that is not happening.

The winter of 2014-2015 in the U.S. and in much of the northern hemisphere is experiencing increased cooling with record-breaking and record-setting low temperatures, snow and ice. This trend is due to the normal cycle of the Sun's and Earth's.

Global warming and climate change trumpeters continue to beat out their lies in order to transform the global economic system from capitalism, the most effective creator of growth and wealth, to socialism, a pathetic, failed system of income redistribution controlled by a central government.

Real climatologists, meteorologists, and scientists paying attention to both the past and to present events are forecasting more intense and longer winters—a Little Ice Age.

The Brundtland Commission chaired by Gro Harlem Brundtland, Norway's socialist former Prime Minister, who also served as vice-chair of the Socialist International created the definition of sustainability as: Sustainable Development is development that meets the needs of the present without compromising the ability of future generations to meet their own needs.

Carol Browner, President Obama's Energy and Environment Czar, also served with Socialist International.

Sustainable development is a socialist idea, that demands redistribution of land, resources and private property into government hands. One particularly odious quote is: "*Land, because of its unique nature and the crucial role it plays in human settlements, cannot be treated as an ordinary asset, controlled by individuals* and subject to the pressures and inefficiencies of the market. *Private land ownership is also a principal instrument of accumulation and concentration of wealth and therefore contributes to social injustice;* if unchecked, it may become a major obstacle in the planning and implementation of development schemes. Social justice, urban renewal and development, the provision of decent dwellings-and healthy conditions for the people can only be achieved if land is used in the interests of society as a whole.*"

The Brundtland Commission included Maurice Strong (Canada's version of George Soros, an oil billionaire who, has the destruction of the West), William Ruckelshaus (first head of the EPA – the only American) and luminaries from such enlightened states as   , Communist China, the USSR, Algeria, Saudi Arabia and Cote D'Ivoire.

Sustainable Development" has become the buzzword for a strategy to completely control every aspect of our lives, including resettling entire populations. The 1976 U.N. Conference on Human Settlements called for population redistribution:

Sustainability is code word for communism.

Monsanto is a major player in Agenda 21 with designs to control the worlds food supply and thus population.

Land conservation is one arm of U.N. Agenda 21. All across the U.S. land is locked in conservation projects and easements contracts are convenient financial hooks to take land out of agricultural use in perpetuity under the guise of protecting it.

Marxism survives because they re-package the same ideas in flowery or obscure language. Consider the following phraseology. Everything in quotes comes directly from UN sustainability documents:

"Social Justice" assures the right to benefit equally from the resources afforded us by society and the environment = equal distribution of wealth = communism.

"Social Justice" assures that every worker/person will be a direct capital owner = dictatorship of the proletariat = communism.

"Sustainability" means that individual rights will have to take a back seat to the collective. "collective" = communism.

"Public/private   partnerships"   = Government   subsidized   competitive advantage, wipes out competing private business, allows for monopoly government control = communism.

Monsanto & Agenda 21

Food Domination and Depopulation: Monsanto's Monopoly

MONSANTO

NO FOOD SHALL BE GROWN THAT WE DON'T OWN

Under the guise of "saving the earth" the socialists have explicitly demanded redistribution of income.

Agenda 21's **Millennium Development Project** requires developed countries, to donate 0.7 percent of GDP every year, in 2002 that was $103B; an amount that would fund the Departments of State, Justice and Energy, as well as the entire Legislative and Judicial branches of the U.S. government or the departments of Homeland Security, Interior and Housing and Urban Development.

The United States contributes the largest share of any nation to the U.N. Budget. We provide the largest contribution to the International Monetary Fund, the World Bank, and every other similar organization. We provide billions in loans, subsidies and grants to other nations through separate programs within multiple federal agencies and offer private loans subsidized or guaranteed by the government. The result - everyone still hates us. Money really cannot buy you love!

The U.N. has always been anti-American. Agenda 21 attempts to dictate every aspect of our lives *and we are paying for most of it.*

Just as socialism mindlessly reduces life to a tug-of-war between the haves and have-nots, Agenda 21 reveals the real agenda of its authors; and it is a Trojan horse. Socialists see life as a zero sum game: if someone is wealthy, he must have taken it from the poor; if we are rich today, it must follow that future generations will be weaker. Current generations greedily sap our resources, leaving less for the future. The sustainable development crowd has transformed this complaint into public policy, "Anthropogenic Climate Change" to force the issue.

Below the "water-line" of the Sustainability Iceberg

- What you see ➡ · Green / · Everything ➡ · **Effect:** Marketable Window Dressing

- **Their Premises (excuses)** ➡ · Catastrophic Global Warming & Sea Level Rise / · Social Justice Demands ➡ · **Effect:** Create Fear

- **Their A21 "Sustainable" values** ➡ · Environment; Economy Social Equity ➡ · **Effect:** Collective trumps the Individual

- **Their Antidote** ➡ · Government Control: Production & Consumption (Marxism) ➡ · **Effect:** Arrest capitalism & freedom

Man-caused Global Warming has been scientifically and solidly disproved. It is a hoax. Caught in a lie, socialists rebranded 'Global Warming' as 'Climate Change' to advance their agenda of control and profit. The truth is, climate change is a natural cycle of the Earth – a NATURAL cycle, not caused by man. But evil uses it today to advance evils agenda.

AGENDA 21 Eco Terrorism

Agenda 21 is satan's old trick; create a state of fear – call it Eco-Terrorism and divert attention from what is really happening. AKA sell the Rose but hide the Thorns or a spoonful of lies help make the medicine go down.

A common theme of college courses in environmental conservation is the "greediness" of American consumer society. They repeat the mantra that "America consumes 25% of the world's resources but is only 5% of the world's population." The implication is that America is wasteful and unfair. We should only consume 5% of our resources. However, what happens to countries exports to America when they drop from 80% to 5%. Their economies collapse.

A better way to look at this issue is that America consumes 25% of the world's resources to produce 25% of the world's GNP. America's economy buoys all others.

History reveals that during the Great Depression, U.S. GDP declined by 27 percent. World industrial production fell 31 percent as a result. Worldwide calamity ensued, culminating in World War II. What if America reduced GDP by 80 percent?

The Cap and Trade bill will cause a catastrophic decline in living standards. Every country that adopts the socialist/communist model so far has become an environmental disaster area. Socialism's true objective is power. The sustainability agenda will certainly destroy world economies, in the process of doing so it will hand absolute power to the people promoting it.

Environmentalism' has become a convenience beat down tool of progressives to advance their One World Order (OWO) toward tyranny; blame the greedy West, redistribute the wealth so everyone becomes poor subjects to the OWO leaders.

Following are three examples of how environmentalism has been used, DDT, Ozone and climate change - and there outcomes:

DDT - Environmentalisms origins have roots in Rachel Carsons' book published in 1962, The Silent Spring in which she argued that DDT was accumulating in our environment causing the thinning of the eggs of birds resulting in fewer bald eagles. It was also accused of increasing cancer risks in children. During the time of its use DDT virtually eliminated malaria; a leading cause of death in the world.

Driven by Carson's theory, politicians do what politicians do. They acted swiftly to save eagles and children and outlawed DDT. The result was the return of malaria, particularly in poor nations.

Here is what we now know. In 2010 nearly 220 million Africans caught malaria and 660,000 died. After 25 years and 50 million preventable deaths, The World Health Organization has reversed its position. It now advocates painting the inside walls of home with DDT in high risk areas.

Ozone - The 1970s scientists observed that the ozone layer in the stratosphere above Antarctica thinned at times. It was argued that less ozone allowed more ultraviolet rays to reach the earth increasing our risk of skin cancers. The culprit was chlorofluorocarbon (CFC) used in freon for coolants in air conditioning. It was thought that chlorine escaped from the CFC molecule reacted with the ozone and caused it to become thinner.

In 1987, 25 nations signed the Montreal Protocol to protect the ozone layer. They outlawed freon.

Here is what we now know. Ozone filters out UV-B rays and they are not the rays that cause skin cancer. UV-A rays cause skin cancer and they are unaffected by ozone filtration. Ozone is not a chemical reaction but a result of normal atmospheric changes.

Climate Change – It started with the guilt-trip man-caused global warming scheme that scientists throughout the world debunked. So progressives changed their tactic and now call is man-caused climate change, supposedly caused by CO_2 emissions from burning fossil fuels. John Kerry calls climate change is the "world's most fearsome destructive weapon."

While it is true that uncontrolled burning of coal emits sulfur into the atmosphere that can damage ecosystems 100's of miles downwind and compromises air quality as in Bejing, there is no evidence that fossil fuel burning precipitated current climate change.

The global warming/climate change alarm tactic was built on the same fear mongering as the ozone hole. The Montreal Protocol to ban freon was the warm-up exercise for the Intergovernmental Panel on Climate Change (IPCC). IPCC alarmists gained recognition by badgering the U.S. Congress into supporting the Montreal Protocol. They used dramatized, phony scientific claims like 'ozone holes over Kennebunkport'" (President Bush Sr.'s seaside residence in New England). Fear mongering sunk to new lows when IPCC advocates used dying polar bears, shrinking arctic ice caps to advance their agenda. Educators frighten and brainwash children into the same man-made global warming fantasy, using cuddly and lonely polar bears floating on ice floes as examples of a vanishing species due to global warming, when in reality the polar bear population has increased five-fold.

Agenda 21 is a financially motivated political scam advanced by Al Gore. It is based not on science, but on contrived computer models, manipulated climatological data and fear. The objective – to gain power and control through the Chicago Exchange, to redistribute wealth and bring down the West – of course except for those in control.

Here is what we now know. Millions of years ago the atmosphere had more than four times the CO_2 that is currently in our atmosphere yet there was no industrial activity or humans to cause it. Computer models cannot duplicate the known climate. Earth has experienced times when the CO_2 levels were 50 times greater than the present level and survived. There are about 20,000-25,000 polar bears in the artic today compared with 5,000 to 10,000 in the 1950s. The arctic ice cap is expanding. Ottmar Endenhofer, an IPCC official advised: "...one has to free oneself from the illusion that international climate policy is environmental policy. Instead, climate change policy is about how we redistribute de facto the world's wealth..."

This author believes that we do need to make continuous improvements in our stewardship of 'mother Earth.' After all, there is 'No Away'. We are a closed system. Our Earth is the best planet living option we have. Therefore, we had better take care of it. Earth provides ecosystem services that sustain all life. We must repent of our past polluting ways. We must create human cyclical systems in bio-mimicry of Earth's ecosystems. However, we must fight against the socialistic use of sustainability and the environmental movement. Satan uses socialism to persuade and communism to force people to comply. God uses freedom of choice coupled with stewardship of Earth's resources to invite people to care for the Earth. Capitalism provides the options for people to choose with their wallet and drive the free market toward a greener, more sustainable future. We must add the triple bottom line – people, planet & profit - to capitalism to produce more sustainable living on Earth.

American Arrogance – really?

Obama apologizes to Europe and the Middle East that our country is "arrogant"! Perhaps if he reminded those of our sacrifice he wouldn't confuse arrogance with leadership.

Consider the following facts: American Soldiers who died to free other people from the tyranny of Adolf Hitler's Nazi German Third Reich:

1. The American Cemetery at Aisne-Marne, France... A total of 2289
2. The American Cemetery at Ardennes, Belgium... A total of 5329
3. The American Cemetery at Brittany, France... A total of 4410

5. Cambridge, England... A total of 3812

6. Brookwood, England - American Cemetery... A total of 468

7. Epinal, France - American Cemetery... A total of 5525
8. Flanders Field, Belgium... A total of 368

9. Florence, Italy... A total of <u>4402</u>

10. Henri-Chapelle, Belgium... A total of <u>7992</u>

11. Lorraine , France... A total of <u>10,489</u>

12. Luxembourg, Luxembourg... A total of <u>5076</u>

13. Meuse-Argonne... A total of <u>14246</u>

14. Netherlands, Netherlands... A total of <u>8301</u>

15. Normandy, France... A total of <u>9387</u>

16. Oise-Aisne, France... A total of <u>6012</u>

17. Rhone, France... A total of <u>861</u>

18. Sicily, Italy... A total of <u>7861</u>

19. Somme, France... A total of <u>1844</u>

20. St. Mihiel, France... A total of <u>4153</u>

21. Suresnes, France... A total of <u>1541</u>

The total count is <u>104,366</u> dead, brave Americans.

How many French, Dutch, Italians, Belgians and Brits are buried on American soil after defending us against our enemies? We don't ask for praise...but we have no need to apologize!

Our Upside Down World

Sadly, America has become the land where special interest rules and double standard applies.

Consider the following:

- Politically correct is the new term for avoiding truth.
- Crisis are no longer dealt with, they are exploited for political gain.
- If The President or Congress lies to us its politics. If we lie to them it a felony.
- We take money from those who work and give it to those who won't.
- If blacks are racist, its their first amendment right. If whites are racist, game over. (The truth is racism is wrong. Period.)
- The government spends millions to rehabilitate criminals and do almost nothing for victims. Often criminals have more rights than victims.
- Schools can teach homosexuality is just another form of human relations. But they may not use the word God or the Bible to teach.
- You can kill an unborn child, but almost never execute a murderer.
- Instead of burning books some burn the Flag and rewrite books.
- We relabeled socialists and communists as progressives.
- We cannot close the US/Mexican border but we protect the 38th parallel in Korea.
- Pornography on the TV or internet is OK but don't put a nativity scene is a public park.
- Criminals are called sick people. Radical Muslim terrorists are freedom fighters.
- We can use a human fetus for medical research but not animals.

Summary Points:

- America IS clearly in an Awful Situation as the evidence testifies.

- America is in this awful situation because we have turned from God, ignored His laws, and failed to adhere to the U.S. Constitution.

- This chapter is far from a complete compilation of all the evidences of our awful situation, but it should suffice any reader to reveal our awful situation.

- Progressives' evil has infiltrated our lives 1 degree at a time over the past 100+ years throughout our society. Like 'slow cooking a frog' we now find ourselves almost thoroughly 'cooked' our loss of freedoms and the overflowing scourge of evil in our once great country.

- God speaks to us in a small voice that is more often felt than heard. If we do not heed His voice He raises His voice and frequency of delivery until we do listen. God's messages come in the testimony of earthquakes, in the voice of thunderings, and lightnings, and tempests, and waves of the sea heaving themselves beyond their bounds. We have 'heard' ample evidence of God speaking to us in the recent decade.

- America is at a critical - life altering - fork in the road of history, Will we choose to return to 'the path less traveled by' that prospered us as a nation for the first 100 years, or choose the well-worn path we have slipped down the past 100 years - a path traveled by many former nations - all which ended in their destruction.

- The choice for America is Cleansing and Restoration or Succumbing and Enslavement

Action Steps:

Note: 'Facts' can seldom be verified with total certainty in this world using evidence and reason alone. Much information presented as 'fact' in this world is false. I have done 'due diligence' with resources available to determine truth. The following 'Fact checkers' have been consulted to verify truth insofar as it is possible: snopes.com, factcheck.org and truthorfiction.com. All have liberal left leanings and some are partially funded by George Soros, an enemy of capitalism, freedom and a One World Order advocate. Sometimes they tell the truth. Sometimes they spin it a little. Sometimes they report truth as false. Each of these 'fact checkers' differ on various points; some conclude 'false', some 'true', and some report a mixture of truth and falsehoods. Yet they are some of the best sources to check for truth. However, remember the obligation of the reader to seek truth from the source of all truth presented in Chapter 1.

Remember that this world is filled with 'gross darkness that covers the minds of people.' Therefore, it is essential that the reader apply Chapter 1 teachings to verify truth from the source of all truth, even these.

1. Have you applied Action Step #3 from Chapter 1? If not, please do it!
2. Take the truth of our awful situation as weapons to defeat the enemy.
3. Repent where we need to, individually and as a nation.

End of Chapter

8

What We The People
MUST Do & CAN Do NOW

Where there is no vision, the people perish:
but he that keepeth the law [Gods Commandments], *happy is he.* Pro 29:18

My people are destroyed for lack of knowledge Hosea 4:6

If my people, which are called by my name, shall humble themselves, and pray, and seek my
face, and turn from their wicked ways; then will I hear from heaven, and will forgive their sin,
and will heal their land. 2 Chronicles 7:14

"...choose you this day whom ye will serve...but as for me and my house, we will serve the Lord.
Joshua 24:15

Every government degenerates when trusted to the rulers of the people alone.
The people themselves are its only safe depositories.
Thomas Jefferson

"The troubles of the world may largely be laid at the doors of those
who are neither hot nor cold; who always follow the line of least resistance;
whose timid hearts flutter at taking sides for truth...there can be no neutrality."
John A. Widtsoe

"All that is necessary for the triumph of evil is for good men to do nothing."
Edmund Burke

"The price of freedom is eternal vigilance." Thomas Jefferson

"*We The People* are the rightful masters
of both Congress & the courts, not to overthrow the Constitution,
but overthrow the men who pervert the Constitution."
Abraham Lincoln

"Freedom is never more than one generation away from extinction. We didn't pass it to our
children in the bloodstream. It must be fought for, protected, and handed on for them to do the
same, or one day we will spend our sunset years telling our children and our children's children
what it was once like in the United States where men were free."
Ronald Reagan

Understand The Truth about America

To change direction of America's crisis and restore health to America's Tree of Liberty We The People must act on truth. The chapter introductory quotes provide the guiding light. We must severely prune the roots and branches of falsehoods and evil that produced the bitter fruits of our current lives.

America is not just another nation on Earth. America is a choice land above all other lands that God has reserved for habitation of a free people that would keep Him first in their lives. It is a land with a spiritual foundation and a prophetic history. America is a nation with a great mission to perform for liberty-loving people everywhere. The United States of America is the last bastion of real freedom – the only effective protection against the world's greatest evil – the godless socialist-communist conspiracy that seek to destroy the liberty and freedom of all mankind.

Understand The Real Problem

The real problem is not 'out there'. It seldom is. The real problem is in us; We The People.

Our problems are not political, or economic or social. Our root problem is spiritual.

American was founded by Christians. Americas justice system is based primarily on the Bible. America's moral code of conduct for nearly 300 years was based on the Bible. Our primarily Founding Fathers established the Constitution based on the yardstick of Biblical morality. America became great because America was good. Now, America has become morally rotten and weak because we have turned away from that which made us good.

John Dickinson, a signer of the Constitution, warned *"Political slavery is ever preceded by sleep."* John Jay, president of the American Bible Society, the original Chief Justice of the U.S. Supreme Court and one of the Founding Fathers counseled, *"....it is the duty of our Christian nation to select and prefer Christians for their rulers."* The Reverend Charles Finney admonished, *"Politics are a part of religion in such a country as this, and Christians must do their duty to the country as part of their duty to God...God will bless or curse this nation according to the course Christians take in politics."*

We are in the current mess because the 86% declared Christians went to sleep and assumed our freedoms would always be there. That has proven to be a false assumption. As Edmund Burke reminds, *"The only thing necessary for the triumph of evil is for good men to do nothing."*

In 1803 the Reverend Matthais Burnett taught *"...let the wise counsel of Jethro {Exodus 18:21]...be your guide. Choose ye out from among you able men, such as fear God, men of truth and hating covetousness and set them to rule over you."* In 1791the Reverend Chandler Robbins taught that *"...rulers be just men, fearing God...haters from holding bribes...because a gift blindeth the eyes of the wise, and perverteth the words of the righteous."* Less than half the Christian community now votes and thus have abdicated their responsibility to God and Country.

Good government is the result of good leaders who fear God and live according to His teachings. Good leaders have to be elected by good people who do likewise. When God fearing people depart their values depart with them. When ungodly individuals enter their corrupt values enter with them. Leaders make decisions based on the values they hold inside. Corrupt values lead to corrupt decisions that enslave people. Pure values base on God's established standard of morality led to the Declaration of Independence and the US Constitution which are now hanging by a thread of government corruption.

No institution has intrinsic value. No institution is of itself good or bad. It is the people who rule in institutions that determine its direction. Whether it is good or bad is measured by God's immutable standards, not man's moral relativism. If government is bad it is because it is led by people with wrong values. Like cars, governments take on the nature of whoever is at the wheel; they reflect the values of those involved.

George Mason, the Father of the Bill of Rights – affirmed that God holds people accountable for what they do. Similarly, He holds communities, states, and nations accountable for what is done by public officials.

George Washington stated in his Inaugural Address *"the propitious (favorable) smiles of Heaven can never be expected on a nation that disregards the eternal rules of order and right which Heaven itself has ordained."*

Following the 1963-63 Supreme Court mandate separating students and public venues from religious principles resulted in - among other pertinent metrics of a healthy society – violent crime skyrocketed nearly 700%. Consequently prison funding is now one of the fastest growing expenditures for state government.

A majority of We The People elected the representatives who make false promises they cannot keep to take more from those who work and give more to those who refuse to work. A majority of Americans have become dumbed-down, ill-informed entitlement mentality slaves living on Uncle Sam's Plantation.

Therefore, We The People must take accountability for electing corrupt leaders.

Understand The Game Being Played On YOU

It is critical to understand the 'game' being played on YOU. The stakes are high; YOUR freedom or slavery, YOUR liberty or bondage.

The author of the game is the same one who tried to enslave us before, he just works through power-mongering men here. The tools of destruction used are ancient; deceit, lies, coercion, guilt-tripping, manipulation, force and control. The players using these tactics have some modern and some historic names; progressives, socialists, communists, Nazis, fascists. And they use laws.

Lawyers write laws. They dominate the Democratic political party. Their skill in in spinning the facts to win the day, not necessarily see that justice is done.

Laws are supposed to be created by Congress. However, socialist power mongers have found ways to circumvent Congress through Executive Orders, through government bureaucrat regulations from the EPA, FDA etc. They do not want these laws to be observed. They want them to be broken!

Socialists, progressives and communists want power at any expense; to them the ends justify the means. There is no way to rule innocent men. Therefore, they create the kind of laws that can neither be observed nor enforced nor objectively interpreted, and so many laws and regulations that people break them unknowingly. Then government has the tool to crack down on criminal law-breakers. Then you create a nation of law-breakers that you can control through guilt and punish them when you catch them.

Part of the game was authored in mortality by Karl Marx. It is simply to create a problem, then step in and provide a solution that looks like they're a savior but instead enslaves.

Divide and conquer is another tactic of the adversary of freedom. As a result of applying this tactic to divide, most recently by hate fomenters such as Obama and his cohort in crime Al Sharpton, and by George Soros and his minions.

Two Americas have emerged over it history. It can be summarized in the following way: The America where people work, produce, is independent, contribute, and have acquired things by their industry, the businessman, entrepreneur, merchant, craftsman, those who provide service to others. The other America is where people don't work, don't produce, are dependent, don't contribute and therefore don't have anything except from those who produce; the entitlement mentality. The division is givers and the takers. It is also manifest in two political parties; one who preaches hate, greed and victimization in order to win office. They love power more than country, The other party who promote individual enterprise.

The difference is not about income inequality, it's about civic responsibility. It is about the producer and the parasite.

Educate Ourselves

"If a nation expects to be ignorant and free, it expects what never was and never will be. Experience has shown that even under the best form of government, those entrusted with power have in time, by slow operations, perverted it into tyranny, and the most effectual means of preventing this would be to illuminate, as far as practicable, the minds of the people at large." The Real Thomas Jefferson, p.82, 2008, National Center for Constitutional Studies

People perish for lack of truth. Many wander about in search of truth but stumble because they know not where to find it. We must educate ourselves about America's true history. We must read from original sources, because liberal-left progressive revisionists have rewritten our history over the past 100 years to further their socialistic agenda. Good sources include David Barton's website 'Wall Builders' http://www.wallbuilders.com/, the National Center for Constitutional Studies – The Real series – George Washington, Thomas Jefferson, and books from the Bibliography.

An example of liberal left brainwashing is that many people think we live in a democracy. We do not! A democracy is rule of the majority (mob rule). Democracies always end in tyrannical violence.

America is a Republic; a government in which supreme power resides in body of citizens entitled to vote and is exercised by elected officers and representatives responsible to them and governing according to law (rule of law).

The United States Constitution, Article IV, Section 4., states, "The United States shall guarantee to every State in this Union a Republican form of Government..."

George Washington taught that *"A primary object...should be the education of our youth in the science of government. In a republic, what species of knowledge can be equally important? And what duty more pressing...than...communicating it to those who are to be the future guardians of the liberties of the country?"*

We must continually feed the roots of the tree of Liberty to keep it healthy.

Know The Real Dangers To America

America's danger lies mostly within. They include failure to follow God's moral compass, entitlement mentality, and ignorant citizens. We need to wake up and live the principles that are the Judeo-Christian foundation of American greatness; self-rule, responsibility and accountability. We must not give up freedom to choose for security.

An ancient prophet warned that in our day *"...there shall be great pollutions upon the face of the earth.."* he went on to innumerate them as murders, robbing, lying, deceit, whoredoms, and all manner of evil abominations.

Darrell Scott, father of Rachel Scott, a victim of the Columbine High School shootings in Littleton, Colorado, addressed a Congressional subcommittee. The following is a portion of the transcript:

"Since the dawn of creation there has been both good & evil in the hearts of men and women. We all contain the seeds of kindness or the seeds of violence. The death of my wonderful daughter, Rachel Joy Scott, and the deaths of that heroic teacher, and the other eleven children who died must not be in vain. Their blood cries out f or answers.

"The first recorded act of violence was when Cain slew his brother Abel out in the field. The villain was not the club he used. Neither was it the NCA, the National Club Association. The true killer was Cain, and the reason for the murder could only be found in Cain's heart.

"In the days that followed the Columbine tragedy, I was amazed at how quickly fingers began to be pointed at groups such as the NRA. I am not a member of the NRA I am not a hunter. I do not even own a gun. I am not here to represent or defend the NRA - because I don't believe that they are responsible for my daughter's death. Therefore, I do not believe that they need to be defended. If I believed they had anything to do with Rachel's murder I would be their strongest opponent.

"I am here today to declare that Columbine was not just a tragedy -- it was a spiritual event that should be forcing us to look at where the real blame lies! Much of the blame lies here in this room. Much of the blame lies behind the pointing fingers of the accusers themselves. I wrote a poem just four nights ago that expresses my feelings best.

> *Your laws ignore our deepest needs,*
> *Your words are empty air.*
> *You've stripped away our heritage,*
> *You've outlawed simple prayer.*
> *Now gunshots fill our classrooms,*
> *And precious children die.*
> *You seek for answers everywhere,*
> *And ask the question "Why?"*
> *You regulate restrictive laws,*
> *Through legislative creed.*
> *And yet you fail to understand,*
> *That God is what we need!*

"Men and women are three-part beings. We all consist of body, mind, and spirit. When we refuse to acknowledge a third part of our make-up, we create a void that allows evil, prejudice, and hatred to rush in and wreak havoc. Spiritual presences were present within our educational systems for most of our nation's history. Many of our major colleges began as theological seminaries. This is a historical fact. What has happened to us as a nation? We have refused to honor God, and in so

doing, we open the doors to hatred and violence. And when something as terrible as Columbine's tragedy occurs -- politicians immediately look for a scapegoat such as the NRA. They immediately seek to pass more restrictive laws that contribute to erode away our personal and private liberties. We do not need more restrictive laws. Eric and Dylan would not have been stopped by metal detectors. No amount of gun laws can stop someone who spends months planning this type of massacre. The real villain lies within our own hearts.

"As my son Craig lay under that table in the school library and saw his two friends murdered before his very eyes, he did not hesitate to pray in school. I defy any law or politician to deny him that right! I challenge every young person in America, and around the world, to realize that on April 20, 1999, at Columbine High School prayer was brought back to our schools. Do not let the many prayers offered by those students be in vain. Dare to move into the new millennium with a sacred disregard for legislation that violates your God-given right to communicate with Him. To those of you who would point your finger at the NRA -- I give to you a sincere challenge. Dare to examine your own heart before casting the first stone!"

We must purify ourselves; inside first and then our outside environments. We must clean up our thoughts, desires, appetites, and passions. When we are clean on the inside our words and actions will be honorable. We have a stewardship for the time we spend on Earth. We are accountable to God for how we use our time, how we treat others and how we care for the gift of life and for this Earth that sustains our life.

Know God's Voices

When we are righteous and seek God's instruction, He speaks to us in a still small voice, a whisper, that is more often felt than heard. If God cannot get our attention that way He increases the volume and intensity – like many mortal fathers do with disobedient children! If the majority of the people become evil, God cleanses them from the earth to provide a fresh start for a new generation of His children. Following are a few of God's words, actions and warnings:

"Ye shall hear of wars and rumours of _wars. ...For nation shall rise against nation, and kingdom against kingdom: a_nd there shall be _famines, and pestilences, and earthquakes_, in divers places.

"All these are the beginning of sorrows. ..._then shall be great tribulation_, such as was not since the beginning of the world to this time, no, nor ever shall be. And except those days should be shortened, there should no flesh be saved: but for the elect's sake those days shall be shortened" (Matt. 24:6, 8, 19, 21–22).

God's 'voice' is sometimes 'heard' in natural and man-made disasters like 9.11, tsunamis, volcanoes, earthquakes, wars, famines, disease, hailstorms, tornados etc. designed to get our attention and have us repent and turn back to Him. Remember how we all felt on 9.12? Most of us returned to prayer, to our churches and synagogues, to unite in prayer for the victims, to unite in power against evil. Are we listening? And waking up to reality?

Fulfill Our Duty To God

"Next to being one in worshiping God there is nothing in this world upon which [we] should be more united than in upholding and defending the Constitution of the United States." President David O. McKay *(America In History & Prophecy p 41)*

"I am grateful for the Constitution of this land. I am grateful that the Founding Fathers made it clear that our allegiance runs to that Constitution and the glorious eternal principles embodied therein. Our allegiance does not run to any man, to a king, or a dictator, or a president, although we revere and honor those whom we elect to high office. Our allegiance runs to the Constitution and to the principles embodied therein" Ezra T. Benson (America In History & Prophecy, p. 41)

Our duty to God is to stand as witnesses for God in all things. We must elect righteous men and women to represent us in government. Our duty is to be informed about the issues and candidates, and vote for those candidates who most fully align themselves with the laws of happiness defined by God in the Gospel of Jesus Christ.

Many of our current government leaders are men of cunning device and men of many flattering words. They lead away the hearts of many people to do wickedly. They seek to destroy faith in God and create faith in government. They create dependence on government rather than independence. They seek to destroy the foundation of liberty – the U.S. Constitution - which God granted to us.

Three civilizations have already been swept off this land of America when they became ripe with iniquity. Will we be next? The answer depends on how we act NOW!

Most politicians seek office for power and when in office do everything possible to keep their power and become career politicians. They seek to stay in office by buying votes with our tax dollars from whomever they can; illegal aliens, welfare dependents, voting fraud, etc.

In the days of our Founding Fathers, political office was not sought after. It was an honor to SERVE We The People. After they served they went back to their regular jobs. We The People recommended who we wanted to serve us to office. How far we have descended from those days of more honorable men!

We The People must pull down the accumulated centralized power of the self-professed nobility of the Washington 'elite' and restore power to We The People where it rightfully belongs according to the U.S. Constitution.

We must remember ... *"The power under the Constitution will always be in the people."* George Washington

We The People need to take back OUR Power! The 10th Amendment states: *"The powers not delegated to the United States by the Constitution, nor prohibited by it to the States, are preserved to the States respectively, <u>or to the people.</u>*

Repent

"Righteousness exalteth a nation; sin is a reproach to any people" [Proverbs 14:34]

Our sins severed the roots of The Tree of Liberty. Therefore, we MUST REPENT and re-connect the source of life of the Tree of Liberty – God, His religion, and His morality.

The place to start is to fix ourselves first. Righteousness brings God's blessings and support. Without God, we cannot succeed. With God, we cannot fail.

Consider the world if everyone lived by the Golden Rule - do unto others as you would have others do unto you - embodied in God's second great commandment of The Law. It requires humility, stripping ourselves of pride and greed. It requires living God's laws of happiness and it leads to peace, prosperity and joy.

Return to 'the faith of our Fathers" – the American faith – develop a relationship with Your Father In Heaven. He is God. We must know Him, serve Him and live according to His moral laws to have Him on our side in this fight to restore our Republic.

We are in a battle between good and evil. The only thing that can defeat evil is good. Therefore, first and foremost, repent America and turn back to God who give us life and strengthens and protects us as a nation as we honor Him by living His commandments.

We must decide from the 'opposition in all things' what trees we will allow to grow in our lives...

THE TREE OF TRUTH	OR	THE TREE OF FALSEHOODS
THE TREE OF CLARITY	OR	THE TREE OF DISTORTION
THE TREE OF LIBERTY	OR	THE TREE OF TYRANNY

Righteous people in God's eyes have His spirit to be with them. They will not be confounded.

We The People must repent, become righteous in God's eyes. Then we will have courage to ACT and cut down every tree that does not bring forth good fruit and cast them into the fire!

Rise Up & Act America – Especially The 86% Christians

"Silence in the face of evil is itself evil. God will not hold us guiltless. Not to speak is to speak. Not to act is to act." Dietrich Bonhoeffer

A wise prophet foresaw our days and wrote: *"For behold, at that day shall he [Satan will] rage in the hearts of the children of men, and stir them up to anger against that which is good. And others will he pacify, and lull them away into carnal security, that they will say: All is well ...all is well— and thus the devil cheateth their souls, and leadeth them away carefully down to hell. And behold, others he flattereth away, and telleth them there is no hell; and he saith unto them: I am no devil, for there is none—and thus he whispereth in their ears, until he grasps them with his awful chains, from whence there is no deliverance."*

Beware of false prophets, which come to you in sheep's clothing, but inwardly they are ravening wolves. Ye shall know them by their fruits. Every tree that bringeth not forth good fruit is hewn down, and cast into the fire. Matt 7:15-19 KJV This ancient counsel is valid today.

Thomas Jefferson counseled that America's foreign policy be "*Peace, commerce, and honest friendship with all nations — entangling alliances with none.*" Should we really be in other parts of the world now that we have avenged 9.11.2001?

Abraham Lincoln, widely regarded as one of America's wisest and best presidents said that "*The principles of Jefferson are the axioms of a free society.*"

 "Never give up, for that is just the place and time that the tide will turn" Harriet Beecher Stowe

"I would unite with anyone who does right and with nobody to do wrong." Frederick Douglass

Never. Never. Never. Give up the fight for liberty and to restore the Constitution of the United States of America!

Enlist the Power of God

Benjamin Franklin remarked, *"God governs in the affairs of men. And if a sparrow cannot fall to the ground without his notice, is it probable that an empire can rise without his aid? We have been assured, Sir, in the sacred writings that "except the Lord build they labor in vain that build it."*

A corollary in our time, 'is it probable that America can be restored without God's aid?' The answer is resoundingly...NO!

Let us keep faith in God's ability to deal with tyrants. If 10% of America's Patriots wake up and act to intercede with God in prayer we can swiftly change the course of events and restore our Declaration of Independence and the U.S. Constitution as the supreme law of the land.

Patrick Henry reminds us that ***"...we are not weak, if we make a proper use of the means which the God of Natures hath placed in our power...we shall not fight our battles alone. There is a just God who presides over the destinies of nations and who will raise up friends to fight our battles for us. The battle is not to the strong alone, it is to the vigilant, the active, the brave...there is no retreat but to submission and slavery! Our chains are forged. Their clanking may be heard....why stand we here idle?...Is life so dear, or peace so sweet, as to be purchased at the price of chains and slavery? Forbid it, Almighty God! I know not what course others may take,; but as for me, give me liberty, or give me death!"***

Remember that ***"...with God all things are possible."*** Matt 19:26

Therefore, let us remember to be on our knees daily as individuals, and families and plead with God to help us restore our morality and Republic.

Stand up Christians - Practice Your Religion & Repeal Obamacare

The first Amendment of the Constitution states "Congress shall make no law respecting <u>the establishment of religion,</u> **or** <u>prohibiting the free exercise thereof</u>..."

One of God's Ten Commandments reminds us "<u>Thou shalt have no other gods before me</u>." Ex 20:3

Obamacare sets up a false god – government death panels - where decisions are made as to who lives and who dies based on their 'worth' to society and the cost of providing health care to them.

The truth is that God is the author of life. Only God has the right to grant life and take it away.

Muslims have the 'right' to exclude themselves from un-Constitutional Obamacare because of their doctrine of dhimmitude. Therefore, if Muslims can be excluded from Obamacare because of their doctrine of dhimmitude, Christians can be excluded from Obamacare because of our doctrine in the Ten Commandments.

Christians founded America. America's history has deep roots in The Bible. It is overwhelmingly Christian today. 86% of America are Christians. We have the right to practice our religion under the supreme law of the land; the U.S. Constitution. Yet we allow one or few opposing voices to destroy our right to celebrate our Christian religion.

For example, Georgia Tech constructed a carillon in central campus, and during Christmas holidays, it played Christmas music, that is until one Pakistani professor objected. The president of the college supported him and shut down Christmas music! WHY?

If Christians went to Pakistan, or Iraq, or Iran or any other predominately-Muslim country and complained about Islamic music or religious practice, do you think they would stop their countries' religious practice because of our hurt feelings? NO! Instead, you would be deported, or beheaded!

Everyone in America has the right to practice their religion according to the dictates of their own conscience, as long as that practice does not interfere with the rights to life, liberty, and property of another.

I advocate the use of common sense in defining what to allow in the public square as long as it is not dictated by government as the only allowed religion. We should respect America's 86% Christian population, Christian history, Christian values, and principles that made America great. We should allow the free exercise of that major religion in public and throughout government as it was from the beginning of our country.

If people with other religious beliefs do not like America's Christian beliefs and practices, including Christmas music and Nativity scenes and the Ten Commandments in the public square, go find another country where you are more comfortable! However, do not complain about OUR Christian foundations or practices. God reserved America for a people that would worship Him. Without God we will fall.

Stand up Christians and demand OUR rights!

Apply The Solution

The solution in summary is for the majority of We The People to repent of our wicked ways. We must keep God's Law - His Commandments. We must choose to serve the God of this land. We must educate ourselves, gain knowledge and exercise wisdom so that we do not perish and are not destroyed. We must become 'hot' in the service of our country and in defending our freedoms under the U.S. Constitution. Good men must DO much good! We must overthrow those who pervert the U.S. Constitution at the ballot box. We The People must rise up & act!

I care not for power, but to tear it down. We must tear down centralized federal government to the level defined in the U.S. Constitution. Reposition power to the States and local governments - to We The People.

Our Founding Fathers never intended supreme court justice appointments to be permanent until death. We must remove all supreme court justices from position when they legislate from the bench and fail to uphold and defend the Constitution of the United States of America.

The U.S. Constitution is clear that only Congress and make laws. Thus the unconstitutional executive actions taken by Obama and others that by-pass Congress must be rescinded.

The U.S. Constitution states that only Congress can declare War. Thus, every war since WWII has been unconstitutional. They have been entered into by presidents without authority to do so. Therefore, American has never won a war since WWII. They were not about winning. They were about government bending to warlords and big business who made billions supplying armaments to our troops. But, they also funded and supplied armaments to the communists who used them to kill our boys in uniform. That is Treason!

We must root out the evil that has infected our government and society from top to bottom. Evil in the form of communists, socialists, progressives, Marxists, Nazis, radical Islam's Sharia and other similar ideologies; all of which are in opposition to the U.S. Constitution.

Prepare

The Boy Scout Motto – BE PREPARED – is wise counsel for us today.

To know God is to know wisdom. Heed His instruction to prepare; spiritually and physically for the coming great tribulation.

We must live so that we can be found worthy to call upon God for divine protection. We cannot expect God's help if we are unwilling to keep His commandments.

Preparation includes both spiritual and physical. We prepare spiritually by keeping God's laws. We must put on *"...the whole armour of God, that ye may be able to withstand in the evil day, ...having your loins girt about with truth, and having on the breastplate of righteousness; And your feet shod with the preparation of the gospel of peace; Above all, taking the shield of faith, ...the helmet of salvation, and the sword of the Spirit, which is the word of God: Praying always with all prayer and supplication in the Spirit."* Eph 6

We prepare physically by living within our means, saving for a rainy day, storing a year's supply of water, food, clothing, shelter and other necessities, 6 months cash reserves, and if able, add gold, silver, guns and ammo. These preparedness parameters have been taught for years by many ecclesiastical & secular leaders.

Know What Makes Our Republic & Capitalism Work

Too many people – primarily those 'in charge' of our Country, our supposed representatives in Washington, Wall Street Banksters, heads of massive corporations - have failed to respect the roots of the Tree of Liberty; they have become greedy. In turning from God to greed they have become Satan's agents to gain prestige, power and position, often at the expense of the American worker.

The enemies of freedom will try to convince you that liberty and capitalism has failed, and that they have a better, more secure way. The way is the way of Satan. It is called by many names; communism, socialism, fascism, Marxism, Nazism and in modern days - progressivism. These ideologies are parasitic cancers and the roots of the Tree of Tyranny that have produced the current bitter fruits of our lives.

Freedom and capitalism ignite entrepreneurs, stimulate creative minds, is the rising tide that lifts all ships. Only those on higher ground can life others. Application of love thy neighbor as thyself betters all mankind. The slavery of communism, socialism, Marxism etc. destroys the human spirit, deaden creativity and sink all ships.

Abraham Lincoln said *"God must have loved the common man, because He made so many of us."* God knew what He was doing! The common man is basically good; we outnumber those 'elite' who see to destroy the freedom and liberty of all mankind. Some 'elite' banksters, politicians and big businessmen manipulate us 'sheeple' to their advantage. Generally we have let them. But NO MORE!

Remember what happed to the people in Austria who elected Adolf Hitler as president of the National Socialist Party by 98% of the popular vote. Hitler came to power during an economic depression. He promised hope and change; prosperity and work for everyone. Hitler provided the hope and change through government jobs. Five years later, the Austrians woke up to find themselves subjects to the one of the worst tyrannical dictators of all time.

Obama is using the same strategy that Adolf Hitler used to rise to power. Obama's actions – along with his like-minded 'team' of czar conspirators – are right out of the progressive, communist, Marxist, socialist, fascist, Nazi manual of operations to seize power over the people. Obama's promise of hope and change was unfolded to be hope for his union buddies, and expanded government jobs and dependency. He has methodically stifled and killed small businesses that provided 70% of all jobs in America.

Remember the following truths:

1. You cannot legislate the poor into prosperity by legislating the wealthy out of prosperity.
2. What one person receives without working for, another person must work for without receiving.
3. The government cannot give to anybody anything that the government does not first take from somebody   else.
4.   You   cannot   multiply   wealth   by   dividing   it!
5. When half of the people get the idea that they do not have to work because the other half is going to take care of them, and when the other half gets the idea that it does no good to work because somebody else is going to get what they work for, that is the beginning of the end of any nation.

It is time to WAKE UP AMERICA & Choose wisely!

Consider Wal-Mart Vs. Washington

Consider Wal-Mart's record:

Americans spend $36,000,000 at Wal-Mart every hour of every day,

That's $20,928 profit every minute!

Sells more from January 1 to St. Patrick's Day (March 17th) than Target sells all year.

Is bigger than Home Depot + Kroger + Target +Sears + Costco + K-Mart combined.

Employs 1.6 million people,

Is the world's largest private employer and most speak English.

The largest company in the history of the world.

Sells more food than Kroger and Safeway combined, and keep in mind they did this in only fifteen years. During this same period, 31 big supermarket chains sought bankruptcy.

Has approximately 3,900 stores in the USA of which 1,906 are Super Centers; this is 1,000 more than it had five years ago.

7.2 billion different purchases will occur at Wal-Mart stores in 2011. (Earth's population is approximately 6.5 Billion.)

Consider Washington's record:

The U.S. Postal Service was established in 1775. You have had 235 years to get it right and it is broke.

Social Security was established in 1935. You have had 75 years to get it right and it is broke.

Fannie Mae was established in 1938. You have had 72 years to get it right and it is broke.

War on Poverty started in 1964. You have had 46 years to get it right; $1 trillion of our money is confiscated each year and transferred to "the poor" and they only want more.

Medicare and Medicaid were established in 1965. You have had 45 years to get it right and they are broke.

Freddie Mac was established in 1970. You have had 40 years to get it right and it is broke.

The Department of Energy was created in 1977 to lessen our dependence on foreign oil. It has ballooned to 16,000 employees with a budget of $24 billion a year and we import more oil than ever before. You had 33 years to get it right and it is an abysmal failure.

The U.S. Administrations and the Congresses are either incompetent, corrupt or both. Washington, you have failed in every "government service" you have shoved down our throats while wasting our tax dollars.

Politicians have lost their minds to "Political Correctness"! We're 'broke' and 'can't' help our own seniors, veterans, orphans, and homeless, yet in the past year we have provided billions of dollars in aid to Egypt, Haiti, Chile, and Turkey, Pakistan and many other foreign countries, many of whom hate America. Our retired seniors living on a 'fixed income' receive no aid.

Maybe we should hire the guys who run Wal-Mart to fix the economy.

Remember Canadian Tribute To The United States of America

America: The Good Neighbor....editorial broadcast from Toronto by Gordon Sinclair, a Canadian television commentator. ... Printed in the Congressional Record: Originally broadcast during the Vietnam War in 1973 and re-printed in a Canadian Newspaper on 13 Sep 2001 in the wake of the Attack on America of 11 September 2001...

"This Canadian thinks it is time to speak up for the Americans as the most generous and possibly the least appreciated people on all the earth.

"Germany, Japan and, to a lesser extent, Britain and Italy were lifted out of the debris of war by the Americans who poured in billions of dollars and forgave other billions in debts. None of these countries is today paying even the interest on its remaining debts to the United States.

"When France was in danger of collapsing in 1956, it was the Americans who propped it up, and their reward was to be insulted and swindled on the streets of Paris. I was there. I saw it.

"When earthquakes hit distant cities, it is the United States that hurries in to help. This spring, 59 American communities were flattened by tornadoes. Nobody helped.

"The Marshall Plan and the Truman Policy pumped billions of dollars into discouraged countries. Now newspapers in those countries are writing about the decadent, warmongering Americans. I'd like to see just one of those countries that is gloating over the erosion of the United States dollar build its own airplane. Does any other country in the world have a plane to equal the Boeing Jumbo Jet, the Lockheed Tri-Star, or the Douglas DC10? If so, why don't they fly them? Why do all the

International lines except Russia fly American Planes? Why does no other land on earth even consider putting a man or woman on the moon? You talk about Japanese technocracy, and you get radios. You talk about German technocracy, and you get automobiles. You talk about American technocracy, and you find men on the moon - not once, but several times and safely home again.

"You talk about scandals, and the Americans put theirs right in the store window for everybody to look at. Even their draft-dodgers are not pursued and hounded. They are here on our streets, and most of them, unless they are breaking Canadian laws, are getting American dollars from ma and pa at home to spend here.

"When the railways of France, Germany and India were breaking down through age, it was the Americans who rebuilt them. When the Pennsylvania Railroad and the New York Central went broke, nobody loaned them an old caboose. Both are still broke.

"I can name you 5000 times when the Americans raced to the help of other people in trouble. Can you name me even one time when someone else raced to the Americans in trouble? I don't think there was outside help even during the San Francisco earthquake.

"Our neighbors have faced it alone, and I'm one Canadian who is damned tired of hearing them get kicked around.

"They will come out of this thing with their flag high. And when they do, they are entitled to thumb their nose at the lands that are gloating over their present troubles.

"I hope Canada is not one of those." ***"Stand proud, America!"***

Understand Freedom's Enemy & The U.S. Constitution

President David O. McKay Warned Americans in 1956 that "*...groups are organizing within the United States to take over the government and destroy our freedoms. The tactic they use is to sow discord and contention among men with the intent to undermine, weaken, and destroy our Constitutional form of government. Timely references and appropriate warnings have been given on the danger and evils of war. There is another danger even more menacing than the threat of invasion of a foreign foe. It is the un-patriotic activities and underhanded scheming of disloyal groups and organizations within our own borders. Secret, seditious, scheming of an enemy within our own ranks, hypo-critically professing loyalty to the government, and at the same time plotting against it, is a cancer from within.*" (America In History and Prophecy)

Elder Mark E. Peterson, said that *"To save the Constitution, either when it hangs by a thread [we must] understand the Constitution and be willing to accept the provisions set forth therein. [We must] understand the Constitution and be whole-heartedly converted to the high principles of free government which it embodies."* (America In History and Prophecy)

President Ezra T. Benson said in 1979 that "*...God's hand has been in our destiny... freedom as we know it today is being threatened as never before in our history. ... this land of the Americas must be protected, its Constitution upheld, [we must] preserve our liberty.*" "*Now I tell you it is time the people of the United States were waking up with the understanding that if they don't save the Constitution from the dangers that threaten it, we will have a change of government.*" (America In History and Prophecy, p. 49)

"Government is like a baby. An alimentary canal with a big appetite at one end and no sense of responsibility at the other." President Ronald Reagan

Understand The U.S. Constitution's 3/5ths Clause

Modern progressives, democrats and liberals use slavery to bash the Constitution and the Founding Fathers as slave owners. They have brainwashed the Black people into believing that the Founding Fathers and republicans were racist. They have intentionally mis-interpreted the 3/5ths clause in the U.S. Constitution as evidence of racism.

The exact opposite is true! The truth is that 70% of the Founding Fathers were republican abolitionists; they were against slavery. Thomas Jefferson tried to abolish it seven times through the courts of law and Congress.

Concerning the 3/5ths clause that is so often misunderstood. The 3/5ths clause in the U.S. Constitution is ANTI-SLAVERY. The truth is that the Founding Fathers wanted to abolish slavery. The progressive liberal left lie about this clause to win votes from the Black population. The Northern states wanted to abolish slavery. The Southern states were the primary holders of slaves and wanted to keep slavery. They dug in their heels and would not join the union because the Northern states were not going to count slaves toward states representation in Congress. In order to persuade the Southern states to join the United States of America the North conceded to the South to include slaves on one condition; the condition was the 3/5ths clause. Thereby, each slave counted only as 3/5 of a full person when counting the total population of each State. The number of representatives each State could send to the House of Representatives in Congress as based upon the total State population. Thus, the Southern States who supported slavery were punished for holding slaves. Thus the 3/5ths clause served both to unite the States into the United States, and as an incentive to the South to abolish slavery. It did NOT mean that slaves were only worth 3/5 of a man to the Founding Fathers as is commonly taught by progressive democrats. For more information See: http://americasblackfounders.com/ThreeFifthsClause.aspx

Frederick Douglass, a former Black slave, worked toward abolishing slavery with President Abraham Lincoln before the Civil War and became a highly respected friend. In fact after Lincoln's second inaugural address Douglass records this visit in his own words, *"I was invited into the East Room of the White House. A perfect sea of beauty and elegance, too, it was. The ladies were in very fine attire, and Mrs. Lincoln was standing there. I could not have been more than ten feet from him when Mr. Lincoln saw me; his countenance lighted up, and he said in a voice which was heard all around; 'Here comes my friend Douglass.' As I approached him he reached out his hand, gave me a cordial shake, and said: 'Douglass, I saw you in the crowd today listening to my inaugural address. There is no man's opinion that I value more than yours; what do you think of it?' ... I said: 'Mr. Lincoln, it was a sacred effort,' and then I walked off. 'I am glad you liked it,' he said."*

Frederick. Douglass a century ago reminded blacks: **_"The Republican Party is the ship, all else is the sea." 'I am a dyed in the wool Republican."_**

Douglass had great authority on the subject of the Constitution. He was a brilliant man, born a slave in 1818, but taught himself to read when he was 6 years old (without the benefit of the public schools). He was a man who valued liberty, and escaped from slavery when he was 20, in 1838.

Then he worked for the liberty of others, and at the same time, educated himself. He read the Founding documents of our nation, and commentaries on them, like the Federalist Papers. After 1840, he was able to get his hands on Madison's Notes on the Federal Constitution.

"Let me tell you something. ***Do you know that you have been deceived and cheated? You have been told that this government was intended from the beginning for white men, and for white men exclusively; that the men who formed the Union and framed the Constitution designed the permanent exclusion of the colored people from the benefits of those institutions.*** *Davis, Taney and Yancey, traitors at the south, have propagated this statement, while their copperhead echoes at the north have repeated the same. There never was a bolder or more wicked perversion of the truth of history. So far from this purpose was the mind and heart of your [Founding] fathers, that they desired and expected the abolition of slavery.* ***They framed the Constitution plainly with a view to the speedy downfall of slavery.*** *They carefully excluded from the Constitution any and every word which could lead to the belief that they meant it for persons of only one complexion.*

"The Constitution, in its language and in its spirit, welcomes the black man to all the rights which it was intended to guarantee to any class of the American people. Its preamble tells us for whom and for what it was made."

Frederick Douglass (June 1863) http://teachingamericanhistory.org/library/index.asp?documen...

In perhaps his most famous "Fifth of July Speech," Douglass declared: "Fellow-citizens! there is no matter in respect to which, the people of the North have allowed themselves to be so ruinously imposed upon, as that of the pro-slavery character of the Constitution. In *that* instrument I hold there is no warrant, license, nor sanction of the hateful thing; but, interpreted as it *ought* to be interpreted, **the Constitution is a GLORIOUS LIBERTY DOCUMENT."** Fredrick Douglass

Know Our Citizens' Right, Power & Responsibility To Act

From the Declaration of Independence – "We hold these truths to be self-evident, that all men are created equal, that **they are endowed by their Creator with certain inalienable Rights** that among these are Life, Liberty and the pursuit of Happiness. — That to secure these rights, Governments are instituted among Men, **deriving their just powers from the consent of the governed, — That whenever any Form of Government becomes destructive of these ends, it is the Right of the People to alter or to abolish it, and to institute new Government, laying its foundation on such principles and organizing its powers in such form, as to them shall seem most likely to effect their Safety and Happiness. ...But when a long train of abuses and usurpations, pursuing invariably the same Object evinces a design to reduce them under absolute Despotism, it is their right, it is their duty, to throw off such Government, and to provide new Guards for their future security."**

"... God forbid we should ever be twenty years without such a rebellion. The people cannot be all, and always, well informed. The part which is wrong will be discontented, in proportion to the importance of the facts they misconceive. If they remain quiet under such misconceptions, it is lethargy, the forerunner of death to the public liberty.... And what country can preserve its liberties, if its rulers are not warned from time to time, that this people preserve the spirit of resistance? Let them take arms. The remedy is to set them right as to the facts, pardon and pacify them. What signify a few lives lost in a century or two? The tree of liberty must be refreshed from time to time, with the blood of patriots and tyrants." **-** Thomas Jefferson Papers, 334 (C.J. Boyd, Ed., 1950)

"Resistance to tyrants is obedience to God." – Thomas Jefferson

The government does not endow citizen rights. They are endowed to us by God. Therefore, government cannot deprive us of our rights. Government gets its power from We The People - not the other way around!

"I think we have more machinery of government than is necessary, too many parasites living on the labor of the industrious." -_Thomas Jefferson Letter to William Ludlow, September 6, 1824

"The Constitution is not an instrument for the government to restrain the people, it is an instrument for the people to restrain the government." - Patrick Henry

We Americans must remember that America is a land of promise; a gift of God. Whoever lives here must serve God, or they shall be swept off when they become evil and ripe in iniquity.

We must seek for honest and wise men to serve as our public servants, and hold them accountable!

"Any people that would give up liberty for a little temporary safety deserve neither liberty nor safety." - Benjamin Franklin

"Confidence is everywhere the parent of despotism. Free government is founded in jealousy, and not in confidence. It is jealousy and not confidence which prescribes limited constitutions, to bind down those whom we are obliged to trust with power... Our Constitution has accordingly fixed the limits to which, and no further, our confidence may go... In questions of power, then, let no more be heard of confidence in man, but bind him down from mischief by the chains of the Constitution." - Draft of Kentucky Resolutions, October, 1798

"It [is] inconsistent with the principles of civil liberty, and contrary to the natural rights of the other members of the society, that anybody of men therein should have authority to enlarge their own powers, emoluments (income)... without restraint." --Thomas Jefferson: Virginia Allowance Bill, 1778.

Restore & Preserve American History

America's Tree of Liberty has been infected with the roots of the Tree of Tyranny, The Tree of Falsehoods and The Tree of Satan's power. We must restore and preserve American history in order to keep the Tree of Liberty alive and well.

Let us recommend to our representatives to assign David Barton of Wall Builders (America's encyclopedia of American History from original sources) to spearhead an initiative to restore American history from original sources, and to develop a required K-College curriculum. We must require our representatives to legislate that the Library of Congress or other existing departments preserve in perpetuity our real American history so that America never loses touch with its real roots. This is the only influence the Federal Government should have on education; to restore and preserve true American History. All other education should be governed at the local and state levels with parental guidance and approval.

Restore The U.S. Constitution

A former supreme court justice, State of Utah, offered five suggestions of citizen responsibility to the U.S. Constitution: 1. to understand it; 2. to support the law; 3. to practice civic virtue; 4. to maintain civility in the political discourse; and 5. to promote patriotism.

The divinely inspired Constitution MUST be upheld as the law of the land. It must be understood by EVERY American to be upheld so that never again can progressive, liberal left, socialist, communist, Nazi, fascist and Marxists erode its prominence to the dustbin of history as they almost have done.

We The People must repent of our ignorance of the Constitution. Read it, learn it, know it, live it. Teach your children about it. Measure every politician's words and actions against it. They took the oath of office to uphold it. Let us hold them accountable to fulfill their oath of office.

Remember a key purpose of the Second Amendment....

"The strongest reason for the people to retain the right to keep and bear arms is, as a last resort, to protect themselves against tyranny in government." Thomas Jefferson

"When the people fear their government, there is tyranny; when the government fears the people, there is liberty." Thomas Jefferson

"Towards the preservation of your government...it is requisite...that you resist with care the spirit if innovation upon its principles, however specious the pretexts. One method of assault may be to effect, in the forms of the Constitution, alterations which will impair the energy of the system, and thus to undermine what cannot be directly overthrown." (George Washington)

This warning is especially relevant today. Obama cannot directly overthrow the Constitution; but he had circumvented Congress and the Constitution by utilizing executive orders. He and his kind in Congress have forced Obamacare down American throats even after poll after poll revealed that 66% of Americans were against it. Furthermore, Obama cannot eradicate Congress, but he continues to by-pass Congress thus rendering them impotent. And America has never been in such a mess! It is time to read and apply the owner's manual; The United States Constitution!

Raise A Banner Of Liberty

We must restore the U.S. Constitution to its rightful place in government.

Our representatives in Washington have undermined the Constitution for decades because it limits their power. The Constitution was written INTENTIONALLY to limit the federal government's power so as to avoid the rise of another King George of England under whom American Colonies were suppressed.

Government does not create wealth. Government only takes OUR wealth, keeps most for itself, and then redistributes the rest to those for whom there is political benefit; to stay in power. Such a system creates a demeaning and initiative-sapping welfare system that traps the poor.

Our Federal government has become a huge parasite that feeds on the labors of We The People. We must pull down that power to where it belongs – to the States and to We The People.

Let us remember Thomas Paine's stirring words during the first American Revolution and apply them to the current revolution to restore our Republic. *"THESE are the times that try men's souls. The summer soldier and the sunshine patriot will, in this crisis, shrink from the service of their country; but he that stands by it now, deserves the love and thanks of man and woman. Tyranny, like hell, is not easily conquered; yet we have this consolation with us, that the harder the conflict, the more glorious the triumph. What we obtain too cheap, we esteem too lightly: it is dearness only that gives everything its value. Heaven knows how to put a proper price upon its goods; and it would be strange indeed if so celestial an article as FREEDOM should not be highly rated."*

George Washington, during the Constitutional Convention of 1787 said "*Let us raise a standard to which the wise and honest can* [support]; *the event which is in the hands of God.*"

Let US, We The People, in our day, raise a **BANNER OF LIBERTY, in memory and honor of the U.S. Constitution, of our American religion, of freedom, of peace, for our wives, our children and posterity yet unborn.** True American Patriots will bow themselves to the earth, and pray mightily unto our God for the blessings of liberty to rest upon us, so long as there should a band of Christians remain to possess the land of America. Let **The BANNER OF LIBERTY** fly on our homes, on bumper stickers, on the internet and be spread throughout American. Let it be a symbol to which Patriots can gather unto; a symbol of restoration of our beloved Constitution and Republic.

Implement Proposed Washington Reforms:

- **Remove all un-Constitutional authority assumed by the federal government**
- **Repeal un-Constitutional Obamacare** - Obamacare is un-Constitutional. Period. Not to mention it is criminal, controlling and destructive of capitalism.
- **Abolish the unconstitutional Federal Reserve** (see entry below for why and how)
- **Abolish the un-Constitutional Environmental Protection Agency (EPA)** and return power to the States and to the people where it belongs under the Constitution - The EPA has long been overstepping its bounds; it is used as an Executive Branch's arm of force when the President cannot get his way through legislation. The latest atrocity is the EPA now considers CO2 and other so-called greenhouse gases to be pollutants because of their role in propagating human caused climate change. The real reason why the EPA did this is to pander to politicians and big business that stand to make trillions of dollars per year on the Cap & Trade fiasco. The Chicago Climate Exchange is proposed to be a $12 Trillion industry with the potential of making the Al Gore's of this world and Obama and his consortium of Crime Inc. that Glenn Beck points out our government has become, with untold wealth and power, while making the common man paupers. And all this political maneuvering is based on false science, and they know it!
- **Abolish the un-Constitutional department of Health, Education and Welfare (HEW)** and return power to the States and to the people where it belongs under the

Constitution - The un-Constitutional department of <u>Health</u> has anything but health in mind. They are in bed with big-pharmaceutical companies who make their billions from treatments, not cures. People are their cash-cows. Curing disease cuts their own throats, income would decline and they would lose power. Only continued treatment of disease insures their survival, at the expense of course, of our health. The un-Constitutional department of <u>Education</u> has been feeding progressive propaganda to our children from pre-K through post-doc. The strings the HEW holds is federal funding for meeting certain federal standards. The intent is to create an ever tightening noose about the necks of educators in order to brainwash our children with progressive/socialist/Marxist /communist philosophies. For example, college professors who dare speak of creation in addition to the theory of evolution are ostracized, demoted, re-assigned and in some cases, dismissed based on concocted offenses. More than 75% of our education tax dollars are confiscated by the Federal Government to pay bureaucrats. (<u>Restoring the Heart of America</u>, Cleveland & Noyes p. 59) Therefore, abolish Washington's Department of Education and let our tax dollars be utilized at the State and local level to educate our children under our supervision. Remember, it was a communist, Joseph Stalin, who noted that *"Education is a weapon whose effects depend on who holds it in his hands and at whom it is aimed."* We must get education OUT of the hands of Washington progressives and INTO the hands of We The People. (more details found later in this chapter) The un-Constitutional department of <u>Welfare</u> is the third evil to be abolished. They keep most of our tax dollars for 'administrative' costs and destroy dignity of recipients and incentive to become self-reliant. Health, education and welfare are best administered at the local and state levels where We The People can be directly involved in how our tax dollars are spent.

- **Abolish the un-Constitutional Food and Drug Administration (FDA)** and return power to the States and to the people where it belongs under the Constitution - 60% of all people seeking medical treatment are seeking it from alternative sources, because western medicine controlled in large part by the pharmaceutical companies has failed the people. Yet the FDA has, unconstitutionally, assumed power to dictate that only MD's can diagnose and only drugs can treat a disease. Who's in bed with whom here? We The People must abolish the FDA to pull down its tower of power and restore it to the people. What mother hasn't diagnosed and treated her child's illness with her own remedies. The fact is western medicine is mostly about drug treatments and surgery. It is not about prevention, healing, health and wellness.
- **Get the United States out of the United Nations and the United Nations out of the United States.** 85% of UN members vote against the US, and we continue to give billions of USD in aid to our enemies. Bring that money home to the U.S.A. to recover our own economy. Our mantra should be 'the U.S. out of the U.N. and the U.N. out of the U.S.'
- **Institute Term Limits for Politicians:**
12 years only, one of the possible options below.
Two Six-year Senate terms
Six Two-year House terms
One Six-year Senate term and three Two-Year House terms
- **No Tenure / No Pension for Politicians**
- **A Congressman collects a salary while in office and receives no pay when they are out of office.**

- **Congress (past, present & future) participates in Social Security.**
- **All funds in the Congressional retirement fund move to the Social Security system immediately.**
- **All future funds flow into the Social Security system, and Congress participates with the American people.**
- **Congress purchases their own retirement plan, just as all Americans do.**
- **Congress will no longer vote themselves a pay raise.**
- **Congressional pay will rise by the lower of CPI or 3%.**
- **Congress loses their current health care system and participates in the same health care system as the American people.**
- **Congress must equally abide by all laws they impose on the American people.**
- **All contracts with past and present Congressmen are void effective 2015.** The American people did not make the current contract with members of Congress. Congressmen made all these contracts to benefit themselves. Serving in Congress is an honor, not a career. The Founding Fathers envisioned citizen legislators, so ours should serve their term(s), then go home and back to work.
- **Politicians shall make no more money than U.S. Military volunteers who protect our freedoms.** The average income of the US Army - $22.676
- **The average income of U.S. Federal government employee shall be no higher than the average U.S. private income.** Considering the following facts:
- Average US private income - $50,462. Average US Federal government employee (public servant) average income - $74,403.
- **Establish English as the official language**
- **All government agencies and businesses will offer their services in English only.**
- **Outlaw Lobbyists** – Our is government OF the People, BY the People and FOR the People. Not government OF big business, BY special interest groups and FOR foreign governments! Lobbyist control politicians who have power because of their 'deep pockets'. We The People are a distant second concern. Lobbyists are the source of bribes to politicians and influence government in favor of big business. The bigger the business the more the influence. Campaign contributions 'buy' candidates. Unions get candidates elected who are then beholden to them. This MUST end. We MUST return power to We The People.
- **Abolish the Internal Revenue Service & Institute the Fair Tax**. The Progressive notion that the more you raise taxes on the rich the more revenue for government to line their pockets and redistribute a token amount to the poor is false because it results in less production by those who actually work (non-politicians). Reaganomics proved that lower taxes increase production and increase revenue to the government. The Fair tax is uniform and taxes consumption; the more you buy the more you pay tax that is embedded in the cost of the good. Just think...NO more April 15th deadlines and spending countless hours and billions of dollars of lost revenue to fill out tax forms. And all those IRS employees, tax preparation people and tax lawyers can find jobs that actually increase the national GDP!
- **Reduce federal government to Constitutional size.**
- **Incentivize that which you want to happen. Our** current government dis-incentivizes growth and production by taxing entrepreneurs with higher taxes!

Currently 20% of the 'rich' (people making over $250k) already pay 70% of the taxes and 51% of the lower wage earners pay NO taxes!

- **Pass the Marriage Amendment to the Constitution** – 'Marriage is between a man and a woman'. The continued attempts to destroy traditional marriage by equalizing same-sex marriages are "the highway to hell". (Glenn Beck) Satan's attempts to redefine traditional marriage to include homosexual unions is just the next step in destroying every other freedom, including the right to free speech, the right to worship, the right to preach from the scriptures, the right to read the scriptures. Here is Satan's strategy. IF homosexuals have the legal authority and right to be married, then they have the right to adopt children, then they can force enactment of laws against homophobic hate speech. Since God in the Bible condemns homosexual practice, use of the Bible in the public realm, preaching form the Bible in church and reading from the Bible in private all constitute homophobic hate speech and homophobic indoctrination. These religious practices will then be outlawed and the Bibles burned. The truth is that in the beginning God created Adam and Eve. He blessed them with marriage. Since that time marriage between man and woman has been the foundation of civilizations. History confirms repeatedly that when traditional marriage is not honored people suffer, freedoms are lost, families decline, societies unravel and civilizations fall. The following excerpts from 'The Proclamation on the Family' reveal truth on this issue: "...*marriage between a man and a woman is ordained of God and that the family is central to the Creator's plan for the eternal destiny of His children. ALL HUMAN BEINGS—male and female—are created in the image of God. Each is a beloved spirit son or daughter of heavenly parents, and, as such, each has a divine nature and destiny. Gender is an essential characteristic of individual premortal, mortal, and eternal identity and purpose. THE FIRST COMMANDMENT that God gave to Adam and Eve pertained to their potential for parenthood as husband and wife. We declare that God's commandment for His children to multiply and replenish the earth remains in force. We further declare that God has commanded that the sacred powers of procreation are to be employed only between man and woman, lawfully wedded as husband and wife. WE DECLARE the means by which mortal life is created to be divinely appointed. We affirm the sanctity of life and of its importance in God's eternal plan. THE FAMILY is ordained of God. Marriage between man and woman is essential to His eternal plan. Children are entitled to birth within the bonds of matrimony, and to be reared by a father and a mother who honor marital vows with complete fidelity. WE WARN that individuals who violate covenants of chastity, who abuse spouse or offspring, or who fail to fulfill family responsibilities will one day stand accountable before God. Further, we warn that the disintegration of the family will bring upon individuals, communities, and nations the calamities foretold by ancient and modern prophets. WE CALL UPON responsible citizens and officers of government everywhere to promote those measures designed to maintain and strengthen the family as the fundamental unit of society.*"

- **Abolish the Two Party System.** George Washington warned not to adopt a two party system because it would divide the country. And so it has. America does not need or want Republican or Democrats. American wants moral, honest representatives who are not influenced by lobbyists or any other influence except by us. We must have representative who love correct principles over love of party and power.

- **Funding for candidates seeking office shall come from the general fund, and from NO other source:** Each candidate shall have equal funding from the general treasury and equal airtime to present his/her platform.
- **Allow the free market to provide health care alternatives.** Offer at least two different programs. One for those who choose to abuse their bodies with alcohol, drugs, fast food, overeating etc. Another for those who choose to care for their bodies through preventative health practices. The high cost of insuring body abusers should not be paid for by those who care properly for their bodies.
- **Abolish the 17th Amendment and revert to original practice of the State legislatures appointing Senators to Congress to represent the States.**
- **Legalize drugs.** Let's face it, the war on drugs is a colossal failure like prohibition was in the 1930's. We should use the model that works. America finally legalized alcohol and laws hold people accountable for their use of it. We should do the same for drugs. JAMES P. GRAY is a retired judge of the Orange County Superior Court, Why Our Drug Laws Have Failed: A Judicial Indictment Of War On Drugs, who said *"No one, absolutely no one, is even remotely talking of increasing young people's access to harmful drugs. But what we are doing simply isn't working. The way things are now, young people tell me it's easier for them to find marijuana or cocaine than it is alcohol. The War on Drugs isn't winnable, but it's fundable...It's not only the Drug Enforcement Administration's nearly $20 billion annual budget but government agencies of every kind receive extra funding for drug enforcement...things must change; it is impossible to have both a free society and a drug-free society. We will have drugs; either with drug lords or without them. The answer is to hold people accountable for their actions, as we do with alcohol. And let's get rid of this enormous and expensive bureaucracy. If you really think about it, most drug related problems stem from drug prohibition; not drugs."* Jim Wood, Coast Magazine Interview - Judge James P. Gray, (June 2001) Prohibition 1 (on alcohol) just made the business of selling and transporting alcohol very profitable, just like the prohibition 2 on drugs is doing today for drug traffickers. *"Violence in drug sales is caused by prohibition, not by the drugs themselves. Conservatives who care about the right to bear arms should also care about repealing drug prohibition. Besides the fact that prohibition drives the violence that's behind the sentiment to ban guns, drug prohibition and gun prohibition are rooted in the exact same social philosophy. Instead of regulating violent behavior, prohibitionists want to regulate inanimate objects. Historically, gun control is intimately linked to drug prohibition, as when alcohol prohibition led to the gangster violence, which became a pretext for passage of the 1934 National Firearms Act, the first federal gun legislation to apply to the general population. Liberals who are sensitive to the injustices of drug prohibition should also be wary of gun restrictions. Our police departments suffer corruption as a direct result of drug prohibition. The most obvious problem is that police officers can make big money dealing drugs, protecting drug dealers, or simply looking the other way."* (Drug War Addiction, Notes from the Front Lines of America's #1 Policy Disaster, Sheriff Bill Masters) 40% of the nation's local police agencies depend on seized assets as a budgetary supplement. Property owners do not need to be charged with a crime for property to be seized if drugs are suspected, or used as an excuse to seize property. And their personal property is seldom restored if the people are innocent. This gives law enforcement a strong financial incentive to raid whenever they have an opportunity. (Common Sense Revisited, Cleveland, Finkelstein, Morrow, Cook 2009))

The U.S. is by far the most criminal country in the world. The U.S. has 5% of the world's population and 25% of its prisoners. (Common Sense Revisited, Cleveland, Finkelstein, Morrow, Cook 2009)) The federal government has NO constitutional role or authority to be involved in people's personal choices that do no harm to others. However, laws should be enacted that form the foundation of civilizations, for example, a law that defines marriage as between a man and a woman.

- **End all government funding of the ACLU**
- **Get America out of all secret societies**
- **Become Energy Independent –** America is dependent on foreign oil, mostly from countries hostile to us. We should develop our own God given natural resources and use them in an environmentally sustainable way. We sent a man to the moon in 1969, surely we can learn to burn fossil fuels without degrading the Earth until we find a more sustainable way to power our society. (SEE REPORT BELOW THIS SECTION ON ANWAR)

Coal - Based on U.S. coal consumption for 2010, the U.S. recoverable coal reserves represent enough coal to last 249 years. However, U.S. Energy Information Administration projects in the most recent Annual Energy Outlook (April 2011) that U.S. coal consumption will increase at about 1.1% per year for the period 2009-2035. If that growth rate continues into the future, U.S. recoverable coal reserves would be exhausted in about 119 years if no new reserves are added. AND YET – Obama's Cass Sunstein has forged ever restrictive EPA regulations that have caused our coal power plants to shut down!

Natural Gas - Based on data from U.S. Energy Information Administration, the annual US consumption of natural gas is about 23 TCF (23 trillion cubic feet). The proven natural gas reserve, is 237.726 TCF. So that's roughly 10 years worth of natural gas left in the USA. However, the NaturalGas.org claims that the US natural gas reserve estimate is 1747.47 TCF. So if you divide that number by annual usage of 23 TCF, you have 76 years' worth of natural gas. http://www.naturalgas.org/overview/resources.asp The Granada Forum (Lindsey Williams) reports there are 200 years of natural gas reserves in Alaska alone if we do not use any of our natural gas reserves in the lower 48 States.

Electricity – under Obama's energy plan Obama said **"electricity would necessarily skyrocket."** Do we really want that future?...especially with all the proven reserves we have in the USA that generate electricity!

Oil - There is enough crude oil on the north slope of Alaska alone to supply the USA for 200 years. Since that report explorers found another oil field on Gull Island, Alaska that is as large as the first. (The Granada Forum - Lindsey Williams). There is no such a thing as 'peak oil'. **Oil would be $1.50/gallon in one years' time if we release our own oil reserves, AND we would be energy independent of foreign supplied energy**. See 'The Energy Non-Crisis' on YouTube and a book by Lindsey Williams. http://video.google.com/videoplay?docid=5541564304553695985#docid=334027469716701 1147 It costs $3 a barrel to extract oil from Alaska and $5 a barrel to extract oil from Saudi Arabia. One barrel of oil is 42 gallons. That's 7-12 cents per gallon! USGS found an additional 4.3 billion barrels of oil in the Bakken Reserve. So why do we pay $4.00 a gallon at the pump? Who is making the big profits soaking the American public? The oil companies do make a lot, but nothing compared to what the International Monetary fund and the World Bank make. Henry Kissinger coerced oil producing countries to buy American debt with part of the profits they would make off of America buying their oil. All countries except Iraq signed up. That is why George Bush initiated the first Gulf War, to bring Saddam in line with the other OPEC countries. **International banksters - the IMF and the World Bank control our lives and steal our wealth by controlling the price of oil. They make over $60 billion per year! Then they buy our national debt with those profits - and own us!**

We must become energy independent by using America's own resources. A portion of the profits from doing so should be allocated to developing sustainable energy sources. For more information on oil see ANWR entry below:

ALASKA'S Arctic National Wildlife Refuge (ANWR) OIL

Environmentalists have forced gas prices up to an impossible rate, forcing us to buy oil from our enemies empowering them, making us weaker.

There is enough oil in ANWR to supply the US at our present rate of usage for more than 200 years. The space that ANWR occupies in Alaska is equivalent to a postage stamp in the Mojave Desert. ANWR is 19.2M acres. Oil drilling will occupy 2,000 acres; that's 0.0001% of ANWR.

A new pipeline across Alaska is NOT required since the location for drilling in ANWR is about 160 miles from the North Slope Prudhoe Bay pipeline where it would be connected. Wildlife love the pipeline since it is heated and provides a shelter during the worst times during the winter.

Check out the following comparison: NOTE the size of ANWR.

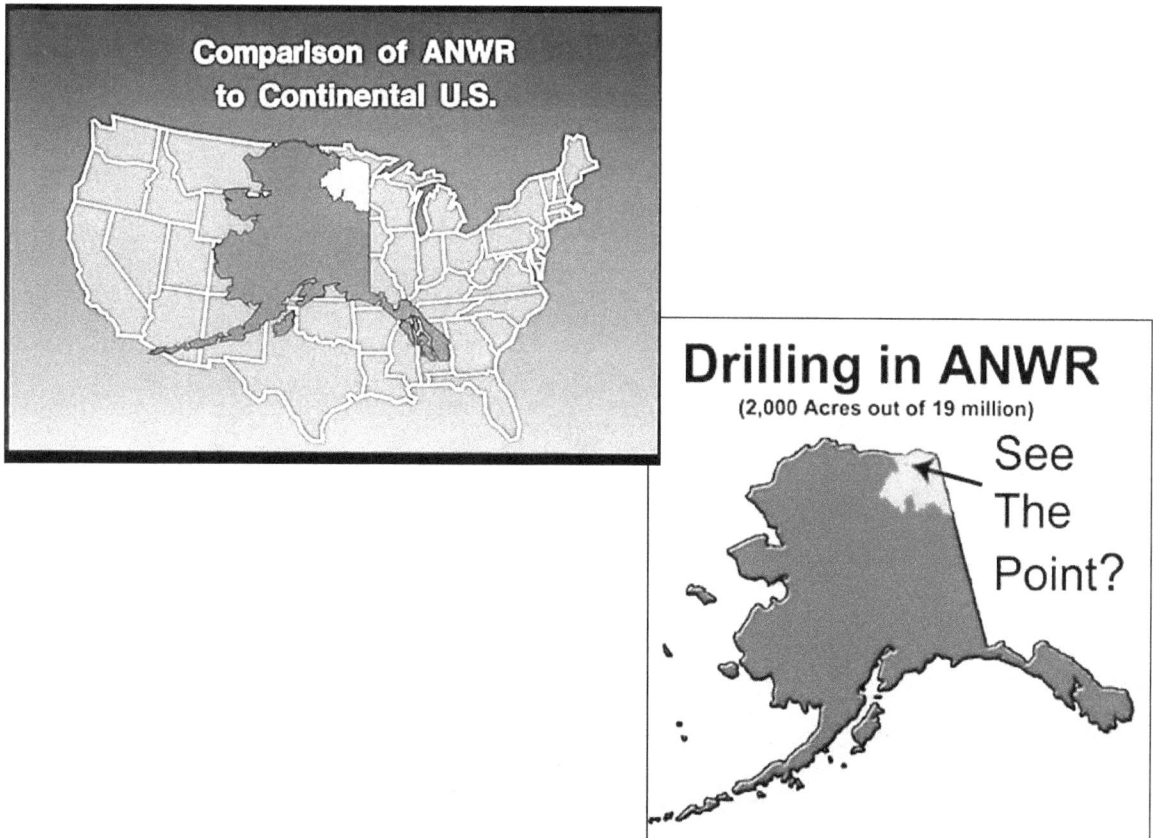

Comparison of ANWR to Continental U.S.

Drilling in ANWR
(2,000 Acres out of 19 million)
See The Point?

The proposed development area is in the "ANWR Coastal Plain"

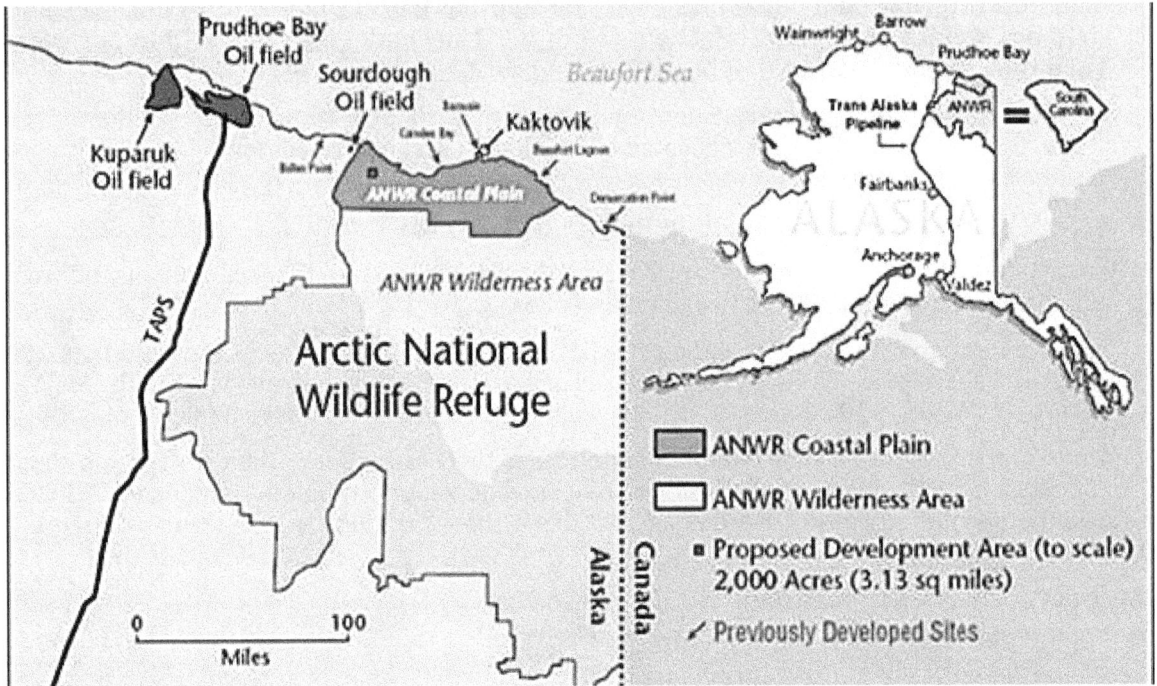

Below is what the Democrats, liberals and environmentalist "greenies" show you when they talk about ANWR and they are right these are photographs of ANWR: ANWR is beautiful. These are pics of **the mountain regions of ANWR.**

Drilling is proposed in ANWR Coastal Plain. This is what the proposed exploration area actually looks like in the winter:

And this is what it actually looks like in the summer:

The proposed drilling area is a barren wasteland.

And what about local wildlife? Here are photos (Summer & Winter) of the "depleted wildlife" situation created by drilling around Prudhoe bay: The caribou seem right a home.

The Prudhoe bay area accounts for 17% of U.S. domestic oil production. Now, why do you think that the Democrats are lying about ANWR? Remember when Al Gore said that the government should work to artificially raise gas prices to $5.00 a gallon? Well Al Gore and his fellow democrats have almost reached their goal! Now you know that the Democrats have been lying.

Can you now see the world wide evil involved in dumbing down the sheeple through controlled liberal left media to milk the sheeple of their wealth by controlling everything in our lives?

American sent men to the moon. We CAN use oil and coal emission free and obtain it from our own country without hurting life on Earth. This will provide us time to develop sustainable energy resources.

Abolish The Federal Reserve

"If the American people ever allow private banks to control the issue of their currency, first by inflation, then by deflation, the banks and corporations that will grow up around the banks will deprive the people of all property - until their children wake-up homeless on the continent their fathers conquered." Thomas Jefferson

Folks – we are there! The Federal Reserve is a PRIVATE BANK CORPORATION.

Our President and government, our very lives, are controlled by this 'invisible government' – The Federal Reserve and the International Banksters. Therefore, We The People MUST destroy this destroyer of the freedom and liberty of all mankind. We must institute our own money supply according to the Constitution of the United States.

In 2007, Ron Paul Introduces H.R. 2755: To Abolish the Federal Reserve. Repeal of Federal Reserve Act- this enactment of this simple directive would be the most earth shattering and economic liberating action seen in the lifetime of everyone alive.

This is probably the best thing we can do to restore our Republic, but it may not be the first. I invite honorable Patriots who know the legal system to implement this change. We The People – 360 million strong - will support the effort to overthrow this evil that has infected our way of life and hangs over our heads robbing us of our wealth, destroying our lives and futures of all mankind. There would be no more worthwhile endeavor or service to mankind than to achieve this monumental worthy goal.

Just let We The People know and We The People will raise of a force sufficient to overpower this evil.

We must return to the Constitution - Article 1 - The Legislative Branch, Section 8 - Powers of Congress. "The Congress shall have Power To coin Money, regulate the Value thereof, and of foreign Coin, and fix the Standard of Weights and Measures; To provide for the Punishment of counterfeiting the Securities and current Coin of the United States;...."

We must pressure Congress to fulfill its Constitutional authority...to coin money, ...and provide for the punishment of counterfeiting and abolish the Federal Reserve! Restore the Constitution to its proper place. Get the power out of the hands of international banksters and the Federal Reserve whose goal it is to destroy American economy and institute their One World Order.

Amend The U.S. Constitution

For information, the 26th amendment (granting the right to vote for 18 year-olds) took only 3 months & 8 days to be ratified! Why? Simple! The people demanded it. That was in 1971...before computers, before e-mail, before cell phones, etc.

Of the 27 amendments to the Constitution, seven (7) took 1 year or less to become the law of the land...all because of public pressure.

We The People must pull down the accumulated centralized power of the self-professed nobility of the Washington 'elite' and restore power to We The People where it rightfully belongs according to the U.S. Constitution.

THE AMENDMENT PROCESS

The first method is for a bill to pass both houses of the legislature, by a two-thirds majority in each. Once the bill has passed both houses, it goes on to the states. This is the route taken by all current amendments. Because of some long outstanding amendments, such as the 27th, Congress will normally put a time limit (typically seven years) for the bill to be approved as an amendment (for example, see the 21st and 22nd).

The second method prescribed is for a Constitutional Convention to be called by two-thirds of the legislatures of the States, and for that Convention to propose one or more amendments. These amendments are then sent to the states to be approved by three-fourths of the legislatures or conventions.

Power, authority and process of how to accomplish this amendment process is spelled out in The Constitution of the United States, Article V, which reads *"The Congress, whenever two thirds of both Houses shall deem it necessary, shall propose Amendments to this Constitution, or, on the Application of the Legislatures of two thirds of the several States, shall call a Convention for proposing Amendments, which, in either Case, shall be valid to all Intents and Purposes, as part of this Constitution, when ratified by the Legislatures of three fourths of the several States, or by Conventions in three fourths thereof, as the one or the other Mode of Ratification may be proposed by the Congress; Provided that no Amendment which may be made prior to the Year One thousand eight hundred and eight shall in any Manner affect the first and fourth Clauses in the Ninth Section of the first Article; and that no State, without its Consent, shall be deprived of its equal Suffrage in the Senate."*

Regardless of which of the two proposal routes is taken, the amendment must be ratified, or approved, by three-fourths of states. There are two ways to do this, too. The text of the amendment may specify whether the bill must be passed by the state legislatures or by a state convention. Amendments are sent to the legislatures of the states by default.

The Constitution, then, spells out four paths for an amendment:
1. Proposal by convention of states, ratification by state conventions
2. Proposal by convention of states, ratification by state legislatures
3. Proposal by Congress, ratification by state conventions
4. Proposal by Congress, ratification by state legislatures (most often used)

At no point does the President have a role in the formal amendment process (though he would be free to make his opinion known). He cannot veto an amendment proposal, nor ratification. This point is clear in Article 5, and was reaffirmed by the Supreme Court in *Hollingsworth v Virginia* (3 US 378 [1798]): *The negative of the President applies only to the ordinary cases of legislation: He has nothing to do with the proposition, or adoption, of amendments to the Constitution.*

We need to seek out good people who know the political and judicial system well enough to lead the process of implementing these changes.

READER - this is your and my opportunity - to make good change happen. Let us rise up and act!

Remember Civility In Public Discourse

As elections near and politicians' race for the prize, the world is aflame with mudslinging and the liberal left media spins stories to advance their agenda. Economies are tumbling. Public trust is falling off a cliff. Individuals feel vulnerable and the social fabric of civilization is coming unraveled. Rage and agitation resound on the radio, TV and streets. What we need are voices of reason, balance and moderation.

Renowned educator and scholar who received four honorary doctorate degrees, Thomas S. Monson, who was also appointed by President Ronald Reagan to the U.S. President's Task Force for Private Sector Initiatives, reminds us to generate a spirit of goodwill within and to unite with people on a common problem the results will be enhanced. Presidential Medal of Honor Recipient Gordon B. Hinckley, taught that the hallmark of civilization is working respectfully with others in communities with concern for one another's needs.

Often we see the world how we are, not how it is. We must have the right paradigm; the lens through which we see the world. Truth creates paradigm shifts. Understanding enables civilized discourse.

Civilizations rise and decline. Various peoples repeat the cycle of prosperity, pride and fall. In almost every case, the seeds of decay begin with the violation of the simple rules of civility. Cooperation, humility and empathy gradually give way to contention, strife and malice.

Therefore, we must treat our neighbors with respect, work cooperatively and avoid partisan politics. Focus on principles and values that form the foundation of civilizations and promote peace, prosperity and the good of the people. Partisan politics divide and destroy. It is the tool of the adversary. However, progressive policies have proven repeatedly that they destroy people, communities and countries; remember Chapter 6 expose on Detroit? That city and the 10 worst run cities in the United States have been run by progressive democrats for decades. Progressives are found in both parties. Watch out for them and vote them out. Progressives always act to grow government, raise taxes, institute more government regulations, 'take care' of you and ultimately control you.

We must unite on common principles and values which are found by some candidates of all parties. Vote for the person, not for the party. My objective is ... that we eliminate the weakness of one standing alone and substitute for it the strength of people working together.

Pray For All Our Representatives

Some of them are being controlled by the Invisible Government - international banksters, secret societies, the illuminati etc. Our President and leaders must be set free from the control of international evil in order to represent We The People. They also must stand before the judgment bar of God and will be held accountable for their actions. Unless they repent, it likely will not be well for them. After all they are our brothers and sisters who have lost the right way and succumbed to Satan's lust for power, position, prestige and property.

Reinstate God's Morality & Get Government Out of Our Way

Benjamin Franklin - _"The longer I live, the more convincing proofs I see of this truth: 'that God governs in the affairs of men.' And if a sparrow cannot fall to the ground without His notice, is it probable that an empire can rise without His aid?"_

In our day, is it reasonable that America can be restored without God's aid?

We must recognize that we are a nation of laws. All laws are an imposition of someone's morality. Thus, the statement 'you can't legislate morality' is absurd. However, it is correct that you cannot apply a political solution to a spiritual problem. We must return to high moral standards, but whose? The liberal left uses the argument that the right wing extremists are trying to impose their morality on society. But the truth is, the left is trying to do the same thing! Homosexuals pushing for same sex marriage are trying to impose their laws on society. Atheists have no moral code but their own.

Whose morality is best for society? The answer was given long ago by God as the Ten Commandments; proven over the course of 6,000+ years as the best system of morality on which to base society. For God to govern in our affairs we must keep His moral laws.

Ronald Regan - _"if we ever forget that we are a one nation under God, then we will be a nation gone under."_

We must return to 'the faith of our Fathers." The American religion that Benjamin Franklin defined.

We must educate our citizens as Thomas Jefferson stated. The basic purpose of his plan of education [note: NOT public education from a centralized governmental authority that we have today to which Jefferson expressed both fear and scorn, but rather education from private enterprise which manages so much better than government] is to qualify people **"to understand their rights, to maintain them, and to exercise with intelligence their parts in self-government. The people...are the ultimate, guardians of their own liberty"** The Real Thomas Jefferson, p.85, 2008, National Center for Constitutional Studies

After we have reinstated God's morality in our lives, then we can remove all authority from government except those responsibilities expressly stated in the U.S. Constitution, which are:

1. Secure OUR inalienable rights.

2. Establish and maintain military in order to provide for the common defense

3. Promote (NOT PROVIDE) for the general welfare by reducing taxes and creating a climate for entrepreneurial spirit of capitalism to thrive.

4. Provide a stable currency (a Congressional duty)

5. Establish post offices

6. Create courts

7. Regulate (meaning to make regular - not to control!) commerce between the states

8. To declare war

9. To raise money

10. Set and implement foreign policy for the 50 United States.

"...the truth is that outside of its legitimate function, government does nothing as well or as economically as the private sector." Ronald Reagan

"To take from one, because it is thought his own industry and that of his fathers has acquired too much, in order to spare to others, who, or whose fathers, have not exercised equal industry and skill, is to violate arbitrarily the first principle of association, the guarantee to everyone the free exercise of his industry and the fruits acquired by it." – Thomas Jefferson Letter to Joseph Milligan, April 6, 1816

"We are determined to foment a rebellion, and will not hold ourselves bound by any laws to which we have no voice or representation" Abigail Adams (John Adams wife)

"I think we should obtain the confidence of our fellow citizens in proportion as we fortify the rights of the people against the encroachments of the government." James Madison

Solve The Illegal Invasion Problem

Require illegal aliens to do as Thomas Jefferson counseled. Those *"Born in other countries, yet believing you could be happy in this, our laws acknowledge...your right to join us in society, [but you must]* **conform...to our established rules***."* The Real Thomas Jefferson, p.367, 2008, National Center for Constitutional Studies

*"'In the first place, we should insist that if the immigrant who comes here in good faith becomes an American and assimilates himself to us, he shall be treated on an exact equality with everyone else, for it is an outrage to discriminate against any such man because of creed, or birthplace, or origin. **But this is predicated upon the person's becoming in every facet an American, and nothing but an American...There can be no divided allegiance here. Any man who says he is an American, but something else also, isn't an American at all. We have room for but one flag, the American flag... We have room for but one language here, and that is the English language.. And we have room for but one sole loyalty and that is a loyalty to the American people.**'"* Theodore Roosevelt 1907

Is it right, just and fair for those who illegally sneak across our borders to be granted citizenship while those who come in the front door legally wait years, take citizenship classes, raise their right arm to the square and pledge allegiance to The United States of America, pay large sums of money and wait years to obtain citizenship?

Solve Illegal Immigration The Missouri Way

Missouri has no illegal aliens. Why?

In 2008 Missourians passed a constitutional amendment by a 90% vote designating English as the official language for all governmental agencies. Missouri highway patrol is required to verify immigration status of any person arrested and inform federal authorities. Illegal immigrants do not have access to taxpayers' benefits like food stamps and health care. In 2009 a law passed that insured that no financial aid would be given to illegal aliens. After all, they are our brothers and sisters who have lost their way and succumbed to Satan's way.

Know Who You Are - Conservative Or Liberal?

A young woman was about to finish her first year of college. Like so many others her age, she considered herself very liberal, and among other liberal ideals, was very much in favor of higher taxes to support more government programs, in other words redistribution of wealth. She was deeply ashamed that her father was a rather staunch conservative, a feeling she openly expressed. Based on the lectures that she had heard, and the occasional chat with a professor, she felt that her father had an evil, selfish desire to keep what he thought should be his.

One day she was challenging her father on his opposition to higher taxes on the rich and the need for more government programs. The self-professed objectivity proclaimed by her professors had to be the truth and she indicated so to her father. He responded by asking how she was doing in school. Taken aback, she answered rather haughtily that she had a 4.0 GPA, and let him know that it was tough to maintain, insisting that she was taking a very difficult course load and was constantly studying, which left her no time to go out and party like other people she knew. She didn't even have time for a boyfriend, and didn't really have many college friends because she spent all her time studying. Her father listened and then asked, "How is your friend Audrey doing?" She replied, "Audrey is barely getting by. All she takes are easy classes, she never studies and she barely has a 2.0 GPA. She is so popular on campus; college for her is a blast. She's always invited to all the parties and lots of times she doesn't even show up for classes because she's too hung over."

Her wise father asked his daughter, "Why don't you go to the Dean's office and ask him to deduct 1.0 off your GPA and give it to your friend who only has a 2.0. That way you will both have a 3.0 GPA and certainly that would be a fair and equal distribution of GPA."

The daughter, visibly shocked by her father's suggestion, angrily fired back, "That's a crazy idea, how would that be fair! I've worked really hard for my grades! I've invested a lot of time, and a lot of hard work! Audrey has done next to nothing toward her degree. She played while I worked my tail off!" The father slowly smiled, winked and said gently, "Welcome to the conservative side of the fence."

Consider the following:

If a conservative doesn't like guns, he doesn't buy one.
If a liberal doesn't like guns, he wants all guns outlawed.

If a conservative is a vegetarian, he doesn't eat meat.
If a liberal is a vegetarian, he wants all meat products banned for everyone.

If a conservative is homosexual, he quietly leads his life and respect others rights to live theirs as long as it does not interfere with the life, liberty and property of another.
If a liberal is homosexual, he demands legislated respect.

If a conservative is down-and-out, he thinks about how to better his situation.
A liberal wonders who is going to take care of him.

If a conservative doesn't like a talk show host, he switches channels.
Liberals demand that those they don't like be shut down.

If a conservative is a non-believer, he doesn't go to church.
A liberal non-believer wants any mention of God and religion silenced.

If a conservative decides he needs health care, he goes about shopping for it, or may choose a job that provides it.
A liberal demands that the rest of us pay for his.

Abolish The Federal Department Of Education

Neal Boortz says 'sending your kids to public school is child abuse.' Now do not misunderstand. There are many good teachers and good people in public schools. However, the fact is that the liberal left progressives have perverted education by crafting damaging laws. These laws take Federal Tax dollars –OUR MONEY- and demand that schools teach their progressive agenda (revised American History etc.) in order to qualify for Federal funding! Without Federal funding schools can hardly exist. Therefore, Progressives CONTROL much of what is taught in our public schools...and to control what is taught is to shape the future in their elite image of what the future should be. Remember it was Lucifer in the beginning who sought control over mankind. The liberal left lawyer progressives are just using Satan's age-old tactics in today's society.

Therefore, it is essential to take an active role in your child's education. Do not leave it up to the government to educate YOUR Child.

Establish Local-level Principles for Education

Education of children should be in cooperation with their parents. Parental involvement in concert with teachers should establish a set of principles on which education should be based. Worthy of consideration are the following:

- This is an America public school created to educate people to make better American citizens.
- American values will guide this school including clubs. There will be no division based on identities, including race, language, religion, sexual orientation etc.
- Schools will teach in English. – the official language of The United States of America.
- Schools will not prefer one race, ethnicity, gender, or religious affiliation over another.
- Individual identity – the content of your character, not the color of your skin, or origins of your ancestors - is the identity that will be respected.
- The only national identity this school will honor is American; without hyphenations.
- Non-American nationality-based celebrations will not be allowed because they undermine one of American core values – e pluribus Unum – from many, one.
- Political correctness will not be tolerated. PC is code for limited freedom of speech. However, in order to respect others, no obscene language, vulgar language, hate speech, cursing and swearing will not be tolerated. Such language reveals absence of vocabulary and disrespect for others rights and because it degrades dignity.
- Clubs will be based on interest and passions, including art, music, astronomy, debate, recreational pursuits, athletics, sports, languages you do not already speak, vocational skills, etc.
- Schools will have a formal dress code to create a paradigm of respect for learning.
- Self-esteem will be gained by earning it.

- Curriculum will be oriented toward academics, not politics. There will be no more classes to teach victimization due to color or ethnicity or origin. Sex classes will not be taught; morality is the domain of parents, not government.
- Everyone in the school will recite the Pledge of Allegiance every morning.

Recognize Archetypes of Evil

First, how they are not recognized. They are not recognized by race, gender, color, language, ethnicity or geography.

They are recognized by their fruits; the consequences of their words and actions; not the rhetoric, but the results. Satan is a silver-tongued deceiver and his tactics appear in mankind today.

They are ravening wolves in sheep's clothing; hypocrites! They lie repeatedly knowing that if they tell a big enough lie often enough the sheeple will believe it as truth. They are driven by their twisted ideologies and are usually narcissists.

There are two forces at work in our world; good and evil. Their origins are rooted in pre-mortal life when Lucifer rebelled against God. Lucifer was a morning star, a charmer, handsome, persuasive and charismatic. He became Satan through rebellion and led followers to the dead end of continued progression. All mortal conflicts can be traced back to these roots. The force for good seeks the liberty of all mankind. The force for evil seeks the enslavement of all mankind.

Good comes from God, maintains freedom and promotes human progress. Evil comes from Satan, enslaves, forces and dams human progress.

Consider evil of history, Cain, Ghengis Khan, Mao, Stalin, Hitler etc. Their values and passions all originate from the same evil satanic source and have the same tactics; force, control, tyranny, subduing others to obtain power.

Should Christians Support Obama?

America has a Christian history. Our Declaration of Independence, U.S. Constitution and judicial system has their primary roots in the Bible. Obama states that America is not a Christian nation.

Christians value life as sacred. Obama de-values life through promoting abortion with government funding.

Christians value independence. Obama values dependent citizenry.

Christians value the idler shall not eat the bread of the laborer. Obama values re-distribution of wealth – that the idler SHALL be entitled to the bread of the laborer, that illegal aliens deserve the welfare and healthcare and housing fruits of taxpaying Americans.

Christians are by nature humble and try to practice serving others. Obama is arrogant.

Christians value strength through righteousness defined by God in the Bible. Obama values strength through subjugation as preached by Allah in the Koran.

Christians know that God condemns homosexuality but counsels to love the sinner and condemn the sin. Obama supports the homosexual agenda.

Christians support traditional marriage; one man and one woman. Obama supports gay marriage.

Christians try to bring souls unto Christ so that they together can be saved in the Kingdom of God. Obama supports Islam's Allah that teaches conversion to Islam and death to infidels.

Christians stand with the Jewish State of Israel. Obama stands with the Palestinians and the Muslim world.

The Christian view of America is vastly different from Obama's.

Christians have a higher obligation to their God and America and to follow the Bible. Obama has a higher obligation to his Allah and the Muslim world and to follow the Koran.

Christians value the First and Second Amendments. Obama has tried to kill free speech and disarm American citizens.

Christians have a high toleration for opposing views as long as they do not interfere with the U.S. Constitutional rights to life, liberty and property. Obama tolerates anyone and anything that will buy him votes and keep him in power.

Christians see the hypocrisy of most of Hollywood's 'tinsel town' celebrities who typically lean left, with the exception of a few wonderful patriots like Gary Sinese and Clint Eastwood, and many of yesteryears legends like Charles Durning and Jimmy Stewart. Obama embraces the Hollywood liberal left and punk-rapper crowd.

Christians value keeping God as part of public life as the Founding Fathers intended and practiced. Obama and his progressives work to remove God from public life so that the sheeple can be more easily controlled.

However, while Christians' current enemy may be embodied in Obama and his regime, there is a much broader context to be understood. There have been many in the past 100+ years of progressives that have eroded American from it greatness to its current state. The important thing is be good gardeners of our lives. When a weed sprouts pull it out before it grows big and needs to be cut out, thus damaging nearby plants you want to keep. Likewise we must recognize evil when it sprouts, root it out and not to vote it into positions of power.

Billy Graham in his 90th year reminded us that the Bible teaches 'Woe to those who call evil good,' but that is exactly what we have done. He chastened America for losing its spiritual equilibrium and reversed its values. He noted that we exploited the poor and called it the lottery. We rewarded laziness and called it welfare. We killed our unborn and called it choice. We shot abortionists and called it justifiable. We neglected to discipline our children and called it building self-esteem. We abused power and called it politics. We coveted our neighbor's possessions and called it ambition. We polluted the air with profanity and pornography and called it freedom of expression. We ridiculed the time-honored values of our forefathers and called it enlightenment.

The moral foundation of religious doctrine provides essential truths that illuminate the solutions to current issues. Therefore, be not afraid to speak up! Both spiritual and secular voices need to be heard in the public square!

Be Grateful For the American Soldier

He stands on the wall and says to us all –sleep well tonight; nothing will harm you while I am on watch. Too often that watch has led to the deaths of 100's of 1000's who have fought to gain and maintain our liberty since the beginning of America.

We stand today on the shoulders of those who provided our freedom. For those who fought for freedom, liberty is cherished in a way the protected never know.

Let's bring home our troops from foreign wars we have no business being in. Unless the security of our country is at risk or we are provoked by being attacked first, let us do as Thomas Jefferson counselled; develop friendly trade with all, entangling alliances with none. Sticking our nose in other countries business breeds hatred against us. Let us employ our troops to secure our America's borders. Too often we have gone to war over energy resources that we have in more abundance in America than in any country in the world. Let us develop our own resources, use them in ecologically sound ways, promote non-polluting sustainable energy sources and stand independent of all other countries. Let us keep to our own business, except to defend our allies, mainly Great Britain and Israel. If another Hitler type arises let us uproot that sapling Tree of Tyranny while it is small rather than ignore it until it must be dealt with as a mature Tree of Tyranny as in WWI, WWII, WWIII..

Defend The Pledge Of Allegiance

Isn't life strange? I never met one Veteran who enlisted to fight for Socialism!

Only 31 words -- Think about it!

I Pledge Allegiance To The Flag,

Of The United States Of America,

And To The Republic For Which It Stands,

One Nation Under God, Indivisible,

With Liberty And Justice For All!

If Muslims can pray on Madison Avenue, why are Christians banned from praying in public and from erecting religious displays on their holy days? Muslims are allowed to block off Madison Ave, in N.Y.C., and pray in the middle of the street in a monthly ritual!

I believe it is time we stand up for what we believe!

Its time Americans to draw a line in the sand!

Truth, Tolerance and Respect

There are many different religious beliefs. In our interactions, we must stand for truth, but we must do so with tolerance and respect. Presidential Medal of Honor Recipient Gordon B. Hinckley taught that there is common belief among various religious denominations. We all believe in the fatherhood of God and that we are His children; thus brothers and sisters are we of the human family. We must work to build mutual respect and tolerance for differences of doctrinal interpretation and focus on the doctrine and beliefs that unites us. In this way we will be more effective in achieving mutually desired objectives.

Given those guidelines for human interaction, at what point do we 'draw a line in the sand' like Colonel Travis did at the Alamo or state 'you shall not pass' as Gandalf did to the dragon?

When Hitler came for the Jews the Germans did nothing because they were not Jews. When he came for the Christians' they did nothing because they were not Christians. We all know the tragic ending to that abdication of defending other people's rights. The point is we have a moral responsibility to defend other people's right to practice their religion, and for them to live.

In America the U.S. Constitution Bill of Rights Amendment 1 "Congress shall make no law respecting an establishment of religion, or prohibiting the free exercise thereof; or abridging the freedom of speech, or of the press; or the right of the people peaceably to assemble, and to petition the Government for a redress of grievances." That Amendment preserves the right OF RELIGION (not FROM religion), and THE FREE EXERCISE THEREOF, (not the prohibition of exercising religion even in government. In America we allow the free exercise of Christianity, Buddhism, Confucianism, Hinduism, Islam, Jainism, Judaism, Shinto, Sikhism, Taoism, and Zoroastrianism. The common denominator of all world religions – faith, god, goodness, family, serving one another should be a foundation on which we can all stand. These values are the foundation on which civilization rests. Let us not let the lesser differences in doctrine and beliefs divide us; that is just what Satan wants – to divide and cause contention. The 'line in the sand' that all people must be united in drawing is when radical elements of any religion seek to infringe on the LIFE, LIBERTY or PURSUIT OF HAPPINESS of others!

While we must be tolerant of others beliefs we need not be tolerant of their behavior if it crosses the line of the 'inalienable right that we have been endowed with by our Creator' – among those are the right to life, the right to liberty and the right to property. All people have a right to live as long as their actions do not deprive others of their rights - the rights stated in the U.S. Constitution.

Be careful of the use of the word tolerant. Those who use it as a weapon to advance their agenda rarely return tolerance. Gays demand tolerance but are typically intolerant of those who stand for Biblical teachings against homosexuality. Often the face of sin wears the mask of tolerance. Do not be deceived; behind that façade is heartache, unhappiness, and pain. There is right and wrong, and God – the Father of us all - defines what is right and what is wrong. No disguise, however appealing, can change that.

Our Father gives commandments to bless and guide us from pain and suffering. They are not intolerant restrictions. They are blessed guardrails and sign posts along the path of life.

Today we face Muslim leaders like Akmud Ahmadinejad (former President of Iran) and Yusuf Al-Qaradawi (religious leader of 60 million Muslims) saying that the Jews (Israel) are cancers of society, the enemies of Allah, and that they must be removed from off the face of the Earth. Ahmandinejad practices rape, torture and murder in his prisons. He is a murderer. The Koran demands jihad of infidels (non-Muslims). Ahmadinejad is pushing for world-wide bloodbath of infidels to bring about the 12th Imam who will establish a world-wide caliphate. The words of Ahmadinejad and Al-Qaradawi reveal evil in these madmen who hate and believe they are doing the will of Allah.

Do we stand idly by while it happens? Or do we remember the world consensus after Hitler's Holocaust was exposed – NEVER AGAIN!

We MUST remember. We MUST be determined that a holocaust will NEVER AGAIN happen, be it against the Jews, Christians, Buddhists, Hindus, Muslims or atheists.

Remember, we are engaged in the war between good and evil. In this ideological war and sometimes physical war, there can be no middle ground. We must stand for that which is true, good and right.

In our upside down society where 'political correctness' rules the day, TRUTH is the new hate speech. *"During time of universal deceit, telling the truth becomes a revolutionary act."* (George Orwell) Now IS the time to stand for truth to expose evil forces, doctrines, programs, policies and ideologies that have the effect of destroying the liberty and freedom of all mankind.

Political correctness PC is absolute non-sense. It is exposed in two short sentences: We are advised TO NOT judge ALL Muslims by the actions of a few radicals. But, we are encouraged TO judge ALL Gun Owners by the actions of a few radicals.

We constantly hear about how Social Security is going to run out of money, but we never hear about Welfare running out of money. What's interesting, the first group "worked for" their money, the second didn't. It's time to tell the truth and expose PC for what it is.

Stand With Israel

Yes it is a complex issue, but is boils down to this:

It is well to remember the covenant God made with Abraham. *"The Lord had said unto Abram... I will make of thee a great nation, and I will bless thee,...I will bless them that bless thee, and curse him that curseth thee: and in thee shall all families of the earth be blessed."* Gen 12:1-3 The promise of God was extended to Abraham and through his legitimate descendants; Isaac, Jacob (who was renamed Israel) and to the rest of the twelve tribes of Israel.

America, we had better stand with Israel; our best, and last friend, in the Middle East.

End Radical Muslim Terrorism

For the past 30 years radical Muslim terrorists have fomented WW III. Especially since 9.11.2001 America and the World has overwhelming reason to question Muslim loyalty to freedom. Some say 'well, it's only the radical Muslims who are doing this. Most Muslims are peace loving. So why worry about the few radicals?' That is true. Now consider other facts. Most of the Chinese were peace loving when Mao slaughtered 70M Chinese. Most of the Russians were peace loving when Stalin murdered 20M Russians. Most Germans were peace loving when Hitler's Nazi's annihilated 13M Jews, Christians, Gypsies and other undesirables.

The point is that the silent majority of peace loving populace are irrelevant when it comes to stopping evil. We must decide where we stand, with freedom or slavery; with the US Constitution or with Sharia Law. WWII fought the Nazi's, not all Germans. WWIII must fight Islamic terrorists, not all Muslims.

There are 1.2B Muslims in the world. Best intelligence sources estimate there are 'only' between 15-25% radical Muslims. That means there are between 180M-300M radical Muslims in the world – close to the population of the United States of America – and they are hell-bent on destroying freedom and our way of life. THAT is why we should pay attention to these 'few' radicals. THAT is why we should wage war to we achieve complete victory over radical Islam.

Muslim terrorism is not a new problem. By the 7th year of George Washington's presidency, Muslim terrorists were seizing, killing, and capturing our merchant ships. We had no navy to defend ourselves. Washington was paying 16% of the Federal budget to the Muslim terrorists to leave our ships alone. Washington went before Congress requesting funding for a navy stating, *"Would to heaven we had a navy able to reform those enemies [Muslim terrorists] to mankind or crush them into non-existence."* Washington then said *"to be prepared for war is one the most effectual means of preserving peace."* Washington received funding and built a navy and his term ended. The next president, John Adams did nothing to combat the Muslim terrorists because he thought the American people did not have the stomach for it.

Thomas Jefferson was an ambassador during that time of Muslim terrorizing. He asked the Muslim ambassador why they continued attacking our ships since we did nothing to provoke them. The Muslim ambassador replied, because Allah demands it, our Koran teaches it and to die in Allah's cause is our greatest honor and insures us going to heaven. Jefferson ordered a copy of the Koran because he could not believe there was a religion that fomented such evil. When Jefferson became president, the Muslim terrorists were extorting 20% of the Federal budget. Jefferson would not stand for it, sent our navy and marines to Tripoli for two years, and hammered the Muslim terrorists into submission, which ended Muslim extortion of the U.S.A. This was the first War on Terror that America fought.

The problem America, and the rest of the world faces, is the apparent conflict in Islamic doctrine.. In the first half of the Quran Mohammed taught peace. In the second half, Mohammad advocated jihad and violence to get to heaven. How does one account for a peaceful loving god turning into a violent murderous god in the Quran's teachings? Koran experts say that Mohammad was led astray by Satan, the god of this world, in the latter half of his life.

There is a glaring difference in the doctrine of Christianity and Islam. Christianity teaches that in order to get to heaven Christians should accept Jesus Christ as their savior, be baptized in His name and live His teachings. We should love God with all our might, mind, and strength, and love our neighbor as ourselves, serve others and help others come unto Christ so that their sins can be washed clean. Thus, we can dwell with them together in heaven. Islam teaches that in order to get to heaven and enjoy 72 virgins you have to blow yourself up to kill those who do not believe as they do. Actions of the past 30 years clearly reveal who seeks peace and who seeks violence.

The problem IS that Muslims do not separate Islam (Muslim religion), Caliphate (Muslim government), and Sharia (Muslim law). In their ideology, they are inseparable. A good Muslim is bound to convert or destroy all infidels (non-believers) by violent jihad if they will not convert. Muslim ideology and subsequent terrorist actions violate OUR God given inalienable rights to life, liberty, and property. The Islamic ideology of force and control is directly opposite to America's freedom of religion, the U.S. Constitution, and the Biblical roots of our judicial system.

The evidence presented is not intended to foment hatred toward Muslims. However, truth compels exposure of the inseparable trilogy of Islam, Caliphate & Sharia and its intent to take over the world under the banner of Islam.

We must fight against any form of religion, government, or law that seeks to overthrow the freedom and liberty of all humankind. Specifically, Americans have a duty to uphold and defend the Constitution of the United States against all enemies, foreign and domestic. The Muslim Islam-Caliphate-Sharia constitutes America's enemy.

There is ample evidence for America not to trust Muslims including WW III, 9.11, Fort Hood, Al-Takeyya, ISIS brutality in Iraq and Muslim silence concerning these heinous actions.

Let us be very clear on this issue. In this war between good and evil, there is no middle ground. Either you stand with America or you stand with terrorists.

To be accepted in America, peaceful Muslims must do the following:

1. They must speak out against radical Islam.
2. They must not teach jihad in their Mosques nor foment hatred for America.
3. They must pledge allegiance to the flag of the United States of America and to the Republic, for which it stands, one Nation, under God, indivisible, with Liberty and Justice for all.
4. They must pass the citizen test.
5. They must demonstrate <u>by their actions</u> that they have fully become Americans in allegiance, language, and culture, and defend the U.S. Constitution.
6. They must fight with us to eradicate Islamic radical terrorists from the Earth.
7. They must renounce the doctrine of al-takeyya [aka Taqiyya].

If Muslims do these things then America will defend Muslim's right to practice their religion, as long as it does not violate our Constitutional rights of life, liberty, property and the pursuit of happiness.

If Muslims are not willing to become Americans and renounce violent evil jihad, then we invite them to leave and go to a country where they can practice their religion, government, and law.

Since the beginning, American's have the right to expect immigrants to become Americans in every way. There should be no cultural isolation, no secret fomenting of hatred toward Americans. Tyrannical hypocrites will be dealt with like Hitler and Hirohito.

"Every society has the right to fix the fundamental principles of ties association, and to say to all individuals that if they contemplate pursuits beyond the limits of these principles, and involving dangers which the society chooses to avoid, they must go somewhere else for their exercise; we want no citizens...on such terms. We may exclude them from our [Country], as we do persons infected with disease." The Real Thomas Jefferson, p.367, 2008, National Center for Constitutional Studies

Understand America, Christianity & Islam

The God of America is Jesus Christ to the Christians and Jehovah to the Jews; the same God. He is a God of peace. Allah is Muslim's name for God. We all worship the God of Abraham, Isaac and Jacob; Jehovah of the Old Testament, Jesus Christ of the New Testament and Islam's Allah.

Isaac was the firstborn legitimate child of Abraham and his wife Sarah. Ishmael was an illegitimate son born of Sarah's handmaid Haggar. However, both lineages received blessings of Abraham to become great nations. Why then should the children of Abraham – brothers and sisters - fight with each other? Why are the descendants of Ishmael seeking to kill the other descendants of Abraham? This should not be. The fact is that we are all children of the same Father in Heaven. Our understanding of what God wants us to do is different. God does not condone sin like cowardly terrorism. The true God, our Father in Heaven does not condone murder. To live in harmony those with murderous doctrine must renounce violent jihad, repent of this evil, and seek peace.

Muslim terrorists focus on the violent portion of Koran doctrine to justify committing heinous acts of murder, rape, mutilation, and destruction in the name of Allah. They need to repent of these evil acts and renounce the doctrine that led to committing them to live peacefully in this world.

Christians seeking freedom from persecution in Europe founded America under the guiding hand of God. As long as we Americans serve the God of this land, He will not suffer America to be overthrown by evil forces.

Christianity started with Adam and Eve; it is over 6,000 years old on Earth. They offered sacrifices in similitude of the sacrifice of Jesus Christ who would come as the Lamb of God suffering for our sins in the meridian of time. Every prophet from Adam to Christ prophesied He would come and looked forward to that event. Every prophet since Christ testified that He did come and looked back on Christ's Atonement and forward to His Second Coming. Christianity is over 6,000 years old. In fact, it began in the pre-mortal life before the world was and before time was measured when we voted to accept Jehovah as our savior and redeemer.

Islam is a relative new-comer to the world scene; it began 700 A.D. It is only 1,300 years old. Its founder, Muhammad (c. 570 A.D. – June 8, 632 A.D.), is believed by Muslims to be the last prophet through whom Allah spoke to restore original doctrine. For the last 22 years of his 62 year life, Muhammad claimed to receive messages from Allah which were memorized and recorded by his companions. During this time, Muhammad preached to the people of Mecca, imploring them to abandon polytheism. Thus, God the Father, God the Son and God the Holy Ghost – three separate Gods that form the Christian Godhead in heaven is not what Islam teaches. Islam has only one God, Allah. After Muhammad's death, war broke out over who should be his successor. The result was the larger Sunni sect and smaller Shia sect.

It is interesting to note that there are quite a few similarities between Christian and Islamic doctrine. We should develop a world built on this common ground.

America extends an invitation to people of the world; come to America legally, embrace our ideals, live according to our laws, be loyal to our Flag and the U.S. Constitution, speak English, work to build America as Americans, and seek peace. American's will accept no less.

Require Drug Testing For All Welfare Recipients & Members Of Congress

Florida is the first state that is now going to require drug testing for welfare! Some people are crying this is unconstitutional. It's completely legal that every other WORKING person had to pass a drug test in order to SUPPORT those on welfare!! Let's get welfare back to the ones who NEED it, not those that just WANT it!

Congress should also comply with drug testing.

Feed The Right Wolf

One evening an old Cherokee told his grandson about a battle that goes on inside people. He said, 'My son, the battle is between **two 'wolves'** inside us all.

One is Evil. It is anger, envy, jealousy, sorrow, regret, greed, arrogance, self-pity, guilt, resentment, inferiority, lies, false pride, superiority, and ego.

The other is Good. It is joy, peace, love, hope, serenity, humility, kindness, benevolence, empathy, generosity, truth, compassion and faith.'

The grandson thought about it for a minute and then asked his grandfather: 'Which wolf wins?'

The old Cherokee simply replied, "The one you feed."

Maintain Our Faith In God

God has a way of working all things toward good for them that believe.

Following is a beautiful story that helps you understand that things happen for a reason.

The brand new pastor and his wife, newly assigned to their first ministry, to reopen a church in suburban Brooklyn, arrived in early October excited about their opportunities. When they saw their church, it was very run down and needed much work. They set a goal to have everything done in time to have their first service on Christmas Eve.

They worked hard, repairing pews, plastering walls, painting, etc, and on December 18 were ahead of schedule and just about finished.

On December 19 a terrible tempest - a driving rainstorm hit the area and lasted for two days.

On the 21st, the pastor went over to the church. His heart sank when he saw that the roof had leaked, causing a large area of plaster about 20 feet by 8 feet to fall off the front wall of the sanctuary just behind the pulpit, beginning about head high.

The pastor cleaned up the mess on the floor, and not knowing what else to do but postpone the Christmas Eve service, headed home. On the way he noticed that a local business was having a flea market type sale for charity, so he stopped in. One of the items was a beautiful, handmade, ivory colored, crocheted tablecloth with exquisite work, fine colors and a Cross embroidered right in the center. It was just the right size to cover the hole in the front wall. He bought it and headed back to the church.

By this time, it had started to snow. An older woman running from the opposite direction was trying to catch the bus. She missed it. The pastor invited her to wait in the warm church for the next bus.

She sat in a pew and paid no attention to the pastor while he got a ladder, hangers, etc., to put up the tablecloth as a wall tapestry. The pastor could hardly believe how beautiful it looked and it covered up the entire problem area.

Then he noticed the woman walking down the center aisle. Her face was like a sheet. "Pastor," she asked, "where did you get that tablecloth?" The pastor explained. The woman asked him to check the lower right corner to see if the initials, EBG were crocheted into it there. They were. These were the initials of the woman, and she had made this tablecloth 35 years before, in Austria.

The woman could hardly believe it as the pastor told how he had just gotten "The Tablecloth".

The woman explained that before the war she and her husband were well-to-do people in Austria

.

When the Nazis came, she was forced to leave. Her husband was going to follow her the next week.

He was captured, sent to prison and never saw her husband or her home again.

The pastor wanted to give her the tablecloth; but she made the pastor keep it for the church.

The pastor insisted on driving her home. That was the least he could do. She lived on the other side of Staten Island and was only in Brooklyn for the day for a housecleaning job.

What a wonderful service they had on Christmas Eve. The church was almost full. The music and the spirit were great. At the end of the service, the pastor and his wife greeted everyone at the door and many said that they would return.

One older man, whom the pastor recognized from the neighborhood continued to sit in one of the pews and stare, and the pastor wondered why he was not leaving.

The man asked him where he got the tablecloth on the front wall because it was identical to one that his wife had made years ago when they lived in Austria before the war and how could there be two tablecloths so much alike.

He told the pastor how the Nazis came, how he forced his wife to flee for her safety and he was supposed to follow her, but he was arrested and put in a prison. He never saw his wife or his home again all the 35 years between.

The pastor asked him if he would allow him to take him for a little ride. They drove to Staten Island and to the same house where the pastor had taken the woman three days earlier.

He helped the man climb the three flights of stairs to the woman's apartment, knocked on the door and he saw the greatest Christmas reunion he could ever imagine.

Vote on Principles not Politics, Gender or Color

Following are who voted for Obama:

95% Blacks	66% Single	51% Married
84% Democrats	63% Asians	43% Whites
78% Jews	56% White Females	41% White Males
66% Hispanics	54% Young White voters	24% White Evangelicals
66% under 30 yrs old	54% Catholics	

We MUST stop voting for color, party, or gender.

We MUST use our heads, forget the rhetoric, analyze the principles, values and track record of candidates. Then vote for those who most align with God's principles and values.

Dr. Martin Luther King said he looked forward to the day when a man would be "judged by the content of his character, not the color of his skin." How true those words are and applicable today.

Considering the long, racist past of the Democrat party, despite the fact that Republicans passed the 13th, 14th, and 15th Amendments, numerous Civil Rights bills, and bills to punish the KKK, it is very strange indeed that black Americans overwhelming vote Democrat. The number one question remains, "What changed the black vote from Republican to Democrat? The answer lies with Arthur W. Mitchell, a black politician con artist who used political spin to advance his own career at the expense of telling the truth about Democrat racism. The content of a man or woman's character IS what counts the most; their principles and values.

Government programs designed to 'take care of us' under the disguise of entitlements are traps leading to government slavery; socialism then communism. Those who are able to work should do so to the extent of their ability in order to maintain their personal dignity. Only those not able to work should accept government welfare. Generations of welfare recipients with entitlement-mentalities destroy their own sense of self-worth, and destroy the fabric of self-governing society. In the end socialists run out of other people's money because it is a society of consumers with not producers; takers without givers.

Remember history....*"Any man who thinks he can be happy and prosperous by letting the government take care of him better take a closer look at the American Indian!"* Henry Ford

Understand The Message Of The Ant And The Grasshopper

This one is a little different ......Two Different Versions..... Two Different Morals

OLD VERSION:

The ant works hard in the withering heat all summer long, building his house and laying up supplies for the winter. The grasshopper thinks the ant is a fool and laughs and dances and plays the summer away. Come winter, the ant is warm and well fed. The grasshopper has no food or shelter, so he dies out in the cold.

MORAL OF THE OLD STORY: Be responsible for yourself!

MODERN VERSION:

The ant works hard in the withering heat and the rain all summer long, building his house and laying up supplies for the winter. The grasshopper thinks the ant is a fool and laughs and dances and plays the summer away. Come winter, the shivering grasshopper calls a press conference and demands to know why the ant should be allowed to be warm and well fed while he is cold and starving. CBS, NBC , PBS, CNN, and ABC show up to provide pictures of the shivering grasshopper next to a video of the ant in his comfortable home with a table filled with food.

America is stunned by the sharp contrast. How can this be, that in a country of such wealth, this poor grasshopper is allowed to suffer so? Kermit the Frog appears on Oprah with the grasshopper and everybody cries when they sing, 'It's Not Easy Being Green. 'ACORN stages a demonstration in front of the ant's house where the news stations film the group singing, We shall overcome. Then Rev. Jeremiah Wright has the group kneel down to pray for the grasshopper's sake. President Obama condemns the ant and blames President Bush, President Reagan, Christopher Columbus, and the Pope for the grasshopper's plight. Nancy Pelosi & Harry Reid exclaim in an interview with Larry King that the ant has gotten rich off the back of the grasshopper, and both call for an immediate tax hike on the ant to make him pay his fair share.

Finally, the EEOC drafts the Economic Equity & Anti-Grasshopper Act retroactive to the beginning of the summer. The ant is fined for failing to hire a proportionate number of green bugs and, having nothing left to pay his retroactive taxes, his home is confiscated by the Government Green Czar and given to the grasshopper.

The story ends as we see the grasshopper and his free-loading friends finishing up the last bits of the ant's food while the government house he is in, which, as you recall, just happens to be the ant's old house, crumbles around them because the grasshopper doesn't maintain it.

The ant has disappeared in the snow, never to be seen again. The grasshopper is found dead in a drug related incident, and the house, now abandoned, is taken over by a gang of spiders who terrorize and ramshackle, the once prosperous and peaceful, neighborhood.

This story has relevance to America today. Our Nation will collapse bringing the rest of the free world with it if we continue to act like grasshoppers. We must repent and act like industrious ants.

Know The Truth About Wall Street Occupiers Vs. The Tea Party

The '**Occupy Wall Street**' agitators disrupt business and break laws as part of their protests. They are disheveled, dirty, and disrespect the public streets and parks they occupy. They defecate on the American flag and police cruisers on Wall Street. They litter and then expect someone else to clean up their mess. They are selfish and inconsiderate people who poison workplaces and neighborhoods. They disparage the greatness of this country even as they enjoy the benefits of our freedoms. Their protests continue with no end in sight because they are unemployed or they are being paid by socialist, anti-capitalist, progressive, Marxist backers. Following is a list of '**Occupy Wall Street**' supporters and backers:

Communist Party USA

American Nazi Party

Ayatollah Khamenei, Supreme Leader of Iran

Lisa Fithian (Left-wing anarchist – "What do I do? I create crisis.")

President Barack Obama ("We are on their side.")

Government of North Korea

Debbie Wasserman-Schultz   Member of Congress/Chairwoman of the Democratic National Committee.

Louis Farrakhan Jew-hating leader of Nation of Islam

Revolutionary Communist Party

Bill Ayers Marxist/former domestic terrorist who said to Occupy Chicago, "Every revolution seems impossible in the beginning."

David Duke Jew-hating former Grand Wizard the Ku Klux Klan

Hugo Chavez Communist ruler of Venezuela.

Black Panthers Organization of radical black nationalists

Socialist Party USA

Nancy Pelosi Democratic House minority leader who said of the Occupy Wall Street protestors, "God bless them."

Communist Party of China

Hezbollah Anti-Jewish terrorist organization

Stephen Lerner Militant labor activist/leading mastermind behind Occupy Wall Street - "How do we take down the stock market?"

International Bolshevik Tendency
Van Jones Avowed communist/former senior advisor to Obama White House – "I'll drop the radical pose to achieve the radical ends."

Harry Reid Senate Majority Leader (D-NV)

International Socialist Organization

Frances Fox Piven Marxist professor/honored elder stateswoman of the Democratic party – "It's okay to use violence." Marxist Student Union

The protesters then moved to the Washington Mall where YOUR tax dollars are being used to provide food stamps so the protesters can eat expensive crab legs! Are you mad yet?

In contrast, businesses compete to host **Tea Party functions** because they are considerate and spend money. Tea Party Patriots are law abiding, they secure permits for rallies, they leave the places that they rally cleaner than they found them, and then they return to their jobs. They are patriotic and honor our military. They proudly sing the national anthem and say the pledge of allegiance. They are frustrated with corruption and dirty politicians, but they are thankful for the opportunities that this great nation has provided.

The Tea Party has successfully begun a takeover of the Republican Party by challenging and beating corrupt establishment Republicans. In contrast, establishment Democrats have endorsed and cheered 'the Wall Street occupiers.'

These are the facts. Yet despite these facts, the big-government propaganda machine has been driving a completely different narrative; by calling good evil and evil good.

Vote With Your Wallet For The Triple Bottom Line

Big business is powerful because of their money. Money is power. Big business is driven by the bottom line of profits in $$$$. Big business is driven by Wall Street to keep increasing their bottom line. Many do it at the expense of people. That is why pharmaceutical companies are so powerful. They use people as their cash cows by first creating diseases in league with the FDA and contaminated food supply, then selling the drugs to treat but not cure the disease.

The problem is we let them by buying into their lies. The problem also is the focus of their bottom line is ONLY money. That must be changed to the triple bottom line.

The triple bottom line for all business should be people, planet and profits. Or in other terms, society, Earth and economy. If the first question all businesses asked is 'is this good for people?' the product offerings would be better. The next question is, 'is this good for the Earth's ecosystems that support our life on this planet?' The last question is 'is this profitable?' All three must be positive for it to be 'good business'.

We The People have the power to drive this preferred triple bottom line with our wallets. Choose to buy products from businesses who use the triple bottom line only. If we do, others will either fall into line or go out of business.

Remember The Power Of Good

Listen to the link below and envision how it could be in America again! Then act to make it happen!
Opera Company of Philadelphia "Hallelujah!" Random Act of Culture

Take a couple of minutes and watch this video. The Opera Company of Philly, PA showed up at Macy's on October 30, 2010 with 650 opera singers and sang the Hallelujah Chorus. Shoppers were taken by surprise, but many cheered, teared up and even raised their hands and started praising the Lord. They called it "a random act of culture". You'll be blessed. By the way, I heard the Wanamaker Organ is a permanent fixture in Macy's – you'll see a quick picture of it at the beginning of the video. It is gorgeous! http://www.youtube.com/watch?v=wp_RHnQ-jgU

Consider this Governmental Customer Service Future

GOOD MORNING, WELCOME TO THE UNITED STATES OF AMERICA, a pre-dominantly Christian nation, land of the free and home of the brave.

How may I help you? Press '1' for English. Press '2' to disconnect until you learn to speak English

Remember only two defining forces have ever offered to die for you, Jesus Christ and the American Soldier.

Christ died for freedom of your soul to choose and immortality.

The American Soldier fought and some died for freedom from tyranny in the world.

A Nation of Sheep Breeds a Government of Wolves!

Serve Others

Following is a short story to illustrate a key point:

Two groups of people sat in two separate rooms seated at banquet tables full of the most delicious foods imaginable. Both groups were given utensils with handles longer than their arms.

The first group feasted fabulously. They used the long-handled utensils to feed each other. It was heaven! The second group starved to death. They food from the long-handled utensils into their own mouths! It was hell.

The point of this short story is: the difference between heaven and hell is simple. It is selfless service vs. selfish service.

America, we must remember who we are. Like the Boatlifters, American's help each other.

THE POINT: Selfless service is a key ingredient to healing our Republic.

Remember The Abundance Of Good In America

It's easy to lose faith and hope watching the 6:00 o'clock news! Remember, there is more good in America than you glean from the news media. Thank God!

Remember the love of family and friends. The kind acts of service of neighbors. The wonderful traditions in America; Christmas, Easter, the 4th of July, Memorial Day, Labor Day, Thanksgiving. Keep your traditions alive. They anchor the soul in good times.

Good will triumph over evil, but we must remember Edmund Burke's quote "The only thing necessary for evil to triumph is for good men to do nothing." Good men, we must rise up and act!

Summary Points:

- We must know the truth. Know who God is. Know who you are and where you stand.

- Know your relationship with God and your accountability to Him.

- Educate ourselves on all the issues of our time

- Repent of evil and wrong doing so that WE become the moral and religious people for which the U.S. Constitution was designed.

- The foundation on which one stands determines the extent and accuracy of the archers' arrow. On quicksand the arrows flight tends to be short and inaccurate. On solid rock the arrows flight tends to be longer and more accurate. Likewise the foundation of emotion often leads to poor choice, whereas the foundation of carefully considered choice brought to the Lord for verification leads to better choices.

Action Steps:

1. Seek truth of American history from original sources. David Barton's Wall Builders website is excellent – www.wallbuilders.com.
2. Plant our feet on the foundation of TRUTH, then let our arrows of choice fly.
3. Vote for the person based on their values, principles and record – not on their rhetoric, charm, looks, vain promises, color or gender.
4. Apply the principles and values of the Gospel of Jesus Christ because they are true and have proven over millennia that they are most effective in producing peace and happiness.
5. Look for freedom of choice vs. force and control; God's way vs. Satan's way. And vote for candidates who represent God's way!
6. Perform random acts of kindness. Love is powerful. Service is love. "America is great because America is Good!" Let us be good again America and restore our greatness!
7. Watch this short video from 'one of the founding Fathers on his views of our current world affairs: (made in 2008 so the debt level is not up to date but the principles are true. "Common Sense – The Second America Revolution" on YouTube. I do not agree with his separation of church and state comment for reasons documented earlier in this book. https://www.youtube.com/watch?v=pKFKGrmsBDk
8. Read The Blaze online. It is the only media outlet of truth that is not bought and paid for by international business interests.
9. Obtain as many signatures as possible to **A Petition of Patriotism and Warning to Washington by We The People** in Appendix A. Send it to all 535 representatives in Washington.
10. Join Freedom Works. They empower We The People to take back OUR Country.
11. Remember, although evil exists, there are great pockets of good. There is more good in America than evil. Resist evil wherever it is found. Overcome evil with good.
12. Rise UP & ACT to save our Republic!

End of Chapter

9

Summary

Since the only thing for evil to triumph is for good men to do nothing...
Therefore, good men and women, Patriots among We The People MUST...
Know the TRUTH - Defend the TRUTH - Rise UP and ACT!

Truths To Remember:

- It is the obligation, and opportunity, of the reader to verify the truth of all things, including the things presented in this book. I realize there are inclusions that people have opposite opinions on. Some simply cannot be verified. Case in point: Area 51 still has legitimate opposing viewpoints. Therefore, after all you can do to research, examine and ponder on information, it is essential to seek final confirmation of the truth from the source of all truth, who is God.

- There is an opposition in ALL things. We are in a war between opposites: good and evil, truth and falsehood, God and Satan. In the end only good, truth and God will win. Evil, falsehoods and Satan will lose.

- The way to choose is simple. Examine where choices will lead. If it flows from force and fear it leads to control and slavery - it is from Satan. If flows from love and choice it leads to freedom and independence - it is from God.

- To know good, truth and God apply the required formula- seek for them out of the best books (the scriptures is a good place to start), ponder, pray to God (the source of all truth) and receive His enlightenment.

- We took part in the pre-existent War in Heaven and voted in favor of God's Plan of Happiness and for Jehovah to become our Savior & Redeemer. Part of that Plan was retention of our God-given freedom to choose - moral agency.

- Lucifer (Satan) presented his plan which was based on force and control. Lucifer was a handsome, 'silver-tongued', highly intelligent devil who professed almost all the right things – his position was just a 'little off' of Heavenly Father's Plan of Happiness. Satan wanted to force. Heavenly Father insisted on the eternal law of moral agency; the right to choose.

- 2/3rds of us choose Our Father in Heaven's Plan and were born on Earth with physical bodies. 1/3rd of our brothers and sisters in the pre-mortal life choose Lucifer's plan and were cast out down to this earth never to receive physical bodies.

- In the pre-mortal life God established the eternal principle of moral agency (the freedom to choose with consequences and accountability for those choices.) The War in Heaven was fought over this principle.

- God created this Earth so that His spirit children could be born on Earth, gain physical bodies to house their eternal spirits, be tested to see if they will live by God's commandments, and if they choose well, to progress and become more like Him.

- God created the land of America choice above all other lands and reserved it for those who would worship Him and keep His commandments. Two previous civilizations inhabited America and failed in their attempts to live righteously. Will ours be next?

- God established the U.S. Constitution through good men in order to provide a place where His children would have the freedom to worship God free of conscience according to the dictates of their own hearts. We have accountability to God for how we treat our freedoms.

- America became great because her citizens were rooted in the Trees of Truth, Clarity, God's Power and Liberty.

- Thus, the real roots of America lie in the pre-mortal life with God. The threads of freedom are woven into the fabric of America's Declaration of Independence and the U.S. Constitution.

- God inspired the Founding Fathers of this Country to write the U.S. Constitution. There was none other like it for nearly 5,000 years on this Earth. We are the beneficiaries of this great document. The USA is what it is today largely because of the freedoms the U.S. Constitution insures.

- 95% of the Founding Fathers were practicing Christians.

- 29 of the 56 signers of the Declaration of Independence held seminary or Bible school degrees.

- The Christian history of the U.S. was deeply rooted from Columbus to today.

- The war that started in heaven continues on Earth from Cain to today. The actors on the stage change, but the root cause of fighting is the same – freedom vs. slavery.

- The forces of good and evil which divided us in the preexistence (God and Satan) still exist today and are manifest in mankind's' attitudes and actions.

- Whenever good arises, so also does evil– the required 'opposition in all things' that compel us to use our moral agency and choose.

- Moral agency - our right to choose - is God's eternal principle. We must choose sides now – God or Satan - good or evil - there is no middle ground.

- Satan teaches people to lust for power, position, property and prestige. To gain these ends he teaches them to create a state of fear (never let a good crisis go to waste) then enter the scene as a 'savior' (born on Krypton like Obama-ha!) to protect and provide for the people. The ignorant sheeple will succumb to such tactics by evil wolves cloaked in sheep's clothing. The game is always the same – create fear, cause the problem, blame the good guy as the cause, offer a solution of 'safety' for the good of the people, and then control the suckers who accept it. One strategy evil employs is destroy the economy, create food shortages, and control the supply of money and food. Then unprepared dependent people will sell their goods, their homes and their souls to eat. It worked in ancient Egypt, it is working today.

- The progressive/liberal left/socialist/communist movement which started in the early 1900's revised American History to advance their own evil agenda of control and eroded the moral foundations upon which America prospered. Their movement is a strategic evil plan, methodically implemented, to destroy the foundations of America and to supplant it with a false religion (worship of power, prestige, position & property) and immorality (anything goes mentality). The ultimate goal of these people along with their secret societies and international banksters (the IMF, World Bank & Federal Reserve), is to establish their own New World Order, with them, the 'elite' of the world, as controlling kings.

- Communists/socialists/Marxists/fascist/Muslim radicals/sharia law/the liberal left media (NY Times, Washington Post, ABC, NBC, ABC etc.) are controlled by and are propaganda outlets for Satan as he works through George Soros, banksters and international corporations.

- Satan's goal is to overthrow the works of God. The overall goal of these anti-Christ persons and organizations is to destroy the U.S. Constitution (established under God's inspiration) and free market capitalism. Evil's next step is to institute One World Order – a global controlling government. Israel and the United States of America are the two last obstacles – the last bastions of freedom - to achieving evil's goal.

- America descended from being a light on a hill because its citizens progressively drew evil from the Trees of Falsehoods, Distortion, Satan's Power and Tyranny.

- The evidence presented in Chapter 6 makes it clear that we are in an awful situation where evil has infiltrated our government, business and much of society.

- Historically, when mankind has reached such a state of depravity as we have, God out of His infinite love of His children, cleanses the world of evil through wars and calamities in order to purify His children. Catastrophes often bring people to repentance and an awareness of what matters most. What matters most is what lasts longest. Love and family matter most. Remember your change of heart and thoughts on 9.12? We all felt differently after 9.11. This disaster happened because America had a chink in its armor of righteousness. We must repent of our evil in order to have the ultimate protection – God's protection – over our country. If God does not periodically wake us up through suffering disasters that leads to repentance of unrighteousness, He will take the next step and cleanse evil from the land when we are ripe with iniquity. If we continue to add more sin to our lives we will receive even greater condemnation at God's Judgment Bar.

- We have severed ourselves from the roots of the Trees of Truth, Clarity, God's Power and Liberty by turning from God toward Satan. Thus, the roots of the Trees of Falsehoods, Distortion, Satan's Power and Tyranny have infected good trees with evil roots. We must repent, sever the roots of evil in our lives and reconnect with God's good roots so that our Trees of Truth, Clarity, God's Power and Liberty will bear good fruits for America's future.

- We MUST not lose our freedoms to evil. The way to combat evil is to know the truth, defend the truth, rise up and act to establish truth.

- We must repent and turn back to God, live His laws and uphold and defend the U.S. Constitution – the foundations of human happiness and progress.

- Prepare to be independent of government control. Store water, food, clothing, tools, cash, guns, ammo, gold & silver. Have the ability to produce your own food.

- Watch out for the handsome, persuasive, charming, 'silver-tongued devil' political candidates who say all the right things and then promise that the government will take care of you. They use manipulation, force and control. It is a trap. It is enslavement.

- The U.S. Constitution, capitalism and liberty are in direct opposition to communism, socialism, Marxism, the Islam's Caliphate, sharia law and slavery.

- The U.S. Constitution and capitalism have not failed. We have failed to be a religious and moral people for whom the Constitution was designed.

- Greed, dishonesty, corruption from international secret societies, progressives/liberal left/socialists/communists/Marxists/ Nazis have infiltrated our government, businesses and undermined the foundation of America.

- Use your buying power to promote truth by purchasing products from companies who sponsor truth. Do not buy products from companies who sponsor (advertise) on liberal left media programs.

- Buy products only from businesses who use the 'triple bottom line' – people, planet & prosperity (society, Earth & economy).

- Join the Tea Party and support it with your wallet and your presence.

- Require Muslims to do the following to be accepted as Americans:
  1. They must speak out against radical Islam.
  2. They must not teach jihad in their Mosques nor foment hatred for America.
  3. They must pledge allegiance to the flag of the United States of America and to the Republic, for which it stands, one Nation, under God, indivisible, with Liberty and Justice for all.
  4. They must pass the citizen test.
  5. They must demonstrate <u>by their actions</u> that they have fully become Americans in allegiance, language and culture, and defend the U.S. Constitution.
  6. They must fight with us to eradicate Islamic radical terrorists from the Earth.
  7. They must renounce the doctrine of al-takeyya [aka Taqiyya].

- Departure from God's laws has destroyed our ability for self-government and separated us from God's support.

- 73% of Americans say we are going in the wrong direction.

- 87% of Americans disapprove of Congress.

- Historically 6-10% of the population can bring about major change....witness the American Revolution! Therefore We The People can succeed in this quest to restore our Republic. If We The People are on God's side, "With firm reliance on the protection of Divine Providence" WE CANNOT FAIL!

- Bring our troops home, protect American borders and root out evil within.

- We MUST not fall into the One World Order crowds trap. What they want is for us to be part of the insurrection, to cause chaos, to be evil and be dependent on them. Therefore, prepare, be righteous – that is our best defense; to be on God's side.

- Remember what *George Washington* said, "***The thing that sets the American Christian apart from all other people in the world is he will die on his feet before he'll live on his knees.*** " Thank God for the America Christian who would rather live free, or die before he subjects himself to the tyranny of a foreign king, or to a president or government who assumes the role of king in our own country. America will NEVER be ruled by kings. Patriot's will defend our Republic to the death before bowing to evil.

Proposed Washington Reforms:

1. Abolish the Federal Reserve. Return America to the gold standard.
2. Institute Term Limits for Politicians.
3. No Tenure & No Pension for Politicians.
4. Require Congress (past, present & future) to participate in Social Security.
5. Require Congress to purchase their own retirement plan, just as all Americans do.
6. Rescind Congressional authority to vote themselves a pay raise. Pay should be determined by We The People based on performance and adherence to the U.S. Constitution per their oath of office.
7. Congress loses their current health care system and participates in the same health care system as the American people.
8. Congress must equally abide by all laws they impose on the American people.
9. All contracts with past and present Congressmen are void effective January 2, 2012.
10. Politicians shall make no more money than U.S. Military volunteers who protect our freedoms.
11. The average income of US Federal government employee income shall be no higher than the average US private income.
12. Outlaw Lobbyists.
13. Establish English as the official language..
14. Abolish the Internal Revenue Service & Institute the Fair Tax.
15. Pass the Marriage Amendment to the Constitution – 'Marriage is between a man and a woman'
16. Abolish the Two Party Systems.
17. Funding for candidates seeking office shall come from the general fund, and from NO other source.
18. Repeal un-Constitutional Obamacare.
19. Allow the free market to provide health care alternatives.
20. Abolish the un-Constitutional Environmental Protection Agency (EPA) and return power to the States and to the people where it belongs under the Constitution.
21. Abolish the un-Constitutional department of Health, Education and Welfare (HEW) and return power to the States and to the people where it belongs under the Constitution.
22. Abolish the un-Constitutional Food and Drug Administration (FDA) and return power to the States and to the people where it belongs under the Constitution.
23. Get the United States out of the United Nations and the United Nations out of the United States.
24. Abolish the 17th Amendment and revert to original practice of the State legislatures appointing Senators to Congress to represent the States.
25. Legalize drugs.
26. Remove all authority assumed by the federal government that is un-Constitutional.
27. End all government funding of the ACLU
28. Get America out of all secret societies
29. Become Energy Independent by using our own resources.

U.S. Constitution Authorized Roles Of The Federal Government

1. Secure OUR inalienable rights.
2. Establish and maintain military in order to provide for the common defense
3. Promote (NOT PROVIDE) for the general welfare by reducing taxes and creating a climate for entrepreneurial spirit of capitalism to thrive.

4. Provide a stable currency (a Congressional duty)
5. Establish post offices
6. Create courts
7. Regulate (meaning to make regular – not to control!) commerce between the states
8. To declare war
9. To raise money
10. Set and implement foreign policy for the 50 United States.
11. Preserve American history. (assign David Barton of Wall Builders to spearhead an initiative to restore American history from original sources, and to develop K-College curriculum required to be taught for each of those 16 years so that America never loses touch with its real roots.)

Let us, We The People, hold our elected representatives accountable to fulfill these Federal Government functions, uphold their Oath of Office, and do no more than what is Constitutional.

Strip all other non-Constitutional powers from the Federal government. It will aid in our becoming what we were supposed to be.

The Constitution of the United States of America is The Law that is to go forth from this 'Shining City on a Hill' to all nations of the Earth so that all nations can be similarly blessed by adopting their own versions of the U.S. Constitution. A key word here is that other nations should *'adopt'* not have it forced upon them. America has tried to force our Constitution in the past and it has failed. It failed not because the U.S. Constitution was no good. It failed for two reasons: [1] it was 'forced' upon people and force sows seeds of future rebellion, and [2] the people were not a religious and moral people. The U.S. Constitution was designed ONLY for a religious and moral people WHO LIVE THEIR RELIGION AND ACT ACCORDING TO ITS MORAL PRINCIPLES.

The ultimate end of following the principles of morality found in religion upon which the U.S. Constitution is based, is to prepare the people of the Earth to adopt the full Gospel of Jesus Christ. Christ's Gospel, when lived, can produce a civilization in the future like it has in the past where as an ancient prophet recorded among his people who lived the Law, that *"...there was no contention in the land, because of the love of God which did dwell in the hearts of the people. And there were no envyings, nor strifes, nor tumults, nor whoredoms, nor lyings, nor murders, nor any manner of lasciviousness; and surely there could not be a happier people among all the people who had been created by the hand of God."*

A former Utah State Supreme Court Justice, noted that the U.S. Constitution was the model for every nation's written constitution in the world, except six.

The progressive/liberal left/socialist/communist/Muslim argument that the U.S. Constitution and capitalism are a bad and failed system is like saying that an automobile is a bad vehicle because it provides the opportunity to kill and destroy. An automobile becomes deadly in the hands of a drunk driver. Likewise, capitalism becomes a system that does not work when people become irreligious and immoral.

The Constitution of the United States of America – and its economic system is for a religious and moral people. It is wholly inadequate for any other!

Let us become the religious and moral people for which our Constitution was designed and we will rise again to become the Light on a Hill America was created to be.

Let us know truth, and measure our choices against the principles of freedom vs. force; AND ALWAYS CHOOSE FREEDOM!

Action Steps:

- Learn the truth

- Stand for truth

- Christians & Jews - Rise UP and ACT. Our voices must be silent no more!

    - Practice your religion and destroy Obamacare as described in Chapter 7.

    - Take the Petition to Washington to your pastor, minister, rabbi etc. and ask then to spearhead petition signing by your congregation and sending it to Washington. Let OUR voices be heard!

- Remember there is so much good in America! Let that good motivate you to action to restore and preserve the reason for America's greatness; Goodness!

- Serve! Serve! Serve....each other!

- Act on truth to restore our Republic

- **Patriots**, let us raise again...

-

We The People raise
The Banner of Liberty
for our peace, religion, families and freedom.
The Constitution of the United States of America,
Now and Forever!

End of Chapter

Petition of Patriotism and Warning
to Washington by
𝔚e 𝔗he 𝔓eople

Following Petition is intended for use by American Patriots.
Make copies of it and compile names & signatures
of people who support its message.
Then send it to all 535 representatives in Washington
to wake them up to the demands of We The People

A Petition of Patriotism & Warning
to Washington by
𝔚𝔢 𝔗𝔥𝔢 𝔓𝔢𝔬𝔭𝔩𝔢

This Petition is sent in accordance with direction from the Founding Fathers of The United States of America and The Declaration of Independence wherein Thomas Jefferson stated:

"Prudence, indeed will dictate that Governments long established should not be changed for light and transient causes; and accordingly all experience hath shewn, that mankind are more disposed to suffer, while evils are sufferable, than to right themselves by abolishing the forms to which they are accustomed. <u>BUT when a long train of abuses and usurpations, pursuing invariably the same Object, evinces a design to reduce them to absolute Despotism, it is THEIR RIGHT, it is THEIR DUTY, to throw off such Government, and to provide new Guards for their future security.</u>"

We The People recognize that we are at the critical juncture spoken of by Thomas Jefferson. And **We The People** choose liberty over government slavery – freedom over government control. Therefore, **We The People** of the Republic of the United States issue this Petition of Patriotism and Warning to our leaders in Washington D.C. Our intent is:

- To re-establish the blessings and liberties bestowed by our Creator God to us and to our posterity.
- To return OUR government to the principles of our Founding Fathers as stated in The Declaration of Independence and the U.S. Constitution.
- To return our Country to the principles of religion and morality, for as President John Adams stated on October 11, 1798: *"... no government armed with power capable of contending with human passions unbridled by morality and religion. Avarice, ambition, revenge, or gallantry, • would break the strongest cords of our Constitution as a whale goes through a net. Our Constitution was made only for a moral and religious people. It is wholly inadequate to the government of any other."*
- George Washington, in his 1797 farewell address warned our generation with these words. *"Of all the dispositions and habits which lead to political prosperity, <u>religion and morality are indispensable supports</u>; in vain would that man claim the tribute of patriotism, who should labor to subvert these great pillars of human happiness, these firmest props of the duties of men and citizens... Let it simply be asked, where is the security for property, for reputation, for life, if the sense of religious obligation desert the oaths which are the instrument of investigation in courts of justice? And let us with caution indulge the supposition that morality can be maintained without religion. What may be conceded to the influence of refined education ... reason and experience both forbid us to expect that national morality can prevail in exclusion of religious principles."*
- To re-form and to restore to the citizenry a more perfect union.

Now, after a long train of abuses have been forced upon the people of this land in an attempt to reduce the citizens of this United States to absolute despotism, **We The People**, exercise our right according to the Declaration of Independence and to uphold our sacred duty to the God of this Land, to ourselves, to our families, to our communities and to our posterity do hereby petition the whole of the Government (both Federal & State) to either change its course or endure revolt by vote, demonstration and protest until it reverses course or is removed by popular demand of the patriotic citizenry of this great nation.

Beginning with Woodrow Wilson, the U.S. Government has in varying degrees over ensuing decades, and most especially the current White House Administration and its Czar appointees, including the majority of representatives in the House and Senators in the halls of Congress, and the Judicial Branch, have passed legislation and orders that effectively rendered OUR Constitution nearly obsolete and hanging by a thread.

Washington has been and continues to be destructive to the sovereignty, health, welfare, indeed the very existence of the United States of America, as an independent society based upon God-given inalienable universal rights of the people as stated in our Declaration of Independence and U.S. Constitution.

It is a sad day as one soberly considers the current state of affairs of this nation. We have lost our religious, spiritual, moral and ethical moorings. Some of the loss is intentionally orchestrated by anti-American individuals serving in Washington, D.C. and by groups including, but not limited to, the ACLU, SEIU, Acorn etc.

Most of our representatives have demonstrated to be two-faced, hypocrites and enemies of The United States of America. You have enacted laws and orders that destroy the U.S. Constitution which in your oath of office you swore to "...uphold and defend". Some of you have intentions and secret combinations (criminal conspiracies) under the disguise of 'Progressivism' which is simply re-labeled 'socialistic-communism'. You seek to overthrow the freedom of all people, lands, nations and countries, and to bring destruction on all peoples, Satan is the father and you are his agents. Your actions are acts of treason against the United States of America.

Therefore, it is necessary for the citizenry to chastise our government and change our representatives if you do not repent of this evil.

Now it is necessary for the people, <u>with whom the power resides</u>, to serve notice to the elected officials of this great nation; From the President to the Congress, to the Courts, to Governors, City & County Seats, and Town Mayors - from the White House to the local Courthouse.

We The People, are no longer willing to sit idly by while you make decisions behind closed doors, secretly, in the middle of the night, and force votes from legislators without providing adequate time to read, analyze, debate and consider voluminous pages of pork laden bills, and use OUR TAX DOLLARS to bribe congressmen to secure their votes, and to use extortion and threats to wives and other family members of congressmen to secure votes against the will of the people.

We will not stand for politicians and presidential appointees who break the law and who are therefore untrustworthy, to be assigned positions of authority and trust. We will not allow Presidential appointees who are avowed communists, Marxists or socialists to occupy positions of leadership.

No one is above the Law. We will not allow you to set aside the U.S. Constitution for your political expedience. You have lost our trust and respect by trashing Our U.S. Constitution and advancing your blend of Socialist/Fascist/Marxist/Communist agenda. We will no longer allow you to rip from this society the religious and moral freedoms and rights, the very fabric upon which all civilizations depend. We will not sit silently by and allow you to further pervert, twist and destroy our Republican form of government long ago established by the Founders, Fore-Fathers and Framers of this great nation; men who were both Churchmen and Statesmen, Political & Religious; business men who considered it a temporary honor, not a career, to serve as OUR representatives.

Patrick Henry's words are worthy of rehearsing:

"The Constitution is not an instrument for the government to restrain the people, it is an instrument for the people to restrain the government – lest [government] come to dominate our lives and interests."

We The People are aware of our 'professed Christian' leaders who are wolves in sheep's clothing. Remember, 92% of US Citizens believe in God and 86% are registered Christians. We know about your allegiance and membership and oaths to secret societies such as: the Skull & Crossbones, the Bilderberg Group, the Bohemian Grove, the Trilateral Commission, the Council on Foreign Relations, the Thule Society and the Illuminati – all created with the sole purpose to destroy people's freedom, the U.S. Constitution, religion and morality; and to supplant it with political, economic and social slavery in the form of One World Order blend of communism, Marxism, socialism and fascism.

Your atrocities have awakened **We The People** - a sleeping giant - and we will not stand for your hypocrisy any longer.

The long train of abuses of our freedoms started with the first 'Progressive' - Woodrow Wilson. We know of the illegal Federal Reserve. Evidence of recent Federal Government's abuses that has precipitated our ire and has come to dominate our lives includes:

1) Our Federal Government have refused to close down the southern border and stop illegal immigration and to do what is necessary to address the problem of the already 22 million illegal aliens living in this country.
2) *As written in the Declaration of Independence under abuses*; Obama and Congress have called together *"legislative bodies at places unusual, uncomfortable and distant from the depository of the public record"* for the sole purpose of enshrining his own agenda.
3) Senator Obama voted 'present' 129 times which is un-Constitutional. The Constitution requires a vote Yea or Nay – not 'present'!
4) Obama and Congress have forced passing legislation, in the dead of the night, leaving no time for proper reading and understanding such legislation, under the poor disguise to 'keep the country from disaster' when in actuality no disaster was truly imminent. This is a clear misuse of power to 'let no crisis - real or created - go to waste' to gain more control over the People.
5) Obama, Congress and the Fed have has forced banks to accept bailout monies when it was not necessary, and in a few instances, when bank officials tried to refuse such monies.
6) Obama and Congress gave away billions to AIG also without pre-conditions.
7) Obama has nationalized major industries; [banks, insurance, and automobile] fired CEO's from their positions and replaced them with his own incompetent and inexperienced comrades in crime.
8) Obama and Congress have forced nationalized health care upon the individuals of this nation without concern for their own wishes. Recent polls indicate that 81% of the people are happy with their current health care and are opposed to socialized medicine, which is a universal failure in every country that has enacted it.
9) Obama told Acorn and union member implants in the town meetings to use "twice the force" of the resistance they encounter to this bill, and promote confrontation with opponents.

10) Obama and Congress have characterized peace-loving, patriots of the Constitution and America who are concerned at the methodical dismantling of our Republic by a combination of socialists and communists currently in government, as GOP mobs and potential terrorists. Thus, our government has become a gang of thugs using war-time propaganda to further their own un-popular un-Constitutional agendas which are designed to gain control over the People.

11) Obama stated that under his healthcare plan, no abortions would be funded. Soon after Obamacare was passed we learned that government funded abortions were happening in Pennsylvania, California and several other states. Obama Lied.

12) Obama appointed Donald Berwick head of health care. Berwick is a socialist, death panel advocate and redistribution of wealth advocate.
As of this writing:

26 States have voted against requiring their citizens to be forced to accept Obamacare.

21 States have banded together stating that Obamacare will bankrupt both the States and the Federal government.

Over 700 'select' (read unions, friends of Obama) have been exempt from the requirements of Obamacare which gives them unfair advantage over other businesses who are forced to comply.

13) Obama apologized to every country he can for what he perceives to be national arrogance while never mentioning how this great country has given aide, supplies, military and medical help, spilled the blood of its men & women who while fighting for the freedoms of others, many of whom gave the ultimate sacrifice in death.

14) Obama promised 'no new taxes for 95% of the American people'. Yet virtually everything he has done raises taxes on everyone. Raising taxes in a deep recession with rampant inflation on the horizon is economic suicide.

15) Obama and Congress's Health Care Reform Bill/Affordable Care Act dramatically raises taxes - but the bill says they will not call it a tax. [A tax by any other name is still a tax.] Obama and Congress proposed Government Health Program will burden those who live responsibly to pay for those who choose to live irresponsibly by paying for their bad choices – including the ill-effects of smoking, drugs and alcohol use, provide for death councils, ration service, provide entitlement for illegal aliens using OUR money, and a host of other atrocities all designed to further control People and destroy the Republic. Everything the Federal Government has taken over to run it has run to ruin. Social Security, United States Post Office, AmTrak & Medicare are all bankrupt!

16) Obama offended all Patriotic Americans by refusing to put his hand over his heart or recite the Pledge of Allegiance to the United States Flag.

17) Obama praised the Marxist Daniel Ortega.

18) Obama endorsed the Socialist Evo Morales of Bolivia.

19) Obama announced we would meet with Iranians with no pre-conditions.

20) Obama insulted everyone who has ever loved a Special Olympian.

21) Obama announced a termination of the space defense system the day after the North Koreans launched an ICBM.

22) Obama, despite the urgings of his own CIA director and the prior 4 CIA directors, released information on intelligence gathering.

23) Obama selected five cabinet members who cheated on their taxes and two others withdrew after they couldn't take the heat.

24) Obama appointed a Homeland Security Chief who quickly identified as "dangers to the nation" groups including veterans of the military, and opponents to abortion. He also ordered that the word "terrorism" no longer be used but instead referred to such acts as "manmade disasters".

25) Obama lied to the Mexican President that the violence in their country was because of us. Obama stated that 96% of drug related guns were from the U.S. The correct number is 17%.

26) Obama politicized the census by moving it into the White House from its Department of Commerce origins to be administered by Acorn. The new Census questions are Un-Constitutional. They ask for private details of People's lives that is none of the government's business. The definition of Census is population count – period!

27) Obama was a community organizer for and supports Acorn. Acorn is under indictment in 11 states for voter fraud, has used $35M in taxpayer money with no accountability, chairman Wade Rafkee plays shell games with our money and his brother embezzled $1M but never had to repay it.

28) Obama appointed Eric Holder as Attorney General; the man who orchestrated the forced removal and expulsion to Cuba of a nine-year old whose mother died trying to bring him to a life of freedom in the United States.

29) Obama announced that members of the Bush administration will stand trial for water boarding a terrorist who had played a part in killing 3000 Americans.

30) Obama flies Air Force One over New York City terrorizing citizens and wasting $325,000 of OUR money.

31) Obama sent his National Defense Advisor to Europe to assure Europe that the U.S. will not support Israel in a special manner and they are on their own in the midst of Muslim countries who want to destroy them.

32) Obama chose Marxist friends and professors in college,

33) Obama sought the endorsement of the Marxist party in 1996 as he ran for the Illinois Senate,

34) The 'Rev.' Jeremiah Wright taught Obama liberation theology for twenty years and spewed hatred for America,

35) The Palestinians in Gaza, set up a fund raising telethon to raise money for Obama's election campaign which is un-Constitutional,

36) Obama's has taken numerous un-Constitutional actions against the Second Amendment.

37) Obama disguised his campaign funding sources,

38) Obama received endorsements from radicals including Louis Farrakhan and Mummar Kaddafi and Hugo Chavez,

39) Ignorant people referred to Obama as a messiah and children in schools were taught to sing his praises,

40) Obama surrounded himself in the White house with advisors who were pro-gun control, pro-abortion, pro homosexual marriage, anti-capitalism, anti-free markets, pro-government control over everything and sought to curtail freedom of speech to silence opposition,

41) Obama favors sex education in Kindergarten, including homosexual indoctrination,

42) Obama's first act as President, literally within 5 minutes of taking office, he signed executive order #13489 that sealed his own records, (what does he have to hide?),

43) Obama had association in Chicago with Tony Rezco, a man of questionable character, who is now in prison and had helped Obama to purchase of his home which he could not afford,

44) Barney Frank destroyed Fannie Mae and Freddie Mac by forcing them to make sub-prime loans at the expense of the American taxpayers and then conspires to give them a carte blanche credit for future operations.

45) Barney Frank removed shower stall curtains in the men's shower in the US Capitol for his viewing enjoyment. Perversion of God's standards of moral conduct affects the security of our Nation.

46) George Soros, a multi-billionaire Marxist, funded a large portion of Obama's election,

47) Obama appointed czars that were radicals, revolutionaries, and even avowed Marxist/Communist,

48) Obama had trained ACORN workers in Chicago and served as an attorney for ACORN. Acorn has been exposed as corrupt using tax dollars to support prostitution.

49) Obama appointed a science czar, John Holdren, who believes in forced abortions, mass sterilizations and seizing babies from teen mothers,

50) Obama appointed Cass Sunstein as regulatory czar and he believes in "Explicit Consent", harvesting human organs without family consent, and to allow animals to be represented in court, while banning all hunting,

51) Obama appointed Kevin Jennings, an overt homosexual, and organizer of a group called Gay, Lesbian, Straight, and Education Network, as 'safe school czar'.

52) Obama appointed Mark Lloyd as diversity czar who believes in curtailing free speech, redistribution of wealth and who praises Hugo Chavez's control of media,

53) Obama selected Valerie Jarrett, senior advisor, his right-hand woman was born in Iran, has ties with terrorist William Ayers, and her father-in-law, Vernon Jarrett is a card-carrying communist party member and associate of Frank Marshall Davis, the controversial Communist Party activist who was Obama's childhood mentor. While a student at Stanford University, Jarrett admitted her loyalty to Islam and continues to object to any negative statements aimed at any part of her 'religion of peace'. She "seeks to help change America to be a more Islamic country...using freedom of religion in America against itself."

54) Obama selected Anita Dunn as White House Communications director who said Mao Tse Tung was her favorite philosopher and the person she turned to most for inspiration,

55) Obama appointed Carol Browner as global warming czar, and she is a well-known socialist working on Cap and trade as the nation's largest tax hike in history,

56) Obama appointed Van Jones, an ex-con and avowed communist as green energy czar, who since had to resign when this was exposed,

57) Obama traveled around the world criticizing America and apologizing for her actions,

58) Obama's threw our only mid-eastern ally, Israel, 'under the bus',

59) Obama offended America' greatest ally in the world, Great Britain, by returning a bust of Winston Churchill,

60) Obama upset our European allies by removing plans for a missile defense system against the Russians,

61) Obama played politics in Afghanistan by not sending required troops requested by the Field Commanders,

62) Obama spent us into unsustainable debt,

63) Obama took a huge spending bill under the guise of stimulus and used it to pay off organizations, unions and individuals that supported his election,

64) Obama forced the takeover of insurance companies, car companies, banks, etc,

65) Obama nationalized student loans,

66) Obamacare is a national disaster,

67) Obama set into motion a plan to take over the control of all energy resources in the United States through Cap and Trade. When Congress did not pass it, Obama did and end-run around Congress with EPA regulations to achieve his objective,

68) Obama and Congress tried to conceal the largest tax increase in the history of American under the guise of Clean Energy HR 2454 - a voluminous 1,500 pps.- 300 of which were

added at 3am the day of the vote! – and forced a vote without providing adequate time to read and analyze the contents.

69) Every decision made and every bill signed into policy by the current president and the out of touch Congress has the effect of turning this Republic into a blend of the following ideologies Marxism/socialism/fascism/communism.

70) Obama allocated $2 billion of OUR money to Petrobras Brazil to drill for deep ocean deposits of oil to support George Soros's hedge fund, while stifling America oil exploration,

71) Obama promised 'transparency' in his administration. In reality, Obama's administration is all about deception, shell games, show 'em your left hand but don't let them see what the right hand is doing. In short, Obama is our Country's worst presidential hypocrite.

72) The arrogance of many elected representatives in Washington is depicted by Rep. Pete Stark, D-California in his June 2010 Town Hall meeting making fun of his constituents and the Minute Men trying to protect our borders.

73) Gulf Oil spill – Obama refused 15 countries help for 78 days to let the situation get far more serious than is should have. Obama also refused to send one of our own sweeper ships in Norfolk VA harbor capable of sweeping up 500K gallons of oil/day! Why all this intentional neglect? In the words of Rahm Emanuel, White House Chief Of Staff: *"You never want a serious crisis go to waste. What I mean by that is it's an opportunity to do things you couldn't do before."* Obama's exacerbates the oil spill crisis by refusing to waive the Jones act to receive help from other countries in order to create political capital to further his Green agenda and destroy capitalism.

74) Obama Administration sues Arizona on upholding US Immigration laws!

75) Obama Administration submits Arizona Immigration Law to U.N. Review –another Un-Constitutional act.

76) The Obama administration and Department of Justice turns their back on the Black Panthers intimidating voters and their hate speech advocating... *"You are going to have to kill some crackers. You might have to kill some of their babies."*

77) Michelle Obama's White House assistants list *add up to $6,364,000 for the 4 years of office.* Michelle Obama spends $242,000 - plus additional expenses - for her and her daughter Sasha, several long-time family friends, her personal staff and various guests to vacation in Spain. She enjoyed a $2,500.00 per night suite at a 5-Star luxury hotel, including 70 additional rooms for our friends, staff and family. Plus she used Air Force 2 and 70 Secret Service personnel. Air Force 2 at a cost of $11,500 per hour to operate and each additional plane for guests. It used 47,500 gallons of jet fuel for this trip and carbon emissions were 1,031 tons of CO_2. This outrage in a time of severe economic depression! And the Obama's have the audacity to ask us to sacrifice! This act of extreme hypocrisy and scores of others by the Obama's and many of the Washington politicians and bureaucrats outrage the American people!!

78) Obama supports the Ground Zero Mosque, which is an insult to the 3,000 people who died there because of Muslim terrorists!

79) Obama's preaching of Social Justice is in direct opposition to God's Individual Justice.

80) Obama's preaching of Collective Salvation is in direct opposition to God's Individual Salvation.

81) Obama's forced redistribution of wealth is in direct opposition to God's voluntary contributions to help our neighbor in times of need. Even the Pope stated that when government assumes the role of redistribution of wealth it becomes demonic.

82) Obama has broken almost all of his campaign promises to the America people. For example: He promised on 5.7.2009 that he would cut the federal deficit in half by the end of his first

term. Yet, in the first 19 months of his first term he has added more federal debt than all the President's from Washington to Reagan – combined. A debt that is unsustainable.

83) Obama has supported the riots in the middle east through the efforts of Richard Trumpka – President of the AF-CIO (organized labor unions_ who visits the White House 2-3 times per week and is in phone contact with them daily – and in concert with Code Pink and the liberal left – to support the Muslim Brotherhood in overthrowing middle eastern governments and establishing a Muslim Caliphate. One of the goals of the Muslim Brotherhood is to annihilate the Jews in Israel (the little Satan, and then The United States of America (the big Satan). Obama said he would side with the Muslims – since his is one – and he has. In doing so he has alienated Israel, a former United States ally.

84) Nancy Pelosi – stated "We have to pass the Healthcare bill to see what is in it!" – political insanity!

85) Obama lied to the America people when he said "If you like your healthcare, you can keep your healthcare."

86) Barack H. Obama and his accomplice, Eric H. Holder, Jr., 82nd Attorney General, have – for the first in American history –sided with a foreign government; a direct violation of the oath of office. This act of treason is un-Constitutional. They sided with Mexico and its drug cartels against the State of Arizona and the citizens of the United States of America by suing the State of Arizona for upholding Federal Immigration law that the Federal Government refused to do. One-third of Arizona prisons are filled with criminal invaders from Mexico. The Presidents' duty to the United States is to protect the citizens of the United States from foreign criminal invaders. Obama and Holder have done the opposite in aiding a abetting the enemy. (See Arizona Senate Bill 1070 and Arizona House Bill 2162, taken from Federal Law since 1940, Section 8 USC 1304 paragraph C,D,E,F.)

87) When Obama took office gas was $1.68/gal. It has soared to $4.23/gal.; a 152% increase!

88) When Obama took office unemployment was 7.6%. Now it is 9.7% - but the real number counting those who stopped working is 23% - only 2% less than during the Great Depression.

89) Obama administration spent $20 million to create 14 'green' jobs.

90) Obama administration, including Holder, involved in Mexican gun runner 'Fast and Furious' project responsible for killing American agent.

91) Obama administration deeply involved in IRS, NSA and Solyndra scandals.

92) August 24, 2011 – the first audit of the Federal Reserve revealed that the Fed gave away $16 TRILLION dollars of OUR MONEY, much of it to our enemies. This wholesale plunder of OUR wealth is an act of treason and sole reason enough to foment a revolution against the tyrannical dictatorship under which **We The People** have suffered far too long.

The Constitution of the United States – excerpts on treason and impeachment follow:

Article II SECTION. 4. The President, Vice President and all civil Officers of the United States, shall be removed from Office on Impeachment for, and Conviction of, Treason, Bribery, or other high Crimes and Misdemeanors.

Amendment XIV SECTION 3. No person shall be a Senator or Representative in Congress, or elector of President and Vice President, or hold any office, civil or military, under the United States, or under any State, who, having previously taken an oath, as a member of Congress, or as an officer of the United States, or as a member of any State legislature, or as an executive or judicial officer of any State, to support the Constitution of the United States, shall have engaged in insurrection or rebellion against the same, or given aid or comfort to the enemies thereof. But Congress may by a vote of two-thirds of each House, remove such disability.

The sum of all these criminal and un-Constitutional actions is clear; international banksters, secret societies (combinations), and the Obama administration are determined to destroy capitalism and America by using the Cloward & Piven approach to overload the system – under the disguise of HOPE & CHANGE - and then to re-make America over into a socialistic society and institute One World Order.

We The People have sought and found the truth about our government. America's CANCER are socialists, communists, fascists & Marxists, masquerading as PROGRESSIVES with a promise of Hope & Change.

Never before in the history of America have we been confronted with problems so huge that the very existence of our country is in jeopardy. Rasmussen pole reports in July 2010 that 84% of mainstream voters say America is on the wrong track.

Our biggest enemy is not China, Russia, or Iran. No. Our biggest enemy is corrupt politicians in Washington DC. It is our Constitutional duty to act to restore our Republic.

Therefore, **We The People** will all now unite to overthrow this secret combination of evil that has control in our government.

We The People will act to return The United States of America to its Christian foundation of the Declaration of Independence and the God-inspired United States Constitution.

BIG GOVERNMENT IS NOT THE SOLUTION.

BIG GOVERNMENT IS THE PROBLEM.

Therefore, **We The People**, draw a line in the sand; a line of demarcation that marks the end of a long train of abuses. We, the heretofore silent majority, will no longer be silent while our freedoms are stolen daily and supplanted by social, economic and political slavery.

We will fight by vote, peaceful demonstration and protest and by making our presence known in the halls of Washington and at the front gate of the White House.

We The People, after many meetings and conversations, pleading with the Almighty, the God and Father of our Lord & Savior, Jesus Christ who is the Supreme Judge and Legislator, with one voice demand that this government cease and desist from its current course and ideologies and listen to the voice of moral truth & reason. It must take time to consider the already mounting abuses against the U.S. Constitution that lay at the feet of this Congress and Administration. It must return to the United States Constitution, uphold its principles, follow its guiding light and reduce the Federal Government to the U.S. Constitutionally defined limits; delegating all other power to the States.

We The People underscore the fact that the United States Government works for us. We do not work for you.

We The People are fed up with Washington representatives who will not listen. We are fed up with taxation without proper representation. We are fed up with both political parties unbridled spending of OUR MONEY and mortgaging our future and our children's future and our grandchildren's future.

You have led us and are leading us toward destruction. *We demand that you stop - NOW!*

We The People support of the divinely inspired United States Constitution. You have led us away from it toward socialism, fascism and communism. In that regard you are aiding and abetting the enemy – treason!

Therefore, **We The People** *demand the following of our elected representatives:*

1. Remove all socialists, communists, etc. out of the White House and out of ALL political positions throughout America.
2. Abolish the Federal Reserve, replace with a true Federal Bank that operates under the U.S. Constitution. Return to the gold standard backed USD.
3. Institute Term Limits for Politicians.
4. No Tenure & No Pension for Politicians.
5. Congress (past, present & future) participates in Social Security.
6. Congress purchases their own retirement plan, just as all Americans do.
7. Congress will no longer vote themselves a pay raise.
8. Congress loses their current health care system and participates in the same health care system as the American people.
9. Congress must equally abide by all laws they impose on the American people.
10. Politicians shall make no more money than U.S. Military volunteers who protect our freedoms.
11. The average income of US Federal government employee income shall be no higher than the average US private income doing similar jobs.
12. Outlaw Lobbyists - a $9 billion/year manipulation of OUR representatives.
13. Establish English as the official language.
14. Abolish the Internal Revenue Service & Institute the Fair Tax.
15. Pass the Marriage Amendment to the Constitution – 'Marriage is between a man and a woman'
16. Abolish the Two Party System which has divided America. We the People want statesman, not politicians.
17. Repeal un-Constitutional Obamacare.
18. Allow the free market to provide health care alternatives.
19. Abolish the un-Constitutional Environmental Protection Agency (EPA) and return power to the States and to the people where it belongs under the Constitution.
20. Abolish the un-Constitutional department of Health, Education and Welfare (HEW) and return power to the States and to the people where it belongs under the Constitution.
21. Abolish the un-Constitutional Food and Drug Administration (FDA) and return power to the States and to the people where it belongs under the Constitution.
22. Get the United States out of the United Nations and the United Nations out of the United States.
23. Abolish the 17th Amendment and revert to original practice of the State legislatures appointing Senators to Congress to represent the States.
24. Remove all authority assumed by the federal government that is un-Constitutional.
25. End all government funding of the ACLU
26. Get America out of all secret societies
27. Become Energy Independent by using our own resources.
28. STOP the insane headlong dive toward socialism, fascism, Marxism and communism under the guise of 'Progressivism'.
29. Re-establish The Constitution of the United States as the guiding light that drives decisions.

30. Uphold The Constitution of the United States as you have sworn to do in your oath of office..
31. Repeal the drug assistance program that mortgages our future for the benefit of the drug companies. Stop funding drug companies with our tax dollars. Let the world of natural healing arts and science take at least equal place on the stage so people have a choice for their health care needs.
32. Outlaw and destroy secret combinations that will prove the downfall of this nation – including skull & crossbones, CFR, Trilateral Commission, Thule society, Bilderberg Group and Illuminati, etc. – by whatever names and sub-sets they operate and whatever un-Constitutional ideologies they promote – including communism, Marxism, socialism, & fascism.
33. Require Congress to balance the Federal Budget.
34. Stop the insane unbridled spending in Washington of OUR MONEY that is going to BANKRUPT the United States of America.
35. Prohibit our tax dollars from being given to illegal aliens and enemy countries.
36. Enforce our borders. Stop the illegal invasion. Require all illegal aliens to return to their own country. If they want to return, require them to do legally. And learn English!
37. Prohibit our tax dollars from providing discounted loans to 'special privileged' foreigners to start businesses here.
38. Stop rewarding banks, business and States - failures and lawbreakers - with bailouts using OUR MONEY.
39. Establish a level playing field for would-be political candidates where each receives and equal amount to conduct their campaigns from a pool of tax dollars set aside for that purpose. Establish a law for it to be a crime to receive election funding from any other source.
40. Re-establish the practice of recognizing God, Nature's God etc. in public places – including schools, Congress, the Supreme Court and the White House. This has and must be done without establishing a national religion.
George Washington, First President of the United States: _"True religion offers to government its surest support . . . It is impossible to rightly govern the world without God and the Bible."_

Our justice system of laws was derived primarily from the Bible. Keep it that way.

41. Change the incredibly wasteful, utterly failed Federal welfare program. Institute a new one after The Church of Jesus Christ of Latter-day Saints Welfare program that President Ronald Regan was so impressed with and which he sought to institute. This system gives a hand UP, not a hand OUT, where dignity is retained, the degrading dole is abolished, help is temporary (not provided for generations of welfare parasites) and recipients are required to pass drug tests and work to the extent of their ability for what they receive.
42. Monitor the teachings of all Moslem Mosques. Virtually all the terrorist actions in the past 30 years have been perpetrated by Muslim males 17-40 years old. Muslim clerics teach hate and death to the infidels (non-Muslims), and espouse the advent of the Third Jihad to overthrow America and place it under Sharia rule.

We The People demand that Our representatives hold a Constitutional Convention to adopt the above itemized policies and practices to return Our Country to a foundation of freedom, liberty and prosperity.

We do humbly submit this Petition to the president of the United States, Barack Hussein Obama and the sitting Congress of the House and Senate with reliance upon our Creator God, who sees all things, will acknowledge our cause as just and will therefore uphold this righteous action.

You - our representatives who work for us - shall be held accountable by Almighty God for the exercise of trust placed upon you in governing this choice land above all other lands of Earth.

With hope that the union of this great nation will be restored and so avert any further moral, spiritual, financial and emotional damage than has already been incurred and that restoration of our government will be achieved through a change of course by the government representatives - or else - **We The People** shall work to overthrow all non-Constitutional adhering representatives at the polls. Your acts are monitored and for those who will not act in accordance with this Petition, your days are numbered.

We The People oppose slavery - in any form. Our great country fought The Civil War to decide the freedom of all men. Freedom Won! Let us never backslide to slavery again - including slavery of the people to all un-Constitutional Federal Government control.

One last thing....if you who consider yourselves 'elitists' in Washington who regard yourselves as better than the average Citizen - still don't get it, let **We The People** spell it out. **THIS IS OUR COUNTRY! The Government works for US - not the other way around.**

Thomas Jefferson and the Founding Fathers put **We The People** is in unusually large font size in the Declaration of Independence for a reason. It was to remind you politicians in Washington that **YOU REPRESENT US. YOU WORK FOR US. We The People DO NOT WORK FOR YOU.**

Therefore, **We The People** declare that we uphold and demand that you uphold your oath of office:

We The People raise
The Banner of Liberty
for our peace, religion, families and freedom.
The Constitution of the United States of America,
Now and Forever!

"'Tis better to die standing as a Patriot fighting in the cause of truth and freedom,

than to live kneeling as a coward in submission to lies and slavery."

Appendix B

DEFINITIONS

de·moc·ra·cy noun \di-'mä-krə-sē\ plural de·moc·ra·cies
1a : government by the people; especially : rule of the majority (Mob rule)

1b : a government in which the supreme power is vested in the people and exercised by them directly or indirectly through a system of representation usually involving periodically held free elections

re·pub·lic noun \ri-'pə-blik\

1a: a government having a chief of state who is not a monarch and who in modern times is usually a president

1b: a political unit (as a nation) having such a form of government

1c: a government in which supreme power resides in body of citizens entitled to vote and is exercised by elected officers and representatives responsible to them and governing according to law.

sheeple [slang] noun - People who act like sheep – they follow the leader even when the leader is leading them to slaughter

banksters [slang] noun –Bankers who are gangsters. Criminals who control money to gain wealth and power at the expense of those who work.

Marx·ism noun \'märk-,si-zəm\ Definition of MARXISM: the political, economic, and social principles and policies advocated by Marx; especially : a theory and practice of socialism including the labor theory of value, dialectical materialism, the class struggle, and dictatorship of the proletariat until the establishment of a classless society

Na·zism noun \'nät-,si-zəm, 'nat-\ Definition of NAZISM : the body of political and economic doctrines held and put into effect by the Nazis in Germany from 1933 to 1945 including the totalitarian principle of government, predominance of especially Germanic groups assumed to be racially superior, and supremacy of the führer

com·mu·nism noun \'käm-yə-,ni-zəm, -yü-\ Definition of COMMUNISM 1 a : a theory advocating elimination of private property, b : a system in which goods are owned in common and are available to all as needed 2 capitalized a : a doctrine based on revolutionary Marxian socialism and Marxism-Leninism that was the official ideology of the Union of Soviet Socialist Republics b : a totalitarian system of government in which a single authoritarian party controls state-owned means of production c : a final stage of society in Marxist theory in which the state has withered away and economic goods are distributed equitably d : communist systems collectively

so·cial·ism noun \'sō-shə-,li-zəm\ Definition of SOCIALISM 1 : any of various economic and political theories advocating collective or governmental ownership and administration of the means of production and distribution of goods 2 a : a system of society or group living in which there is no private property b : a system or condition of society in which the means of production are owned and controlled by the state 3 : a stage of society in Marxist theory transitional between capitalism and communism and distinguished by unequal distribution of goods and pay according to work done

fas·cism noun \'fa-,shi-zəm also 'fa-,si-\ Definition of FASCISM 1 often capitalized : a political philosophy, movement, or regime (as that of the Fascisti) that exalts nation and often race above the individual and that stands for a centralized autocratic government headed by a dictatorial leader, severe economic and social regimentation, and forcible suppression of opposition 2 : a tendency toward or actual exercise of strong autocratic or dictatorial control <early instances of army *fascism* and brutality — J. W. Aldridge>

Bibliography

Jefferson, Thomas, *The United States Declaration of Independence,* 1776

The Constitution of the United States of America, 1787, 1789, 1791

Lillback, Peter, *George Washington's Sacred Fire,* Providence Forum Press, 2006

Allison, Andrew, Maxfield, Richard, Cook, DeLynn, Skousen, Cleon, *The Real Thomas Jefferson,* National Center for Constitutional Studies, 2009

Paine, Thomas, *Common Sense, Rights of Man*, Signet Classics, 2003

McPheters, Mike, *Cartels and Combinations,* Bonneville Books, 2010

Griffin, G. Edward, *The Creature From Jekyll Island*, 1994.

Hayek, F.A., *The Road to Serfdom,* University of Chicago Press, 2007

Skousen, Cleon, *The 5000 Year Leap-A Miracle that Changed the World,* National Center for Constitutional Studies, 2007

Skousen, Cleon, *The Naked Communist,* Ensign Publishing, 1958

Beck, Glenn, *Glenn Beck's Common Sense,* Mercury Radio Arts, 2009

Coulter, Ann, *The Church of Liberalism Godless,* Crown Forum, 2006

Cleveland, Clude, Finkelstein, Eliyah, Morrow, Corey, Cook, Jonny, *Common Sense; Revisited,* 2009

Kimber, Glenn & Julianne, *America In History and Prophecy,* God*Family*Country Publishing, 2007

Shatzer, Vaughn, *The Truth Behind the Declaration of Independence*, Beacon of Truth Publications, 1995

Beck, Glenn, *Arguing with Idiots,* Mercury Radio Arts, 2009

Flood, Robert, *The Rebirth of America*, Arthur S. DeMoss Foundation, 1986

The Invisible Committee, *The Coming Insurrection,* Editions La Fabrique, Paris, 2007

Huntsman, Jon M., *Winners Never Cheat,* Pearson Education Inc., 2009

Ramsey, Dave, *The Total Money Makeover,* Thomas Nelson, 2007

Hamilton, JoAnn, *Personal Revelation,* Covenant Communications, 1998

Farah, Joseph, *Taking America Back,*WND Books, 2005

Boortz, Neal, Linder, John Linder, *The Fairtax Book,* Reagan Books, 2005

Nelson, Russel M., *The Power Within Us*, Deseret Book, 1988

Covey, Stephen, R., *Spiritual Roots of Human Relationships*, Deseret Book, 1970

Covey, Stephen, R., *The 8th Habit*, Free Press, 2004

Covey, Stephen, R., *Principle Centered Leadership*, Simon & Shuster, 1991

Covey, Stephen, R., *The 7 Habits of Highly Effective People,* Simon & Shuster, 1989

Holland, Jeffery R. & Patricia T., *On Earth as it is in Heaven,* Deseret Book, 1989

Worth, Grant A., *Do Your Prayers Bounce off the Ceiling?,* Deseret Book, 1982

Beck, Glenn, Ablow, Keith, *The 7 Wonders that Will Change your Life,* Mercury Radio Arts, 2011

Lund, Gerald N., *Hearing the Voice of the Lord,* Deseret Book, 2007

Schiff, Peter D., *Crash Proof,* John Wiley & Sons, 2007

Beck, Glenn, *Broke,* Mercury Radio Arts, 2010

Hannity, Sean, *Deliver Us From Evil,* Reagan Books, 2004

Crichton , Michael, *State of Fear,* Harper Collins, 2004

Bush, George W., *Decision Points,* Crown Publishers, 2010

Palin, Sarah, *Going Rogue,* Harper Collins Publishers, 2009

Weiss, Martin, *The Ultimate Depression Survival Guide,* John Wiley & Sons, 2009

Talmage, James, E. *Jesus The Christ,* Desert Publishing, 1982

Hagee, Matthew, *ResponseABLE*, Charisma House, 2011

Rand, Ayn, *Atlas Shrugged*, Plume Printing, 1957

GBTV

The Holy Bible - King James Version

Standard Works of The Church of Jesus Christ of Latter-day Saints

Writings of prophets, apostles, evangelists and ministers

The Quran (Koran)

Benson, Ezra Taft. *An Enemy Hath Done This*. Compiled by Jerrald L. Newquist. Salt Lake City; Parliament Publishers, 1969.

"Muslim Mafia: Inside the Secret Underworld That's Conspiring to Islamize America," a WND Books publication by counter-terrorism investigator Dave Gaubatz and "Infiltration" author Paul Sperry, documents

Barton, David, *America:To Pray or Not to Pray*, Wall Builder Press, Aledo, TX, 1991

www.ingramcontent.com/pod-product-compliance
Lightning Source LLC
Chambersburg PA
CBHW081145270326
41930CB00014B/3044